I Rea

GRAPHIC DESIGN MUSEUM

valiz

I Read Where I Am
Exploring New Information Cultures

Compiled by
Mieke Gerritzen,
Geert Lovink,
Minke Kampman

Graphic Design Museum, Breda
Valiz, Amsterdam

I Read Where I Am
Mieke Gerritzen and Geert Lovink

691 words | 2:39 mins

We are street readers. Look at us, info junk dealers, as we zip through the telephone, scan a newspaper we've just read, leaf through a magazine. We are the new generation of readers. Not dumber, just faster. We whiz through three lives at once. Let's be honest: reading has become a different experience. Reading has become looking and vice versa. Information has become tactile. You don't have to remember anything, you just look it up. Could it be that the average person (still) doesn't like reading? Can you call what people do on Facebook and Twitter reading? Absorbing books and newspapers was something from which you traditionally became wiser, because unusual opinions, special thoughts, new developments, and fantasies were revealed. But there have always been good and bad books. Quality and pulp have always existed.

We are info junkies. People don't know where to draw the line and, in today's consumer society, are constantly fighting for control. Information, following food and the environment, may be next in line for an analysis on sustainable development. Information has become a consumer product because it is linked to the form in which it appears. New platforms and formats are appearing with greater frequency on the market. Text, video, sound, and graphics intermingle. Everybody is busy answering, uploading.

We all know the main lines of info evolution, from the printing press to the iPhone. By now the information is drifting through space and there are new tools for reading and writing, which each time combine the multimedia mix in a different way. Each change is in itself large and has consequences for the economy, politics, and the social status of our existence.

In I Read Where I Am the Graphic Design Museum, together with the Institute for Network Cultures, investigates recent developments in the field of information design. The book is produced under the Infodecodata programme, an exhibition about information design that was launched in 2010 in the Graphic Design Museum. Infodecodata presents new developments on the cusp of text and image.

Much discussion took place in the twentieth century about the relationship between art and science, but it often did not go further than good intentions. Engineers do not want to involve artists in crucial stages of the research and artists in turn are all too determined to remain *autonomous*. But now we see them actually coming closer together. This has not happened because good intentions have all at once been turned into deeds. It is the technology itself that develops form and content simultaneously and considers it to be a whole. Different types of content and readers ask for different forms and experiences. The question remains: which form will it assume and what experience do you want?

In I Read Where I Am, 82 invited authors, artists, critics, and designers present a wide range of observations, inspirations, and critical notes about how we daily consume and produce our information. We intended to leave the justified nostalgia for what it is and asked the expert-amateurs to look further than the current hype around the iPads and Kindles. This publication does not only reflect the current state of affairs but also speculates about the significance and importance of new forms of image-text in the future. Let us together place them in the world and not wait for ready-made products from Silicon Valley. The reflections presented here are explicitly intended to be read as a guideline for the

following generations of *reading machines*. All that remains is for us to design them –without losing our attention.

--

Mieke Gerritzen is designer and director of the Graphic Design Museum.

Geert Lovink is media theorist, net critic and director of the Amsterdam-based Institute of Network Cultures.

Contents

Indexes

Index on First 140 Characters of Essay | p 16
Index of Word Frequency | p 22
Index on Related Subjects | p 178

82 essays

01 | p 50
Gathering Up Characters
Arie Altena

02 | p 51
Better Stories
Henk Blanken

03 | p 53
From Books to Texts
Andrew Blauvelt

04 | p 54
I Read More Than Ever
Erwin Blom

05 | p 56
Encoded Experiences
James Bridle

06 | p 57
Watching, Formerly Reading
Max Bruinsma

07 | p 60
If Words, Then Reading
Anne Burdick

08 | p 60
Flowing Together
Vito Campanelli

09 | p 62
Highway Drugs and Data Visualization
Catalogtree

10 | p 64
The Revenge of the Gutenberg Galaxy
Florian Cramer

11 | p 66
Where Do You Read?
Sean Dockray

12 | p 67
Pancake
Paulien Dresscher

13 | p 69
Between Reality and the Impossible: Revisited
Dunne & Raby

14 | p 70
Weapons of Mass Distraction
Sven Ehmann

15 | p 73
Reading Beyond Words
Martin Ferro-Thomsen

16 | p 74
We Left Home; Why Shouldn't Ideas?
Jeff Gomez

17 | p 75
Delectation
Denise Gonzales Crisp

18 | p 76
Welcome to the Digital Age. What Changed?
Alexander Griekspoor

19 | p 77
Non-linear Publishing
Hendrik-Jan Grievink

20 | p 78
Subtitling
Ger Groot

21 | p 80
Ambient Scholarship
Gary Hall

22 | p 82
Set the Text Free: Balancing Textual Agency Between Humans and Machines
John Haltiwanger

23 | p 83
Educate Well, Read Better
N. Katherine Hayles

24 | p 84
Reading the Picture
Toon Horsten

25 | p 85
Apples and Cabbages
Minke Kampman

26 | p 86
How Will We Read?
Lynn Kaplanian-Buller

27 | p 88
Screening
Kevin Kelly

28 | p 90
I Don't Read on My Bike
Joost Kircz

29 | p 91
Reading As Event
Matthew Kirschenbaum

30 | p 91
Reading the Network
Tanja Koning

31 | p 93
Nearby and Global in Its Impact
Steffen Konrath

32 | p 95
The Interface of the Graphic Novel
Erin La Cour

33 | p 97
Minimal and Maximal Reading
Rudi Laermans

34 | p 99
Reading Apart Together
Warren Lee

35 | p 100
Unexpected Ways
Jannah Loontjens

36 | p 101
Consume Without a Screen
Alessandro Ludovico

37 | p 103
The Networked Culture Machine
Peter Lunenfeld

38 | p 104
From Noun to Verb
Ellen Lupton

39 | p 106
The Role of the Hardware
Anne Mangen

40 | p 107
From Reading to Pattern Recognition
Lev Manovich

41 | p 109
Reading *For the Sake of It*
Luna Maurer

42 | p 111
The Matrix: Three Subjective and Intuitively Selected Pointers for Building Blocks for The Script in Which We Live
Geert Mul

43 | p 113
Horses Are Fine So Are Books
Arjen Mulder

44 | p 115
Shapes
Caroline Nevejan

45 | p 117
Achievement Unlocked!
David B. Nieborg

46 | p 119
U-turn
Kali Nikitas

47 | p 119
The Epitaph or Writing Beyond the Grave
Henk Oosterling

48 | p 121
Jumping Frames
David Ottina

49 | p 123
Pictures and Words
Peter Pontiac

50 | p 125
The Grammar of Images
Ine Poppe

51 | p 127
The Many Readers in My Body
Emilie Randoe

52 | p 129
Arrangements
Bernhard Rieder

53 | p 130
Desecration of Reading
Paul Rutten

54 | p 131
Epi-phany Plea for a Counter-culture of Un-reading and Un-writing
Johan Sanctorum

55 | p 133
Savouring Thoughts
Louise Sandhaus

56 | p 134
The Stutter in Reading (Call for a New Quality of Reading)
Niels Schrader

57 | p 135
I Read in the Mind
Ray Siemens

58 | p 135
Full Circle
Karin Spaink

59 | p 137
Books
Erik Spiekermann

60 | p 138
The New Orality and the Empty House
Matthew Stadler

61 | p 140
Letter en geest / Letter and Spirit
F. Starik

62 | p 141
Social Reading
Bob Stein

63 | p 144
Is the Role of Libraries in Reading Innovation Fading?
Michael Stephens & Jan Klerk

64 | p 146
Slow Reading
Carolyn Strauss

65 | p 147
Cyclops iPad
Dick Tuinder

66 | p 149
Context Is King; Content Is Queen
Lian van de Wiel

67 | p 150
Reading Becomes Looking
Bregtje van der Haak

68 | p 152
The Library Is As Large As One Half of the Brain
Els van der Plas

69 | p 155
Classic Canon
Rick van der Ploeg

70 | p 156
Content Economies
Daniel van der Velden

71 | p 157
Do Images Also Argue?
Adriaan van der Weel

72 | p 158
Read Me First
Erwin van der Zande

73 | p 160
Designing a New Stratification of Information
René van Engelenburg

74 | p 162
Dancing Words
Francisco van Jole

75 | p 163
Books Are Bullets in the Battle for the Minds of Men
Peter van Lindonk

76 | p 165
Reading Surroundings
Koert van Mensvoort

77 | p 166
Reading with Electronic Blinkers
Tjebbe van Tijen

78 | p 168
Better Tools
Dirk van Weelden

79 | p 170
E-Stone
Jack van Wijk

80 | p 172
Mushrooms and Truffles
Astrid Vorstermans

81 | p 173
Book It
McKenzie Wark

82 | p 174
Danger: Contains Books
Simon Worthington

Indexes

Index on First 140 Characters of Essay

01 | p 50
Reading behaviour changes, also because of the influence of technology. Empirical research has shown that a screen-based reading behaviour h

02 | p 51
When man began to speak, around fifty thousand years ago, the earth was already billions of years old. That the word was *in the beginning*

03 | p 53
It took about 300 years for the codex (the book as a set of bound pages) to rival the popularity of scrolls and another 300 years to replace

04 | p 54
I like reading. I'm crazy about print. Everyday, two newspapers fall onto the doormat, every week I buy a pile of magazines during my weekly

05 | p 56
Books are changing, and the nature of reading, what we take away from it, is changing too. Books used to be physically malleable things that

06 | p 57
I don't read, someone I know well told me. She meant that she doesn't read the way *readers* read. People who can spend hours on end with a

07 | p 60
If interface, then navigation. If disguise, then disclosure. If map, then itinerary. If resource, then use. If environment, then wayfinding.

08 | p 60
Maybe it's trite but when I reflect on the evolution of reading modalities I cannot do without thinking that, in the present historic moment

09 | p 62
Experts do not need visualization to be able to read data. A musician can hear the music as he reads a score. The rest is at the mercy of gr

10 | p 64
Let's be clear, reading is not limited to alphabetic language, but is actually any act of visual or tactile perception involving interpretat

11 | p 66
I read where I am but sometimes I'd rather read where you are. I'd rather sit on your lap and have you read to me. I want to see what you un

12 | p 67
When, in 2007, I decided to resume studying after a break of 15 years, I discovered with a shock that I could no longer write without a comp

13 | p 69
What human beings are and will become is decided in the shape of our tools no less than in the action of statesmen and political movements.

14 | p 70
I love reading. That is why I took three books along on a recent vacation. Three books that I picked carefully from my library and was sure

15 | p 73
My literature professor understood reading as a relative concept: One might grasp the words without yet comprehending the meaning. Ideally t

16 | p 74
A hundred years ago books were pale shut-ins, escaping overstuffed shelves only sparingly; maybe one or two volumes at a time but never en m

17 | p 75
Type well used is invisible as type, wrote Beatrice Warde in the early 1930s. Like a clear glass goblet, a crystalline window, and a perfe

18 | p 76
Scientists read a lot. In fact the entire academic 'workflow' is based on publishing papers, a drive that acts as both the final goal and th

19 | p 77
The books that I find interesting are more likely to be printed collections than linear stories and are also consumed as such. Traditional c

20 | p 78
The misconception that a picture says more than a thousand words is based on the idea that it is immediately clear what a picture means. You

21 | p 80
Today knowledge and information are increasingly being externalized onto complex, multilayered, distributed systems of computers, databases,

22 | p 82
The computer has eaten typography, just as it has eaten everything else. The ramifications of the coded extensions we wrap our text in are b

23 | p 83
Literacy is not without neurological consequences. Recent research in fMRI studies indicates that reading changes how the brain functions. M

24 | p 84
When Hergé, the creator of Tintin, was interviewed in the seventies, he wasn't certain of things. The comic strip, and Tintin in particular,

25 | p 85
We didn't need dialogue, we had faces. A sentimental line by Norma Desmond in the movie Sunset Boulevard, explaining why silent movies wer

26 | p 86
As text appears everywhere –even beamed on the wall while we exercise or onto the ceiling as we lie in bed– we read faster and faster. In

27 | p 88
In the morning I begin my screening while still in bed. I check the screen near my pillow for the time, my wake-up alarm, and also to see wh

28 | p 90
I read the whole day long and tease my brain, a neurological fruit salad consisting of various pieces of tasting, touching, feeling, hearing

29 | p 91
Reading is an event, not an act. Books are incidental (in the fullest meaning of the word). Texts are signals, transmissions. This is where

30 | p 91
As editor of an independent magazine, I am naturally crazy about paper; nothing is as fine as the smell of a new magazine. Yet when it came

31 | p 93
Many people have stopped reading newspapers on a daily base. Circulation figures are on the decline worldwide. Don't worry. It is a declinin

32 | p 95
I was first drawn into the world of graphic novels while working as an editorial assistant at a New York based publishing house where I was

33 | p 97
Nowadays, information is not scarce –there is far too much of it, or rather, far too many information possibilities, as I will explain. But

34 | p 99
Books have in many ways become an integral part of my life; I have been in the book business now for forty years. I have done just about eve

35 | p 100
How and where we encounter literature determines how we approach the text. Not only do our physical surroundings influence our reading exper

36 | p 101
Since the arrival of electronic media, visionaries have speculated on ways to expand our physiological reading limits beyond the constraints

37 | p 103
The growth of blogs, Twitter, and Facebook considered in tandem with Tumblr and other social softwares that enable posting and tagging accou

38 | p 104
Over forty years ago, the author was brutally slain in the streets of Paris. It was 1968. The times were dark; the turtlenecks were darker.

39 | p 106
These are challenging times for reading research. For a long time, we have felt comfortable with developing theories of reading and models

40 | p 107
The emergence of social media creates a radically new opportunity to study cultural processes and dynamics. For the first time, we can follo

41 | p 109
The longer I think about what reading actually means to me, the more insoluble situations I encounter. Everything I do daily –communicating

42 | p 111
The experience of reality is mediated by a script. This script is the grammatical equivalent of a placebo: a form that channels the content/

43 | p 113
In the thirties, Marshall McLuhan read all the writings of the Church Fathers in Latin and all the great books of the Western world in thei

44 | p 115
Clutter
In the summer of my 26th year I completely lost the capacity to read. I had hit my head badly and a severe concussion made me instan

45 | p 117
It is a question that keeps recurring among game critics. What if games had the same social status as literature? A gamer can search through

46 | p 119
Alternative paths towards reading to achieve maximum knowledge, in the shortest period of time, with approval from peers on content consumed

47 | p 119
We browse a lot. What used to be written in thick books hidden away in shadowy libraries and which could only be consulted after negotiating

48 | p 121
My experience of reading is dominated by the experience of browsing the web. I meander, dipping into conversations then jumping out to essay

49 | p 123
Asked to share his or her views on reading, no serious comic strip artist can ignore the bad reputation comic art (or *sequential art* as Wi

50 | p 125
When I was asked to write something about *the future of reading*, I googled to see what has already been published about this subject and w

51 | p 127
My father was a passionate typographer who, during his time at the academy, managed to pick up an antique English printing press and, during

52 | p 129
Having been part of collections, libraries, and catalogues for centuries, the book is increasingly embedded into digital databases of variou

53 | p 130
Information consumption, and that includes reading, can in principle take place everywhere. Electronic networks offer information to the far

54 | p 131
The advance of Internet and the new *social networks* regularly leads to culture-pessimistic deliberations: we shall no longer be capable of

55 | p 133
I admit it. I've stopped reading. Well, not really perhaps. I consume words. That's not the issue. They come in through my ears, my eyes, an

56 | p 134
Reading is the process of consuming information. It cannot exist without the action of producing information and the two can simply not be a

57 | p 135
I read in the mind. For all the physical locations of reading one might choose (at home, at the office, in the garden), for all the bodily p

58 | p 135
I used to read whenever and wherever I could. You were only allowed to borrow four books a week from the library-for me, a measly ration.

59 | p 137
Lots of important people have pronounced the book dead. And lots of less important people – the average consumer – believe them because they

60 | p 138
There is anxiety about the book, but little about writing. Text flourishes. We read and write everywhere. Recall sitting in a room with a ha

61 | p 140
There are two types of people: readers and lookers. And all just push against doors on which scribbles are scrawled,
everyone does it. The r

62 | p 141
Beginning in 2005 The Institute for the Future of the Book began a series of experiments under the rubric of *networked books*. This was the

63 | p 144
Michael Stephens and Jan Klerk share some thoughts about the future of reading and libraries.
Michael, I would like you to consider the foll

64 | p 146
By definition, *reading* goes well beyond the grasping of written characters and the realm of ideas they express. Applied to environments, s

65 | p 147
When we open the classic book, it has the proportions of a landscape. The way that landscape-like format works is not only determined by wha

66 | p 149
Tablet, e-reader, laptop, smartphone. Add to that the information overload from Google, Twitter, and Facebook, combined with the overruling i

67 | p 150
Recently, a friend (26) told me that when reading a book, her eyes will intuitively drift to the top right-hand corner of the page, as she e

68 | p 152
If an old man dies in Africa, a library disappears. This is a well-known African proverb, where oral tradition ensures that history and st

69 | p 155
By reading, you find peace, you come into a different world, experience and feel things you would otherwise never dream of. Reading is aston

70 | p 156
In recent years the economies of offline print and online content have merged as networks invade the book's former sovereignty. Google Books

71 | p 157
The screens that dominate our lives demand literacy. How else would we utilize our digital tools, or the social media that have become so im

72 | p 158
I read more today than ever before. This contradicts the general idea that we are currently reading less and less. And yet it's true. I watc

73 | p 160
There may very well be drivers who are an exception, but I think that for most, observing traffic signs along the road is an automatism. You

74 | p 162
In the second half of the twentieth century, the arrival of vinyl and the transistor made music permanently available to everybody. And the

75 | p 163
What inspires more? A picture or a text? Stupid question, of course - sometimes a picture and sometimes a text. But almost everybody thinks

76 | p 165
Anybody wishing to know the future of reading must consult the past. I will skip grandma's era; the age of printed paper was nothing more th

77 | p 166
This morning, an academic e-reader (MyiLibrary) again annoyed me by putting me in blinkers and only allowing me to read a few pages. I was s

78 | p 168
In the past, when most people were only moderately lettered and read slowly and out loud (obeying the rules according to the holy printed wo

79 | p 170
Text is a fantastic invention. The idea is simple: in its minimal form, text is nothing more than a short or long sequence of around one hun

80 | p 172
How do illiterates and young children read? They don't read text, but can often point out pictures with the best of them. I spoke to a woman

81 | p 173
I define book as any fairly long, more or less continuous act of reading with some more or less consistent thread.

It is probably always the

82 | p 174
The recent proliferation of digital reading devices has led to extreme format paranoia, as if the book is an endangered species, under threa

Index of Word Frequency

Reading 50-52, 54-60, 62, 64-66, 70-75, 77, 80-81, 83-94, 97-101, 106-107, 109-111, 114, 116, 118-121, 123-130, 133-137, 139, 141-151, 155-156, 158-159, 164-169, 172-174
Read 50-58, 62, 64-67, 71-72, 75-77, 79, 83, 85-87, 90-91, 93, 96, 98-100, 106, 108-110, 112-116, 120, 122, 126-130, 132, 135-138, 143-144, 147, 150-154, 157-160, 164-170, 172-173
Can 51, 54-59, 62, 64, 67-71, 73-74, 76, 80-81, 83-84, 86-92, 94-96, 102-103, 107-115, 117-119, 122-124, 127-130, 132, 134, 137-138, 140, 143-144, 147, 149, 151-152, 154-155, 158-160, 164, 167-173, 175
Book 50, 53-54, 56-58, 60-62, 65-66, 72, 74, 77-79, 81, 85-88, 92, 95-96, 99-102, 106, 110, 113-115, 118, 124, 128-132, 135-144, 147-151, 153-154, 156-160, 164, 166-168, 173-175
Text 50-51, 54-55, 57-59, 61, 66-67, 69, 73-75, 79-82, 84-86, 89-91, 96, 100, 102-106, 109-115, 122, 131-132, 138-139, 142, 144, 148-150, 152, 157-158, 161, 163-165, 167-172
Will 50-54, 56-57, 59-60, 62, 69, 72-74, 77, 80-81, 84-88, 90-91, 93-95, 97, 99-100, 102, 114, 119, 122-123, 134, 138, 140, 143-145, 148-152, 155-156, 158-161, 163-165
Information 52, 54-55, 64, 66, 68, 71-72, 76, 80-81, 87, 92-98, 100-104, 108-110, 113, 119, 121, 127-128, 130, 134, 144, 147, 149-151, 156, 160-161, 167, 169-170, 172
Books 53-54, 56-57, 63, 70-71, 73-75, 77, 87, 91, 99, 109-110, 112-115, 118-119, 121, 127-129, 132, 135-138, 140, 142, 144, 148-149, 151-152, 154, 156-157, 159, 163, 172-175
New 51, 53, 55, 59, 61-62, 69-71, 73, 76-77, 82, 84, 86, 88, 90-96, 99-101, 103-105, 107, 109-110, 113-114, 122, 124, 127, 130-132, 134, 138-140, 142-143, 148, 156, 160-161, 163-164, 170-172, 174-175
One 51, 55, 57, 62-64, 69-70, 72-74, 78, 83, 87, 89-90, 92, 98-99, 102, 105, 109, 111, 114, 116-118, 120, 123-128, 133, 135, 139, 142, 144, 146, 148-149, 151-152, 154, 156, 159, 164, 166-167, 169-170, 174-175
Also 50-51, 54-55, 58, 61, 67-69, 72, 76-77, 79, 82, 86, 88, 93, 97-102, 108-110, 114, 120, 123-125, 129, 131-132, 136, 141, 147-149, 151, 153-154, 157, 160-161, 163-164, 166-168, 170-171, 174
Time 50-52, 54-55, 61, 71-72, 74, 76-77, 81, 86, 88, 93-97, 99, 101, 106-108, 110, 114-116, 119-120, 127-130, 135, 142, 144, 146-147, 152, 159-160, 162-164, 166, 168
Digital 50, 52-55, 57, 66, 68, 73-74, 76-77, 82-86, 88, 91, 101-102, 105-107, 109-110, 113, 118, 126, 129, 137, 139-140, 145, 150, 152, 157-159, 161, 170, 174-175
Like 52-54, 56, 58-60, 62, 65, 71-73, 75, 87-90, 92-94, 96, 102, 105, 109-110, 116, 120-123, 129, 132, 139, 142, 144, 148, 153-154, 156, 159, 161-162, 167, 169-170, 174
Media 50-53, 55-56, 58, 60, 62, 65, 68-69, 72-73, 77, 81-82, 86, 96, 100-104, 107-109, 111, 113, 115, 123, 127, 129-130, 133, 143-145, 155, 157-161, 164-165, 168-169, 172
Image 50, 54-55, 58-59, 78-80, 90-91, 97, 108-109, 111-113, 122-123, 125-126, 140, 149-151, 154, 157, 161-164, 166-167, 170-172
Way 51, 57, 59, 66, 68, 70, 76, 79, 84, 90, 92, 95, 99-102, 104, 109-110, 112-113, 117-118, 121, 124, 126, 129, 132-133, 137, 143-144, 147, 149-150, 155, 159, 161, 165-166, 169, 172, 174-175
World 53, 57, 59, 65, 68, 70, 77-80, 95, 105, 109-110, 112-115, 117-121, 130-131, 134, 143, 146-147, 149, 151, 154-155, 160-161, 164, 168, 170
Words 50-54, 56-58, 60, 62, 64-71, 73-80, 82-88, 90-91, 93, 95-101, 103-104, 106-107, 109-111, 113, 115-117, 119, 121, 123-125, 127, 129-135, 137-138, 140-141, 144, 146-152, 155-158, 160, 162-174
Just 50, 52-53, 57-58, 60, 68, 71-74, 82, 86-87, 89-90, 96, 99, 103, 109, 124-126, 128, 133, 137, 139-142, 144, 148, 153, 156, 158, 161, 164, 166, 172, 174-175
Us 52, 58-59, 63, 68, 74, 78-79, 83, 85, 87-88, 92, 94, 96-97, 108, 127-128, 142, 144-147, 149, 154, 157, 159-160, 165, 169-170, 175
Data 51, 57, 59, 61-64, 71-72, 81, 92, 107-108, 121, 129-130, 145, 151-152, 160, 172
People 50, 52, 55-57, 62, 64, 68-70, 78, 93-94, 100, 104-105, 107-108, 113, 115, 122, 126-127, 132, 136-137, 139-140, 153, 160, 162, 164-166, 168-169
Now 54, 57, 59, 65-71, 73-74, 84-85, 91, 93-94, 99, 101-102, 104, 107, 110, 116-117, 119, 125, 129, 136-137, 140, 149, 154-159, 165-166, 168-169, 175
Screen 50-51, 56, 79, 84, 88-90, 92, 94, 101, 103, 105-106, 119, 121, 138, 143, 149, 155, 161, 168, 171-172, 174
Word 50-53, 60, 64-65, 79-80, 82, 86, 91, 97, 104-105, 112, 122, 124, 129, 139, 150-152, 162, 168-169, 171
Texts 53-54, 66-67, 86-88, 90-91, 98, 103-109, 114, 116, 119, 122-123, 129, 131-132, 134, 143, 145, 157-158, 168, 170
Experience 50, 54-57, 71-72, 81, 83, 85-87, 99-100, 110-111, 114, 116, 121, 133, 138, 143-146, 148, 155, 161, 166, 172-173
Become 52, 58-60, 67, 69, 74, 79, 83, 96, 99, 103-105, 107, 118, 123, 126, 129, 139, 143, 145-146, 149, 152, 154-157, 159, 165
Even 53, 58-59, 61-62, 64-65, 68, 70-71, 74, 77, 81, 85-87, 95, 98, 104, 114, 116, 118-120, 124, 135-136, 142, 145-147, 150, 158-159, 164-165, 175
Reader 57, 63-64, 71, 73, 79, 84, 104-105, 114, 120, 122, 124,

132, 136, 138, 140-143, 148, 151, 168, 170, 175
Content 55-56, 58, 62, 64, 77-78, 93-94, 96, 102-103, 105, 108, 111, 114, 119, 138, 145, 149-150, 154, 156-157, 160-161, 165, 172, 175
Years 50-51, 53-54, 56, 62, 65, 67-68, 73-79, 89, 99, 102, 104, 111, 113-114, 127, 137-139, 152, 156, 160-161, 163, 166, 170, 175
Rather 52, 55, 66, 69-70, 72, 81, 83, 86, 96-99, 101, 107, 111, 114, 118-119, 122, 130, 132, 134, 139, 142, 149-152, 156, 174-175
Still 50-51, 65, 68, 72, 76, 78, 80, 85, 88-89, 93, 99, 102-103, 110-111, 114-116, 120, 123, 125, 127, 133, 140, 149, 152-153, 159, 167, 170, 172
Different 50, 58, 62, 65, 69-70, 72, 81, 84-86, 88-90, 92, 102, 106, 108-110, 116, 118, 122, 132, 134, 144, 147, 151, 155, 169-170, 172
See 55, 59, 61, 66, 68, 72, 75, 78-80, 86, 88-92, 94, 115-116, 122-123, 125, 127-130, 147, 159, 162, 164, 166, 169, 171
Language 54, 64, 69, 79, 96, 109-110, 113, 116, 125-126, 132, 134, 154, 162-163, 169
Something 50, 52, 55, 58-60, 62, 64, 68, 79-81, 98-99, 109, 113, 125, 127, 133, 144, 147-148, 151, 158, 164-165, 168-169, 173-174
Make 56, 63, 68-69, 71-72, 83, 85-86, 89, 92, 95, 102-103, 115-116, 119, 123, 129, 142-143, 148, 160-162, 168-169, 172-174
Stories 51-53, 74, 77, 88, 93-94, 117, 122, 124, 131, 149, 152-154
Knowledge 51, 74, 79-81, 91, 107-109, 113-114, 119, 121, 124, 126-127, 129, 138, 143, 149, 152-154, 157
Paper 55, 57, 67-68, 73, 76-77, 87-88, 91, 99, 102, 114, 118, 126, 128, 138, 147-149, 156-157, 165-166, 170, 172
Writing 52, 61-62, 66-68, 80, 88, 92-93, 104, 119, 122, 126, 129, 134, 138-139, 143-145, 149, 162, 166-167, 169, 173, 175
Culture 52-53, 59, 65, 79, 95-96, 103-104, 111-113, 118, 120, 122-123, 125-126, 130-132, 140, 143, 145, 149, 152, 155, 161
Readers 50, 57-58, 74, 94-96, 98, 100-101, 105, 117, 120, 122-124, 127-129, 138, 140, 142-143, 145, 160, 168, 170
Much 50, 54-56, 58, 68, 71, 73, 85-86, 92-93, 95, 97, 101-102, 114-115, 126, 129, 142-143, 145, 162, 164, 170, 172, 174
Print 54, 72-74, 76, 83, 85-88, 101-102, 125, 127, 142, 149, 156-157, 172, 174
Want 51, 53-55, 60, 66-67, 74, 86, 89, 97, 100, 113, 128, 138, 140, 144, 149-150, 154, 163, 167, 170-171
Many 54, 57, 61-62, 66, 69, 72, 77-79, 93, 96-99, 107-108, 117-118, 124, 127, 133, 138, 144, 149, 151, 153, 166, 173
Page 54, 56-57, 62, 64, 66, 68, 75, 85-87, 114, 133, 135, 138-140, 142-143, 148, 150, 156, 166-167, 174
Form 57-58, 61-62, 66, 70, 72, 75-76, 81, 93, 96, 103, 110-111, 114, 118, 120, 130, 134, 143, 147-148, 155, 167, 170, 174
Picture 58, 71, 78-79, 84, 98, 118, 124-126, 140, 151-152, 159, 163-164, 166
Social 55-56, 61, 69, 74, 80, 93, 98, 102-103, 107, 117, 122-123, 131, 137, 139, 141, 143, 145, 157-158, 164, 174-175
Future 50-51, 54, 57, 65, 69, 71, 77, 80, 86, 93, 95, 103, 106, 125-128, 134, 141, 143-146, 150, 165
Printed 50-51, 54-55, 61, 73, 77, 99-100, 103, 106, 130, 138-140, 143, 153, 156-159, 165, 167-168
Story 53, 63, 72, 77-78, 84-85, 89-90, 93-94, 109, 112-114, 122, 124, 126, 148, 170
Without 59-63, 65-68, 73, 80, 83, 93, 101, 103, 106, 110-112, 114-115, 121, 125-126, 134, 157, 168
Always 52, 55, 64, 71-72, 75, 78-79, 83, 92-93, 97, 110-111, 114, 124, 126, 131-132, 137, 144-145, 149, 163-164, 173
Well 57, 60, 64, 67, 69, 71-72, 75-76, 81, 83, 85, 87, 94, 99, 105, 124, 133, 145-146, 148, 154, 160, 169
Internet 50, 52, 55, 65, 68, 94, 113-114, 117, 122, 131-132, 136-137, 154-156, 158, 163, 172
Know 57-58, 61, 64, 66-67, 81, 87, 90, 95, 99-100, 127-128, 140, 144, 150, 154, 163, 165, 167, 169
Made 51, 63, 78, 87-88, 92, 103, 112-113, 115, 121, 125-126, 128, 135, 152-153, 156, 159, 162, 166, 169
Think 54, 56, 69, 71, 76, 78, 91-92, 109, 111, 121-122, 125-126, 143-144, 146, 160-162, 165, 167, 169, 173-174
Yet 51, 58, 64, 73-74, 78, 85, 89-90, 92, 98, 100, 102, 114, 118, 121, 124, 157-158, 161, 163, 165
First 52, 54, 58, 63-64, 67, 94-95, 107, 113-114, 116, 120, 128, 136, 141-142, 158-159, 162-163, 167, 170
Library 50, 71, 73-74, 81, 112-113, 130, 136, 144-145, 151-154, 157
Long 50-51, 56, 60, 89-92, 96, 100, 106, 114, 122, 124, 127, 133, 138, 154, 158, 164, 170, 173-175
Meaning 50, 73, 82, 91, 98, 104, 110-111, 116-117, 120, 132, 139, 141, 149, 151, 162
Perhaps 52-53, 56, 58-59, 63, 86, 96-97, 106, 118, 132-133, 143, 145, 147, 161, 167, 171, 173
Less 52, 55-56, 58, 66, 69, 73, 96, 98, 124, 137, 146, 158-159, 173
Old 51, 53, 55, 59, 61-62, 76, 89-90, 103, 120, 139, 146, 149, 152-155, 161, 172
Place 51-52, 59, 61, 63, 67, 73, 77, 84, 91-92, 100, 117, 129-130, 133, 135, 141-143, 147, 149, 161
Tools 67, 69, 71-72, 77, 82, 89, 102, 105, 107-109, 147, 150, 157, 168
Written 61, 64, 69, 75, 87, 95, 104, 112-113, 119, 122, 126, 132, 139, 146, 148, 162-163, 169
Day 55, 57, 63, 79, 84, 87, 89-90, 92-94, 109, 116, 124, 136, 144-145, 151, 153, 171, 175

Every 54-55, 61, 73, 78, 97, 102-103, 120, 122, 127-128, 133, 151, 154, 160, 171, 175
Find 66, 71, 77, 81, 86, 97, 99-100, 108, 110, 124, 129, 131, 139, 149-150, 155, 172-173
Means 57-59, 61, 63-64, 66, 74, 78, 80, 86-87, 96, 109, 120, 134, 153, 162
Pages 53, 55, 66, 76, 109, 129, 136, 140, 142-143, 151-152, 156-157, 166-167, 173
Two 54, 58-59, 63, 74, 77, 85-86, 102, 107, 128, 134, 136-137, 140, 146, 148, 154, 159, 164
Used 56, 58-59, 62, 65, 75, 90, 99, 104, 119, 129, 135, 155, 162, 164, 167
Work 55-57, 64, 66, 71, 83, 87, 89-91, 94, 100-101, 109-111, 150, 153, 160-161, 163, 173
End 52, 54, 57, 61, 65, 71, 76, 84, 94, 97, 99, 114, 119, 128, 130, 136-137, 148, 156, 164, 174
Process 54, 60, 67, 77-78, 94-96, 98, 107, 115, 123, 126, 130, 134, 147, 149, 156
Things 50, 52, 56, 58, 67, 70, 74, 84, 112, 116, 126, 131, 144, 149, 155, 165, 172
Visual 58-59, 64-65, 71-72, 77, 93, 95-96, 108-109, 142, 148, 150, 152, 154, 164, 166
Better 51-53, 55, 71, 83, 85-86, 88, 90, 96, 101, 105, 118-119, 126, 143, 148, 150, 168
Ever 50, 52-54, 56, 72-73, 96, 103, 113, 136, 143, 146, 148, 155, 157-158, 161-162, 171, 173
Format 51, 53, 74, 76-77, 82, 134, 138, 142, 147-148, 162, 167, 174
Moment 55, 60, 71, 74, 84, 92, 98, 104, 112, 119, 128, 133, 139, 142, 149-150, 158, 174
Need 51, 53, 62, 64, 70, 72, 81, 85-86, 89, 101, 115, 126, 138, 144, 147, 150, 159, 163-164
News 53, 73, 88-89, 93-94, 119, 129, 136, 145, 152, 159, 164, 168, 172
Open 57, 81-82, 87, 93, 104, 107, 109, 114, 123, 137, 139-140, 147, 152, 166-167
Really 51-52, 60, 76, 79-80, 88, 109, 119, 127-129, 133, 153, 155, 163, 167, 173
Space 59, 66, 69-70, 91, 94, 96, 101-102, 110, 113-114, 122, 132-133, 135, 140, 142, 157, 167, 170
Take 56, 61, 63, 67, 74, 86, 88-89, 119, 130, 133, 136, 143, 149, 154, 159, 169-170
Via 50-52, 94-95, 101, 109, 120, 131, 145, 149-150, 164, 172, 175
Able 52, 55, 61-63, 86-87, 106, 108, 116, 125, 127, 132, 138, 152, 162, 164, 169
Becomes 54, 61-62, 78, 80, 82, 98, 102, 109-110, 120, 150, 155, 166-167
Fact 58, 61, 66, 76, 83, 95, 100-102, 118, 121, 123-125, 139, 142, 148, 157, 174
Get 51, 55, 67, 73, 76, 79, 88, 90, 127, 133, 137, 151, 155, 159-160, 171
Images 50, 58, 64-65, 86, 96, 98, 103, 107-109, 125, 131, 157-158, 162-164, 172
Longer 53-54, 56, 58-60, 67, 76, 78-79, 81, 100, 107, 109, 113, 126, 131, 136-137, 140
Screens 74-75, 88-90, 130, 135, 145, 157, 160-161, 171, 173
Use 51, 60, 63, 69, 72, 79, 83, 96, 108, 124-125, 134, 162, 172, 174
Author 71, 74, 77, 81, 87, 95, 100-101, 104-105, 109, 112, 142-143, 146, 170, 174
Back 54, 72, 74, 76, 86, 95, 102, 105, 113, 116, 119-121, 128, 151, 159, 165, 167
Increasingly 55-56, 58, 69, 80-81, 83, 87, 100, 129, 146-149, 152, 156, 158, 164
Looking 58, 66, 80, 86, 98, 116-117, 120, 150-151, 153, 164, 167, 173
Often 63, 66, 73, 87, 96, 99-102, 112, 129, 137, 158-159, 167, 171-172
Pictures 58, 99, 123-126, 151-154, 157, 159, 163, 172
Right 50, 71-73, 76, 79, 84, 90, 108, 113, 127, 142, 148-152
Search 81, 98, 102, 105, 108, 114, 117, 132, 135, 150, 152, 161-162, 168, 171
Ways 55, 69-70, 77, 83, 99-101, 103, 105-106, 129-130, 138, 142, 147, 151, 157
Around 51, 63, 67, 74, 76-79, 89, 99, 132, 136, 143, 147, 149, 170
Art 51, 54, 57-58, 64-65, 88, 107, 111, 113, 119, 123-124, 126-127, 134, 140, 161, 173
Change 61-62, 68, 77, 110-111, 113, 125, 127, 134, 137, 139, 142-143, 151, 158, 164
Come 61, 72, 81, 85, 113-114, 128, 130, 133, 137, 142-144, 155, 159, 167, 175
Cultural 61, 66, 69, 90, 97, 101, 103, 107-108, 123, 126, 129-132, 174
Everything 56, 61, 80, 82, 99, 103, 109, 112, 121, 128, 131-132, 143, 154, 168, 170
Online 50, 55, 57, 67-68, 72, 77-78, 81, 93, 102, 112, 118, 142, 145, 150, 156-157, 160, 166
Script 111-113, 120
Together 56, 58-62, 77-78, 85, 89, 92, 94, 99, 114, 120-121, 127, 131, 140, 146, 156, 173
Enough 53, 74, 80, 93, 95, 110-111, 118-119, 127-128, 152, 163, 172-173
Good 53, 63, 66-68, 73, 88, 92, 97-98, 118, 146, 150, 154, 169, 175
Possible 63, 69-70, 72, 86, 98, 101, 103, 107, 110-111, 113, 121, 126-127, 162, 171
Sometimes 66-68, 74, 90-91, 102, 121, 135-136, 140, 152, 163-164, 170-171
Technology 50, 69, 75, 96, 101, 103, 117, 121, 126, 130, 140, 159, 165, 170-171
Completely 51, 53, 57, 63, 65, 84-85, 90, 110, 112, 115, 132, 155, 161, 163
Design 54, 58, 60, 64, 69-70, 72, 75, 78, 92, 104-105, 109-110, 119-120, 126, 133-134, 138, 142, 147, 155-157
Electronic 66, 81, 87, 90-91, 99-101, 103, 113, 115, 130, 135, 139, 143, 160, 166-167, 170-171
Literature 73, 80, 83, 95, 100-101, 111, 115, 117, 124, 147, 155
Medium 56, 65-66, 73, 84, 102-103, 111-112, 114, 120, 123, 148, 150, 170
Network 52, 68, 78, 91-94, 131, 157, 161, 175
Possibilities 55, 61, 68-70, 84, 97-98, 102-103, 123, 161, 171-172
Question 50, 83, 95, 117-118, 122, 128, 149, 163-164, 166
Seems 58, 73, 79, 83, 86, 100, 110, 112, 122, 133, 167-168, 173
Set 53, 61, 63, 82, 93, 104, 108, 114, 122, 138, 147-148, 152, 166, 170, 174
Structure 62, 68, 91, 96, 111-112, 114, 126, 129, 134, 142, 151
Access 50-51, 81, 93, 102, 105, 108, 113, 126, 129, 131, 145
Attention 88, 91, 93, 96-97, 101, 108, 116-117, 159-160, 169, 172
Faster 52, 86, 96, 116, 148, 150-151, 169
Graphic 75, 95-97, 102, 105, 113, 119-120, 124, 138, 167, 170-171
Look 55, 63, 68, 80, 88,

102, 116-117, 123, 125, 135, 141, 150, 164, 169, 175
Never 74, 79, 86, 111, 115, 117, 128, 132, 139, 141, 153, 155, 158, 161
Nothing 56, 62, 73, 90-91, 111, 115, 118, 132, 137-138, 151, 165, 170
Order 64, 66, 68, 70, 100-101, 106, 112, 132, 136-137, 150-151, 166
Part 77, 79, 81-82, 96, 99, 105, 109-110, 112, 114-115, 123, 129, 144, 157, 162
Publishing 54, 72, 74, 76-77, 82, 91, 94-95, 105, 115, 174-175
Simply 79, 84, 98, 103, 119, 122, 124, 128, 134, 151-152, 154
Today 61, 68, 72-74, 78, 80, 95, 101, 104-105, 108, 131, 141, 146, 149, 152, 158, 164, 169
Using 51, 63, 72, 75-76, 81-82, 92, 96-97, 109, 124, 145, 159
Actually 57, 64, 78-79, 97, 109, 118, 128, 144, 157, 160, 163, 166, 173
Comic 84, 123-125, 127, 140, 154
Communication 62, 66, 73, 96, 117, 119, 121-122, 131, 134, 155, 158
Game 61-62, 88, 115, 117-118, 143, 156
Man 51, 79, 98, 125-126, 140-141, 152-155
Must 53, 61, 63, 110, 112-113, 148, 164-165, 171
Physical 54, 56, 74, 76, 100, 135, 138, 148, 156-157, 160, 165-166
Reality 59, 69-70, 73, 79, 100, 111-112, 149, 161, 165
Turn 65, 75, 78, 85, 88, 90, 94, 98, 105, 123, 135, 142, 153, 174
Various 61-64, 74, 90, 96, 102, 129, 145, 161, 166, 172
Write 50, 58, 67, 100, 122, 125, 138, 143, 153, 157, 164, 168
Another 53, 63, 66, 73, 79, 83, 87, 92, 106, 116, 118, 123, 139, 168
Available 55, 71, 82, 93, 96, 113, 119, 130, 145, 162, 175
Eye 79, 86-87, 97, 120, 135-136, 166-169
Google 53, 72, 81, 105, 109, 129, 149-150, 154, 156-157, 162
Home 66, 74, 76, 81, 90, 99, 128-129, 135-137, 140
Human 64, 69, 73, 75, 82, 96, 104-105, 107, 115, 126, 151, 165
Ipad 74, 84, 127-129, 135, 147-148, 154-155, 164
Keep 52, 72-73, 87, 90, 114-115, 134, 136, 167, 169, 171
Least 50-51, 75, 89, 95, 106, 108, 125, 127, 136, 162, 174
Libraries 74, 119, 129, 144-146, 153-154
Making 64, 69, 71, 83, 92-93, 98, 130-131, 139, 156, 162, 164
May 90, 105, 121, 132, 145-146, 156, 160, 164
Point 62, 74, 76, 99, 112, 125, 130, 141, 147, 150, 172
Problem 51, 76, 103, 113, 128, 142, 151, 153, 164, 171
Real 51, 59, 71, 85, 87, 93, 99, 112, 128-129, 149
Speed 63, 86, 90, 132, 160, 164, 168-170
Whether 65, 68, 74, 94, 102, 109, 114, 127-129, 149, 163, 169, 174
Along 54, 61, 63, 70, 79, 86, 89, 104, 107, 151, 160, 164, 167
Already 51, 54, 67, 79, 93-94, 98, 109, 123, 125, 174
Although 64, 67-68, 70, 73, 84, 90, 97, 110, 114, 117, 121
Based 65, 76, 78, 95-96, 106, 125, 134, 150, 157, 169
Complex 68, 70-71, 80, 83, 116, 126, 133, 138, 143, 147
Computer 63, 66-67, 76, 82, 84, 104, 106, 108, 136, 162, 164, 171
Course 50, 55-56, 64, 70, 122-123, 144, 156, 163, 165, 167
Devices 74, 77, 87-88, 94, 105-106, 117, 135, 145, 156, 174
Full 74-75, 81, 83-84, 88, 99, 113, 115, 135-137, 164
Hours 52, 57, 63, 83, 94-95, 101, 116, 136-137, 142, 144
Learn 96, 115, 126, 134, 143, 149-152, 164, 172
Life 70, 85, 87, 99-101, 109, 114-115, 120, 124, 127, 144
Might 65, 72-73, 81, 87, 123-124, 135, 145, 158
Music 62, 67, 90, 102-103, 111, 152, 159, 162
Offer 55, 72, 84, 96, 104-105, 130, 149-150, 167, 171-172, 175
Past 50, 81, 115, 120-121, 128, 165, 168-169
Sense 71, 87, 89, 97-98, 116, 120, 126, 132, 139, 151, 173
Since 58, 64-65, 74, 89, 101, 112, 127, 159, 175
Small 52-53, 78, 88, 90, 107, 126, 144, 154, 167, 175
Therefore 55, 61, 66, 96, 98-99, 114, 134, 145, 151, 153-154
Thought 58-59, 61, 73, 79, 110, 113, 126, 133, 146, 155, 161, 163
Twitter 52, 56, 65, 103, 106, 108, 145, 149, 161, 164, 170
Web 72, 83, 104-105, 121, 125-126, 146, 152, 170
Whole 57, 67, 79-80, 86, 90, 113-115, 118, 150
Working 62, 70-72, 83, 89, 94-95, 132, 171
Africa 93-94, 125, 152-155
Ago 51, 55, 62, 65, 74, 78, 103-104, 114, 139, 165, 170
Current 50, 55, 59, 75, 80, 111, 121, 123, 126, 130, 141, 160, 167
Designers 54, 69-72, 92, 105, 118, 161
Everybody 79, 108-109, 119, 130-131, 154, 162-163, 171, 174
Hand 50, 68, 79, 87, 98, 119, 128-129, 132, 166, 168, 170
History 51, 104, 107, 111, 115, 134, 152-153, 158, 166, 174
However 54, 62, 84, 106-108, 117, 122, 124, 138, 143, 161
Important 58-59, 77, 109, 126, 128, 137, 152, 157, 171
Instead 66, 71, 76-77, 81, 110, 138, 144, 162, 170, 175
Letters 58, 113, 116-117, 138, 151, 170
Live 53, 70, 74, 95, 97, 99, 111, 145, 148, 151, 155-156
Material 50-51, 82, 91, 94, 119-120, 135
Message 82, 93, 109, 121, 132, 162, 171
Messages 56, 66, 68, 88-89, 92-93, 132, 139, 158-159
Mind 73, 79, 110, 132, 134-135, 139, 146, 152, 163
Mobile 63, 66, 72, 86, 94, 117, 145, 155, 164, 171
Moving 65, 68, 98, 103, 142-143, 147, 154, 164, 174
Novel 83, 95-96, 100-101, 103, 124-125
Publishers 55, 74, 76, 103, 118, 146, 149, 156, 167, 174-175
Quality 72, 76, 82, 117, 134, 159, 170
Say 52, 57, 59, 98, 100, 124, 145, 155, 163-164, 169
Touch 63, 75, 89, 92, 110, 119, 121-122, 124, 132, 146, 160
Understand 59, 96, 101, 126, 132, 134, 143-144
Across 72, 108, 120, 132, 135, 137, 145, 167, 173, 175
Act 64, 87, 91, 118, 134-135, 145-146, 167, 173
Age 57, 66, 74, 76, 96, 98, 104, 133, 136, 140, 155, 165, 172
Almost 71, 85, 92, 94, 99, 101, 113, 136, 139, 163
Authors 71, 100-101, 104, 118, 122
Best 63, 72, 89, 132-133, 135, 149, 153, 155, 172
Certain 50, 68, 81, 84, 123, 125-126, 132, 167, 172

Clear 58, 63-64, 75, 78, 96, 142, 154, 175
Context 61, 90, 104, 112, 122, 128, 149, 151, 165, 167, 172
Create 77, 90, 94, 107, 109, 118, 122, 132, 150
Easily 51, 64, 70, 79, 81, 94, 100, 144, 159, 168, 172
Example 72, 83, 92, 101, 108, 153, 158, 163, 170-171
Follow 65, 93-94, 103, 107, 111, 114, 121, 142, 168, 175
Free 51, 54, 82, 123, 137, 140, 150-151, 159-161
Games 84, 90, 117-118, 143
Help 52, 59, 63, 85, 105, 108, 118, 129, 165, 175
High 52, 75, 79, 93, 112, 126, 153, 156, 159
Interesting 63, 70, 77, 95, 97, 108, 111, 145, 149, 160, 174
Last 52, 56, 62, 77, 127-128, 140, 144, 175
Left 73-74, 89-90, 115, 132, 140, 146, 148, 151
Line 56, 63-65, 85, 101, 114, 126
Lot 68, 76, 89, 99, 109, 117-119, 174
Networks 53, 80, 92, 102, 109, 130-131, 145, 156, 175
Number 92, 95, 112-113, 125, 144, 149, 170, 174
Patterns 81, 97, 107-109, 129, 146, 168
Printing 50, 52-53, 61, 75, 88, 99, 127, 149, 156
Production 67, 103, 109, 123, 138, 143, 157, 174
Quickly 64, 67, 76, 81, 83, 93, 110, 114, 138, 152, 171
Rules 61-62, 112, 162-163, 168
Second 58, 66-67, 102, 109, 119, 129, 154, 162, 169
Slow 90, 128, 144, 146-147, 151, 156, 159, 168
Slowly 51, 55, 115-116, 148, 160, 166, 168-169
Society 53, 69, 72-73, 97-98, 107, 117, 149, 157, 169
Started 51, 67, 94, 99, 115, 124, 136, 153, 172
Thanks 52, 80, 92, 115, 127, 159, 162
Understanding 64, 74, 90-91, 116, 131, 142-143, 147, 155
Visualization 62-64, 71, 92, 108, 148, 171
Watching 57-60, 85, 89, 144-145, 149
Audio 55, 62, 72, 75-76, 96, 145, 159, 164
Became 51, 65, 72, 76, 92, 140, 142, 162, 164
Bit 86, 89, 98, 116, 127-128, 133, 136
Changes 50, 77, 83, 93, 96, 121, 139, 145, 149
Comes 59, 94, 114, 122, 132, 159, 169, 174
Connected 57, 59, 68, 93-94, 110, 146, 148
Digitization 54, 56, 61, 123, 130, 139, 159, 162
Eyes 58, 80, 86, 89, 120, 133, 138, 143, 150
Field 71, 80, 109, 147, 163-164, 166-167
Film 69, 84-85, 90, 101, 111, 124, 128, 137
Forms 61-62, 73, 75, 83-84, 100, 113, 124, 143
Go 57, 68, 85, 90, 102, 114, 127, 140, 165, 170
Idea 58, 70, 78, 96, 126, 147-148, 154, 158, 170
Interest 55, 83, 93-95, 108, 126, 128, 148, 166
Interface 60, 65, 86, 89, 95-96, 101-102, 159, 165, 174
Later 75, 113-114, 136-137, 142, 163, 170-171
Linear 61, 67, 77, 106, 121, 134, 150-151, 167
Links 53, 59, 78, 89, 126, 131, 139, 173
Little 52, 58, 72, 93, 117, 138, 146, 154, 160
Lives 69, 79, 87, 100, 104, 139, 157
Makes 63, 89, 107, 111, 114-115, 124, 151, 169, 171
Newspaper 55, 57, 116, 127-129, 132
Next 53, 62, 77-78, 87, 99, 125, 135, 161, 165-166
Recent 68, 70-71, 83, 108, 152, 156, 160, 174-175
Research 50, 66, 76-77, 83, 91-92, 106, 109, 130, 135, 146-147, 167, 174
Room 89, 93-94, 136, 138-139, 159
Software 51, 71, 77, 82, 85, 102, 105, 108-109, 125
Symbols 65, 89, 120, 132, 161, 165, 170
Thing 50, 58, 112, 116, 122, 125, 128, 143, 162, 173
Though 70, 72, 85, 101, 118-119, 121, 125, 139, 142
Thousand 51, 71, 78-79, 124, 163-164
Times 60, 73-75, 92, 104, 106-107, 144, 155
Told 53, 57, 63, 117, 150, 153-154, 175
True 58, 104, 124-125, 140, 145, 154, 158, 160, 165
Turned 56, 67, 74, 78, 128, 136, 142, 148
Value 55, 94, 99, 101, 124, 127, 143, 147, 149
Within 61, 68-69, 80, 120, 128, 139, 142, 154-155
Becoming 59, 68, 111, 126, 145, 148, 157
Beginning 51, 62, 112, 114, 116, 121, 141
Believe 56, 62, 101, 137, 146, 160, 164
Contemporary 61, 97, 102, 104, 106, 140, 143, 151-152, 156
Designed 99, 105, 115, 138, 161, 170-171
Enormous 63, 132, 151, 154-155, 161, 166, 168
Fast 87, 102, 110, 114, 126, 146, 164, 168
Flow 61-62, 67, 94-95, 123
Following 50, 65-66, 76, 84, 103, 112, 144, 166
Half 55, 90, 136, 140-141, 148, 152, 154-155, 162, 167
Ideas 74-75, 105, 107, 120, 143, 146, 156, 165
Imagination 74, 107, 112, 114, 124, 148
Individual 72, 97, 107, 122, 132, 161, 164
Large 74, 78, 81, 95-96, 108, 115, 125, 152, 171
Learning 80, 116, 126, 134, 149-150, 164
Living 69, 73, 93-94, 104, 114, 136, 140, 144
Lost 57, 67, 102, 110, 115, 120, 146, 148
Love 53, 55, 62, 70, 76, 99, 137, 170
Mass 52, 62, 65, 70, 73, 132
Million 53-54, 78, 108-109, 151
Perception 64, 97, 166-167
Personal 68, 72, 89, 103, 117, 144-146, 160
Photos 93, 103, 108, 152, 158
Power 52-53, 114, 120-121, 127, 131
Put 95, 115, 117, 122, 130, 142, 159, 162, 164
Reads 50, 62, 73, 79, 97, 120, 128, 141, 170
Role 70, 104, 106, 122, 142-145, 161, 167
Scanning 50, 58-59, 83, 109, 149, 159
Share 53, 55, 87-88, 118, 123, 144-145, 175
Short 56, 92-93, 98, 112, 115, 134, 148, 164, 170
Simple 51, 80, 106, 142, 155, 160, 170
Somebody 67, 127, 161, 168-169
Study 80-81, 107-109
Taken 54, 66, 84-85, 99-100, 146, 157, 159
Tell 52-53, 63, 108, 117, 153, 169
Video 53, 55, 93, 102, 109, 145, 152, 159, 170
Virtual 59, 89, 93-94, 118, 121, 156, 160
Watch 60, 85, 89, 95, 128, 158-159, 164
Went 52, 55, 63, 67, 116, 142, 165
Youtube 65, 85-86, 108-109, 145, 158-159, 162
Ability 52, 81, 87, 102, 122, 135, 162, 169
Alphabet 61, 65, 105, 113, 132, 150-151, 171
Away 56, 85, 88, 99, 110, 119, 139
Behaviour 50, 55, 128, 159, 174
Behind 59, 61, 66, 72, 116, 136, 160, 174
Beyond 70, 72-74, 98, 101, 119, 121,

138, 146
Call 58, 101, 117, 123, 133-134, 147, 155, 164
Case 72, 81, 90, 137, 164, 173
Certainly 92, 96, 114, 125, 159, 164
Classic 79, 83, 102, 147-148, 155, 157, 161
Concept 66, 73, 109, 134, 142, 145, 151
Days 67-68, 83, 114-115, 137, 142, 173
Environment 55, 60, 89, 93, 98, 103, 117, 161
Facebook 56, 65, 81, 103, 129, 136, 145, 149
Far 55, 93, 97, 121, 128, 138, 143
Getting 51, 55, 58, 71-72, 96, 157, 168
Going 57, 65, 81, 93, 106, 136, 149
Impossible 63, 67, 69-70, 75, 103, 123, 166
Interpretation 61, 63-64, 98, 132, 154-155
Kindle 74, 99-100, 137, 145, 156
Knows 59, 79, 89, 98, 110, 154, 167, 169
Landscape 92, 147-148, 165-167
Limited 64, 96, 103, 110, 113-114, 154, 156, 170
Literacy 66, 72, 83, 139-140, 157
Massive 66, 76, 107-108, 123, 150
Matter 55-56, 84, 92, 109, 121, 127, 158
Naturally 91, 128, 136, 148, 159, 167
Newspapers 54-55, 93, 114, 117, 136, 164
Object 103-104, 129, 148, 156-157, 167
Offers 68, 96, 100, 114, 120, 132, 138, 159
Project 54, 62, 67, 78, 92-93, 104, 126, 151, 155, 157, 175
Questions 69, 90, 93-94, 150, 172, 174
Reach 52, 68, 88, 128, 149, 153-154, 169
Said 50, 63-64, 71, 85, 99, 143, 169
Seem 79, 84, 87, 100, 136, 139, 144
Seemed 65, 67, 84, 101, 116, 142
Sentences 57, 110, 114, 129, 132, 167, 173
Shape 69, 77, 97, 115-116, 133
Shapes 115-116, 161
Shift 50, 76, 83, 95, 142-143, 148, 152
Sms 65, 92, 104, 162, 164, 170-171
Sound 55, 85, 149, 158
Sources 72, 94, 110, 126, 134, 152, 157
Start 59, 137, 144, 151, 155, 169, 173
Subject 52, 63, 111, 125, 162, 164
Surroundings 100, 154-155, 165
Table 61, 81, 88-89, 128, 143, 156
Three 63, 65, 70, 75, 111, 127, 136
Types 63, 65-66, 72, 75, 107-108, 140
Typography 75, 82, 91, 110, 167, 172
Ultimately 77, 79, 97, 121, 135, 151
Voice 75, 79-80, 99, 104
Add 85-86, 88, 118, 133, 149, 173
Alone 70, 74, 76, 96, 111, 140, 144
Appear 52, 58, 84, 106, 166, 171, 175
Bed 86-88, 90, 137, 140
Blog 78, 93, 108, 132, 142, 156
Blogs 56, 73, 80, 95, 103, 108, 136, 157
Brain 83, 86, 90, 116, 133, 152, 154
Called 58-59, 78, 82, 139, 153, 165, 173
Carefully 71, 73, 81, 138, 140, 170
Century 52, 65, 119, 162, 168
Challenge 70-71, 96, 106, 110, 131, 171
Changing 56, 121, 154, 161, 165
Collections 74, 77, 107-108, 129-130, 171
Comments 114, 142, 156
Companies 95, 108, 129-130, 161
Consider 74, 76, 109, 134, 143-144, 156
Considered 75, 96, 100, 103, 124, 136, 138
Consume 95, 101, 103, 119, 133, 164
Creating 54, 62, 88, 97, 110-111, 156
Depth 55-56, 59, 107, 118, 121, 138
Difference 52, 58, 66, 83, 92, 98, 172
Disappear 77, 79, 102, 106, 115, 148, 153
Dynamic 55, 74, 106, 111, 144, 152
E-Reader 114, 118, 148, 159, 164, 166
Early 55, 66, 71, 75, 101, 170
Else 52, 67, 70, 82, 89, 109, 157, 169
Everywhere 71, 86, 113, 115, 130, 137-138
Expensive 51, 54, 103, 156, 158, 165
Experiences 54, 56-57, 88, 93
Files 76-77, 90, 102, 105, 166
Focus 69, 77, 100, 102, 116, 118, 167, 174
Forward 52, 86, 89, 143, 147, 159, 167
Friends 52, 88, 94, 118, 137-138, 164
Fully 64, 83, 119, 126, 144, 150
Glance 59, 63, 67, 89, 162, 167
Ground 58, 61, 104, 121-122, 139, 150
Immediately 64, 78, 90, 94, 137, 147
Inside 73-74, 78, 88, 110, 132
Invention 50, 53, 61, 68, 74, 156, 170
Lead 81, 94, 103, 122, 148, 168
Level 79, 98, 103, 116, 121-122, 142
Magazines 54-55, 78, 116, 136, 164
Mean 50, 58-59, 83, 145, 151, 164
Modern 82, 118, 148, 158-159, 171
Networked 78, 92, 103, 118, 123, 142, 157
Objects 74, 87, 99, 138, 143
Ones 88-89, 122, 125, 129
Opened 94, 99, 116, 148, 167
Orality 138-140
Original 63, 79, 87, 105, 113, 119, 141, 170
Pdf 76-77, 82
Percent 73, 103, 139, 153, 157, 174
Phone 139, 157, 160, 164, 171
Play 70, 88, 106, 143, 161, 167
Potential 74, 95, 122-123, 130, 145, 164
Private 51, 87, 100, 107, 130, 139, 144
Processes 57-58, 71, 106-107, 147
Recently 59, 68, 92, 99, 101, 150, 165
Relationship 130, 139, 142, 147, 153, 170
Remains 73, 80, 131, 133, 149, 165, 167
Says 57-58, 78-79, 152, 163, 165
School 65, 67, 76, 89-90, 92, 97, 127, 148, 168, 174
Science 52, 61, 70, 81, 108, 120, 171
Sentence 67, 86, 110, 118, 163, 169
Sequence 89, 114, 134, 151, 170
Show 62-63, 89, 108, 125, 147, 154
Sorts 122, 144, 148-149, 166, 173
Speaking 66, 75, 79, 89, 118, 134
Spoken 64-65, 79, 85, 104, 126, 162
Stream 88, 94, 158, 161, 170
Systems 80-81, 87, 108, 146, 160
Technological 57, 70, 103, 134-135, 146
Thus 58, 69, 92, 96, 98, 132, 139
Took 53, 64, 70, 99, 101, 128, 142
Transitory 59-60, 62, 120, 155, 159, 171
Unique 53-54, 78, 114, 143, 148
View 56, 59, 76, 83, 112, 115, 124
Week 54, 116, 128, 136
Writer 53, 56-57, 60, 75, 80, 84, 101, 109, 112, 115, 124, 131, 137, 140-141, 148, 152, 157, 163, 165
Writers 74, 104-105, 112, 118, 159, 168
Action 69, 104, 134, 140-141, 166
Active 63, 94, 142-143, 147, 166
Allows 70, 82, 93, 129, 143, 170
Animation 60, 75, 84, 149
Appeared 65, 84, 115, 123, 132, 162
Articles 57, 76, 95, 125, 128
Average 57, 117-118, 137, 159, 168
Beings 65, 69, 107, 151, 165
Booking 173-174
Came 77, 92, 99, 136, 163
Car 81, 89
Centuries 74, 129, 146-147, 153
Changed 68, 76, 85,

124, 144, 164, 175
Channels 55, 72, 111, 145, 159, 175
Check 51, 68, 88-89, 93-94
Child 87, 116, 125, 159, 164
Chinese 132, 151-152, 164
Cloud 50-51, 130, 171, 174
Cold 78, 86-87
Coming 94, 99, 164, 167
Concerned 55, 68-69, 75, 94, 98
Constantly 108, 118, 139, 144, 166-167
Continue 80, 86, 114, 134, 169
Creative 73, 83, 105, 122, 131, 147, 167-168, 175
Decide 70, 93-95, 114, 129
Developed 59, 68, 92, 123, 171-172
Development 65, 93, 115, 126, 130, 161, 163
Dutch 60, 79, 117, 120, 137, 146, 150, 153, 155, 157-158
Ebooks 54, 56, 74, 99, 145
Era 93, 100, 113, 130, 165
Et 72, 77, 124, 145, 149
Exist 51, 112, 114, 134, 149, 153
Favourite 88-91, 128, 145
Feel 71-72, 99, 102, 155, 159
Figures 59, 63, 81, 93, 95
Found 71, 82, 99, 113, 125
Given 114, 119, 121, 138, 147
God 102, 111-112
Graphics 62, 71-72, 103, 170
Greater 98, 115, 118, 142, 164
Hardly 78, 111, 116, 136, 151, 159
Head 53, 58, 66, 69, 85, 115, 153, 155
Heart 87, 115, 141, 151, 163
Huge 74, 95, 101, 103-104, 143
Infinite 112-113, 131, 159
Insight 59, 111, 118, 155, 159
Larger 79, 107-108, 114, 147, 173
Leads 63, 84, 129, 131, 135, 163
Light 51, 135-136, 143, 172
Linked 58, 78, 96, 103, 126, 154
Literally 74, 80, 92, 154, 169
Machine 82, 87, 103-104, 115, 154, 162, 171
Magazine 50, 90-92, 103, 108, 112, 116, 160, 163
Minimal 97-98, 102, 170
Mother 73, 87, 127, 144, 153, 164
Multiple 82, 95, 102, 122, 134, 145
Nature 56, 61, 77-78, 96, 156, 165
Novels 74, 95-97, 101
Numbers 55, 65, 134, 139, 151, 159
Others 89, 119, 126, 130, 143, 166
Otherwise 63, 87, 134, 153, 155
Outside 57, 61, 111, 131, 143, 147
Oversight 59, 105
Particular 64, 80, 84, 97, 106, 118
Pass 73, 81, 89, 94, 117
Piece 89, 92, 105, 127, 144, 163
Pieces 63, 90, 109, 116, 136-137
Political 69-70, 111, 113, 132
Practice 60, 82, 108, 126, 142, 163, 171
Present 60, 75, 108, 110, 118, 139
Press 52-53, 69, 99, 104, 123, 127, 156
Provide 56, 94, 131, 160-161
Public 67, 78, 132, 136, 160-161, 175
Readership 95-96, 101, 122
Relationships 62, 77, 122, 131, 146
Release 60, 87, 101, 109, 112, 153
Relevant 69, 76-77, 81, 160-161
Remain 57, 61, 77, 85, 160, 165
Screening 88-90
Series 62, 84, 98, 118, 124, 141
Shows 79, 84, 88-89, 100
Significance 58-59, 119, 148, 172
Signs 64-65, 115, 151, 160
Sit 61, 66-67, 128, 136
Situation 83, 87, 99, 147, 173, 175
Smell 73, 91-92, 148, 172
Son 89-90, 151-153, 165
Sounds 85, 98, 116-117, 151
Specific 61, 93, 102, 130, 162
Stage 85, 116-117, 131
Static 74, 77, 96, 106, 139-140
Status 61-62, 104, 117, 130, 173
Strip 84, 123, 125, 154
Symbolic 65-66, 165
System 63, 96, 167, 169, 175
Tablet 93, 105-106, 118, 147, 149
Tablets 51, 84, 138, 158, 174
Techniques 83, 108, 129, 156, 168
Technologies 57, 68-69, 105-106, 135
Ten 63, 65, 68, 78, 114, 164
Thinking 60, 69, 91, 124-125, 173
Thoughts 67, 87, 95, 110, 133, 144
Title 71, 77, 87, 97, 154
Traffic 63, 89-90, 160
Transition 50, 76-77, 136
Transmission 56, 75, 139-140
Try 85, 90, 116, 122, 144
Type 61, 75, 132, 158, 168
Videos 107-108, 145, 152, 158-159
Virtually 67, 106, 119, 126, 159, 166
Works 51, 88, 147, 151, 169
Worlds 69, 74, 85, 102, 107
Young 104, 118, 124, 127, 164, 172
Absorb 87, 101, 109, 170, 172
Abstract 63, 65, 126, 129, 163
Accessible 130, 134, 154-155
According 68, 111, 124, 159, 168
Activity 58-59, 80, 86
Added 55, 85, 94, 127, 149
Advertising 79, 110, 160, 163, 175
Anyone 59, 73, 89, 94, 158
Approach 62, 78, 100-101, 107
Architecture 54, 60, 92, 156-157, 161
Area 93-94, 110, 112
Arrival 101, 113, 158-159, 162
Artist 71, 113, 123-126, 140-141, 148, 161
Began 51-52, 67, 141
Begin 70, 88-89, 161
Black 76, 105, 126, 157
Blur 115-116
Body 68, 81, 101, 117, 127, 162
Bottom 65, 68, 79, 142, 151
Break 66-67, 71, 131, 137
Browsing 50, 59, 109, 121, 134
Buy 54-55, 81, 127-128
Cetera 72, 77, 145, 149
Characters 50, 107, 118, 124, 146, 151
Choose 59, 100, 107, 135, 169
Claimed 104, 124-126, 175
Collected 63, 127, 129, 157
Collecting 119-120
Condition 61-62, 139, 156
Consumed 77, 109, 119, 164, 172
Consumption 52, 102-103, 110, 130
Contained 56, 75, 79, 81, 109
Countries 50, 79, 153
Creates 96, 103, 107, 114, 167
Crucial 61, 68, 77, 110, 150
Daily 79, 93, 109, 111, 127
Deep 52, 73, 98, 107, 116
Definition 70, 75, 146, 151, 159
Designing 59, 69-70, 109, 160
Developments 50, 81, 107, 134, 150
Device 59, 72, 93, 106
Differently 58, 96, 106, 158, 168
Difficult 72, 99, 122-123, 143
Dinner 90, 128, 143
Display 88-89, 105-106
Distribution 55, 77, 135, 146, 164
Done 56, 87, 99, 118, 137
E-Mail 63, 66, 169-170
Easy 53, 68-69, 72
Effort 64, 71, 126, 142, 151
Elements 62, 102, 110, 124
English 91, 99, 105, 127, 173
Events 72, 154, 156, 165
Eventually 53, 120, 134, 156, 173
Existence 82, 85, 94, 120-121
Express 107-108, 146, 162
Expression 61, 120, 129, 140, 143
Feeds 52, 80, 108, 159, 161

Filter 105, 129, 160-161
Finally 52, 74, 79, 89, 130
Finding 71, 101, 146, 171
Fixed 54, 62, 66, 149, 151
Flat 98, 133, 140-141
Frames 96, 121-123
Front 113, 136, 150-152
Function 61, 122, 150, 164, 171
Generally 50, 65, 124, 153, 158
Generated 82, 90, 102, 105, 158
Generation 58, 80, 87, 103-104
Gives 114, 120, 166, 168, 171
Groups 52, 107, 136, 142
Happen 51, 142, 158, 164
Herzog 125
Hold 50, 87-89, 104
House 95, 99, 138-139, 162
Hundred 74, 128, 137, 151, 170
Illiterate 65, 115, 120, 124, 172
Individuals 51-52, 81, 123, 143
Journalists 52-53, 71
Key 50, 62, 103, 150, 171
Kind 70-71, 87, 123, 173
Latest 55, 93, 129, 138, 172
Leading 65, 74, 76, 78, 142, 161
Learned 81, 99, 126-127, 172
Link 59, 88, 115, 131, 151
Listening 64, 90, 144-145
Losing 58-59, 128, 146, 156
Mainly 106, 113, 153, 158-159
Map 60, 63-64, 128
Meanings 59, 98, 120, 122, 151
Mediated 69-70, 75, 111, 117
Methods 77, 107, 149-150
Morning 55, 88-89, 145, 166
Move 70, 87, 93, 117, 123
Movies 85, 144, 148
Needed 56, 76-77, 97, 108
Nevertheless 64, 81, 97, 102, 149
Newsroom 93-94
Nobody 50, 64, 114, 125
Onto 54, 75, 80, 86, 155
Passing 51, 128, 138, 153, 168
Period 71, 81, 119, 127, 165
Preferable 70, 163
Publisher 57, 93-94, 145, 150, 159, 165, 173
Realize 60, 97, 142-143, 174
Recognition 90, 107, 150, 152, 168-169
Replaced 52, 64, 100, 148
Required 64, 117, 142, 156, 164
Russian 79
Sales 54, 95, 139, 156
Saw 85, 128, 137, 160, 171
Saying 55, 58, 86, 99, 140
Scarce 53, 97-98, 153, 163
Scholars 80-81, 152, 168
Searching 65, 88, 120, 152, 162
Seen 111-112, 118, 124, 138
Senses 75, 96, 102, 147
Sent 63, 92, 137, 166, 171
Side 58, 73, 88, 142, 151
Single 119, 148, 151, 166-167
Size 107, 114, 138, 147, 175
Smart 72, 119, 127, 151, 158
Smartphone 93-94, 149, 171
So-Called 65, 85, 118, 153, 166
Soon 86, 136-137, 155, 166
Statistics 52, 94, 107-108, 152
Suddenly 84, 101, 136, 142, 164
Sure 67, 71, 88, 129
Talking 85, 104, 139, 149, 159
Technique 83, 86, 149, 168, 171
Terms 59, 82, 147, 167-168
Textual 82, 91, 95, 110, 135, 158
Thousands 63, 76, 119, 151
Top 63, 73, 138, 150, 174
Topic 85, 93-94
Traditional 77, 110, 142, 166
Train 81, 137, 140, 155, 172
Understood 59, 73, 79, 98, 132
Universe 80, 108, 120, 129
User 65, 96-97, 149, 162
Variety 98, 106, 108, 169
Visible 80, 92, 95, 121
Wants 54, 140, 150, 154
War 78, 104, 118, 148
Websites 57, 105, 136, 160, 164
West 94, 105, 151, 154
Wherever 93, 135, 137, 155
Yes 57, 67, 76, 95, 133
Absorbed 87, 127, 149
Absorbing 58-59, 109-110
Academic 76, 166-167
Activities 144-145, 149
Adding 56, 85, 118, 149
Advance 75, 88, 131, 167
Affordances 103-104, 106, 143
African 93, 152-153
Aggregate 97, 105, 122
Allowed 74, 120, 135, 137
Allowing 76, 142, 155, 166
Amazon 129, 137, 156-157
Among 97-98, 117, 143
Analysis 97, 108, 139
Answer 57, 106, 128, 164
Anything 74, 85, 99, 169
Apparently 52, 55, 67, 116
Appears 86, 118, 173, 175
Ask 99, 148, 153, 162
Aspect 79, 143, 156
Associated 100, 135, 175
Authority 81, 169
Automatically 79, 105, 161, 163
Aware 58, 93, 126, 132
Balance 82, 148, 159, 167
Basis 120, 125, 149, 152
Blind 120, 125, 136
Bound 53, 74, 106, 173
Built 81, 122, 137, 169
Business 99, 124, 150, 170, 173
Carrier 92, 114, 148
Carriers 91, 117, 127, 172
Carry 74, 99, 110, 136
Chance 122, 160-161
Charge 51, 87, 150, 159
Chat 55, 95, 139, 146
Cinema 65, 85-86, 137
City 84, 92, 109, 141, 168
Close 88, 107, 139, 170
Closely 72, 89, 96, 111
Codex 53-54, 66
Colleagues 94, 142
Collection 54, 121, 159, 171
Combination 84, 96, 103, 120
Comics 96, 119, 124
Compared 86, 99, 115, 159
Compiled 77, 92, 119, 122
Complete 112, 127, 162-163
Computational 107-108, 123, 130
Concentrate 51, 81, 147, 169
Concentrated 50, 81
Concentration 102, 139, 159, 172
Concepts 59, 129, 134
Concern 67-68, 119, 136
Conditions 73, 91, 122-123
Configurations 62, 106, 117
Consequence 113, 124, 141, 148
Consequences 69, 83, 102
Constant 94, 146, 161
Consumers 70, 105, 145, 156
Contains 109, 115, 121, 132, 174
Continuous 103, 149, 173
Contrast 68, 73, 83
Created 110-111, 121-122
Critical 69, 72, 76, 105, 156
Critics 58, 101, 117, 130
Dance 89, 162-163
Death 127, 174
Decline 52, 93, 149
Deeper 89, 97-98, 155
Degree 50, 68, 98
Demands 79, 82, 162, 170
Depends 91, 97, 149
Desk 76, 78, 95, 136
Develop 72, 114, 134, 169
Developing 81, 106, 108, 161
Digitally 54, 83, 102, 114
Distraction 70, 73, 144, 159, 169
Distributed 80-81, 134, 171
Door 130, 136, 140
Download 51, 88, 128, 155
E-Readers 51, 137, 166
Easier 110, 123, 159, 164
Ebook 54, 129, 145, 167
Economy 97, 156-157
Editing 94-95, 126

Efficient 53, 66, 150, 162
Either 86, 96, 103, 171
Emerge 70, 80, 86, 116
Emotions 87, 112, 169
Enable 81, 103, 114, 147
Enjoy 71, 82, 119, 126
Ensure 50, 84, 105, 162
Entire 74, 76
Environments 103, 105, 146, 170
Established 102, 135, 151, 171
Exact 63, 76, 98, 107
Except 89, 99, 127, 165
Exclusive 56, 85, 102, 164
Existing 58, 78, 106, 132
Expanding 82, 108, 110, 151
Explain 97, 106, 110, 152
Explains 52, 91, 128, 140
Explore 69, 108, 129-130
Extent 83, 100, 106, 157
Facts 72, 138, 169-170
Fear 90, 119, 133, 152
Fifty 51, 75, 136
Films 84, 111, 126, 149
Final 76, 82, 130
Fine 87, 91-92, 113, 149
Fit 73-74, 126, 145
Five 73, 96, 136
Flickr 65, 108
Flows 81, 89, 117
Forget 71, 144, 159, 164
Formats 51, 77, 105, 162
Forty 99, 104, 172, 175
Four 75, 84, 135, 137
Freedom 105, 162, 168
Gamer 117, 142, 174
Gathering 50, 59, 71, 86, 109
General 64, 97, 134, 158
Give 87, 128, 133, 172
Goes 116, 129, 146, 154
Great 56, 113, 145
Growing 59, 94-95, 98
Handle 67, 72, 106, 116
Hands 89-90, 135
Hard 76, 87, 153
Higher 58, 64, 107, 171
Highly 65, 93, 153, 158
Husband 154
Ignore 89, 123, 132, 148
Immediate 98, 147, 154, 167
Including 72, 84, 96, 154
Increases 76, 86, 98, 124
Industry 65, 76, 95, 175
Inflation 52-53
Influence 50, 78, 100, 150, 161
Initially 82, 159, 166, 170
Ink 82, 127, 148, 163
Intention 87, 91, 98, 131
Journals 76, 87
Kinds 65, 80, 106, 129
Knowing 94, 119, 130, 147
Known 54, 72, 99, 167
Languages 79, 126, 151
Largely 103, 106, 142, 156
Latin 59, 113, 127, 134
Layer 85, 92, 161, 165
Layout 78, 91, 96, 142
Leave 85, 154, 160
Leaves 79, 107, 132, 141
Let 64, 73-74, 88, 99, 165
Lets 77
Letter 115, 117, 135, 140-141, 170
Likely 77, 93, 96, 102
Lines 144, 168, 170-171
Liquid 93-94
Listen 52, 90, 133, 164
Lose 52, 93, 150, 174
Machines 65, 82, 103, 160
Market 84, 137, 171, 174
Masses 52-53
Master 80, 125, 132, 168
Materials 87, 91, 138
Maybe 60, 72, 74, 147
Memory 57, 97, 114, 119
Men 80, 153-154, 163
Millions 107, 129, 159
Movement 87, 95, 131, 167
Moves 77, 82, 140, 167
Multimodal 96, 157-158
Narrative 118, 122, 143, 167
Necessary 63, 82, 86, 169
Needs 91, 133, 149, 151
Northern 93-94
Notion 56, 66, 73, 82
Nowadays 97, 127, 136, 155
Occasionally 57, 133, 161, 168
Offline 77, 156
Offset 157-158
On-Demand 93-94, 149
Opening 116-117
Oral 75, 139, 152
Pan 151-152
Pancake 67-68
Paragraphs 114, 129, 142
Parents 83, 136, 153
Passed 68, 153, 157
Per 78, 128-129, 171
Perspective 59, 73, 122, 147
Pick 94, 114, 127, 160
Plan 60, 92, 109, 126
Platform 65, 74, 85, 94, 96, 155
Poetics 111
Popular 95, 101, 117, 153
Portable 53, 74, 170
Powerful 52, 73, 101, 118
Precise 61, 102, 107
Presented 63, 82, 96, 100
Prevent 62, 68, 72, 118
Probably 50, 68, 152, 173
Problems 67, 127, 143, 146
Produced 51, 138, 171-172
Progress 61, 152, 159, 167
Proper 113, 150, 163, 173
Publications 55, 71, 108, 143
Push 93, 105, 140
Radical 50, 52, 61, 131
Range 62, 72, 83, 172
Reached 94, 99, 107, 172
Receive 88, 118, 171
Remarkably 111, 117, 139, 142
Requires 108, 117, 126
Road 63, 66, 133, 160
Roads 62, 64, 109, 136
Route 65, 89, 160
Several 83, 114, 116, 126
Shared 57, 108, 135, 145
Silent 52, 85, 144
Skills 71, 81, 124, 162
Solution 72, 142, 153, 170
Somewhere 63, 79, 121, 128
Sort 101, 162, 164, 169
South 63, 139, 153
Speak 51, 96-97, 158
Spent 50, 56, 144-145
Standard 76, 102, 142
Stone 91, 170, 174
Streams 90, 110, 130, 161
Streets 104, 115, 130
Strips 84, 140
Students 80, 83
Stupid 83, 111, 163, 169
Survive 87, 145, 152
Takes 51, 73, 129, 143
Telephone 63, 104, 155, 164
Television 78-79, 118, 164
Theories 65, 98, 106
Towards 65, 119, 149, 152
Traces 65, 107, 122, 175
Training 86, 116, 129
Trying 84, 116, 144, 166
Tv 65, 158-160
Tweets 108, 135-136, 171
Twenty 62-63, 67, 102
Typographic 138
Unexpected 100-101, 112, 147
Uses 69, 105, 122, 151
Vision 68, 147, 167
Warm 86-88
Wave 62, 66, 88-89
Woman 125, 140, 154, 172
Women 80, 100, 116, 153-154
Worth 65, 71, 93, 173
Wrote 57, 75, 112, 126, 146
Accounts 51, 103, 175
Acquire 81, 117, 172
Acquiring 95, 113
Ad 101-102, 112
Adapting 61, 116, 134
Admit 58, 90, 133
Air 57, 64, 89
Allow 108, 155, 175
Alongside 65, 96, 102
America 63, 165
Amount 72, 106, 151
Ancient 59, 120, 153
Anybody 108, 165, 169
Anywhere 55, 71, 86
Applications 69, 84, 127
Applied 142, 146, 152
Applies 126, 143, 159
Apps 105, 114, 160
Archives 81, 89, 152
Aristotle 111-112
Arrangement 129, 138, 151
Arrive 130, 146-147
Asked 63, 123, 125
Assumed 61, 100, 147
Bad 52, 101, 123
Barcelona 128
Barriers 123, 131
Bits 54, 133, 144
Bookcase 127, 150, 152
Borges 112-113
Broken 51, 120, 134
Buildings 89, 115, 165
Cabbage 85-86
Calls 95, 139, 165
Capable 125, 131, 154
Capacity 71, 103, 115
Catch 81, 93, 97
Ceiling 86, 90, 121
Centre 90, 106, 117
Chair 57, 60, 89, 91, 119, 135
Challenged 72-73, 144
Characteristic 50, 61, 169
Choice 63, 142, 149
Christian 111-112
Circle 78, 121, 127, 135
Clever 128, 172
Click 75, 119, 130
Closed 112, 114, 140
Code 65, 125, 134
Coherence 156, 164, 173
Coherent 122, 173
Coincide 80, 165, 169
Collectors 99, 120
Combinations 102, 113, 149
Comparison 73, 98, 152
Comprehension 106, 131, 138
Computers 65, 80, 134
Connections 78, 104, 175

Considerable 64, 106, 152
Consistent 173
Consuming 129, 134, 144
Contextual 104, 110, 139
Conversations 107-108, 121
Copy 87, 137
Couple 126, 136, 159
Cover 157, 172
Covers 108, 140, 150
Currently 72, 93, 109, 158
Dancing 162-163
Dark 104, 120, 137
Dating 63, 76
Decades 84, 86, 153
Deliver 75, 104, 175
Demand 93, 157, 161
Density 64, 83, 104
Derived 64, 120, 122
Derrida 61, 79, 104
Designer 60, 72, 75, 77-78, 110, 117, 123, 127, 138, 157, 161
Detail 89, 93, 138
Detailed 89, 107-108
Determined 61, 131, 147
Diagonal 144, 168
Diary 88, 132
Digitize 73, 81, 102, 151
Digitized 74, 139
Direct 88, 118, 169
Discussion 95, 142
Distribute 76, 170, 175
Donald 116
Dots 75, 170-171
Drive 62, 76, 89
Duck 116
Ease 76, 134, 136
Editorial 63, 78, 95, 102, 104
Emergence 61, 81, 107
Emotional 87, 110, 135
Encoded 56-57, 114
Encounter 100, 109, 137
Engaged 107, 142-143
Engine 105, 114, 171
Entirely 58, 82, 89
Equivalent 76, 111
Exists 57, 114, 131
Expanded 101, 147, 175
Expected 80, 83, 166
Expects 64, 150
Experiments 93, 142
Explained 63, 114, 128
Explosion 123, 160
Extra 99, 105, 109
Extremely 84, 126, 158
Fabrics 153-154
Face 92, 147
Fall 54, 90, 148
Family 87-88, 153
Feedback 94, 118, 139
Feelings 87, 107-108
Finger 68, 135, 138
Finite 61, 102, 156
Floating 88, 92, 102
Fluid 61, 103, 139
Flying 90, 125, 154
Font 82, 114, 171
Foreign 79-80, 162
Forgotten 57, 101, 165
Form/Cage 61
Former 60, 63, 156
Foundation 82, 121, 126
Fraction 101, 119, 154
Frame 91, 123, 155
Fresh 67, 70, 88
Futures 69-70
Gained 59, 101, 117
Gamers 117-118
Gave 71, 128, 168
German 105, 116, 127
Gets 87, 89, 157
Global 65, 72, 93, 102
Graphical 65, 102, 142
Gutenberg 54, 64-65, 155
Happy 72, 94
Hear 62, 79, 169
Historical 61, 153-154
Hope 51
Host 81, 105, 140
Hour 90, 155
Html 82, 134
Iconic 65
Ideal 82, 161, 172
Illiteracy 115, 153
Illiterates 140, 154, 172
Imagine 85, 145, 147
Imagining 70, 146
Immersed 58, 85, 116
Implications 69, 80, 117, 142
Importance 76, 148-149
Importantly 72, 96, 157
Increasing 101, 144
Inevitably 61, 64-65
Ingredients 90, 151
Instant 53, 106
Integrated 94, 132, 152
Intense 97, 125, 162
Interaction 74, 96, 123, 135
Interactions 56, 69, 156
Interfaces 102, 105
Involving 64, 87, 101
Ipads 55, 127, 160
Irritation 166
Issue 103, 133, 152
Journalism 52-53, 95
Jumping 121, 123, 166
Keeps 99, 117, 169
Kept 63, 127-128
Led 95, 144, 174
Legible 80, 138
Levels 69, 95, 160
Libre 82
Limitless 59, 74, 106
Limits 101-102, 145
List 128, 164
Lithography 157-158
Lived 62, 154
Logical 55, 111, 148
Looks 84, 136, 175
Loud 50, 168-169
Magic 110, 169
Magnified 125-126, 165
Mail 56, 63
Manage 119-120, 173
Managed 86, 127, 153
Mandatory 128, 131, 164
Margins 66, 114, 142
Materiality 54, 104, 123
Matters 56, 67, 148
Maximal 97-98
Mcluhan 65, 113-114
Meaningful 69, 80, 140
Meant 57-58, 140
Meantime 72, 94, 137
Meeting 68, 121, 132
Method 63, 82, 119
Metro 128
Michael 144-146
Milk 88
Minds 63, 143, 163
Minutes 67, 137, 139
Misconception 63, 78
Missing 59, 72, 166
Mix 123, 151
Mode 91, 94, 98
Models 106, 146
Mostly 62, 89, 130
Movements 69, 158, 162
Natural 79, 143, 167
Navigation 60, 134, 160
Near 88, 93, 123
Necessarily 53, 81, 159
Netherlands 69, 78, 92, 137, 157
Night 128, 136-137
Notice 97, 108, 172
Office 89, 135, 160
Older 58, 111
Operate 99, 102, 156
Opportunity 105, 107, 122
Opposite 72, 145, 163
Organize 81, 153, 169
Outlets 72, 100
Panic 67, 120, 164
Papers 76-77
Parallel 69, 99, 126
Pattern 107, 151, 159, 168
Pay 72, 88, 162
Pdfs 76, 156-157
Peace 110, 148, 155
Perfect 75, 112, 138
Perfectly 64, 102, 165
Permanently 68, 130, 162
Person 87, 97, 110, 120
Philosopher 110, 121, 133, 163-164, 170
Physically 56, 103
Pleasure 64, 71, 99
Plot 111-112
Pointer 111-112
Points 63, 98, 135
Practical 61, 82, 148
Practically 115, 128, 162
Practices 83, 106
Predicted 65, 139
Prefer 61, 93, 132
Primarily 50, 95, 148
Principle 130, 164
Prints 62, 64, 125
Probable 70, 118
Produce 87, 157-158
Producing 56, 129, 134
Products 102, 105, 108
Professional 50, 71, 168
Profiles 122, 129, 175
Publish 94, 159-160
Published 93, 114, 125, 132
Purely 51, 103, 122
Rapid 149, 167, 170
Rapidly 66, 126, 151
Rare 82, 148, 153
Rate 87, 96, 149
Realized 115, 142
Received 63, 66, 153, 159
Reception 98, 104
Recognize 89, 115-116
Red 88, 119, 137
Reference 98, 111, 155
Replace 53, 158, 163
Representation 85, 112, 126
Reproduction 63, 140
Resistance 120-121, 169
Resources 81, 108, 135
Rest 62, 81, 114
Results 81, 99, 168
Return 94, 99, 161
Reverse 75, 120, 160
Rid 76, 160
Sake 109-110
Satisfy 112, 151, 162
Save 51, 145, 170
Savouring 98, 133, 172
Scanned 53-54, 80
Scenario 126, 145, 163
Sciences 70, 98, 107, 120
Scientific 132, 146, 167
Scientists 76, 108
Send 93, 132, 171
Sequential 62, 123, 140
Serve 125, 135, 137
Service 145, 151, 171
Shall 113, 131, 149
Sharing 57, 145, 149
Shoe 78
Shop 127
Shorter 78, 129, 157
Similar 162, 171, 174
Sitting 81, 99, 138
Skill 163, 168
Sleep 95, 136
Smaller 72, 89, 175
Sofa 57, 60, 137
Somewhat 58, 80, 166
Speech 104-105, 137, 171

Spend 52, 57, 83
Stand 59, 119, 127
Stands 90, 152, 163
State 75, 91, 116, 146, 155
Stored 76, 114, 122
Storytelling 71, 124, 153
Street 81, 154, 163
Strength 92-93, 111
Stroke 119-121
Subjects 55, 97, 158
Subtle 68, 148, 169
Successful 77, 124, 142
Suggest 65, 126, 129
Supported 53, 84, 148, 158
Suspect 132-133, 137
Talk 52, 92, 100
Targeted 157, 172
Task 95, 143, 148
Tells 78, 93, 154
Tension 110, 112, 172
Term 52, 151, 167
Thick 92, 107, 119
Thirty 139, 157, 166
Titles 72, 128, 164
Tool 146, 170-171
Tragedy 111-112
Transfer 138, 152, 154
Transparent 59, 75, 95
Trick 55, 83, 105
Truly 101, 146, 155
Truth 112, 121
Turning 57, 71, 146
Typesetting 82, 156
Understandable 71-72, 90
Unread 128, 137, 144
Up-To-Date 55, 102, 149
Upon 100, 105, 175
Urge 120
Useful 71, 83, 149
Usually 89, 173
Versions 111, 167
Vibrant 74, 139, 142
Viewers 58
Waiting 81, 137, 140
Wall 86, 88-89
Walls 90, 130, 136
Website 78, 95, 101
Weight 99, 139, 148
Western 111, 113
Whatever 97, 140, 162
Whereas 98, 100, 124
Whereby 78, 81, 170
Wide 68, 100, 121
Window 75, 150, 168
Wisdom 154-155, 163
Wish 70, 109, 132
Wonder 76, 79, 85
Wonderful 69, 85, 113
Workflow 76-77
Worry 52, 93, 139
Wrong 53, 151
Year 78, 115, 144
1990S 65, 101
Absence 87, 98
Absent 110-111
Academy 104, 127, 134
Accidental 132-133
Accumulated 112
Accurately 146, 170
Achieve 119, 149
Achieved 124, 147
Actions 161, 167
Acts 51, 76, 135
Actual 85, 129
Adapt 96, 161
Addition 72, 150
Additional 85, 110
Addressed 118, 134
Adequately 76, 106
Advances 135
Advantages 68, 114
Adventure 90, 115
Advertisements 89, 136
Advice 154
Afraid 124, 170
Agenda 82, 130
Ages 61, 66
Aimed 89, 130
Algorithms 104, 122
Aloud 66, 89
Alphabetic 61, 64
Alternative 70, 119
Alternatives 51, 156
Amsterdam 88, 91-92, 97, 100, 115, 118, 129-130, 134, 141
Analyse 108, 164
Analyze 51, 171
Animations 102, 152
Annoyed 166
Answers 143, 172
Antique 87, 127
Anymore 116, 151
App 94, 149
Appealing 149, 160
Appearance 56, 127
Appearing 57, 75
Appliance 50-51
Approaching 100, 161
Appropriate 71, 150
Arabic 53, 132
Argue 77, 157-158
Arguments 67, 83
Arise 120, 159
Arose 68, 162
Arrange 76, 105
Artists 92, 161
Ascendance 174
Ascendant 139
Aside 114, 152
Asking 65, 70
Asks 125
Aspects 62, 77
Assigned 83, 95
Assume 143, 156
Astonishing 105, 155
Atoms 54, 121
Attempt 102, 142
Attempts 102, 175
Attentive 97, 159
Attract 87, 102
Aura 57
Australia 87
Authorship 122
Awareness 68, 97
Awkward 131, 151
Awkwardly 140
Babel 112
Babylon 161
Bach 144
Background 79, 101
Badly 115, 138
Bag 74, 128
Basic 65, 127
Bc 111
Beautiful 91, 138
Begins 61, 153
Beholder 97, 124
Beloved 90, 128
Benefit 51, 70
Besides 68, 86
Billions 51, 108
Bin 90, 154
Binding 92, 138
Birds 74, 154
Birthday 87, 136
Blood 153
Bookmark 174
Bookshelf 74, 118
Bookstore 100, 157, 165
Bookstores 74, 139
Borders 160, 165
Born 104, 153
Borrow 135, 153
Boss 95, 163
Boxes 96, 139
Boys 128, 151
Branch 121, 172
Brand 54, 93
Brought 112, 159
Browse 57, 119
Browser 68, 113
Bruno 107
Build 77, 161
Cabinets 76, 88
Cages 61, 154
Calculating 120
Calligraphy 75, 152
Capital 82, 123
Capture 60, 97
Carr 83, 159
Carriage 59, 156
Cartels 63
Castells 157
Categories 77, 174
Catharsis 112
Cathedral 68
Causes 166
Cd 76, 159
Cds 76, 144
Celebrate 84, 130
Cereal 88
Chaos 150
Character 109, 118
Checking 159
Children 87, 127, 136, 172
China 120, 151
Chopped 85
Circulation 51, 93
Civil 63-64
Class 145
Classics 124, 155
Clicks 105, 137
Closer 59, 96
Cognitive 106, 159
Collaborating 143, 155
Collaborative 93, 142
Collect 120
Colour 117, 171
Combines 71, 151
Command 65, 145
Commenting 65, 145
Commercial 85, 131
Common 61, 155
Communal 57, 139
Communicating 109, 134
Communicative 69, 132
Communities 97, 160
Comparable 75, 92
Compare 86, 144
Comparing 85, 129
Complicated 64, 163
Components 103, 143
Comprehend 86, 144
Comprehending 73, 96
Comprehensive 86, 143
Computer-Driven 152, 171
Conceptual 58-59
Conclusion 125, 159
Condensed 73, 126
Confirmed 93, 95
Confronted 55, 150
Confusion 68, 132
Conjures 58, 78
Connect 109, 129
Connecting 85, 117
Consciousness 61, 97
Consistency 164, 173
Constitutes 156, 174
Construction 111, 152
Contact 150, 159
Contents 81, 129
Contexts 122-123
Continues 89, 119
Copies 88, 95
Core 124, 148
Corners 119, 130
Counter 131
Counting 90, 120
Countless 105, 109
Covered 64, 160
Crazy 54, 91
Creation 104, 121
Creators 145-146
Crisis 65, 78
Customer 51, 129
Customized 55
Database 129, 135
Databases 80, 129
Daughter 128, 153
De 55, 84, 115, 141, 149-150, 157
Dead 74, 104, 137
Dealing 63, 72
Decided 67, 69, 71
Deciphering 98
Dedicated 71, 130
Deeply 59
Define 86, 173
Definitely 113, 130
Delay 132, 173
Delivery 87, 119
Depending 83, 148
Described 71, 81

Describes 65, 143
Description 107, 165
Desire 99, 102
Despite 61, 71
Details 59, 94
Determine 77, 97
Determines 100, 147
Diagram 69, 89
Dialogue 85
Dies 152-153
Diffused 57, 106
Dimensions 59, 75
Directed 148, 150
Direction 135, 148
Directly 98, 155
Disappearing 75, 125
Disclosure 60, 133
Discover 164, 166
Discovered 52, 67
Discovering 70, 149
Discursive 123, 158
Discussed 100
Disdain 124, 152
Disk 76
Dissolved 66, 130
Dissolves 59, 139
Distance 61, 73
Distinction 64, 77
Distracted 83, 102
Diversity 123, 168
Doctors 125
Documentary 90, 125, 152
Documents 77, 171
Dominant 61, 126
Dominated 121, 132
Doormat 54, 141
Doors 140-141
Double 121, 131
Doubt 127
Dr 110, 124
Dramatically 143, 156
Drastically 55, 154
Drawing 124, 162
Drawings 152
Drawn 95, 124
Dreadful 55
Drivers 89, 160
Drug 63
Dumbing 96, 145
Durable 53, 170
Duties 140
E-Reading 102, 152
E.G 94, 106
Ears 75, 133
Earth 51, 156
East 94, 125
Eat 88, 133
Eaten 82
Economic 65-66
Economies 156
Edges 167
Editor 57, 77, 86, 91, 115, 140, 173
Education 81, 106-107
Effective 102, 149
Effects 149, 171
Efficiency 66, 156
Efficiently 64, 152
Efforts 130, 156
Eisner 123-124
Elevated 73, 112
Elitist 73, 98
Email 109, 162
Embedded 103, 129
Emerging 103, 147
Empty 102, 138-139
Enables 59, 170
Encompass 74, 105
Encourage 70, 83
Engraved 120, 171
Engulfed 87, 160
Enjoyable 103, 128
Enrichment 110
Enter 77, 114
Entertain 133, 145
Entity 111, 123
Ephemeral 62, 106
Epitaph 119-121
Epochal 60, 62
Equally 106, 171
Equipped 148, 165
Escape 97, 151
Escaping 74, 149
Essay 126, 143
Essays 121, 142
Essential 146, 153
Etcetera 56, 164
Eternal 120-121
Event 91, 121
Everyday 54, 79
Everyone 70, 140
Evoke 109, 173
Evolve 85, 134
Exactly 76, 161
Exam 67-68
Examples 61, 171
Exception 79, 160
Exchange 67, 95, 137
Exchanged 111, 159
Exciting 170, 172
Exclusively 164, 171
Exercise 86, 157
Exhibition 69-70
Expands 89, 102
Experiment 73, 126
Expert 63, 163
Experts 62, 81
Exploring 72, 142
Exposed 104, 132
Extract 71, 122
Extreme 83, 174
Fading 58, 144-145
Fairly 64, 173
Familiar 79, 166
Fantastic 62, 170
Fascinates 50, 55
Fashion 119, 131, 155
Father 127, 153
Favour 65, 82
Feat 75, 95
February 71, 153
Feed 94, 105
Feeling 90, 128
Feels 58, 88
Feet 126, 142
Felt 106, 127
Fervent 117, 160
Fiddling 128, 136
Fifties 86, 124
Filled 112, 159
Filtering 79, 113
Finds 101, 157
Fingers 120, 135
Fingertips 74-75
Finish 128, 144
Finished 136, 141
Floor 92, 141
Flowing 60, 62, 147
Focused 105, 142
Followed 170
Follows 107, 125
Forces 107, 114
Foreman 68
Formed 64, 107
Formulating 67, 109
Forth 120, 167
Fortunately 128, 136
Fragmented 81, 144
Fragments 134
Frederick 163
Freed 80, 139
Freer 169
French 97, 116
Frequently 159, 164
Friend 150, 152
Front-End 94
Fundamentally 97, 107
Gain 103, 118
Gains 59, 98
Gaming 87, 118
Gardens 73, 175
Gather 59, 149
Gathered 71, 94
Genres 123
Gentleman 79, 99
Gift 88, 168
Girl 83, 141
Girls 128, 151
Giving 70, 141
Glancing 64, 159
Glass 75, 174
Got 127-128
Grab 89, 117
Gradually 98, 172
Grammar 105, 125, 127
Grapheme 120
Grasping 105, 146
Greatest 131, 136
Greats 155
Grew 127, 129
Grey 118, 171
Griot 153, 155
Griots 153
Guide 79, 94
Hangs 125
Happening 64, 94
Happens 69, 87
Hat 105, 115
Headlines 57, 159
Heard 85, 163
Hearts 87, 154
Hence 106
Hidden 71, 119
Hierarchy 58-59
Highbrow 100
Highlighting 56, 145
Historians 58, 65
Hits 94, 119
Holiday 71, 159
Honest 163
Horizontal 88, 171
Horse 85, 156
Hybrid 103, 175
Hybrids 102
Hypertexts 102
Icon 90, 130
Icons 65, 102
Ideally 73, 143
Identified 61, 122
Illegally 137, 159
Illuminated 119, 170
Illustrations 89, 140
Imaginations 69, 107
Immediacy 80, 132
Immune 105, 169
Impact 93, 116, 161
Implemented 78, 106
Impossibility 132, 167
Impression 58
Impressive 95, 136
Include 108, 152
Included 61, 83
Incomprehensible 79, 161
Increase 58, 142
Increased 96, 165
Indeed 95, 114
Independent 60, 77, 91, 131, 175
Index 66, 114
Indicates 83, 88
Infinitum 101-102
Influenced 147, 149
Influences 101, 159
Informational 151, 157
Informed 55, 94
Ingenuity 129, 169
Initial 55, 77
Inner 104, 107
Innumerable 97, 129
Input 71, 105
Inspired 124, 169
Inspires 71, 163
Instance 82, 106
Instantly 115, 150
Intensive 80, 126
Interactive 106, 111, 118, 129, 161
Interested 95, 166
Interestingly 76
Interests 55, 122
Interpreting 97, 146
Invented 59, 104
Inventions 99, 170
Investigated 84, 108
Involves 64, 98
Iphone 128, 155
Items 60, 83, 168
Jagged 75, 131
James 56-57, 113
Jan 144-146
Japan 139, 164
Japanese 163-164
Jeliya 153, 155
John 82, 112
Jorge 112
Journal 77, 81, 146
Journey 57, 110
Kitchen 88-89
Label 93, 124
Lady 119, 136
Lamp 128, 137
Lap 60, 66

Laptop 149, 160
Laptops 138, 160
Latour 107
Latter 79, 125
Lay 104, 134
Layers 86, 161
Laying 132, 166
Leafing 59, 166
Learns 89, 169
Lecture 59, 67
Liberated 54, 82
Liberation 162
Lie 86, 90
Lies 134, 140
Lightning 169-170
Likes 53, 90
Limit 90, 160
Limitation 106, 110
Linearity 115, 134
Linguistic 50, 54
Lips 65, 154
Lists 135, 167
Literary 83, 112, 117
Located 117, 122
Locations 118, 135
Logic 66, 120
London 99, 170
Looked 56, 157
Losses 98, 103
Lots 137
Loved 139, 144
Lover 140, 154
Low 52
Makers 118, 126
Manipulated 114, 140
Manner 116, 146
Manuscript 87, 135
Margin 128, 174
Marginalia 57, 135
Mark 83, 115
Marketing 52, 163
Marks 97, 167
Mastered 162, 168
Maximum 119, 160
Measure 52, 92
Measurements 63
Measuring 63
Mechanical 61, 140
Mediators 97, 130
Medieval 75, 92
Mercy 62, 104
Mere 74, 138
Merge 158, 172
Mess 53, 67
Messaging 106, 146
Metadata 76, 85
Middle 66, 114
Miss 147, 155
Mobiles 145, 174
Monks 66
Monopolies 175
Mosaic 113, 134
Mosquito 125-126
Motion 72, 140
Motorway 62
Mouse 68, 119
Movie 85, 140
Multidimensional 122
Mutation 65, 174
Mutually 85, 102
Mystery 132
N-Page 143
Name 110, 167, 171
Names 129, 141
Naming 90
Narratives 95, 122
Navigate 105, 152
Negative 69, 154
Neither 67, 124
Neurological 83, 90
Nice 141, 149
Nicholas 72, 83
Non-Fiction 71, 143
Non-Linear 50, 77, 86
Norm 96, 168
Norma 85
Normative 52, 68
North 63, 75, 93
Note 145, 174
Noted 54, 122
Noticed 58, 68
Noun 104, 147
Numbered 142
Observations 78, 167
Observing 59, 160
Occur 62, 122
Ocean 151-152
Offered 114
On-Going 82, 127
Onslaught 99-100
Opinion 61, 169
Options 102, 110
Orally 112, 153
Organic 87-88
Organization 76, 103, 150
Organized 61, 115
Originally 58, 69, 101
Oslo 92
Output 72, 105
Outputs 82, 107
Overload 52, 149
Owning 50, 157
Pad 68
Panels 160
Paradoxically 120, 140
Paragraph 67, 142
Parameters 138
Paris 56, 104
Partial 103
Partly 101, 131
Passages 128, 145
Passive 58, 94
Path 121, 172
Paths 62, 119
Performed 140
Peripheral 116, 167
Persepolis 95-96
Perspectives 70, 145
Phenomenon 59, 92
Philosophy 70, 80, 97
Phones 133, 158
Phrases 105, 124
Pile 54, 128
Piles 76
Pillow 88, 133
Pity 117, 165
Plain 59, 103
Platforms 102, 175
Plausible 70
Played 118
Plus 137, 148
Pocket 74, 93
Poems 88
Poor 76, 120
Popularity 53, 71
Population 125, 153
Portrait 65, 148
Pose 69, 149
Possibility 61, 122
Posting 103, 157
Posts 108
Precisely 118, 165
Prediction 65, 70
Predicts 139, 152
Preferred 102, 123
Pretty 73, 127
Previously 103, 158
Priests 120, 170
Primary 91, 101
Principles 111, 127
Print-On-Demand 102, 105
Printers 55, 163
Problematic 70, 103
Processed 71, 129
Producers 97, 105
Profound 142, 172
Program 60, 160
Progressive 138, 175
Projects 69-70, 168
Proliferation 123, 174
Promise 115, 175
Properly 138, 173
Property 59, 155
Proportions 147, 156
Proprietary 82
Prove 91, 158
Proven 72, 79
Province 63-64
Psychology 107, 121
Purchased 64, 137
Putting 142, 166
Qualities 108, 131, 172
Quantities 101, 171
Quantity 92, 168
Quick 58, 171
Quiet 88, 149
Quite 62, 128
Radio 92, 164
Rarely 111, 143
Reacting 146, 149
Realization 68, 115
Reason 56, 118
Reasoning 114, 134
Receiving 58, 88
Recipe 151
Recognizes 89, 98
Refined 75, 167
Reflect 60, 100
Reflecting 99, 146
Reflection 117, 159
Reflective 51, 59
Reflects 70, 100
Regardless 131, 163
Regularly 68, 131
Reinventing 84, 161
Rely 107, 146
Remained 116, 144
Remember 114, 169
Renaissance 74, 145
Report 71-72
Representations 71, 129
Represents 63, 111
Require 77, 91
Resemble 81, 102
Respect 115, 132
Responsible 63
Restricted 162, 166
Retreat 82, 87
Reveal 132, 146
Revenue 174-175
Reversed 59, 67
Reviewed 100, 145
Reviews 129, 143
Revolution 61, 84
Rhythmic 139, 162
Rich 102, 145
Richness 98, 103
Right-Hand 150-151
Rise 107, 157
Rival 53-54
Round 127, 137
Routes 64, 89
Rss 80, 108
Run 64, 70, 87, 94
Scale 76, 99
Scan 57, 160
Scarcity 55, 162
Scholarship 80-81
Schooling 126
Scientist 71, 166
Scribble 128, 140
Scroll 135, 168
Scrolls 53, 88
Scrutinize 100
Sea 64, 172
Section 136, 147
Seduction 124, 173
Seductive 97, 147
Seeing 59, 111
Seldom 118
Selected 73, 101, 111
Selection 100, 132
Self 117, 144
Sending 105, 164
Sensory 58
Sentiment 85, 108
Serious 100, 123
Servants 63-64
Services 93, 105
Sets 108
Sexy 69, 138
Shadows 122, 139
Shakespeare 124, 155
Shallow 53, 107
Shaped 61, 68
Shawl 154
Shelves 74, 136
Shifting 148, 167
Shops 54, 137
Shortest 73, 119
Shortly 100, 109
Shown 50, 125
Shut 86, 110
Sight 136, 156
Sign 90, 160
Signals 91-92
Significant 59, 70
Silk-Screen 62, 64
Sites 55, 80
Skilled 158, 169
Skimming 83

Slight 67, 84
Slogans 79, 113
Smartphones 138, 160
Sold 55, 95
Solitary 143, 145
Solutions 171-172
Solved 51, 76
Someone 57, 164
Sors 154
Source 82, 109, 172
Spacious 79, 140
Speaks 80
Special 71, 115, 126
Specialist 55, 81, 106
Species 156, 174
Spelling 139, 162
Spoils 120, 123
Spread 61, 170
Stable 61, 174
Statistical 108, 129
Stay 94
Stick 92, 128
Stimulates 134, 167
Stimulating 149, 160
Stimuli 58
Stopped 93, 133
Storage 76
Storyteller 71, 124
Strange 116
Strangely 128, 139
Stratification 147, 160, 172
Striking 131, 139
Stripped 62, 130
Strong 145, 169
Stronger 52, 169
Struck 127, 136
Structures 61, 114
Studies 83, 108-109, 130, 158
Studying 67, 140
Stuffed 128, 137
Subconscious 148, 166
Subtitle 79
Suggests 80, 90
Suitable 84, 171
Summarized 107, 117
Summary 56, 128
Sun 51
Superficiality 59, 98
Superior 124, 127
Supplement 71, 107
Support 93, 135
Supporting 91, 175
Surfaces 138, 173
Survives 54, 101
Swipe 138, 174
Switching 110, 168
Tactile 64, 166
Tagging 65, 103
Tags 52, 64
Tail 53, 175
Taking 52, 66
Talkies 85
Taste 102, 172
Team 92, 94
Technical 122, 138
Technologically 69-70
Telling 79, 124
Tens 63
Texture 172
Theatre 111, 116
Theory 62, 69, 82, 142, 174
Thinks 151, 163
Thread 134, 173
Threat 74, 174
Three-Dimensional 54, 140
Throughout 79, 155
Time-Consuming 144-145
Tintin 84
Tiny 74, 88
Tips 68, 120
Topics 102, 108
Total 124, 151
Totally 144, 147
Tourist 120, 129
Trace 60, 96
Tracks 165, 172
Trade 99, 163
Tradition 131, 152
Traditions 75, 123
Trained 58, 102
Transforms 54, 156
Translates 75, 105
Translation 53, 152
Transporting 63-64
Travel 99, 115
Travels 122, 156
Treasure 87
Trend 72, 149
Twentieth 119, 162
Ubiquitous 54, 146
Ultimate 131, 140
Un-Reader 132-133
Underlying 97, 146
Undoubtedly 134, 152
Unfolding 140, 142
Universal 73, 102
Unnoticed 75, 119
Unwritten 131-132
Updates 93, 119, 136
Updating 72, 94
Upside 125
Upwards 141, 150
Users 70, 166
Valuable 54, 149
Values 70, 149
Vast 105, 130
Vehicle 73, 75
Verb 104, 147
Version 84, 111
Viewing 85
Views 94, 123
Vinyl 159, 162
Visions 70, 90
Visit 55, 155
Visualizations 59, 64
Visualizing 92, 157
Vocabulary 104-105
Voice-Over 79, 95
Volume 154, 157
Wait 169, 175
Walled 73, 175
Walter 57, 139
Wanted 52
Warde 75
Warns 146, 159
Waves 92, 167
Wc 136
Weapons 64, 70, 73
Weekend 136, 145
Weeks 116, 128
Whenever 135, 137
White 76, 133
WiFi 92
Wikipedia 81, 109
Wikis 80, 136
Wise 153-154
Witnessing 60, 142
Workplace 66
Worried 67-68
Worse 86, 159
York 73, 95
Yorker 100
1-Dimensionality 121
1-Page 167
160,000 171
180,000 164
1854-2007 87
1923-2009 108
1930S 75
1970S 157
20Th 65
24/7 160
26Th 115
36,500 152
40,000 165
5,000 160
500,000 95
65Th 84
A325 62
Abandonment 61
Abilities 159
Aboriginals 165
Absent-Minded 132
Absolute 131
Absolutely 70
Absorbs 161
Absorption 110
Academics 101
Accelerate 152
Accept 171
Accepts 170
Accessed 154
Accessibility 155
Accessing 50
Accidentally 132
Accidents 62
Acclaimed 72
Accommodate 106
Accomplished 102
Accusations 105
Achievement 118
Acknowledging 103
Acquaintances 164
Acquired 131
Activated 114
Actively 97
Adaptation 174
Adapted 78, 104
Additions 75
Additive 139
Address 94
Addresses 76
Addressing 146
Adds 128
Adept 98
Adequate 138
Administer 81
Administrators 81
Adoring 142
Ads 102
Adulterous 154
Advanced 108
Advantage 51
Advent 74
Affair 58
Affirming 90
Affordance-Oriented 135
Africans 125
After-Taste 172
Afternoon 125
Afterthought 52
Aggregation 123
Aggregative 139
Agree 125
Aim 110
Aims 151
AI 124
Alarm 88
Albeit 52
Album 84
Albums 127
Alchemy 54
Alert 167
Alerting 81
Alessandro 85
Algorithm 129
Algorithmic 122
Alien 75
Alienating 79
Alike 58
Alliances 64
Alphabetical 66
Alphanumeric 103
Alter 86
Amateur 131
Amateurism 132
Amazed 143
Amazon.Com 157
Ambiance 110
Ambient 80-81
Ambiguous 118
Amorphous 69
Amounts 107
Amusement 84
Amusing 126
Analogized 123
Analogue 86
Analytic 139
Analytical 146
Analytics 108
Analyzed 122
Analyzing 94
Animals 52
Anniversary 84
Annotate 105
Announcement 113
Annoying 71
Annual 72
Answered 118
Antagonists 53
Anthropology 107
Anticipate 89
Antiquated 144
Anxiety 138
Anytime 71
Anyway 67
Apart 53, 99

Apodictic 61
Apparatus 135
Appliances 51
Application 77
Applying 118
Appointments 173
Appreciate 71
Appreciates 132
Approaches 151
Appropriation 104
Approval 119
Approved 88
April 107
Aptly 156
Archaeology 121
Archeology 60
Aren 120
Argued 83
Argument 86
Argumentation 158
Arisen 50
Arises 126
Arm 127
Armed 92
Arms 88
Arnhem 62
Aron 92
Array 105
Arrested 93
Arrived 161
Arrives 109
Arrogant 124
Arrows 141
Artefacts 107
Article 143
Articulate 114
Artifacts 156
Artistic 84, 132
Ascendency 162
Ascertains 152
Ashes 105
Asian 94
Asleep 90
Aspired 112
Assemblages 81
Assemble 139
Assertive 52
Assess 95
Assessing 149
Assistant 95
Associative 52
Assumes 77
Assuming 57
Assumption 95
Asterix 127
Astonishment 98
Astrology 121
Attach 149
Attached 151
Attaches 141
Attend 127
Attraction 136
Attractive 97
Audience 100
Audio-Visual 158
Audiovisual 157
Augmented 165
Aural 103
Austin 155
Authentic 98
Authentically 146
Authenticity 87
Author-Centred 98
Authored 173
Authoritarian 121
Auto 105
Automatism 160
Automobile 59
Autonomous 101
Availability 162
Avalanche 158
Awaits 115
Awful 159
Back-End 135
Bad-Ass 124
Baffles 89
Baghdad 118
Ban 124
Banal 71
Bang 65
Bangalore 89
Bankrupt 165
Banter 133
Barnard 163
Bars 61
Barthes 104
Base 93
Bases 82
Bat 169
Bath 155
Bathroom 88
Bauerlein 83
Bavaria 93
Beamed 86
Bear 87
Bearded 124
Beatrice 75
Beckons 80
Bedside 128
Behaviours 143
Behold 105
Belief 81
Believable 118
Believed 147
Bell 141
Benefiting 175
Benefits 95
Benjamin 57
Berliner 72
Bet 53
Betray 136
Beware 107
Bible 112
Bibliographies 143
Bieri 110
Big 74
Biggest 160
Bigots 124
Bike 90
Billboards 136
Billion 174-175
Biology 70
Biotope 132
Birth 174
Bitmap 75
Blame 169
Bleeding 141
Blend 166
Bliebs 117
Blindly 103
Blinkers 166
Bloated 175
Blockbuster 117
Blocking 115
Blogging 105
Blooms 145
Blu-Ray 159
Blunt 113
Blurry 64
Blush 133
Board 126, 133
Boards 125
Boasting 124
Bodily 135
Boniface 154
Bonus 148
Bookcases 112
Bookdealers 99
Booked 173
Bookmarks 85
Books-Centered 151
Books-On-Tape 139
Booksellers 54
Boost 156
Booster 174
Border 167
Borrowed 144
Borrower 145
Borrowers 145
Bother 159
Boulevard 85
Bound-Together 173
Boundaries 143
Boundary 131
Bowl 88
Braggart 119
Braille 136
Brainchild 164
Brainpower 138
Brains 138
Branches 80
Breakfast 136
Breaking 93
Breaks 137
Breath 67
Breathe 124
Breed 71
Briefcase 99
Brightly 121
Bringing 78
Brittle 82
Broad 161
Broadcast 105
Broadcasting 161
Broadened 105
Broader 155
Broadly 173
Broke 145
Brutally 104
Builds 150
Bulk 81
Bullshit 169
Bump 120
Buried 120
Burning 104
Burroughs 126
Burst 139
Bus 153
Bush 153
Bustling 84
Buttons 174
Buzz 156
Bytes 51
Cadal 151
Cage 61
Caged 74
Calculated 129
Calculates 151
Calculi 134
Camus 73
Cancellations 172
Candle 135
Candy 69
Canon 155
Capabilities 81
Capacities 140
Capitalist 82
Care 101
Carton 88
Cased 87
Cast 122
Casting 161
Casts 150
Catalogues 129
Categorized 96
Cathedral-Like 68
Cathode 171
Cats 137
Caught 59
Cause 167
Caused 78
Causing 123
Celebration 153
Cell 157
Cello 144
Centerpiece 156
Chain 165
Challenging 106
Changeable 151
Channel 175
Chapel 121
Chapter 156
Chapters 114
Charles 65
Charleston 162
Chatter 139
Cheap 102
Cheaply 172
Cheated 136
Checker 68
Cheerful 88
Cheerfully 128
Cherish 124
Choices 118
Chooses 89
Choosing 59
Chronicling 120
Chronological 86
Chronologically 85
Chunks 134
Church 113
Chute 96
Cinemas 161
Circulating 114
Circumstances 161
Circus 169
Citation 81
Civic 119
Civitas 171
Claim 111
Claims 125
Clan 52
Clans 53
Clapping 85

Clarify 69
Classical 66
Classroom 157
Classrooms 142
Claxton 146
Clay 147
Clean 88
Cleared 136
Clearer 86
Clearly 72
Clerics 153
Clips 96
Cloaking 105
Clock 67
Closes 121
Closet 88
Cloth 154
Clothes 98
Clothing 153
Club 101
Clutter 115
Cluttered 115
Cnn 164
Coarse 170
Coast 94
Cobra 161
Coconut 85
Coded 82
Codified 96
Coffee 156
Coincidental 148
Coincidentally 148
Coined 124
Coins 130
Collaboration 175
Collapse 139
Collapsing 123
Collective 142
Collectively 173
College 89
Collins 145
Colonization 82
Coloured 171
Colourful 154
Colours 90
Combating 153
Combative 105
Combinatory 103
Combined 149
Comfort 132
Comfortable 106
Comfortably 140
Comforting 128
Comma 113
Commands 125
Commas 63
Comment 107
Commentators 98
Commercially 166
Commonly 98
Commonplace 78
Communicable 132
Communicated 112
Communications 158
Community 135
Compact 53
Company 56, 77, 124
Comparers 98
Compatible 63
Compensate 138
Compete 84
Competing 105
Competition 97
Compilation 78
Complain 52
Complement 102
Complexity 83
Compose 105
Composition 174
Compounded 123
Compressed 66
Compression 66
Computed 122
Conceivable 156
Conceived 78
Conceptually 148
Concerning 152
Concerns 76
Concrete 93
Concurrently 58
Concussion 115
Condemned 112
Conduct 89
Conference 89
Conferences 139
Confidence 61
Confident 81
Confined 61
Confirm 112
Confront 61
Confrontational 128
Confused 168
Congress 127, 165
Conjectures 173
Conjured 113
Connection 122
Connectivity 105
Cons 100
Conscientiously 136
Conscious 148
Consequently 134
Conservatives 61
Considerably 163
Considering 102
Considers 97
Consist 131
Consisting 90
Consists 159
Consolidate 175
Conspicuous 75
Constitute 61
Constraints 101
Construct 112
Constructed 170
Constructs 105
Construes 151
Consult 165
Consultants 127
Consultations 70
Consulted 119
Consumable 69
Consumer 137
Containing 154
Contemplate 71
Contemplative 66
Content/Meaning/ Energy 111
Contestation 175
Contextuality 74
Contextualizes 78
Contextualizing 72
Continued 137
Continuity 114
Contours 154
Contradicts 158
Contrarily 139
Contrary 102
Contribute 145
Contributing 72
Contributors 78
Control 122
Controlled 168
Conventional 131
Conventions 131
Convergence 102
Conversation 127
Conversationalist 119
Conversely 118
Converted 50
Converting 50
Converts 54
Convey 140
Convinced 101
Convulsions 139
Cooler 143
Coordinated 111
Coordination 156
Coordinator 63
Copied 76
Copious 139
Copying 56
Coquetry 120
Corn 120
Corner 150
Corpora 135
Correct 125
Corrects 139
Corresponding 95
Corridors 64
Cosiness 79
Cosmopolitan 80
Costs 110
Counted 129
Counterculture 54
Counterpart 98
Country 93
Counts 63
Couperus 154
Coupled 98
Cousin 124
Cousins 148
Craft 92
Crave 87
Creativity 146
Creator 84, 104
Creature 126
Creatures 120
Credulous 169
Crept 67
Crime 52
Criteria 132
Criticism 117
Critique 65
Cross 160
Crossed 67
Crouwel 171
Crowd 120
Crown 154
Crumble 52
Crystalline 75
Cuba 78
Culturally 158
Culture-Linked 125
Culture-Pessimistic 131
Cumbersome 158
Cunning 121
Cupboard 115
Curating 94
Curation 72
Curators 71
Curiosity 55
Curious 100
Currencies 156
Cursed 68
Cursory 56
Curve 172
Cut 170
Cut-And-Paste 67
Cuts 127
Cutting 158
Cyberspace 132
Cycle 103
Daldry 101
Dalloway 101
Damaged 166
Dancer 162
Danger 59, 174
Darker 104
Dash 89
Data-Rush 71
Datasets 71
Date 84
Dates 129
Daunting 95
De-Facto 65
Dear 55
Debate 70
Decade 54
December 163
Decentred 97
Decides 70
Deciphered 80
Decision 69
Decisive 138
Declaration 170
Declare 113
Declared 65
Declining 93
Decoded 132
Decoding 132
Decomposes 131
Deconstructionism 61
Decry 98
Dedicating 138
Deemed 124
Deepens 78
Defective 124
Defects 138
Defies 82
Degeneration 130
Degrees 129
Dekoven 96
Delays 172
Delectation 75
Deliberately 68
Deliberations 131
Delivered 137
Deluge 171
Demarcated 115
Democracy 53
Democratization 158
Democratized 157
Denied 124

Denies 61
Denote 165
Dense 68
Denser 89
Dent 120
Department 63
Dependency 68
Deprogram 68
Desecration 130
Designated 173
Designs 54
Desirable 70
Desktop 94
Desmond 85
Desperate 102
Destruction 162
Devastating 56
Develops 126
Deviantart.Com 109
Deviate 111
Devoured 160
Dexterously 120
Dialogues 70
Dictator 93
Died 105
Differences 167
Differentiation 103
Differs 98
Difficulty 56
Digitality 68
Digitizing 130
Dilemmas 118
Dimension 109
Dinosaurs 156
Dipping 121
Directs 125
Disadvantage 83
Disadvantages 68
Disagree 138
Disappears 152
Discard 73
Discarded 120
Discharge 112
Discipline 162
Disciplined 83
Disciplines 123
Disconnected 134
Discouraged 127
Discourse 72
Discourses 122
Discovers 79
Discs 159
Discussing 72
Discussions 156
Disembodied 157
Disengaged 146
Disfigured 136
Disguise 60
Dishwasher 88
Dislike 152
Dismantles 96
Dismissed 96
Dispersed 156
Displayed 134
Disposal 137
Disreputable 100
Dissatisfaction 154
Disseminate 57
Disseminating 95
Dissemination 96
Dissertations 104
Distil 172
Distinguish 51
Distinguished 97
Distinguishing 167
Distractions 174
Distributions 129
Dive 118
Diverse 55
Divided 70
Divine 112
Division 86
Do-It-Yourself 173
Docile 169
Doctoral 104
Document 106
Documentation 140
Dog-Earing 56
Domain 110
Domains 132
Dominate 157
Doom 139
Doorstop 56
Doses 81
Doubled 139
Doubles 174
Doubling 80
Downhill 52
Downloaded 154
Downloading 76
Downwards 141
Dramas 148
Dramatic 77
Drape 165
Dream 155
Dreaming 70
Dressed 88
Drew 63
Drift 150
Driver 161
Drives 133
Driving 93
Drop 139
Dropped 55
Drown 171
Drugs 62-63
Dtp 160
Dubious 105
Due 96
Dumb 160
Duplicating 72
Dusty 76
Duty 117
Dvds 144
Dwelling 60
Dynamics 107
Eager 170
Eagerly 150
Ear 133
Earlier 76
Earthquake 139
Echoes 120
Eclectic 87
Ecologies 146
Ecology 50
Economics 146
Economist 71
Ecstasy 159
Ed 84
Editions 103
Editors 71
Educate 145
Educated 110
Educating 83
Educational 91
Educators 83
Effect 65
Effectively 134
Effortlessly 150
Egypt 153
Eighteen 50
Einar 92
Elaborated 133
Electrified 104
Electronically 99
Electronically-Based 114
Elementary 162
Elephants 74
Eliminated 158
Eliminating 79
Eline 154
Elocution 75
Eloquent 158
Emails 57
Embedding 104
Embrace 117
Embracing 154
Emerged 142
Emerges 132
Emotionally 87
Emphasis 63
Empirical 50
Employ 108
Emulated 138
En 74, 141
Enacting 145
Encapsulated 162
Enclosed 80
Encoding 82
Encountered 67
Encouraging 96
Encyclopaedia 162
Endangered 174
Ending 117
Endless 106
Endured 53
Enduring 140
Energy 111-112
Engagement 106
Engaging 73
Engineer 151
Engineering 75
Engines 108
Enhancements 102
Enhances 91
Enigma 97
Enjoying 72
Enlarged 157
Enlightened 130
Enlightenment 154
Enriches 85
Enriching 155
Enshrined 174
Ensured 153
Ensures 152
Entail 86
Entered 67
Entering 104
Enterprise 139
Entertaining 71
Entities 156
Entitled 71
Entry 150
Environmental 104
Envision 122
Epiphanes 170
Epiphanies 132
Epiphany 132
Epublishing 175
Equal 124
Equality 142
Equation 145
Equipping 105
Equitable 82
Equivalents 54
Erasure 60
Ereader 149
Ereaders 174
Ergonomic 106
Ergonomics 51
Eroded 123
Erodes 123
Eroticism 173
Escalate 102
Escalation 66
Escapes 131
Eschewed 75
Especially 116
Esperanto 124
Espoused 83
Espresso 87
Essentials 150
Est 154
Establish 102
Establishing 62
Estimated 53
Eternity 171
Ethical 69
Ethics 70
Eu 175
Eurostar 99
Evening 136
Evenings 158
Ever-Evolving 134
Ever-Faster 86
Evidence 93
Evolution 60
Evolutionarily 165
Evolutionary 61
Evolved 65
Evolving 139
Exacts 162
Exaggerated 51
Examining 72
Exceptional 98
Excessive 113
Excitement 173
Exclamations 116
Exclusion 166
Excuse 118
Exhausted 94
Exhibitions 72
Existed 126
Existences 61
Exit 62
Exotic 75
Expand 101
Expanse 59
Expansion 157
Expense 50
Experimentation 131
Experimenting 72
Explaining 85

Explanation 126
Exploit 143
Exploitation 122
Explored 66
Explosions 118
Exponential 116
Exponentially 113
Expressed 68
Expresses 114
Expressive 69
Extemporary 62
Extend 72
Extension 126
Extensions 82
Extensive 80
Externalized 80
Extinction 174
Extracted 129
Extraction 129
Extrapolate 114
Eyeglasses 135
Eyelid 169
Fabricate 88
Faces 85
Facilitate 135
Facsimile 87
Factor 138
Failed 63
Failing 83
Faint 168
Faithful 154
Fake 85
Falling 53
Fallujah 118
Fantasies 174
Fantasize 114
Fantasy 149
Fare 101
Farewell 55
Farmers 120
Farming 105
Farther 154
Farthest 130
Fascinating 92
Fashionable 124
Fashioned 89
Fastest 62
Fathers 113
Fathom 60
Fathomed 64
Fathoming 59
Faulkner 101
Favoured 108
Feature 126
Featuring 124
Feestelijk 124
Fell 137
Fellow 168, 170
Felton 72
Feltron 72
Feuilleton 72
Fewer 52
Fiction 83
Fidelity 171
Fields 70
Fight 118
Fighting 119
Figuratively 154
Figure 122
Figured 76
File 105
Filing 76
Fill 160
Filtered 75
Filters 164
Finder 132
Fine-Tune 156
Fingerprints 87
Finnigans 114
Fire 65
First-Person 117
Flash 120
Flashes 78
Flashing 152
Flawless 148
Flemish 133, 166
Flexible 151
Flick 68
Flight 74
Flip-Books 140
Flotsam 133
Flourishes 138
Fluidity 82
Fluidly 82
Flushed 136
Fmri 83
Fold 128
Folders 76
Foley 85
Folio 133
Followers 145
Fonts 170
Food 90
Foolproof 89
Footage 93
Fora 57
Force 146
Fore 77
Forecast 172
Forecasting 65
Foreground 122
Foremost 167
Foresaw 101
Foreseeable 71
Foreshore 62
Foretelling 146
Forgetful 68
Forgettable 103
Fork 133
Formal 111
Formatted 54
Formidable 170
Formulated 109
Fortune 133
Forums 136
Fostering 139
Foucault 104
Fourteen-Year-Old 168
Foxtrot 162
Fragebogen 71
Fragmentary 168
Framed 123
Framework 100
Frankenstein 83
Frankfurt 65
Frankly 124
Fraught 69
Fredric 124
Free-Of-Charge 155
Freeing 140
Freely 113
Freeze 111
Frequency 129
Frequent 63
Friction-Less 121
Friending 146
Frisch 71
Frontispiece 122
Fruit 90
Fuels 76
Fullest 91
Fun 116
Functional 69
Functions 83
Fundamental 58
Fungible 54
Funnel 164
Funnily 172
Furnish 107
Furniture 156
Furthermore 111
Futile 65
Future-Fiction 143
Futureness 69
Futurologist 69
Gadget 74
Gadgets 138
Gaga 119
Gaining 113
Galaxy 64-65
Galleries 140
Galloping 85
Gap 171
Garden 135
Gargantuan 156
Gates 104
Gathers 120
Gaze 89
Gazette 72
Geestelijk 124
Generalize 107
Generalized 61
Generate 95
Generations 61
Generative 82
Generative/Interactive 111
Genes 51
Genre 95, 123
Gentle 119
Genuinely 97
George 153
Geotagged 108
Germ 132
Germany 93
Gestures 90
Ghana 153
Gifts 87
Gigantic 160
Glamorous 72
Glasses 114
Gliding 68
Globalization 126
Globally 93
Gloss 57
Glue 61
Glued 78
Goal 76
Goblet 75
Goethe 146
Gold 71
Gone 113
Googled 125
Gracefully 154
Graffiti 64
Gram 148
Grammatical 111
Grandchildren 143
Grandfather 154
Granite 171
Graphed 122
Graphemes 120
Grasp 73
Grave 119-120
Great-Great 154
Greatly 125
Greed 173
Greek 120
Green 171
Greenberg 96
Grid 170
Groei 124
Groove 120
Grotesque 156
Groundbreaking 156
Group 52
Grow 113
Grown 116
Growth 103
Guardians 145
Guidebook 128
Guides 129
Guru 54
Gutter 96
Guy 146
Habits 134
Hague 134, 154
Half-Dozen 138
Hall 67
Hallway 89
Halo 117
Halves 148
Hammered 78
Hand/Eye 166
Handful 165
Handicap 155
Handier 170
Handling 77
Handwriting 92
Handwritten 96
Handy 169
Hang 92
Happily 100
Happiness 78
Haptic 54
Hara 54
Hardback 54
Hardbound 99
Hardcore 117
Hardcover 149
Harder 82
Hardware 85
Hardware/Software 105
Harness 151
Harper 145
Harvesting 120
Hassle 77
Hasten 139
Haven 88
Haystack 150
Head-Thinking 87
Headlong 125

Headstrong 167
Heaps 104
Hearing 90
Hears 79
Heartbeat 129
Heavier 75
Heavy 156
Held 167
Helpful 157
Helping 72
Helps 87
Herd 74
Hermeneutic 97
Hermeneutics 98
Heroes 53
Hesitate 53
Heterogeneity 61
Hewn 105
Hid 136
Hideous 169
Hierarchies 142
Highlight 96
Highlights 96
Highway 62, 89
Historic 60
Histories 122
Hit 115
Hitherto 106
Hitting 66
Hive 139
Holding 98
Holes 157
Holidays 136
Hollywood 111
Holy 168
Homeostatic 139
Homer 124
Homework 164
Homini 58
Honor 117
Hop 89
Hopefully 70
Hopes 122
Horizon 80
Horror 163
Horseless 59
Hosted 140
Hostile 87
Hot 93
Hugely 86
Human-Biased 82
Humanitarian 119
Humans 96
Humorous 68
Humour 169
Hundreds 107
Hung 140
Hunger 120
Hunting 165
Hurry 128
Husbands 154
Hyde 148
Hype 131
Hyper-Connectedness 74
Hyperlinking 134
Hypermedia 159
Hypermediated 65
Hypertext 83
Hysteria 131
I-Information 155
I.E 143
Ictheological 121
Identify 83
Identifying 50
Identities 61
Ideological 82
Ideology 82
Idolatry 112
Ignores 68
Il 71
Illuminating 156
Illusion 140
Illusorily 62
Illustrated 124
Illustrates 91
Illustrating 96
Illustration 89
Imagery 157
Imagined 101
Imitating 85
Immense 130
Immersive 81
Immortalized 171
Imparted 153
Imparting 153
Imperative 122
Implicit 169
Implies 147
Implosion/Genre 123
Imposed 175
Impressed 51
Impressions 59
Imprint 95
Improve 138
Improved 116
Impure 112
In-Depth 50
Inch 171
Incidental 91
Incidentally 163
Inclination 112
Includes 130
Incoherent 59
Incompetent 169
Incorporate 102
Increments 148
Incursion 174
Indelible 105
Indents 167
Independence 153
Indexes 135
Indexical 65
Indexing 72
India 89
Indicate 96
Indicated 171
Indications 167
Indicator 65
Indiscretion 132
Industrial 61
Industrialization 66
Industrialized 52
Industriously 67
Inert 104
Inertia 139
Inexhaustible 168
Inferior 124
Infiltrating 175
Info-Bellies 175
Informal 152
Informality 104
Informatics 113
Information-Rich 98
Informative 97
Infotomes 121
Infrastructures 175
Ingest 133
Inherent 110
Initiative 108-109
Ink-Like-Ness 133
Inked 75
Innocent 124
Innovation 175
Innovative 77, 142
Inputs 107
Inquiries 107
Inquiry 157
Inquisitive 120
Inscriptions 132
Insecurity 119
Insights 107
Insoluble 109
Inspect 120
Inspire 69
Instances 61
Instantaneous 117
Institute 141
Institutes 130
Institutional 131
Instruct 75
Instructions 79
Insufficient 55
Intact 132
Intangible 73
Integral 99
Integrating 161
Integration 161
Intellectual 117
Intellectuality 103
Intellectually-Centred 135
Intellectuals 152
Intelligence 130
Intelligent 65
Intend 72
Intended 140
Intensively 60
Interact 106
Intercourse 131
Interiors 140
Intermediary 165
Intermediate 132
Internalize 80
Internalized 68
Interpret 126
Interrupted 99
Interruption 98
Intertext 131
Intertwined 79
Interventions 135
Interviewed 84
Intoxicated 136
Introversion 173
Intuiting 146
Intuition 107
Intuitive 146
Intuitively 111, 150
Invade 156
Inventor 132
Inventory 92
Invest 72
Investigative 89
Investment 158
Invisible 75
Invisibly 160
Invite 172
Invites 123
Involuntarily 68
Involved 142
Inward 146
LP 95
IPO 175
iPod 155
Irksome 166
Irony 73
Irresistible 58
Irrespective 174
Irreversibility 68
Islamic 153
Isolated 125
Issued 84
Issues 76
Italian 71
Itinerary 60
Itunes 76
Jacket 164
Jacques 104
Jam 136
Jammed 89
Jars 136
Je 154
Jealous 170
Jean-Claude 130
Jekyll 148
Jetsam 133
Joe 175
Joined 94
Jointly 164
Jonathan 72
Jotting 66
Journalist 71
Journeys 56
Joy 72
Jpeg 157
Jumble 63
Jump 123
Jumped 145
Jungle 105
Junk 103
Just-In-Time 103
Justify 127
Kafka 155
Kaleidoscopic 62
Kenya 54
Keyboard 68
Keyword 65
Keywords 77
Kg 160
Khrushchev 78
Kids 73
Killed 73
Kindles 145
Kitsch 96
Kittler 96
Klerk 144, 146
Knew 79
Knick-Knacks 121
Knife 133
Koblin 92
Koert 77, 165
Korea 139
Korengal 118

Kph 160
Kpn 92
Krauss 96
Labels 136
Laborious 123
Labyrinth 132
Lack 96
Lacking 97
Laden 154
Lament 59
Land 64
Landscape-Like 147
Landscapeness 147
Lapsed 104
Largest 175
Laser 120
Last-Minute 102
Lasts 158
Lato 82
Laughed 99
Launched 54
Law 155
Laxity 104
Layered 80
Lays 169
Leader 84, 92, 151
Leaf 92
Leaning 68
Leather 137
Leather-Bound 87
Leather-Cased 89
Leaving 124
Leds 92
Lees 124
Legacies 75
Legacy 174
Legein 120
Legislator 104
Lesser 159
Lessons 172
Lest 143
Lettered 168
Levelled 163
Leviathan 122
Lezen 120
Liberating 150
Librarian/Archivist 166
Librarians 145
Libya 120
Lie-In 136
Lifestyles 134
Lifetime 152
Light-Hearted 133
Lighter 75
Limbo 102
Limitations 55
Linearly 113
Liquifies 139
Lit 121
Literal 120
Loading 166
Local 89
Localizations 167
Location 161
Locked 82
Locomotives 87
Log 51
Logged 122
Logics 97
Logos 120
Looker 141
Lookers 140
Loops 139
Loss 119
Louis 112
Lovers 163
Loves 141
Lowbrow 100
Lower 79
Lowly 96
Lucky 142
Ludovico 85
Lugubrious 75
Luis 112
Lumbering 74
Luxury 103
Lying 63
Macbook 128
Magnifying 114
Mails 136
Major 65
Majority 52
Malaria 125
Mall 90
Malleable 56
Manager 91, 127
Managers 81
Mandela 153
Mandelstam 71
Manga 109
Manifestations 135
Manipulate 106
Mankind 53, 73
Mann 155
Mantras 174
Manuel 157
Marbel 171
March 153
Marched 92
Marginal 158
Marginalization 175
Mari 154
Marjane 95
Marked 56
Marketplace 69
Marriage 130
Marshall 113
Martinussen 92
Mary 83
Masse 74
Mastering 162
Mastery 163
Matching 55
Materialized 133
Max 57, 60, 71
Mayor 89
Mcgurk 65
Mckenzie 142, 173-174
Meals 90
Meander 121
Meandering 167
Meaningless 121
Meaninglessly 120
Measly 136
Measurement 63
Mechanism 82
Medal 117
Medals 118
Media-Sociological 132
Mediacracy 52
Meet 136
Megalomaniac 120
Melts 79
Members 88
Memoir 95
Memories 78
Memphis 170
Mensvoort 77, 165
Mental 68
Mention 133
Mercilessly 132
Merely 72
Merged 156
Merging 59
Merits 101
Messenger 132
Metal 158
Metaphorical 167
Metaphors 62
Metres 136
Michel 104
Microsoft 82
Midst 156
Migrants 90
Milling 171
Mine 137
Mini 128
Mini-Printing 127
Mining 108
Minor 142
Minus 148
Miracles 168
Miserly 167
Misery 51
Misfortunes 119
Misguided 174
Misperceive 65
Missed 119
Mist 92
Mistake 76
Misunderstanding 56
Mixed 151
Modalities 60
Model 127
Modeled 129
Moderately 168
Modernistic 161
Modes 96
Modification 106
Modulate 97
Modulated 65
Mohicans 128
Mom 88
Momentarily 132
Momentary 97
Mon 154
Monetizing 122
Money 64
Monitored 94
Monocle 72
Monster 63
Month 55
Months 56
Mood 90
Moods 122
Moral 118
Morse 65
Morsels 133
Motive 97
Motoric 166
Motto 124
Mould 107
Mountain 171
Mountains 71
Mountainscapes 171
Mouth 90
Movable 61
Moved 124
Mp3 76
Mrs 101
Mtv 65
Muddles 145
Multi-Medial 152
Multi-Modal 152
Multi-Player 143
Multicoloured 169
Multifaceted 123
Multilayered 80
Multiplied 53
Multiply 143
Multiplying 76
Multisensory 106
Multitask 169
Multitude 68
Murdered 154
Museum 79
Museums 161
Mushroom 172
Musician 62
Must-Read 71
Mutating 103
Myilibrary 166
Mysteries 133
Mystique 139
N-Chapter 143
Nagging 119
Naive 95
Namely 149
Napkin 135
Napster 159
Narration 153
Narrow 161
Narrow-Minded 80
Narrow-Mindedness 169
Nations 78
Native 83
Navigating 106
Necessity 111
Needle 150
Needs-Centered 151
Neglected 106
Negotiating 119
Neighbouring 166
Nelson 153
Neoliberalism 65
Networking 68
Neurology 121
Neurosis 131
Newly 171
News3.0 93
Newsbars 164
Nicolas 159
Nieuwenhuis 161
Nights 133
Nijmegen 62, 80
Nikita 78
Ninety 73
Ninety-Nine 103
Nod 88
Nomad 161
Non-Existent 58

Non-Levelling 132
Non-Observable 97
Non-Obvious 77
Non-Professional 58
Non-World 112
None 71
Nonsense 147
Nooks 145
Normal 123
Norms 132
Nose 169
Nostalgia 156
Nostalgic 73
Notation 112
Notes 73
Notification 93
Noting 149
Notionally 174
Nuggets 71
Numerical 134
Nutritious 172
Obama 171
Obedient 169
Obelix 127
Obeying 168
Objectively 63
Obligation 161
Obliged 114
Oblivion 120
Obscures 143
Observation 167
Observed 147
Observer 97
Obsessive 131
Obsessively 136
Obsolescence 96
Obtain 149
Obtained 107
Obtaining 111
Obtuse 96
Obvious 143
Obviously 62
Occupation 153
Occupying 142
Oceans 105
Odds 156
Offering 164
Official 153
Offshore 175
Omnipotent 102
Omnipresent 130
On-Screen 73
One-Off 131
Ong 139
Ongoing 73
Onomatopoeic 96
Onomatopoetic 65
Ontological 69
Opaque 97
Openly 174
Openness 123
Operations 153
Opinions 107
Opportunities 130
Oprah 100-101
Opt-In 94
Optimism 55
Optimization 105
Option 153
Orations 167
Ordered 61
Ordering 67
Ordinary 100
Organizational 77
Organizations 51
Organizing 77
Originate 53
Originator 104
Orthodoxy 70
Osama 154
Osmosis 101
Ossip 71
Ousted 162
Outcome 123
Outfit 88
Outskirts 132
Overall 98
Overcomes 150
Overdrive 145
Overestimated 111
Overflowing 87
Overlook 83
Overlooks 174
Overly 73
Overruling 149
Overstuffed 74
Overtaken 66
Overvalue 112
Overview 171
Overwhelm 87
Overwhelming 169
Owner 87
Pace 134
Packaging 55
Packed 121
Pads 90
Paint 124
Painting 65
Paints 124
Paired 86
Pale 74
Palm 89
Palpable 75
Pamphlet 127
Panel 88
Paper-Bound 87
Paperback 99
Papyrus 153
Paradigm 52
Paradise 102
Parafoveal 167
Parallels 157
Paranoia 174
Paraphrase 54
Paratextual 118
Parsed 122
Part-Time 166
Parted 73
Participatory 139
Parties 56
Partner 89
Parts 157
Passage 112
Passerby 132
Passes 121
Passionate 127
Passionately 71
Paste 118
Pasting 158
Patchwork 83
Pause 60
PC 94
Pedagogue 127
Pedestal 142
Peers 119
Penetrates 59
Penetrating 59
People/Artefacts 107
Per-Capita 139
Perceptual 106
Performative 139
Perished 162
Permanence 133
Perpetual 122
Persistent 143
Personalize 88
Personalized 87
Personally 150
Personification 145
Pertinent 135
Peter 110
Phantom 68
PhD 76, 97
Philosophized 126
Phoning 168
Photo 140
Photograph 148
Photographer 127
Photographic 64
Photography 92
Phrase 71
Phrasing 169
Physiological 101
Picked 71
Pictograms 140
Picture-Read 152
Picture-Write 152
Pictureless 124
Piled 137
Pinch 89
Pioneer 113, 170
Piss 140
Pissed 104
Pitiful 125
Placebo 111
Placed 110
Places 129
Placing 142
Plagiarism 105
Planned 54
Plasticity 74
Platonic 112
Player 118
Players 175
Players/Readers 143
Playing 145
Playwright 68
Please 143
Pleased 63
Pleases 124
Pleat 120
Ploy 97
Pod 102
Poet 112
Poetry 71
Poignant 95
Pointing 172
Politically 158
Politicians 53
Politics 130
Ponder 128
Pop 93
Popstar 71
Populations 105
Populist 157
Porous 143
Portal 94
Portals 74
Portray 101
Portrays 143
Posimistic 165
Positive 69
Possess 81
Possibly 132
Post-Its 128
Post-Synchronization 79
Postings 156
Postulated 86
Potentiality 121
Pragmatic 135
Praise 71
Preceding 67
Preconditioned 131
Precursor 114
Predetermined 62
Predictable 111
Predicting 143
Predictions 101
Preferably 132
Preference 158
Prejudice 100
Preparation 67
Prerequisite 61
Prescribed 114
Presence 157
Presentation 93
Presentations 166
Presenter 78
Presenting 96
Presently 152
Presents 132
Preservation 102
Preserved 156
Preserving 91
Presses 158
Pressure 144
Presumably 124
Presumes 143
Pretended 136
Pretending 175
Prevailing 70
Previous 87
Prey 165
Price 79
Pried 107
Primacy 157
Prime 175
Printouts 103
Prior 146
Priorities 70
Privileged 62
Proceed 86
Processing 66
Processor 162
Producer 98
Produces 173
Product 52
Professionals 71
Professors 157
Profile 150
Profitable 99
Profusion 59
Programme 78

Programmed 166
Programmer 71
Progresses 148
Progressives 61
Prohibited 160
Prominent 135
Promises 73
Promoted 146
Promotion 138
Pronounced 137
Propaganda 102
Propels 148
Prophetic 113
Prophets 79
Proposed 124
Pros 100
Prose 158
Prosthetic 57
Prosthetization 80
Protect 166
Protected 101
Protection 137
Protesting 166
Proudly 104
Proverb 152
Providers 161
Provides 171
Providing 151
Provincial 64
Provoke 69
Provokes 124
Psychoanalysis 107
Psychologist/Author 146
Ptolemy 170
Publication 78, 140
Publicist 159
Publics 97
Pulling 119
Pulp 82
Pump 87
Punctually 121
Punishment 52
Pupil 127
Purchase 156
Pure 121
Purist 162
Pursued 128
Puzzled 116
Pyjamas 136
Pynchon 71
Q&A-Button 94
Questionable 64
Questionnaires 71
Quicker 96
Quotation 167
Qwerty 68
Racing 119
Racks 76
Radically 107
Railways 163
Raise 89
Raised 75
Raison 175
Ramifications 82
Random 168
Randomly 115
Randomly-Accessible 53
Ranging 108
Rank 129
Ration 136
Ray 135, 171
Re-Inventing 102
Reaching 121
Reaction 79
Reactions 136
Read/See 122
Readable 138
Reading-Related 135
Readings 147
Readings/Interpretations 147
Ready 89
Real-Time 94
Realie 90
Realistically 143
Realizing 157
Realm 146
Realms 173
Reap 175
Reasons 148
Reassembled 139
Reassured 100
Reassuring 102
Rebirth 105
Rebuild 157
Recall 138
Recalls 75
Recedes 122
Receptical 99
Recognizing 168
Recombine 57
Recombining 113
Recommendation 108
Reconceptualized 106
Reconfigurable 133
Reconstruction 60
Recorded 122
Recounting 120
Recovered 78
Recovers 140
Rectangles 133
Recumbent 140
Recurring 117
Recycle 90
Redefine 86
Redundant 86
Refer 54
References 143
Reflections 111
Refrigerator 88
Regard 85
Regarded 174
Registering 120
Registers 116
Regularity 68
Reification 143
Reintroduce 111
Reject 164
Rejecting 82
Relate 150
Related 66
Relation 85
Relative 73
Relax 95
Relaxing 90
Relied 107
Relish 133
Remaining 157
Remarkable 112
Remarked 54
Remediated 82
Remembered 116
Reminded 99
Reminiscent 92
Remixes 109
Remixing 145
Removed 87
Removes 77
Rendering 59
Rent 122
Repeat 55
Repertoire 83
Repetition 153
Replacing 82
Replete 175
Replicate 85
Reported 54
Reporting 103
Repose 91
Represent 154
Representing 92
Reproduce 56
Reproduced 57
Reproductions 57
Repulse 102
Repulsive 169
Reputation 123
Requesting 145
Requisite 66
Rescue 153
Resemblances 139
Resembled 168
Resent 139
Reside 140
Resist 62
Resistance-Less 121
Resolution 91
Resort 156
Resounds 102
Resource 60
Respects 132
Restriction 80
Restricts 171
Resulting 98
Resume 67
Resurgence 66
Retains 97
Retired 100
Retrievable 54
Retrieval 81
Retrieve 76
Retrieved 157
Retweets 94
Reunification 57
Reuse 111
Reusing 91
Reversal 54
Revival 66
Revolutions 175
Reworking 61
Rhetorical 97
Rhythm 172
Richard 68
Richer 50
Ride 86
Ridiculous 86
Rights 56
Rigid 61
Rigorous 160
Rings 141
Ripe 174
Risk 81
Robust 139
Roland 104
Rolls 153
Root 59
Rosetta 170
Routed 122
Routine 129
Row 127
Rows 154
Rss-Feeds 161
Rubric 142
Ruled 102
Ruler 170
Rulers 120
Ruling 102
Running 114
Rural 93
Rushing 125
Rustling 172
Sadly 145
Safe 87
Sahara 153
Salad 90
Sale 130
Salvation 99
Samples 107
Sanctimoniously 136
Sand 165
Sanskrit 132
Sat 99
Satisfied 70
Saturated 98
Saved 87
Saves 53
Savvy 145
Scalability 75
Scalable 54
Scans 120
Scarcest 97
Scares 101
Scarf 88
Scaring 90
Scholar 83
Score 62
Scoundrels 53
Scout 167
Scrambling 105
Scrawled 140
Screaming 136
Screen-Based 50
Scribbles 140
Scribes 75
Scrim 105
Scripted 112
Sculpture 54
Seamlessly 145
Searchable 54
Searches 109
Seat 99
Seclusion 110
Secondary 139
Secret 169
Sections 128
Secure 156
Securing 122
Seek 130
Seeming 65
Seemingly 105
Seer 120

Sees 120
Select 108
Selecting 72
Selective 50
Selectively 50
Selects 97
Self-Invented 162
Sell 51
Selling 63
Semblance 65
Seminal 157
Semiotician 65
Senegal 153
Sensations 148
Sensed 122
Senseless 120
Sensitive 120
Sensorimotor 106
Sensual 96
Sentimental 85
Separate 114
Separated 63
Separately 134
Seriously 99
Serves 175
Setters 168
Setting 116
Settled 99
Settling 121
Seven 78
Seventeen 50
Seventeenth 168
Seventies 84
Seventy 157
Severe 115
Sexier 138
Sexitecture 156
Shackled 74
Shades 118
Shadowy 119
Shaken 65
Sharing/Commenting 145
Sheer 104
Sheet 67
Shelf 74
Shelley 83
Shells 85
Shifted 142
Shimmering 121
Ship 167
Shirt 88
Shock 67
Shocking 72
Shooter 117
Shopping 129
Short-Lived 72
Short-Track 136
Shortchanges 124
Shoulder 168
Showed 92
Shrinks 57
Shut-Ins 74
Shutter 92
Shy 74
Si 154
Sickness 64
Side-By-Side 142
Sides 62
Signal 92
Significantly 175
Signposting 160
Silly 136
Similarity 129
Similarly 158
Simplicity 164
Simulations 104
Simultaneous 95
Simultaneously 113
Singular 98
Sink 79
Sistine 121
Sits 73
Situations 109
Sixteen-Year-Old 128
Sixteenth-Century 121
Sixth 75
Sized 102
Sketch 60
Sketches 113
Skies 165
Skip 165
Skyline 92
Slain 104
Slate 148
Sleeping 90
Sleepless 133
Slower 147
Smiley 163
Smoke 65
Smoking 137
Sms4ever 171
Sneaking 119
Sneve 92
Snippets 156
Snoozing 136
Soaps 100
Sociology 98, 107
Socrates 68
Softwares 103
Softwarestudies.Com 108
Solid 139
Solve 76
Solving 146
Somehow 61
Songs 76
Sony 137
Soothe 133
Sophisticated 72
Sorcery 168
Sorting 76
Souls 99
Soundtrack 84
Southern 93
Sovereignty 156
Soviet 79
Span 96
Spare 155
Sparingly 74
Spatial 109
Specials 78
Specifications 82
Specificities 82
Specified 171
Spectacles 114
Speculated 101
Speculating 70
Speedread 86
Spell 68
Spending 144
Spindle 125
Spirit 123, 140
Spirits 68
Split 164
Spoke 172
Spotify 159
Spreads 108
Springing 168
Sputtered 75
Stad 84
Stake 120
Stalks 120
Stammering 51
Stammerings 52
Standards 105
Standing 150
Stark 73
Stars 145
Starting 76
Starting-Point 78
Starting-Points 86
States 85
Statesmen 69
Statistician 71
Stealing 167
Step 87
Stephen 101
Stephens 144, 146
Steps 159
Stewart 54
Stickiness 93
Stills 140
Stimulate 134
Stimulus 160
Stolen 137
Stop 113
Storify 72
Storing 72
Stormed 104
Storyline 85
Straightforward 168
Strand 143
Strategic 83
Strategies 83
Strategy 150
Strewn 105
Strict 112
Stricter 163
Strictly 127
String 120
Strongly 154
Structurally 118
Struggling 72
Stuart 69
Stuck 146
Studied 101
Stuivende 84
Stumble 73
Stunning 104
Stunted 67
Stuttering 134
Style 134
Subconsciously 148
Subdividing 86
Subjectively 63
Subjectivities 107
Subliming 57
Subordinative 139
Subscribe 136
Subscribing 94
Subsequent 111
Subsequently 162
Substance 56
Substantial 108
Subtitles 79
Subtly 68
Succeeded 111
Successor 65
Sudan 153
Sudden 123
Suffer 53
Sufficiently 143
Suggestion 68
Suggestions 111
Suite 144
Suited 146
Summaries 136
Summer 77, 115
Sunny 88
Sunset 85
Superb 91
Superceded 138
Superimposed 79
Superseded 98
Supplanting 156
Supplements 117
Suppleness 172
Supply 113
Suppose 98
Supposed 70
Suppressed 79
Suppresses 163
Suppression 163
Surely 160
Surface 116
Surfer 132
Surge 96
Surpass 159
Surpassed 54
Surplus 97
Surprised 71
Surprising 169
Surprisingly 146
Surrender 110
Surrendering 109
Survival 105
Survived 153
Suske 84
Sustain 133
Sustained 158
Sustenance 133
Swallow 115
Sweat 53
Swiftly 168
Switch 68
Swoosh 89
Symbol-Centric 66
Symbolism 148
Symptoms 64
Synchronization 166
Synthesis 113
Systematic 120
Systematically 167
T-Shirts 136
Tabs 52
Tackling 119
Tactility 99
Tag 171
Tailback 63
Tails 174
Talked 100
Talks 52
Taller 126

Tandem 103
Tangible 70
Tango 162
Tangram 115
Tantamount 63
Tape 119
Tasting 90
Taught 127
Teach 125
Teachers 83
Teaching 83
Tearing 128
Tears 53
Tease 90
Teased 86
Technicians 81
Technologically-Facilitated 135
Technopolis 132
Techonology 139
Teddy 87
Teeming 105
Telecommunication 66
Telegraph 170
Teletext 170
Telex 170
Templates 105
Temporarily 136
Temporary 62
Tempt 118
Temptation 62
Tenants 141
Territories 146
Terrorized 131
Testify 83
Testimony 79
Testing 108
Texting 139
Texts/Readers 123
Textualities 82
Textuality 82
Thanked 170
Theatres 161
Thematic 78
Thematically 78
Theme 78
Themescapes 171
Theorized 122
Therapeutic 100
Thesaurus 68
Thin 68
Third 63
Thirsting 120
Thirties 113
Thirtieth 136
Thorough 67
Thoroughly 107
Thoughtless 169
Threads 173
Threatens 139
Threw 67
Throw 99
Throwing 139
Thumb 88
Ticker 93
Ticker-Tape 171
Ticket 160
Till 90
Time-Bound 97
Timeless 110
Tired 138
Titled 156
Toilet 141
Toll 146
Tolstoy 101
Tongue 135
Topical 93
Tops 171
Torrent 164
Touched 87
Touches 120
Touching 90
Toxin 170
Traceable 107
Track 128
Tracking 81
Traditionally 143
Trailer 90
Trains 87
Trajectories 61
Trans-Communicative 132
Transcending 123
Transduction 82
Transferring 90
Transform 130
Transformative 158
Transformed 105
Transistor 162
Transitional 87
Transitions 126
Translatable 54
Translated 118
Translating 90
Translations 162
Transmissions 91
Transmit 161
Transpires 171
Transport 69
Transports 63
Travellers 120
Travelling 81
Treating 63
Trends 138
Tricks 172
Tries 88
Trieste 56
Trip 54
Trite 60
Triumphantly 136
Trivia 90
Troubled 70
Trusted 93
Trustworthy 72
Truths 65
Tu 154, 171
Tubes 171
Tumblr 103
Turns 139
Turtlenecks 104
Tv-Centric 65
Tweet 174
Tweeting 146
Twelve 174
Twentieth-Century 75
Twenty-First-Century 103
Twenty-Five 50
Two-By-Two 166
Typeface 82
Typesetters 158
Typewriter 82
Typewritten 158
Typical 132
Typing 68
Typographer 127, 138
Ui 142
Uk 175
Ulysses 56
Un-Associating 131
Un-Authored 105
Un-Linkable 102
Un-Read 132
Un-Reading 131
Un-Writer 133
Un-Writing 131
Unable 136
Unbound 130
Unconsciously 160
Uncouple 69
Underexposed 110
Underline 66
Underlining 56
Underneath 142
Understandings 122
Understands 63
Undertaken 167
Undoes 123
Undulating 166
Uneasy 73
Unfold 134
Unforeseen 106
Unheard 99
Unimaginable 103
Unintended 169
Unintentionally 119
Unit 63
Unite 121
United 78
Unity 173
Universality 111
Unknown 95
Unlike 120
Unlikely 122
Unlimited 88
Unlistened 144
Unlocked 117-118
Unlocking 130
Unmasked 92
Unnatural 102
Unparalleled 164
Unpredictable 102
Unprepared 83
Unqualified 124
Unrecognizable 131
Unrivaled 104
Unseen 144
Unsubstantial 96
Untenable 103
Unwitting 75
Upcoming 72
Update 94
Updated 102
Upended 104
Upends 142
Upgraded 104
Upper 79
Upright 148
Urban 160
Urgent 89
User-Oriented 98
Utilize 157
Utilized 145
Utmost 148
Vacation 70
Vaccination 125
Vagueness 169
Valley 118
Valued 58
Vanity 169
Variability 75
Varied 83
Varieties 102
Vary 94
Varying 170
Vastly 97
Vector 174
Vehicles 160
Vellum 87
Ventures 72
Verbal 106
Vere 154
Verification 167
Verne 124
Versus 64
Vertical 171
Viable 156
Video-Sharing 80
Viewer 79
Village 65
Villages 126
Violence 164
Virginia 101
Virtuosity 67
Visionaries 101
Visitors 78
Visual-Iconic 65
Visuali 58
Visuality 75
Visuals 71, 152
Vividly 85
Vlisco 153
Volatility 120
Volkskrant 55
Volumes 74
Vox 171
Waits 139
Wake 114
Wake-Up 88
Waking 136
Walk 88
Walked 115
Waltz 162
Wander 127
Wanders 167
Wanes 145
Warcraft 143
Warfare 118
Wark 142
Warrant 173
Wasted 158
Water 143
Waters 145
Wax 153
Wayfinding 60
Weakness 99
Wear 98
Weather 172
Weekly 54
Weighing 160
Welcome 105
Well-Known 152

Well-Put 124
Well-Wrought 117
Werner 125
Wertham 124
Wet 135
Wheel 102
Whilst 145
Whoever 160
Whose 104
Wild 105
Wilderness 149
Wilful 75
William 126
Wim 171
Win 163
Winfrey 100
Winning 164
Wins 163
Wipe 88
Wired 55, 90
Wiser 98
Wishing 165
Wiske 84
Withdrawn 139
Witness 157
Witnessed 76
Wordless 135
Work-Arounds 166
Worked 63
Workflows 77
Workings 107
Worldwide 93
Worrying 159
Worthwhile 155
Wound 91
Wrap 82
Wrestle 55
Wrestling 128
Writes 110
Writings 113
Www 93, 121
Wysiwyg 82
Yemen 153
Yesterday 88
Yield 143
Yielded 102
Yourban 92
Youth 65
Yunhe 151
Zeitgeist 145
Zeros 125
Zone 175
Zones 70
Zoom 150
Zurich 56

01

Gathering Up Characters
Arie Altena

487 words | 1:57 mins

Reading behaviour changes, also because of the influence of technology. Empirical research has shown that a screen-based reading behaviour has arisen because we are online so much and read from the screen. A characteristic of this reading behaviour is that more time is spent on browsing, scanning, and identifying key words. Reading is selective, things are not read more than once, and it is generally non-linear. It is said to be at the expense of concentrated and in-depth reading.

That's probably right. Readers in the richer countries read more and more from the screen. The developments of the past twenty-five years have been just as radical as those following the invention of book printing. With the transition from printed material to digital text, there was, to a certain degree, a shift from *owning text* to *accessing text*; from a book or magazine that you hold in your hand, to access to text in the *cloud* –the internet– via an appliance. (I write *to a certain degree* because in the past the *access* to text was primarily for professional readers: you had to be in the library.)

How, then, will we read in the future? No different than in the past –at least as long as it's about converting word images into something with linguistic meaning. That people are reading more from the screen doesn't, of course, mean that concentrated reading is a thing of the past, or that nobody ever reads out loud. When reading selectively, scanning, the word image is converted into meaning. After seventeen to eighteen years of screen reading, the question of how you ensure a concentrated reading experience in the current –and future– media ecology still fascinates me.

I am still not really impressed by the e-readers (the format misery is still a long way from being solved) and the tablets (you can't read from a reflective screen in the sun). The e-readers have a problem with access, the tablets one with ergonomics. It is getting better –but slowly.

I hope that in fifty years we are using reading appliances and accounts in the *cloud* that individuals are completely in charge of, and that there are no organizations that check and log what bytes you download, analyze it in real time, sell on the data, and save it. Or at least, should that happen –and it will happen; that it will benefit to the customer– and that alternatives will also exist. I hope that use will be made of simple data formats and of simple software. I hope that a free circulation of knowledge takes place.

Printed material is text and reading appliance in one. In the future it will be expensive. But once it has been produced, it doesn't get broken very easily. It has one advantage: you only need light if you want to concentrate and read it in private. Light from the sun.

--

Arie Altena writes about art and new media; he works for V2_ in Rotterdam and co-curates the Sonic Acts Festival.

02

Better Stories
Henk Blanken

534 words | 2:06 mins

When man began to speak, around fifty thousand years ago, the earth was already billions of years old. That the word was *in the beginning* is exaggerated, but yet: man became man when he started stammering and passing on his history not purely via his genes but as stories. It is our stories that distinguish

us from
other animals.

Stories help us forward. That went faster thanks to writing and printing, and then we discovered science and finally, as an afterthought, journalism, which began to tell stories as they were taking place.

The word has always been in power, and the power has always had the word. Journalists keep tabs on that power. Things were better when *the press* was able to reach more people. At the end of last century, journalism was stronger and more powerful than ever. And there you have mediacracy.

And then things went downhill with the word. Mass media is the product of an industrialized century, just like mass consumption and mass marketing. But at the end of last century, the mass began to crumble. Rather than a silent majority, we wanted to become assertive individuals.

Thanks to Internet, just as radical as those first stammerings, we could say what we wanted. The paradigm of the mass media –press talks, masses listen– is replaced by something else: we all talk, albeit in small groups. Not the masses but the group –the clan– is the measure of the Internet.

Us and our 287 friends. The word is subject to inflation. The decline in reading has little to do with that. It is a normative term. The hours we spend reading on the Internet do not appear in the statistics. Apparently, there is a difference between *high* and *low* words, just as there is between high and low culture. That perhaps explains why we complain about the decline in reading and at the same time worry about information overload.

Is it really so bad if we read fewer *high* words, less *crime and punishment* and more twitter feeds? If we lose our ability for *deep reading*? Or will that be replaced by associative digital network reading, via tags and *likes* and links, supported by video, or an instant translation from the Arabic, which is a mess but good enough?

I hesitate. Journalists must live with the inflation of the word. And the word, just like the masses, is falling apart. The inflation of the word is the inflation of the power –and of journalism.

What saves journalists is the story. Not necessarily their story. Or that of their antagonists, the politicians. Stories originate in networks, and are not told by the masses, but by small clans. Perhaps society will eventually have enough with these new stories, but I wouldn't want to bet democracy on it.

But journalists will have to tell better stories and tell those stories better than ever. There's more than enough shallow news. Even stories with a head and tail, heroes and scoundrels, sweat and tears are no longer scarce. But the need for stories that tell what we share and do wrong, how we suffer and love, is as old as mankind.

--

Henk Blanken is a journalist and writer of books on digital culture and new media.

03

From Books to Texts
Andrew Blauvelt

282 words | 1:07 mins

It took about 300 years for the codex (the book as a set of bound pages) to rival the popularity of scrolls and another 300 years to replace it completely. This easy to read, efficient, durable, compact, portable, and randomly-accessible format multiplied with the invention of the printing press and endured for the next 1400 years. In 2010, Google estimated that there are about 130 million unique books in the world. In 2011, Google had scanned

more

than

15 million books and planned to have all known books scanned by the end of the decade. In 1971, Project Gutenberg was launched as the first collection of digitally formatted texts (what we now refer to as eBooks). In 2011, many booksellers reported that eBook sales surpassed their hardback equivalents for the first time. It has taken only 40 years for digital texts to rival printed books.

In a reversal of the publishing process, digitization converts an image of a book page back into language –searchable, retrievable, scalable, and translatable text. This linguistic alchemy transforms atoms into bits, the fixed materiality of a book into fungible texts. In the future, most designers will be creating reading experiences not book designs. However, the codex survives for much longer than we think. To paraphrase Kenya Hara, the physical book becomes an information sculpture –a unique, haptic, three-dimensional reading experience. Counterculture guru Stewart Brand once remarked that information wants to be free, but he also noted that it wants to be expensive because it can be valuable. In the future books will be more expensive while eBooks will be ubiquitous –their texts having already been liberated from the codex will want to be free.

--

Andrew Blauvelt is Curator of Architecture and Design at the Walker Art Center, Minneapolis.

04

I Read More Than Ever
Erwin Blom

419 words | 1:40 mins

I like reading. I'm crazy about print. Everyday, two newspapers fall onto the doormat, every week I buy a pile of magazines during my weekly trip along the shops. But I read each of the publications less and less. In the early morning, I can better look at Internet for current information rather than in the newspaper that went to the printers half a day ago. And for depth, I can better visit specialist sites than read magazines that wrestle every month with a scarcity of pages. No matter how much I love the printed media, I increasingly experience that they offer me insufficient added value. I am slowly saying farewell to something which has always been so dear to me.

For digital media can be text and image and sound. With digital media I can chat online with other people about the subjects that interest me. With digital media I can get customized content and therefore more of what fascinates me and less of what doesn't interest me. And digital media are dynamic and can be current at any moment.

As far as newspapers and magazines are concerned, publishers see new distribution channels such as iPads as possibilities to repeat their old trick one more time in a new packaging. It doesn't work. It doesn't work anywhere. Of course people buy Wired or de Volkskrant out of curiosity, but after an initial optimism, the numbers sold have drastically dropped.

It is as logical as can be, but not, apparently, for the publishers of paper. In an environment with new possibilities, I do not want to be confronted with old limitations. I want my media to be diverse (also audio and video), I want my media to be up-to-date (latest information always available), I want my media to be social (be able to share content with people), and I want my media customized (matching my interests).

Is it dreadful that people are reading less, but are getting informed in other ways? No, of course not. Is it dreadful that the reading

behaviour

of people
is changing? No, of course not. The people that think that only a doorstop of a book can provide depth and that a summary of short messages and interactions on Twitter has no substance, have done nothing more than take a cursory view of things. Adding everything together– blogs, Twitter, mail, Facebook etcetera –I read more than ever, but increasingly less with those parties that used to have exclusive rights to reading matter.

--

Erwin Blom is founder of The Crowds, a company specialized in social media.

05

Encoded Experiences
James Bridle

294 words | 1:10 mins

Books are changing, and the nature of reading, what we take away from it, is changing too. Books used to be physically malleable things that we marked, physically, with our experiences: dog-earing them, underlining them, highlighting, and copying out. But the books will not be physical for very much longer.

The great misunderstanding of digitization is to believe that it is only the content and the appearance that matters. That, to reproduce the experience of the book, we needed to make a screen that looked like a page, that turned like a page, that contained words. And the reason that we've had difficulty for so long with the notion of eBooks is that that is not all that books are.

Books are journeys, and encoded experiences. The writer has spent months, perhaps years, producing this work out of themselves. That devastating last line of James Joyce's Ulysses: *Trieste–Zurich–Paris 1914–1921.* And the book is the medium of transmission of that experience, so that the reader, too, can experience it, and go on their own journey.

The books are subliming, they are going up into the air, and what will remain of them is our experiences. That experience is encoded in marginalia, in memory, and in data, and it will be shared because we are all connected now, and because sharing is a form of communal prosthetic memory.

When Walter Benjamin wrote that *what shrinks in an age where the work of art can be reproduced by technological means is its aura*, he was assuming that the aura diffused, that it was lost to the other reproductions. But digital technologies do not just disseminate, they recombine, and in this reunification of our reading experiences is the future of the book.

--

James Bridle is publisher, writer and editor.

06

Watching, Formerly Reading
Max Bruinsma

832 words | 3:19 mins

I don't read, someone I know well told me. She meant that she doesn't read the way *readers* read. People who can spend hours on end with a book in a chair or on the sofa, occasionally turning over a paper page and appearing to have completely forgotten that there exists a world outside the sentences they are reading. No, she's not one of those readers. But, I say, you actually read the whole day through! You scan articles and books, browse through websites and online fora, open and answer emails, gloss over newspaper headlines. Yes, but that's not reading, she says. What it is, then, I don't know, but I do know that on an average day she processes more text than many a *reader*. I am from a somewhat older generation; I know how it feels to be

immersed in a book. But I have to admit that it's been a while. My reading also seems to be less than what it originally meant to be. Yet I would be too quick in saying I don't read –at most that I read too little, but even that is not entirely true. I read differently.

What we used to call *watching* seems increasingly like what we once called *reading*. Then they were different things, with a clear hierarchy. Reading was *absorbing content*, watching was *receiving an impression of something*. The first was a conceptual activity that was valued higher than the second, a more passive, sensory affair. The fact that you do both with your eyes was less important than the thought that reading conjures up a non-existent picture and watching processes existing pictures. Only for trained viewers –art historians and design critics such as myself– the two were alike. Our looking is also reading; for us, a picture is also a visual text. What I've noticed is that since the irresistible increase of the *visual media,* non-professional viewers have also become more and more readers. Concurrently, the idea that the only thing you can read is text is losing ground.

We, the homini visuali, do not only read and write words but also images. The form in which things appear to us has thus become just as much text as text has become image. Perhaps that is why she says that she doesn't read –because reading is no longer what it used to be. Reading has also become a form of *getting an impression of something*. A scanning of visual stimuli, that are linked together in our head into something of significance. These stimuli can be letters or pictures, the difference between the two –once so fundamental– is fading.

That doesn't just mean that we have become more aware of the sensory side of reading; it also means that watching has become a more conceptual, more reflective activity. And that terms that used to stand for superficiality, for absorbing transitory visual impressions at a glance, such as *scanning*, *leafing*, *browsing*, *watching*, have developed into the most significant concepts of our culture.

Here, oversight is becoming more important than insight. You can lament this and say that the depth that was so connected to the old reading –penetrating deeply into a text is fathoming the world behind reality– dissolves in a view without dimensions. But that comes down to rendering a new phenomenon in old concepts. Something like designing the recently invented automobile as a horseless carriage. You see what is missing from the device, but not what you have gained in its place. The new oversight is not, as it used to be thought of, a perspective on an expanse of plain, but penetrates deeply into the transparent and limitless space of data that the world has become. Oversight is: seeing what links or can link the data. Anyone observing the current profusion of data visualizations that help us understand a reality caught in figures –a reality that used to be called virtual but is now becoming more real than the real– knows what I mean: the image has become a text, the real significance of which is in its property of having us understand what it means at a glance. Once we start reading longer, we are in danger of losing our way in incoherent details.

Like text and image, insight and oversight are growing closer together, merging into each other. Perhaps even the old hierarchy will be reversed: reading, then, will be understood as the scanning activity that gains us oversight and enables us from there to gather significance, to choose (gathering and choosing are, after all, two ancient meanings of *lecture*, the Latin root of which means both), and watching

will become the word for what we realize when we pause at something for longer than a transitory moment. If you really want to fathom something, you will have to watch. Long and intensively, just like former times with a book in your lap on the sofa.

--

Max Bruinsma is an independent design critic and editor-in-chief of Items, the Dutch review of design.

07

If Words, Then Reading

Anne Burdick

48 words | 0:21 mins

If interface, then navigation.
If disguise, then disclosure.
If map, then itinerary.
If resource, then use.
If environment, then wayfinding.
If plan, then practice.
If erasure, then reconstruction.
If sketch, then animation.
If architecture, then dwelling.
If capture, then release.
If trace, then archeology.
If program, then process.

--

Anne Burdick is a designer, writer, and editor as well as the Chair of the graduate Media Design Program (MDP).

08

Flowing Together

Vito Campanelli

478 words | 1:55 mins

Maybe it's trite but when I reflect on the evolution of reading modalities I cannot do without thinking that, in the present historic moment, we are witnessing an epochal *change of status*: from the invention of the alphabet to mechanical movable type printing and even to deconstructionism (Derrida, above all), the text was organized into rigid structures that, despite the heterogeneity of their evolutionary trajectories, have come to constitute as many cages. We know that a cage means a condition in which every possibility is ordered to remain confined within it, so that –to take some practical examples– the interpretation of a written text or its reworking, not being able to take place outside that precise form/cage in which the text was shaped, inevitably end in adapting themselves to the rules of the game and to the set of finite possibilities of that very context. The various dominant forms, characteristic of specific ages, have determined the *thought form* of their time, so that alphabetic writing is a prerequisite for the emergence of historical consciousness; the printed book is crucial for the spread of a generalized confidence in the linear progress of science, without which there would be no industrial revolution; and so on.

The form/cage also assumed the function, somehow, of social glue, in fact, old and new generations, conservatives and progressives, despite the apodictic distance of their instances, have had to confront each other from a common ground: they have had to sit at the same table or –if you prefer– behind the same bars. Today, with the digitization of the text, we see a radical change that –in my opinion– must be identified with the abandonment of all form/cage. The text, in fact, becomes fluid and begins to flow along with other data, therefore, together with any other cultural expression and with contemporary identities and existences. Everything is included in a flow which, by its very nature, denies itself to any stable form. Everything

becomes

and in this new condition, establishing new rules of the game (a temptation which many cannot resist) is quite like writing on the foreshore: it is something that will last only until the next wave. Obviously in the last twenty years old media forms and metaphors (such as the page of the book) have been mostly used; however –and this is the key point– no one and nothing can prevent the same content (only illusorily fixed in a form) beginning to flow in a kaleidoscopic range of different configurations. Stripped of any structure, without any predetermined and sequential paths, reading becomes a flowing together with the other elements of the flow, creating temporary (even ephemeral and extemporary, if you like) relationships and configurations. Fantastic, isn't it?

I love this new condition and I believe I have been privileged to have lived on both sides of this epochal *change of status*.

--

Vito Campanelli is new media theorist and teaches Theory and Technics of Mass Communication at the Università degli Studi di Napoli *L'Orientale*.

09

Highway Drugs and Data Visualization
Catalogtree

531 words | 2:07 mins

Experts do not need visualization to be able to read data. A musician can hear the music as he reads a score. The rest is at the mercy of graphics and audio.

A few years ago we were working on a project about the motorway between Arnhem and Nijmegen, the A325. We used a series of silk-screen prints to show various aspects of the motorway. Where did the most accidents occur? Where did people drive fastest? Which approach and exit roads were used most? We made use of data that the province collected 24 hours a day at various measurement points along the road. Three civil servants worked in this measuring department: one was responsible for traffic counts, using a computer system dating from 1977, one was responsible for speed measurements on a system dating from 1992 (not compatible with the former), and a third was the coordinator of the other two.

We kept in touch with them by telephone and e-mail and asked for interesting data. They were pleased to help. They went out in a mobile measuring unit to take measurements that they then sent us by mail. We received an enormous e-mail with tens of thousands of figures, separated by commas. A completely abstract jumble of figures that was explained in the subject line of the mail: *Look, a monster tailback!*

A frequent misconception in data visualization is that treating data subjectively is tantamount to lying. It is often said that data must be presented as objectively as possible, but to our minds that leads to an exact reproduction of the original data set. That is perhaps the best method if you're dealing with the top ten best selling books, but if the visualization represents tens of thousands of pieces of data, that makes a good interpretation impossible. To be able to tell a story means that it is necessary to place the emphasis somewhere, to make an editorial choice, so that the reader understands what is being told without having to be an expert.

Another misconception is that a visualization must be clear at the first glance, otherwise it has failed. We once drew a map about drug transports between South and North America. It had to show which drug cartels were active (around twenty such cartels), what they were transporting (various types of drugs,

weapons,
money, people), how they were transporting them (various means by land, by sea, and through the air), which routes they took, and which alliances they had formed in order to work efficiently. A fairly complicated map of course and one which required some effort from the reader if it were to be fully fathomed. A data visualization can easily have a higher information density than the written word. Yet nobody glancing at a page covered with words expects that the content is immediately clear. You have to read it first.

Although those provincial civil servants didn't need our visualizations to know what was happening on their roads, they nevertheless derived considerable pleasure from our silk-screen prints. They quickly replaced the art in the corridors which had been purchased by the province. *Well*, they said, *this is art that actually means something!*

--

Joris Maltha and Daniel Gross run the multidisciplinary design studio *Catalogtree*, specialized in making information visualizations.

10

The Revenge of the Gutenberg Galaxy
Florian Cramer

470 words | 1:53 mins

Let's be clear, reading is not limited to alphabetic language, but is actually any act of visual or tactile perception involving interpretation of signs: graffiti tags, photographic images, sickness symptoms. Since human perception always, inevitably, involves interpretation, the line between perception in general and reading in particular is perfectly blurry.

Even reading versus listening is a questionable distinction. Our understanding of spoken words is highly modulated by visual reading –the so-called *McGurk effect* describes how we misperceive a spoken word when the speaker's lips suggest a different word. In a world with intelligent beings, forecasting a future without reading might be futile. But it's worth asking how we read now, and what kinds of reading we are moving towards.

Following the semiotician Charles S. Peirce's three basic types of signs –iconic (based on semblance, whether a portrait painting or an onomatopoetic word like *bang*), indexical (based on traces; smoke as an indicator of fire) and symbolic (abstract numbers, the alphabet or morse code)– 20th century media theories generally predicted a crisis of symbolic symbols in favour of icons, going from the mass medium of the book to the mass media of cinema and TV.

This prediction became the bottom line of the Frankfurt School's critique of the culture industry, of McLuhan's TV-centric *global village* after the *end of the Gutenberg Galaxy*, and of the *iconic turn* declared by art historians since the 1990s. Even the development of symbolic machines appeared to follow this route, as computers evolved from the (symbolic) command line to an (iconic) graphical user interface. The future of culture, and of reading, once seemed inevitably visual-iconic.

The Internet alongside economic neoliberalism has completely shaken these seeming truths. Who would have predicted ten years ago that major youth culture media would not be some hypermediated mutation of MTV, but SMS, Twitter, and Facebook? Even MTV's de-facto successor, YouTube, cannot be used by the illiterate because of keyword tagging, commenting, and searching (same with Flickr, the leading Internet platform for still images).

This requisite computer literacy in fact means a massive resurgence of symbolic literacy –the revival of a more or less classical concept of reading following a cultural and economic logic of compression. That is, reading and writing alphabetical text is often the most compressed and therefore efficient way of rapidly processing information, a notion explored early on in the Middle Ages when monks read texts without speaking them aloud. Now, in the form of e-mail and related types of electronic communication, reading and writing has taken over the workplace and dissolved the difference between work and home, between being fixed in space and hitting the road.

The symbol-centric, mobile medium of the text page has overtaken telecommunication, but instead of the monk's contemplative codex, we find a second wave of industrialization and escalation of workplace efficiency.

--

Florian Cramer is director of the Piet Zwart Institute and head of the research programme Communication in a Digital Age.

Florian Cramer having received about 30 work-related e-mail messages while writing this text.

11

Where Do You Read?
Sean Dockray

178 words | 0:43 mins

I read where I am but sometimes I'd rather read where you are. I'd rather sit on your lap and have you read to me. I want to see what you underline and I want to know why. I want to know what's behind those words you're jotting down in the margins. Why are you looking in the index now? Is that another book? Are you taking a break? How many pages do you read at once? In what order do you read them? I want your reading to be my reading, I want to have your reading because the text is good yes, but only as good as sheet music, while what you have is virtuosity. I want to be there when you read, not when you write, but when you read, although I know that you can't read without writing, neither can I. We write when we read and we read when we write, sometimes I'm not sure if this is my breath or yours, or somebody else's and I'm not sure that it matters anyway.

--

Sean Dockray is founder of AAAARG.org, an online archive of texts, as well as founder of the first Public School, a project initiated by Telic Arts Exchange in Los Angeles.

12

Pancake
Paulien Dresscher

450 words | 1:48 mins

When, in 2007, I decided to resume studying after a break of 15 years, I discovered with a shock that I could no longer write without a computer. After days of thorough preparation, I entered the lecture hall to sit my first exam. When it started, I began industriously writing things down, but I quickly encountered problems. The second sentence didn't flow well, it had to be reversed; I crossed it out and started again, turned the sentence around and then went on to the second paragraph. This also turned into a mess. I went to get fresh paper and threw a worried glance at the clock: I had already lost twenty minutes. A slight panic crept over me. Could I handle it?

My concern was not only that I apparently had become so stunted by cut-and-paste tools that linear text production seemed now virtually impossible, but also that the whole process preceding this –ordering my thoughts and formulating arguments– couldn't take

place

without

ten finger tips subtly leaning, gliding, typing over the qwerty keyboard, with the Internet browser, spell checker, and thesaurus within easy reach. Even more confusion arose in me from the realization that I hadn't even noticed that I had changed this much.

Just as Socrates was concerned that the invention of writing would make people forgetful, people today are worried about the degree to which we are permanently shaped by digital technologies. The playwright Richard Foreman recently expressed his concern about digital dependency in his suggestion that we are on our way to becoming *pancake people*, in contrast to those who are cursed with a more *complex, dense, and cathedral-like* mental structure. The pancake people are *wide and thin*, connected to the network of information, while the cathedral people have internalized a personal vision on the world.

The contrast between the words pancake and cathedral is deliberately humorous, but it is also normative. It ignores the multitude of possibilities that the Internet offers us and the irreversibility of media change. A subtle awareness of the advantages and disadvantages of digitality is crucial.

Although, according to Foreman, I have, in recent years, developed into a networking pancake –and probably a lot more besides me– I still now and then go to a meeting in good spirits with a writing pad. I can't prevent my hand involuntarily, but with a certain regularity, moving to the bottom of the paper page to check a phantom mouse pad, to see whether there are any messages or in order to look up something. These days, I deprogram my body more regularly and flick the online switch to *off* sometimes. By the way –I passed that exam.

--

Paulien Dresscher is head of New Media at Cinekid, advisor E-Culture at the Netherlands Film Fund, filmmaker, and researcher.

13 Between Reality and the Impossible: Revisited

Dunne & Raby

405 words | 1:37 mins

> What human beings are and will become is decided in the shape of our tools no less than in the action of statesmen and political movements. The design of technology is thus an ontological decision fraught with political consequences.[1]

What happens when you **uncouple design** from the **marketplace**, when, **rather** than **making technology sexy**, **easy** to use, and more **consumable**, **designers** use the **language** of **design** to **pose questions**, **inspire**, and **provoke** –to **transport** our **imaginations** into **parallel** but **possible worlds?**

The projects in this **exhibition**[2] **focus** on **designing interactions** between **people** and **technology** on **many different levels.** They are **concerned** not only with the **expressive**, **functional**, and **communicative possibilities** of **new technologies**, but **also** with the **social**, **cultural**, and **ethical consequences** of **living within** an **increasingly** technologically mediated **society.** They **explore new** ways in which **design can make technology** more **meaningful** and **relevant** to our **lives**, both now and in the **future**, by **thinking** not only about **new applications** but their **implications** as **well**, both **positive** and **negative.**

The futurologist Stuart **Candy uses** a **wonderful diagram** to **clarify** how we **think** about **futures. Rather** than **one amorphous** space of **futureness**,

1 Andrew Feenberg, [1991] 2002 Transforming Technology: A Critical Theory Revisited. Oxford: Oxford University Press. (p. 3)

2 This text was originally written for the catalogue of the Biennale Internationale Design 2010 Saint-Étienne.

it is

divided into *probable*, *preferable*, *plausible*, and *possible* futures. One of the most interesting zones is *preferable*. Of course, the very definition of preferable is problematic –who decides? But, although designers shouldn't decide for everyone else, we can play a significant role in discovering what is and what isn't desirable.

To do this, we need to move beyond designing for the way things are now and begin to design for how things could be, imagining alternative possibilities and different ways of being, and giving tangible form to new values and priorities. Designers cannot do this alone, though, and the projects here benefit from dialogues and consultations with people working in other fields such as ethics, philosophy, political science, life sciences, and biology.

The idea of probable, preferable, plausible, and possible futures –the space between reality and the impossible– allows designers to challenge design orthodoxy and prevailing technological visions so that fresh perspectives can begin to emerge. The exhibition is absolutely not about prediction, but about asking *what if*, speculating, imagining, and even dreaming in order to encourage debate about the kind of technologically mediated world we wish to live in –hopefully, one that reflects the complex, troubled people we are, rather than the easily satisfied consumers and users we are supposed to be.

--

Dunne & Raby is a design studio run by Anthony Dunne and Fiona Raby.

14

Weapons of Mass Distraction
Sven Ehmann

667 words | 2:40 mins

I love reading. That is why I took three books along on a recent vacation. Three books that I picked carefully from my library and was sure to enjoy: poetry by Ossip Mandelstam, an early Pynchon, and Fragebogen (questionnaires) by Max Frisch. No recent popstar author, no must-read non-fiction title, just books for my pleasure. In the end I read none of them. Instead I decided—surprised and almost frightened—that not reading would make an even better holiday. Instead of gathering more input, I gave myself a break, time to think, time to contemplate, time to forget.

We are in a period of data-rush. Getting information is banal. Data is gathered, processed, and available anywhere, anytime. It can be very useful or very annoying, but finding the time, capacity, and tools for making sense out of the data—for the moment as well as the foreseeable future—is the real challenge. That is why I so very much appreciate the work of dedicated professionals like journalists and editors. Or a new kind of professional that The Economist described in a special report entitled *Data, data everywhere* in February 2010 as *the data scientist, ... [who] combines the skills of software programmer, statistician, and storyteller, [working as an] artist to extract the nuggets of gold hidden in mountains of data.* I praise these authors, curators, and designers who make the effort of turning information into an experience for me as the reader.

What inspires me the most right now is the field of data visualization, information graphics, and visual storytelling as it can be found in publications such as the Italian supplement IL. A new breed of data journalist is passionately working to find appropriate, understandable, and entertaining visual representations for complex datasets or processes. Having said that, I feel that –despite the popularity of the phrase *a picture is worth a thousand words*– visuals are not

always

understandable

and easy to read. We are challenged to develop more sophisticated visual literacy across society, and those currently working in information graphics are helping to do just that. They clearly intend to prevent data graphics from being merely a short-lived design trend. Today's designers, including Nicholas Felton, who became known for publishing personal data in the form of an annual Feltron Report, are closely reading, examining, and discussing the quality of a visual in addition to the quality and story of the data behind it (for example, in Felton's case, those in acclaimed designer Jonathan Barnbrook's The Little Book of Shocking Global Facts). And many other designers are also contributing to this critical discourse.

Beyond the individual story, the joy of dealing with information is the experience one has with different types of media. I am happy to see how some media outlets keep experimenting to make the best possible use of different channels. Glamorous titles such as Monocle as well as smaller ventures such as the online feuilleton Berliner Gazette are using print, web, mobile, audio, motion, events, exhibitions, et cetera to extend a story rather than just duplicating it over and over again.

What I feel is still missing, though, are the right tools for me to handle my data. Getting data is easy, but selecting, storing, indexing, updating, and most importantly contextualizing the information is rather difficult. What is the opposite of Google, the smart output device? Maybe the range of upcoming online curation tools like Storify might offer a solution, but will the amount of time I need to invest in working with these tools ever pay off?

In the meantime I keep struggling, exploring, enjoying other tools and outlets, while always being happy to come back to proven and trustworthy sources. One of the most powerful promises in media sits right at the top left of The New York Times –the printed paper, that is. It reads *All the News That's Fit to Print*. Nothing more, nothing less. Carefully selected, condensed. In comparison to that, most blogs are just weapons of mass distraction.

--

Sven Ehmann is Creative Director at Die Gestalten Verlag.

15

Reading Beyond Words
Martin Ferro-Thomsen

200 words | 0:48 mins

My literature professor understood reading as a relative concept: One might grasp the words without yet comprehending the meaning. Ideally the reader would discard her library every five years, because by then she had elevated her perspective...

That's an elitist notion of reading in stark contrast to the reality of today. Text as a medium is being challenged by ever more engaging forms of communication. And it seems the conditions for deep reading are pretty much being killed by mankind's ongoing experiment to digitize society. Irony, anyone?

Me, I've parted with most of my print library. For good. Ninety percent of my reading now takes place on-screen, although I'm uneasy about digital books living inside those intangible walled gardens. Can I pass them on to my kids, like my mother did with Camus to me? Will they keep my side notes? Will they smell?

Let's not get overly nostalgic just yet. Text remains a universal vehicle for human thought and often it's the shortest distance from one mind to another. But as we stumble

into

digital

renaissance, our understanding of both text and reading will have to encompass more than mere words: hyper-connectedness, vibrant plasticity, social interaction, and dynamic contextuality.

--

Martin Ferro-Thomsen, M.A. is co-founder of Issuu, a leading digital publishing platform.

16

We Left Home; Why Shouldn't Ideas?
Jeff Gomez

200 words | 0:48 mins

A hundred years ago books were pale shut-ins, escaping overstuffed shelves only sparingly; maybe one or two volumes at a time but never en masse. Libraries were huge, shy, lumbering things; as big as a herd of elephants (and just as portable). But today, with the advent of eBooks and devices such as the Kindle and iPad, we have the potential to carry around with us at all times our entire book collections in a digitized format. Whether or not this is a threat to publishers or bookstores (or even to writers) is beyond the point. Let us, for a moment, consider what this means to readers.

Since the invention of print there has never been a back pocket or book bag large enough to fit a bookshelf full of books (let alone an entire library), and yet now all of that text can live inside a tiny gadget. Our various portable screens then become portals to limitless knowledge, imagination, or anything we want them to be. Stories, novels, entire worlds are at our fingertips. And books, for centuries shackled to the shelf (sometimes literally), are turned from static, bound, physical objects to caged birds finally allowed to take flight.

--

Jeff Gomez is author of the book Print is Dead: Books in our Digital Age.

17

Delectation
Denise Gonzales Crisp

180 words | 0:43 mins

Type well used is invisible as type, wrote Beatrice Warde in the early 1930s. Like a clear glass goblet, a crystalline window, and a perfect speaking voice, transparent typography is the *unnoticed vehicle* for *the transmission of ideas*.

Text sputtered onto screens in alien bitmap types some fifty years later. The jagged forms were as exotic and present as lugubrious calligraphy inked by medieval scribes.

Current high definition screens deliver typography comparable to, if not more refined than, early twentieth-century printing, with conspicuous additions: animation, scalability, variability. Wilful visuality. Human voice, too, translates written text to palpable form in audio *books*, an unwitting feat of reverse engineering that recalls oral traditions. Ears read words filtered by elocution.

Reading is, and was always, mediated by form, contained by technology. Heavier at times, and lighter. As legacies instruct we read in four full dimensions using at least three senses (the sixth is not considered here). Touch fingertips to raised dots. Click to advance. See words appearing, and disappearing. Turn the page. Warde eschewed *delectation of the senses* where reading is concerned. Impossible.

--

Denise Gonzales Crisp is a designer, writer, and Graphic Design professor at North Carolina State University, College of Design.

18

Welcome to the Digital Age. What Changed?

Alexander Griekspoor

414 words | 1:39 mins

Scientists read a lot. In fact the entire academic *workflow* is based on publishing papers, a drive that acts as both the final goal and the starting point of research, and also fuels the massive industry of academic journals. Interestingly, more and more of these journals no longer print articles on paper but distribute them as digital PDFs, a transition dating to 1998 that became the standard in the following years, right around the time I was doing my PhD. Back then I still copied physical journals as poor quality black and white pages to read at home or on the way to school.

It's no wonder that both scientists and publishers love the PDF format. Thousands of these files can be stored on your hard disk, so you can get rid of piles of paper on your desk and in dusty old filing cabinets. But does the PDF really solve our storage issues?

Well, yes and no. The PDF format does get rid of the piles of paper, but instead we quickly end up with the digital equivalent of them on our computer. The ease of downloading articles only increases the scale of the problem. Our critical mistake is to think that the transition to a new format alone adequately addresses storage concerns, but this view doesn't consider the importance of organization. I witnessed this exact problem a few years earlier with the shift from audio CDs to digital MP3 files, leading to the digital equivalent of audio CD racks in the form of folders multiplying on your hard disk.

Interestingly, iTunes solved this problem by allowing you to arrange and retrieve songs using relevant sorting information, or metadata. I figured that exactly this is needed in the digital research paper world, which is how I came to build Papers, an application that removes the hassle of handling and organizing PDF files and instead lets you focus on keywords such as paper title, author, journal title, et cetera. Papers is in many ways a non-obvious but crucial part in the successful transition to a new, digital workflow. I would even argue that these tools and the workflow around content will require more dramatic changes than those needed for the initial format transition from paper to PDF. Even more than changes in formats, in distribution methods, or even in the devices we read on, organizational tools and the workflows we create for our documents will ultimately determine the shape of reading in the future.

--

Alexander Griekspoor is the co-founder of Mekentosj, an independent software company that writes innovative software for researchers.

19

Non-linear Publishing
Hendrik-Jan Grievink

245 words | 0:59 mins

The books that I find interesting are more likely to be printed collections than linear stories and are also consumed as such. Traditional categories of publishing disappear, the only relevant distinction is offline or online. Or: does the story remain static or will it change over time and enter into relationships with other stories? For offline media, visual aspects are more important, the designer moves to the fore in the publishing process where he assumes the place of editor. With the Next Nature book[1] that I have compiled in the last two years together with Koert van Mensvoort, the traditional publishing process is

1 Next Nature, Actar, summer 2011, 450 pp.

turned

inside out: from a small blog for publication in one's own circle to a network with many contributors and 1.5 million unique visitors per year with a few thousand shorter and longer observations about what we called *nature caused by people*. The book deepens and contextualizes existing content and is made up of seven magazines glued together, each with its own theme. This compilation process has had in turn a large influence on the design and layout of the blog: the thematic approach has been implemented online, specials from the book are adapted. On the blog, connections are made through links; in the book we do that by bringing the content together thematically, whereby the image is always leading. Ten years ago, a website was conceived for every project; today, being networked is the starting-point –always linked with your public.

--

Hendrik-Jan Grievink is an editorial designer and co-founder of the Next Nature Institute.

20

Subtitling
Ger Groot

225 words | 0:54 mins

The misconception that a picture says more than a thousand words is based on the idea that it is immediately clear what a picture means. You see a shoe, think *shoe*, but what do you actually see? It only becomes clear from the story around it that this is the shoe with which Nikita Khrushchev hammered the desk at the United Nations.

The presenter of the television programme tells us that and so conjures up a world of memories. Cold War, Cuba Crisis, the Netherlands hardly recovered and yet happiness was still commonplace. All this flashes through our mind's eye as a gentleman speaking Russian shows us around the museum of Soviet reality. The man says something in Russian and we read it in Dutch along the bottom of our television screen.

With the exception of advertising slogans and instructions for use, no text has become such a natural part of our everyday lives as subtitles. Everybody reads them throughout the day, so automatically that picture and subtitle have become intertwined and Derrida seems finally to have been proven right: the whole world has become écriture.

There is another way. In many other countries, the viewer doesn't get to hear the Russian guide, or at most somewhere in the background. A voice in the viewer's own language is superimposed, so easily understood that it melts into the picture. And in reaction it seems as if the latter is actually speaking. Word and voice disappear in the testimony of the *thousand words* that seem to be spoken to us by what we see.

And so it seems as if the picture has the upper hand over the text, as the prophets of the image culture have been telling us for years. But that demands a very high price. Filtering out the Russian by eliminating the text in the picture also has suppressed the foreign aspect that the original contained. The world in voice-over never really leaves the cosiness of the familiar. It no longer hears any incomprehensible Russian. It only ultimately knows itself.

No wonder, then, that in countries with post-synchronization, not only is the knowledge of languages at a lower level, but also knowledge of the world. That reality is larger, more spacious, and more alienating than they had always thought simply doesn't sink in.

The classic book reader already knew that, but the subtitle reader discovers that daily. The writing beckons him out of the immediacy in

which

everything

literally speaks for itself. The image is layered thanks to the doubling of the text, which suggests a whole universe between legible writing and foreign voice.

No image speaks for itself and no voice is simple enough to coincide with this. Without text, the visible remains enclosed within the horizon that can be scanned with the eyes. It only becomes meaningful thanks to the word; cosmopolitan thanks to the writing. Looking by itself is, after all, a somewhat narrow-minded activity. Only when the world becomes legible and something can be deciphered in its image can it be freed from the restriction of the look. Only then is there really something to see in its image.

--

Ger Groot is a writer and teaches Philosophy at the Erasmus University Rotterdam and Philosophy and Literature at the Radboud University Nijmegen.

21

Ambient Scholarship
Gary Hall

336 words | 1:20 mins

Today knowledge and information are increasingly being externalized onto complex, multilayered, distributed systems of computers, databases, blogs, wikis, RSS feeds, video-sharing sites, and other kinds of social networks.

What are the implications of this prosthetization of knowledge for the scholars of the future?

Will the men and women of learning who emerge from the current generation of students continue to internalize particular branches of knowledge by means of extensive, and intensive, reading and study?

Will they still be expected to master their field?

Will scholars not come to concentrate more on developing their specialist search and retrieval skills –confident in the belief that, if they need to know something, then they can find the relevant information quickly and easily using Google, Facebook, Wikipedia, as well as a host of open access, open education, open science, and open data resources?

In which case, is there a risk that a large part of their authority is going to pass to administrators, managers, or technicians?

Will scholars themselves increasingly come to resemble such figures: experts who do not necessarily need to possess the knowledge contained in the systems they administer and have access to?

Instead, their authority will rest on their ability to search, find, access, and even buy knowledge and information using online journal archives, full text search capabilities, electronic table of contents alerting, and citation tracking, and to organize the results into patterns, flows, and assemblages?

Or will such developments lead to the emergence of a different form of scholarship, whereby learned individuals no longer acquire the bulk of their information in concentrated immersive doses, as they might have in the past, from sitting down in a library or study and carefully reading a book?

Rather they experience more fragmented and distributed flows of information –at home, in the street, while travelling by car, or waiting to catch a train– that nevertheless enable a certain body of knowledge to be built up over a period of time.

Might this be described as ambient scholarship?

--

Gary Hall is author of Digitize this Book! and Professor of Media and Performing Arts at Coventry University.

22

Set the Text Free: Balancing Textual Agency Between Humans and Machines
John Haltiwanger

215 words | 0:52 mins

The computer has eaten typography, just as it has eaten everything else. The ramifications of the coded extensions we wrap our text in are both practical and ideological.

In a rare ideal, digital text moves fluidly from format to format, expanding to enjoy the material specificities found in, for instance, HTML and PDF. The more locked down a format is, the harder this necessary multiple existence becomes. Microsoft Word is a remediated typewriter with a capitalist agenda, and its outputs are as brittle as ink and pulp in terms of format fluidity.

Modern typography bases itself on a notion of message encoding, meaning that the typeface in which a message is set becomes part of the message itself. This message was initially set in a libre font called Lato. It was generated entirely using libre software, with a method that allows for transduction into not only HTML and PDF but also into any other format for which specifications are available, a material quality not available in the proprietary mechanism of its final typesetting. Generative typesetting demands a retreat from human-biased textualities presented by WYSIWYG tools, replacing it with a more equitable balance between human and machine. A foundation in libre ideology defies the on-going colonization of capital, rejecting the proprietary in favour of liberated textuality.

--

John Haltiwanger engages new media in theory and practice. He is a member of the Open Source Publishing collective.

23

Educate Well, Read Better

N. Katherine Hayles

234 words | 0:56 mins

Literacy is not without neurological consequences. Recent research in fMRI studies indicates that reading changes how the brain functions. My students increasingly read on the Web rather than in print. What difference does this make? The question is not only what they read, but how they read. Reading on the Web seems to encourage skimming. While useful as a technique to identify quickly items of interest, it can become a disadvantage when working with complex digital literary forms. For example, when I assigned my students Shelley Jackson's classic hypertext fiction Patchwork Girl, they were unprepared for the work's density, extent, and complexity. By contrast, when they read Mary Shelley's print novel Frankenstein, they fully expected to spend several hours (or days) with it. Does this mean that reading on the Web is making us distracted, as Nicholas Carr has argued, or in the more extreme view espoused by Mark Bauerlein, that it is making us stupid? Such arguments overlook the fact that strategic reading practices have always included skimming and scanning, as any scholar can testify. The trick is to have a repertoire of varied reading techniques and the experience to shift to one or another depending on the situation. Where we are failing as parents, teachers, and educators is teaching our digitally native students a full range of reading strategies and educating them on how to use them in disciplined and creative ways.

--

N. Katherine Hayles is a professor in the Literature programme at Duke University, Durham, NC.

24

Reading the Picture
Toon Horsten

218 words | 0:52 mins

When Hergé, the creator of Tintin, was interviewed in the seventies, he wasn't certain of things. The comic strip, and Tintin in particular, had had its day. The medium was out of date and the strip story could not compete with the new forms of amusement (including games and animation films).

In the following four decades, it seemed as if Hergé was right. With the digital revolution, it seemed that there wasn't for the moment any place for the combination of picture and text as they appeared in the comic strip. Reading comic strips on a computer screen was trying. But now that the iPad and other tablets seem to have taken over the market for digital reading, the picture suddenly looks completely different. Comic strips appear to be extremely suitable as reading matter on an iPad. Although the possibilities have to be further investigated.

The iPad version of the Suske and Wiske album De stuivende stad [ed. The Bustling City], issued to celebrate the 65th anniversary of the series, leads the way. The comic strip, supported with a full soundtrack and some slight animation, shows which possibilities the new applications can offer for reading comic strips.

They will have to ensure, however, that with all the new possibilities, they don't simply end up reinventing the animation film.

--

Toon Horsten is writer of Het Geluk van de Lezer [ed. Happiness of the Reader] and artistic leader of Strip Turnhout.

25

Apples and Cabbages
Minke Kampman

440 words | 1:46 mins

We didn't need dialogue, we had faces. A sentimental line by Norma Desmond in the movie Sunset Boulevard, explaining why silent movies were so wonderful and so much better than talking movies. Being immersed in the topic of reading as I was when watching the film, I could not help connecting this line to reading as I did with almost anything I saw or read or heard about. With so-called *talkies*, we did not only add spoken dialogue to film, we added foley sounds as well. Fake sounds that are a better representation of the sound than the actual sound itself. We make the story come more vividly to life by adding the sound of chopped cabbage when a head is chopped off or by clapping together two coconut shells for a horse galloping away. Even though the cabbage in itself has no relation to the storyline, this additional layer of sound enriches our viewing experience.

With regard to our reading experience, we're about to leave the stage of sentiment we are in now. A stage in which most of the commercial software and hardware still try to replicate the *real* reading experience by imitating a book and having us turn the page, make bookmarks, and read chronologically. No wonder that we are still comparing the two, as Norma did with silent movies and talkies. Imagine what she would have said about YouTube. A platform in which the metadata has taken over and completely changed our viewing experience, and yet we still go out to watch movies in the cinema.

Alessandro Ludovico states in his text: *Digital and print, while being two different worlds, are not mutually exclusive.* Both will remain in existence and evolve, but should

not be

compared

with each other, just as you shouldn't compare Cinema with YouTube either. Both chronological and non-linear reading is possible in digital and print. The argument that digital would make reading a more mobile activity is ridiculous; you can take your book anywhere and it will never shut down on you. Subdividing reading into digital and analogue seems a bit redundant, but is perhaps necessary to define two different starting-points from which we can proceed further.

Looking at the future of reading also means looking back to see what we want to take along for the ride. We will continue to read; we just add new layers to alter the reading experience for better or for worse. And in decades time perhaps we will be saying: *We didn't need an interface, we had print.* Or we have managed to find our cabbage and are able to redefine what reading can entail.

--

Minke Kampman is an editor, teacher, and new media researcher.

26

How Will We Read?
Lynn Kaplanian-Buller

487 words | 1:57 mins

As text appears everywhere –even beamed on the wall while we exercise or onto the ceiling as we lie in bed– we read faster and faster. In the fifties a technique for speed reading postulated that the brain can comprehend much faster than the eye can see. So training the eye to read a whole page rather than by word or sentence, hugely increases the speed of comprehensive reading. We will all soon speedread, our eyes teased ever-faster forward by texts paired with images.

But besides reading faster and faster, a clearer division between warm and cold reading will emerge. Cold reading is for gathering information involving head-thinking and fast eye movement. Gaming might even pump up the heart rate, but cold reading doesn't open the heart. For cold reading, hard cased electronic devices are fine delivery systems.

Warm reading happens when we open our hearts. As the author's words move us emotionally, we give off an emotional charge which gets absorbed into the paper page. It's a private kind of reading, often done in bed, and we seem to sense that organic materials like paper can absorb and keep the reading experience safe for another day.

Books can act as *transitional objects* –objects which are able to attract, hold, and release emotions that might otherwise overwhelm the person. Just as a teddy bear helps a child to survive the absence of its mother, we often treasure a book as a means to survive an otherwise hostile situation. One can *retreat* into a book and share with it our own feelings as we work them out, one step removed from real life.

We treasure leather-bound, vellum, and antique books because the materials seem to have absorbed the thoughts and emotions as well as the fingerprints of those who read that copy before us. Paper-bound books can do this as well: children's books saved for the next generation, journals written by hand. The authenticity of being able to run your hand over the page touched by the author or previous owner is a warm experience which we will increasingly crave as we are engulfed with cold texts.

The ability to print a personalized original manuscript or facsimile of an eclectic title will produce gifts overflowing with intention. *I know you like trains and that your family lives in Australia, so, for your birthday, I made a copy of Locomotives of Australia 1854-2007 on the Espresso Book Machine.* *Mom, I had

grandma's

poems and
diary made into a book for you. If you'd like to add your poems and diary, we can print new copies for all the family members.*

To receive such a gift feels very different from receiving a link to a *really good download*, doesn't it? Small printing devices will let us fabricate and personalize digital texts on organic paper, creating unlimited warm reading experiences for us and to share. A haven to hold.

--

Lynn Kaplanian Buller is the director of The American Book Center in Amsterdam.

27

Screening
Kevin Kelly

739 words | 2:58 mins

In the morning I begin my screening while still in bed. I check the screen near my pillow for the time, my wake-up alarm, and also to see what news scrolls by. I screen the tiny panel that shows messages from my friends. I wipe the messages away with my thumb. I walk to the bathroom. I screen my new art works on the wall –these are more cheerful and sunny than the ones yesterday. I get dressed and screen my outfit in the closet. It shows me that the red scarf would look better with my shirt. In the kitchen I screen the full news. I like the display horizontal in the table. I wave my arms to direct the stream of writing. I turn to the screens on my cabinets searching for my favourite cereal. A screen floating above the refrigerator indicates fresh milk inside. I reach inside and take out the milk. The screen on the side of the milk carton tries to get me to play a game, but I quiet it. I screen the bowl to be sure it is approved clean from the dishwasher. As I eat my cereal, I nod and the news stories advance. When I pay close attention, the news gets more detailed. As I

screen further and deeper, the text has more links, denser illustrations. I begin screening a very long investigative piece on the local mayor, but I need to take my son to school. I dash to the car. In the car, my story continues where I left off in the kitchen. My car screens the story for me, reading it aloud as I drive.
The buildings we pass along the highway are screens themselves. They usually show advertisements that are aimed only at me, since they recognize my car. I usually ignore them, except when they show an illustration or diagram from the story I am screening. I screen the traffic to see what route is least jammed this morning. Since the car learns from other drivers' routes, it mostly chooses the best route, but it is not foolproof yet, so I like to screen where the traffic flows.
At my son's school, I check the wall display in the hallway. I raise my palm and the screen recognizes me. It shows me my personal interface. I can screen my messages. I glance at the ones I want to screen in detail and it expands those. I wave some forward and others I swoosh to the archives. One is urgent. I pinch the air and I am screening a virtual conference. My partner in India is speaking to me. They are screening me in Bangalore. I finally make it to the office. When I touch my chair, my room knows me, and all the screens in the room and on the table are ready for me. The eyes of the screens watch me closely as I conduct my day. After 16 years of watching me work, they can anticipate a lot of what I do. The sequence of symbols on the screens makes no sense to anyone else, just as my colleague's sequence baffles me. When we are working together we screen an entirely different environment. We gaze and grab different tools as we hop and dance around the room. I am a bit old fashioned and still like to hold smaller screens in my hands. My favourite one is the same leather-cased screen I had in

college

(the screen
is new, just the case is old). It is the same screen I used to create the documentary I did about the migrants sleeping in the mall. My hands are used to it and it is used to my gestures. I can screen a realie in about an hour, speed screening the whole way. You should see the pads and streams go flying. When I get home, I try to slow down. I like to screen relaxing, affirming visions on the walls. Although my son likes to screen adventure games, we limit it to one hour before dinner. During dinner we screen mood colours to centre our meals. I will admit that we'll sometimes screen questions about school work, or food ingredients, or trivia, but we try to keep those screens small. After dinner I like nothing better than to lie in bed and screen my favourite story on the ceiling till I fall asleep.

--

Kevin Kelly is Senior Maverick for Wired Magazine.

28

I Don't Read on My Bike
Joost Kircz

216 words | 0:52 mins

I read the whole day long and tease my brain, a neurological fruit salad consisting of various pieces of tasting, touching, feeling, hearing, counting, naming, scaring, and translating. With the left half of my brain, I read a traffic sign and know that I may Not turn right. No text and yet understandable. I don't read text on the bike, but I do listen to music. This immediately suggests that reading is not listening and that electronic texts are completely different to music files. An image is a cultural recognition in context: the mouth of my beloved, the icon of a recycle bin on my screen, the fear that is generated on the screen by a film trailer. A text stands for naming, understanding, transferring, and reusing. Sometimes an image enhances a text, the image illustrates an intention; sometimes, the image is primary such as a wound. Here the text explains what we see. Text needs space, because reading depends on the textual image. Typography and layout are conditions for understanding. Text structure depends on the supporting material. Stone is beautiful, paper is superb. New materials will prove they can be carriers. Long reading and educational texts require attention and repose. Text is for knowledge; image is for preserving that knowledge. Reading is thinking, is work.

--

Joost Kircz is part-time programme manager electronic publishing at the HvA [Hogeschool van Amsterdam] and director of Kircz Research Amsterdam.

29

Reading As Event
Matthew Kirschenbaum

50 words | 0:16 mins

Reading is an event, not an act. Books are incidental (in the fullest meaning of the word). Texts are signals, transmissions. This is where I am now when I read, not a place but a mode, not a favourite chair but a state and frame. Think of it as resolution.

--

Matthew G. Kirschenbaum is Associate Professor of English (University of Maryland), Associate Director of the MITH, and Director of Digital Cultures and Creativity.

30

Reading the Network
Tanja Koning

314 words | 1:16 mins

As editor of an independent magazine, I am naturally crazy about paper; nothing is as fine

as the smell

of a new magazine. Yet when it came to writing this piece, I didn't think of that. What is fascinating me most about reading at the moment is the new carrier of information: the network. Networks hang over us like a thick mist; we cannot see them, and certainly cannot touch, leaf through, or smell them. And yet it is the carrier of much of our reading matter.

Are networks fine? Is there are difference between one network and another? And when making a network, can we talk about a craft comparable to binding a book or a medieval handwriting? In short: does a network have a face?

A number of artists and designers have recently unmasked the network by representing it as a phenomenon that is almost like a landscape.

A good example of this is the visualization Aron Koblin made of SMS messages on Queen's Day, the Netherlands. Thanks to data from KPN, he made a inventory of the quantity and place where messages were sent and compiled this information into a visualization that is most reminiscent of a skyline, floating like a layer over the floor plan of Amsterdam.

Or the project YOUrban by Einar Sneve Martinussen. Together with the Oslo School of Architecture and Design, he developed a way of visualizing WiFi in Oslo. He marched through the city with his research team, armed with a long stick with LEDs that can measure the signal strength of WiFi through radio waves. Thanks to photography using long shutter times, a screen of these signals became visible and thus showed, literally, *the networked city*. For a moment. And that's what we'll have to make do with for the moment. The face of the network is always different and only visible for a moment.

--

Tanja Koning is freelance programme maker and project leader of Discovery Festival and O.K. Periodicals.

31

Nearby and Global in Its Impact
Steffen Konrath

673 words | 2:41 mins

Many people have stopped reading newspapers on a daily base. Circulation figures are on the decline worldwide. Don't worry. It is a declining interest in a content presentation form not in reading. Demand for stories is still high. While on the move many already prefer access to stories worth reading at the time they like and wherever they are. But the stickiness to a specific story brand, a specific publisher, is also likely to lose its strength. Highly connected and globally aware, people are open for changes, new reading experiments, and experiences. We are already living in the era of News3.0.

A (near) future day –my smartphone is always on. Push services send me short little messages of breaking news to my little device making information available wherever I am and at any time of the day. The latest push notification tells me, without going into too much detail, that the dictator in the North African country has now been arrested. It is enough to catch my attention. My tablet in my pocket allows me to read the follow up on the news online while driving through a rural area in Southern Bavaria, Germany. So far it is only a ticker message without much more concrete information and more and more questions pop up. Who has confirmed the news? Are photos already available as visual evidence or video footage to support what I read before?

The story is *hot* enough for me to decide to open a Liquid Newsroom[1], a virtual on-demand environment for collaborative writing. I label the topic *Northern Africa* and set up the topical *room* for it on-demand and in real time. I quickly check my social network of

trusted

1 The Liquid Newsroom is an open innovation project. It is currently under development and updates will be published on Konrath's blog at www.nextlevelof-news.com.

news sources

–people in the area of interest, Northern Africa–to see whether anyone can be reached and can provide me with details or material. When the new topic working space on the Liquid Newsroom platform is opened, a new portal front-end comes into existence, where readers connected to the Internet via PC or mobile devices can easily check in to stay informed. The Liquid Newsroom is not run by a publisher, it is an on-demand network for publishing news as a team that can vary over time, only connected via the topic they like to address.

A first flow of information hits my virtual desktop in the *Northern Africa* newsroom. News sources have started to pick up the story. But now it is time to guide my readers through the growing stream of information and update it, analyzing the value added by each of the new stories coming in. I publish the information I have gathered almost immediately to the front-end to create a constant flow of what's new to readers who opt-in to the content stream e.g. subscribing to the feed via their smartphone devices. They do not stay in a passive mode. Some are concerned about what's happening and return questions via the integrated Q&A-button in their smartphone app. The questions from the readers connected to the topic stream provide a constant feedback in the editing and updating process. Together with real-time statistics (active views, reading, retweets, and the like) monitored on the screen as well, I decide which stories to follow up. In the meantime, friends working and living in the East and West Coast of the US have joined my *Northern Africa* liquid newsroom to work on the stories as well. I'm exhausted after hours of curating and am happy to pass the story lead on to these colleagues, knowing that they will pass it on in turn to Asian colleagues at the end of their day. In the virtual room we've already started to exchange thoughts via live chat, simultaneous editing of articles, and voice-over IP calls. Our discussion is interesting enough that we decide to make our editing process transparent on the corresponding website, so that readers can watch the process flow. It is time to relax and yes I know that after a few hours of sleep I will be back again.

--

Steffen Konrath is editor-in-chief of nextlevelofnews.com and blogs about the future of journalism.

32

The Interface of the Graphic Novel
Erin La Cour

476 words | 1:54 mins

I was first drawn into the world of graphic novels while working as an editorial assistant at a New York based publishing house where I was assigned to assess the potential sales benefits of acquiring graphic novels for my imprint. This was a daunting task on multiple levels, not least of which was my naive assumption that publishing companies are primarily interested in disseminating poignant new literature, not sales figures. The book my boss put on my desk was Marjane Satrapi's Persepolis, which at the time had sold over 500,000 copies, a huge feat in the publishing industry for any genre, and an even more impressive number for a memoir written by an unknown author. This fact led me to question what it was about the graphic novel that could generate such a large readership.

The growing interest in graphic novels in popular culture further confirmed that there has been a visible shift in the way in which we consume and process information, and a movement from textual to visual narratives. Indeed, today we consume information at a much faster

rate than ever before due in large part to our increased use of technology, where it has become the norm to process information in quicker clips using various modes of communication, often in combination with each other, such as text and graphic, or audio and visual. But while this readership could indicate a lack of attention span or a dumbing down of culture, and certainly comics have long been dismissed as lowly kitsch (Greenberg, Krauss), it was clear that Persepolis, like many other graphic novels, could not be categorized as unsubstantial either in content or form.

What the graphic novel highlights is that with the surge in multimodal dissemination of information, we are perhaps getting closer to a better means of comprehending information available to us that is less obtuse than language alone. By presenting information in multimodal means, which are based on the five senses rather than in just the codified system of language, we are more likely to understand what is presented to us as it is more closely linked to our nature as sensual humans.

Through the structure of its layout, including its *boxes of time* (Chute and DeKoven), frames, gutter space, images, and onomatopoeic words, alongside text that is often handwritten and therefore offers a *trace of the human* (Kittler), the graphic novel creates a new interface, so to speak, for what has long been considered a limited, static media. The graphic novel thus dismantles the idea of the obsolescence of the book in the age of new media, illustrating how the book can adapt to changes in readership, offer a challenge to its readers to learn to read differently, and perhaps more importantly, highlight that the book can be a platform encouraging a new means of interaction between media and user.

--

Erin La Cour is a PhD candidate at the Amsterdam School for Cultural Analysis (ASCA) where she researches graphic novels and cultural memory.

33

Minimal and Maximal Reading
Rudi Laermans

435 words | 1:44 mins

Nowadays, information is not scarce –there is far too much of it, or rather, far too many information possibilities, as I will explain. But why speak of a surplus; what is actually lacking? The scarcest good in an information society is our vastly time-bound individual perception. We live in an attention economy, distinguished by intense competition among innumerable producers and mediators of information. Using every rhetorical ploy, they want to capture and modulate our perception, then aggregate it, creating momentary attention communities or publics. Nevertheless, attention depends on the individual observer: information is in the eye of the attentive beholder. Why does this, and not that, image, title, shape catch a person's notice? It's always an enigma in the end: time and again, we realize that the deeper logics of perception are non-observable. They escape us, although they fundamentally determine what we find interesting, attractive, seductive –in a word: informative. This awareness that our perception in general and attention patterns in particular are ultimately opaque to our consciousness, marks us as decentred subjects, no French philosophy needed.

Whatever the underlying motive, the contemporary information user actively considers, selects, retains, and perhaps also reads, in the genuinely hermeneutic sense of interpreting or deciphering

the overall, or *deeper*, meaning of a series of words, images, or sounds. This level of reading differs from immediate sense making, or minimal reading, that simply recognizes what one already knows. On the other hand, the maximal reading that most reception theories suppose involves a short interruption, a moment concerned with the difference between something's directly understood meaning ('I'm looking at a picture of a man') and one or more other possible meanings, or even absence of meaning ('why does the man wear these clothes?'). The search for an *exact* meaning is commonly coupled with deciphering the intention of the information producer. Whereas minimal reading is user-oriented, maximal reading is author-centred.

In an environment saturated with information possibilities, we read both more and less. As the minimal mode of reading increases, its maximal counterpart becomes rather exceptional (and thus also more *elitist*, even among those holding a university degree). Many commentators decry this growing superficiality. Yet we also process more information in greater variety. It's therefore wiser to say that we're moving beyond *the Age of Hermeneutics*: deep interpretation of some texts is gradually superseded by flat comparison of more information. Readers turn into comparers, with resulting gains and losses. While we have more points of reference, we are less adept at savouring the richness of a singular bit of information. In an information-rich society, authentic astonishment also becomes a scarce good.

--

Rudi Laermans is professor of theoretical sociology at the Faculty of Social Sciences of the Catholic University of Leuven.

34

Reading Apart Together

Warren Lee

361 words | 1:26 mins

Books have in **many ways become** an **integral part** of my **life;** I have been in the **book business now** for **forty years.** I have **done just** about **everything** in the **trade except operate** a **printing press** and I have **learned** that **books** have **souls;** I know this because I know how **difficult** it is to throw one away, if it has reached that **point** of no return at the end of the value scale. There is a voice which keeps saying: ***Find** a way to let me **live** on*.

I **read** for **pleasure** and I would **rather read** a **hardbound book** than a **paperback**, and, I **love well designed books; books** which become **something** more than just a **receptacle** for **words** and **pictures. Books** which **become objects** of **desire**, for which **collectors will** do **almost anything** to own. A weakness that is **well known** to **bookdealers** and **often used** to **profitable results.**

It is the **tactility** of **books** which I **feel will** be their **salvation** in the onslaught of electronic **paper, eBooks**, and **still unheard** of new inventions. I was reminded of this only recently while sitting in the Eurostar coming from **London.** I had **settled** into my **seat** and **taken** out the **book** I was **reading** at that time; an **English gentleman sat** down **next** to me, **opened** his **briefcase** and **took** out his Kindle and **also started reading.** We were both **seriously** into our **reading** for some time but I found myself **reflecting** on our **parallel situation.** There **came** a **point** when I **interrupted** him **to ask** how he found the **experience** of **reading electronically** as **compared** to a **printed book.** He **laughed** and **said:** *But I love **books** and I have a **house full** of them at **home.** I **read** and I **travel** a **lot therefore** I **just** cannot **carry around** the **extra weight** of **real books**,

and

my Kindle
offers me a wide selection to choose from.*

We talked shortly about the pros and cons and then both retired again into our reading. I was happily reassured that the book will not be replaced, but will find its place in the onslaught of the electronic era.

--

Warren Lee is the owner and co-founder of the internationally renowned bookstore Nijhof & Lee in Amsterdam.

35

Unexpected Ways
Jannah Loontjens

345 words | 1:23 mins

How and where we encounter literature determines how we approach the text. Not only do our physical surroundings influence our reading experience, but also the framework in which a text is presented or discussed. If a novel is discussed by Oprah Winfrey, it is easily associated with therapeutic literature and a women's audience; if the same novel is reviewed in The New Yorker it is taken to be more serious. Exposés of the author's life are often associated with lowbrow forms, whereas highbrow outlets are assumed to focus on the work itself. This prejudice no longer reflects reality. Highbrow media also increasingly write about authors' lives. Yet as long as such exposés are printed in, say, The New Yorker, they are not considered a disreputable way of approaching literature. In fact, all media increasingly scrutinize the lives of authors to the same extent as they scrutinize the lives of ordinary people in reality soaps and talk shows.

People seem curious to read about private lives in order to reflect upon their own lives; it seems that readers do not want to know this information about the author in order to understand his work better, but rather to understand themselves better. While the increasing attention for the author scares critics, who believe that the approach of the *autonomous work* is the only possible way to value literature on its own merits, I am convinced that literature does not need to be protected from bad influences. In fact, literature that seemed almost forgotten, or studied only by academics, is finding a new readership through new media. Tolstoy and Faulkner, for example, were suddenly popular, because their novels were selected for Oprah's Book Club, which took care to portray the background of the authors on its website. Virginia Woolf's novel Mrs Dalloway (1925) also recently gained an unexpected new readership, because of the release of the film The Hours (Stephen Daldry, 2002), which is partly about Woolf's life. This is the way literature survives through, in, and via new media, and finds new readers in truly unexpected ways.

--

Jannah Loontjens is a writer and poet.

36

Consume Without a Screen
Alessandro Ludovico

389 words | 1:34 mins

Since the arrival of electronic media, visionaries have speculated on ways to expand our physiological reading limits beyond the constraints of print, in order to absorb, through a sort of cultural osmosis, huge quantities of information in a fraction of time. They foresaw what we now call digital technology, though originally imagined as much more powerful than today's fare and often involving the body as primary interface. In line with their predictions, since the early 1990s we've expanded reading space almost

ad infinitum

through

global networks of hypertexts. Now we're back again, considering the book the perfectly sized medium with a universal *interface*. In fact, after twenty years of re-inventing the wheel, through multiple and unnatural combinations of icons, graphic and animations, contemporary e-reading interfaces resemble the most effective one yet: print.

Our desire for rich digital content on the go has yielded varieties of fast, precise tools that digitize print at will. We have more software options to make online text (often lost in graphical enhancements and ads) that look and feel like paper. Attempts to incorporate *digital* elements in print have also generated various hybrids, such as POD (print-on-demand) files that can be updated every second. Digital and print, while two different worlds, are in no way mutually exclusive; they attract, repulse, and sometimes complement each other. Nevertheless our senses are still not trained for hypertexts and hybrids. Lost in too much information, we are distracted by the ability to search ad infinitum, floating in a limbo of minimal concentration. The finite space of a book becomes reassuring with its limits, its focus on un-linkable topics.

If the digital expands our possibilities and access to content, print is still the preferred medium for preservation. The *convergence* of different media into a paradise ruled by some omnipotent digital god resounds once more like empty propaganda. The ruling classic interfaces operate alongside digitally specific platforms in a desperate attempt to establish a digital standard for print, as was accomplished for music and video. Once established, this standard will likely escalate our taste for and consumption of editorial products, with unpredictable social consequences. But print will not disappear. On the contrary, whether cheap last-minute up-to-date printouts or more expensive, limited editions, the printed medium is simply mutating as a physically enjoyable form and a future luxury: consume without a screen.

--

Alessandro Ludovico is a media critic, editor-in-chief of Neural magazine, and founder of Mag.net (Electronic Cultural Publishers organization).

37

The Networked Culture Machine
Peter Lunenfeld

209 words | 0:51 mins

The growth of blogs, Twitter, and Facebook considered in tandem with Tumblr and other social softwares that enable posting and tagging accounts, creates an environment of *continuous partial production*. As ninety-nine percent of everything ever made is either purely for personal consumption, largely forgettable, or just plain junk, continuous partial production is not a huge problem. What does become problematic is when the new affordances make the old content untenable in the emerging environments.

Acknowledging that there are losses that follow every gain in technological capacity is not the same as blindly following the reporting cycle. The key issue is that our twenty-first-century cultural machines lead to a previously unimaginable level of object differentiation and information richness. The networked culture machine's combination of embedded technology and just-in-time production make possible a novel hybrid intellectuality. Text can be linked to graphics, photos, and moving images in fluid ways impossible a generation ago. The combinatory possibilities of alphanumeric texts, still and moving images, aural components from

music

to spoken word, and even contextual environmental embedding, all of these simulations of other media offer a huge set of affordances for both the creation and reception of meaning. The sheer density of information and materiality of the contemporary moment is unrivaled in history.

--

Peter Lunenfeld, Professor in the Design Media Arts Department at UCLA. He is the creator and editorial director of the MIT Press Mediawork project.

This text is adapted from The Secret War Between Downloading and Uploading: Tales of the Computer as Culture Machine, MIT Press, 2011.

38

From Noun to Verb
Ellen Lupton

423 words | 1:41 mins

Over forty years ago, the author was brutally slain in the streets of Paris. It was 1968. The times were dark; the turtlenecks were darker. Young people stormed the gates of the academy and upended the author's role as originator and legislator of meaning. Roland Barthes, Michel Foucault, and Jacques Derrida pissed proudly into burning heaps of doctoral dissertations that had once claimed to ground the true meaning of written texts in the inner lives of writers. The author was dead; the reader was born. The new generation exposed the text as an open web of connections whose meaning lay at the mercy of history and context, reception, and appropriation.

What status does *the author* and *the reader* hold today? The vocabulary of SMS has upgraded *text* from noun (inert object) to verb (electrified action). The telephone, invented to deliver the living human voice, is now used for writing more than talking. Along the way, text lapsed into the informality of speech, entering an age of stunning laxity.

Algorithms have become authors, too.

Welcome to the world of *black hat* search engine optimization, which uses automatically generated content to trick Google into sending extra clicks to dubious websites. Phrases like *cloaking*, *auto blogging*, and *content farming* are part of a new wild west of un-authored content. One piece of software translates texts from English into German and then back into English, scrambling the vocabulary and grammar of the input to ensure a seemingly original output, immune to accusations of plagiarism. Behold the rebirth of the author.

And what has become of *the reader*? Digital display technologies have transformed readers into hardware/software constructs designed to display, filter, push, feed, and aggregate content. Screen readers turn text into speech. Tablet devices host apps and files hewn from an astonishing array of file formats, competing for survival in a jungle teeming with combative standards.

Today's *author* and *reader* encompass countless digital products and interfaces as well as human producers and consumers of the word. Designers are grasping the opportunity to aggregate content in critical and creative ways or to offer people better ways to navigate, annotate, and filter the digital word. New tools for writers help people compose text in more focused environments or to arrange ideas with both freedom and oversight. Web templates and print-on-demand services have broadened access to the tools of design and publishing. The author may have died, but his ashes were strewn upon the oceans of digital connectivity, equipping vast populations to broadcast ideas through the indelible scrim of the alphabet.

--

Ellen Lupton is curator at Cooper-Hewitt, National Design Museum in NYC and director of the Graphic Design MFA at MICA, Baltimore.

39

The Role of the Hardware
Anne Mangen

209 words | 0:50 mins

These are challenging times for reading research. For a long time, we have felt comfortable with developing theories of reading and models of reading comprehension mainly based on the verbal, linear, printed text. With digital technologies, however, reading has diffused to a virtually limitless variety of processes and practices with an equally endless variety of texts. How and to what extent are existing theories and models of reading able to explain what's going on when we read the kinds of dynamic, interactive, ephemeral texts that appear and disappear in an instant, as in instant messaging and Twitter? The simple answer is that they cannot, at least not without a considerable amount of modification and limitation. Another challenge, hitherto unforeseen and hence largely neglected, is the role of the reading device itself –e.g. the bound book, the computer screen, or the reading tablet. We handle and manipulate the devices differently, for instance in navigating through a document. Hence, in order to accommodate adequately contemporary and future reading practices, reading should perhaps be reconceptualized as a multisensory engagement with a display of static and dynamic configurations, implemented in a device with particular sensorimotor, ergonomic, affordances which in different ways interact with perceptual and cognitive processes at play. As simple as that.

--

Anne Mangen is a reading specialist at the National Centre for Reading Research and Education at Stavanger University in Norway.

40

From Reading to Pattern Recognition
Lev Manovich

577 words | 2:19 mins

The emergence of social media creates a radically new opportunity to study cultural processes and dynamics. For the first time, we can follow the imagination of hundreds of millions of people –the images and videos they create and comment on, the conversations they are engaged in, the opinions, ideas, and feelings they express.

Until now, the study of the social and the cultural (individual beings, individual artefacts, and larger groups of people/artefacts) relied on two types of data: *shallow data* about many (statistics, sociology) and *deep data* about a few (psychology, psychoanalysis, anthropology, art history; methods such as *thick description* and *close reading*). However, the rise of social media along with the computational tools that can process massive amounts of data makes a fundamentally new approach for the study of human beings and society possible. We no longer have to choose between data size and data depth. Rather than having to generalize from small samples or rely on our intuition, we can study exact cultural patterns formed by millions of cultural texts. In other words, the detailed knowledge and insights, which before could only be reached about a few texts, can now be obtained about massive collections of these texts.

In 2007, Bruno Latour summarized these developments as follows: *The precise forces that mould our subjectivities and the precise characters that furnish our imaginations are all open to inquiries by the social sciences. It is as if the inner workings of private worlds have been pried open because their inputs and outputs have become thoroughly traceable.*[1]

1 Bruno Latour, *Beware, your imagination leaves digital traces*, Times Higher Education Supplement, April 6, 2007.

But how do you *read* through billions of Twitter posts, blogs, Flickr photos, or YouTube videos in practice? That is, how do you read for patterns?

Today people use a variety of software tools to select the content of interest to them from this massive and constantly expanding universe of cultural texts and conversations. These tools include search engines, RSS feeds, and recommendation systems. But while these tools can help you to find what to read, they do not show the larger patterns across this universe.

Computer scientists and media companies use a different set of tools and techniques that allow for the detailed study of such patterns. They employ statistical data analysis, data mining, information visualization, and visual analytics. They also have access to substantial computational resources needed to analyse massive data sets. For example, many companies use *sentiment analysis* to study the feelings which people express about their products in blog posts. Recent publications in computer science investigated how information spreads on Twitter (data: 100 million tweets), what qualities are shared by most favoured photos on Flickr (data: 2.2 million photos), and what geotagged Flickr photos tell us about people's attention (data: 35 million photos).

What if everybody had access to such techniques? At present, this requires knowledge of advanced topics in computer science and statistics. However, with the right tools, anybody should be able to at least explore large image collections and notice interesting patterns. At Software Studies Initiative (softwarestudies.com), we have been developing such software tools, and testing them on sets of different types of cultural images ranging from all 4535 covers of Time magazine (1923-2009) to one million manga pages. Currently we are using these tools to study video remixes on YouTube, images from deviantart.com, and spatial patterns in Second Life. We plan to release all tools as open source shortly.

--

Lev Manovich is an author of new media books and director of the Software Studies Initiative at CALIT2.

41

Reading *For the Sake of It*
Luna Maurer

467 words | 1:52 mins

The longer I think about what reading actually means to me, the more insoluble situations I encounter. Everything I do daily –communicating via email, research, or production for work– means that I absorb a lot of text and information, but I do not connect that to the concept of *reading*. And so I read a lot during the day, just like everybody else, everything that arrives via our countless digital networks: browsing, scanning, searches on Google or Wikipedia. These are pieces of information, texts, or images that are consumed. Not only in the digital field, but also on the city roads. I consider all this as *knowledge gathering* or *absorbing information* –and it doesn't really matter whether it is text or image.

The concept of reading *for the sake of it* is different. It's about surrendering yourself in the world of words. That means that language becomes very important. Part of the story is already contained in the way in which something is formulated. Formulating is designing with words. And just as we wish to evoke a message with a visual design, a writer can create an extra dimension with language. Designing with words contains

a character,

ambiance,

or touch of magic that is lost in the *fast* streams of information. If you surrender yourself to reading, you find peace inside, time is absent, a new world is created.

To explain yourself in words and sentences costs time. It is without aim and seems more like a journey. It's not about absorbing information as quickly as possible, but about expanding your mind with thoughts and words. This form of reading is also an emotional enrichment. Peter Bieri, the language philosopher, writes: *An educated person knows how to read books in such a way that they change him... that after reading, he is different than he was before.*[1]

It is easier to read if you shut yourself away. That is why, for me, a traditional book has always been until now the only way to read *for the sake of it*. Then there are no options for switching –to other textual sources or additional contextual information. A sentence must carry enough in itself.

The seclusion inherent in a book (although thought of as a limitation) is crucial for reading. The challenge is in creating space in a *connected* world where you are completely limited and can experience an enrichment by language instead of the absorption of information. How you can work with text and typography in the digital domain is still an underexposed area; a way which does not present reading for consumption or for information, but where words and their meaning are placed in a timeless area of tension, so that it becomes a new way of reading *for the sake of it*.

--

Luna Maurer is a designer under the name Poly-Luna and she is part of the Conditonal Design Collective.

1 'Wie wäre es, gebildet zu sein?', Festrede by Prof. Dr. Peter Bieri, 2005.

42

The Matrix: Three Subjective and Intuitively Selected Pointers for Building Blocks for The Script in Which We Live
Geert Mul

715 words | 2:59 mins

The experience of reality is mediated by a script. This script is the grammatical equivalent of a placebo: a form that channels the content/meaning/energy, but alone is nothing more than a formal structure. In the daily experience, the form (the script) can be exchanged for what it represents, that is its strength. Each culture has its own script. Culture is creating a script. A script is always dynamic and subject to change. Reflections on older versions are interesting for obtaining insight into the entity of the medium *script*, but political suggestions to reintroduce and reuse older versions of the script or to freeze the current version are, I think, rather stupid.

Pointer 1: Aristotle's Poetics, 335 BC

Before the Christian God there was, remarkably enough, Aristotle (335 BC). The script that Aristotle created can hardly be overestimated. We (the western culture) have, in the subsequent 2000 years, rarely succeeded in reading or seeing outside this script. Furthermore, all possible media in this script (text, image, and music) are subject to one coordinated structure. The western history of art (of literature, theatre, film, to generative/interactive art) can do nothing other than work according to the principles of Aristotle's Poetics or deviate from them, but as reference, the Poetics are never absent. All Hollywood films still closely follow the Aristotle script.

About Aristotle's Poetics: *The claim that tragedy makes on universality should (...) be seen as the necessity of a logical construction, without the plot becoming predictable. The

real

tragedy writer

must construct the plot in such a way that the dénouement, the discharge of the accumulated energy, is completely unexpected. The structure of this plot should satisfy strict rules since only then can the aspired tension be brought to a high point in order, in a completely perfect tragedy, to be closed in a moment of catharsis. This catharsis must be seen as a release of the accumulated emotions.*[1]

Pointer 2: John's *In the beginning*, c. 100 AD

In the Christian culture, The Word is elevated to the medium in which the complete world and non-world must be scripted. Writers often have the inclination to overvalue The Word, and since the Bible is a written notation of a culture that, until then, had been communicated orally, it is not remarkable that The Word is made divine. The Image has been condemned in part of the Christian culture to the area of idolatry, as an impure representation of *the truth*, a Platonic view of imagination. But if you read the following passage from John from the context of The Script, then the text seems to confirm that no reality and no world can exist without script (The Word). The script is everything: the script is God.

> In the beginning was the Word and the Word was with God and the Word was God. The same was in the beginning with God. All things were made by him; and without him was not any thing made that was made. (John 1, 1–3)

Pointer 3: Jorge Luis Borges' *The Library of Babel*, 1946

In 1946 the poet and author Jorge Louis Borges wrote a short story: *The Library of Babel*. The story is about an infinite library in which an infinite number of bookcases are filled with an infinite number of books

1 Stofvorm (philosophical online magazine) Ferrari, G. R. F., *Aristotle's Literary Aesthetics* in: Phronesis XLIV/3, 1999, pp. 181-198.

that are made up of all possible combinations of the letters of the alphabet, the full stop, comma, and space. The consequence of this is that all the books that have ever been written and all the books that shall ever be written can be found in this library. This story forms a wonderful synthesis of text, image, and informatics and is almost a prophetic announcement of the digital information culture that, 47 years later, would grow exponentially with the arrival of the first graphic Internet browser (Mosaic 1993). Borges sketches a world in which acquiring knowledge is no longer the problem of gaining access to information (that is available freely everywhere in the infinite library and on the Internet), acquiring knowledge is mainly a problem of recombining in the right way and filtering out the excessive supply of information.

The world is a script and if you want to change the world, you must change the script. And that is why all great art is political.

--

Geert Mul is a media artist and VJ pioneer.

43

Horses Are Fine So Are Books[1]

Arjen Mulder

535 words | 2:08 mins

In the thirties, Marshall McLuhan read all the writings of the Church Fathers in Latin and all the great books of the Western world in their original language before he thought it proper to declare in a number of blunt slogans that the era of the book was over and the electronic era would definitely come into being. In the new media, people would no longer read linearly –from front to back– but a whole culture would be simultaneously conjured up and gone through, something of which James

Joyce's

1 Marshall McLuhan, Counterblast, Rapp & Whiting Limited, Londen 1970.

Finnigans Wake (1939) was the precursor. Yet the book still exists and will continue to exist for a long time to come, and not only as content for the new medium e-reader or other apps. Even McLuhan is only read because his texts are published as books. As a closed medium, the book offers several advantages that the open, electronically-based and digitally encoded text does not have. Certainly, the space in which the reader can enter comments is limited to the margins and the end paper. Certainly, the font and size are given, although these can be manipulated with reading spectacles and magnifying glasses. Certainly, the index is not a fast search engine. And indeed, a sequence is offered, although nobody is obliged to follow it. McLuhan always first read page 69 of a new book, to decide whether he would go through the rest (he could read very quickly). But what makes a book a unique carrier for knowledge and experience is that the form of prescribed beginning, middle, and end forces that which is offered into a structure that expresses more than separate sentences, paragraphs, and chapters could articulate. Such a structure does not so much keep the text together, but rather gives the reader the space to develop, fantasize, or extrapolate a unique world of experience between the sentences, which comes to life in the reader's activated power of imagination and therefore is also stored in his living memory. Through that structure, we can remember what was in a book we read ten years ago, but not what was in the newspapers or circulating on the Internet at the time. The structure creates the continuity that enable the reader to set aside the book and to pick it up again a few days later and to continue reading without first having to have the whole story or the whole line of reasoning explained again. And because of this, the structure of one book can be part of much larger structures, running from your life as a development and travel adventure demarcated by books to the world literature as a whole or the realization of being part of a human history that, with all respect, is very short compared with the greater history and that greater process in which we are but a link. Thanks to its linearity, a book contains time; that is why people keep books in a special designed cupboard: time past (read books) and time that still awaits, as a promise (a book that has still to be read). A book doesn't swallow time, as practically all electronic media do; it makes time, it is a time machine.

--

Arjen Mulder is a media theorist, writer, and editor for V2_Publishing and of De Gids.

44

Shapes

Caroline Nevejan

560 words | 2:14 mins

Clutter

In the summer of my 26th year I completely lost the capacity to read. I had hit my head badly and a severe concussion made me instantly illiterate. As I slowly walked the streets through the heart of Amsterdam in a large hat, I was surprised at how streets appeared to be full of text; I had never realized this before. They were full of cluttered signs randomly organized and blocking the buildings from view. Why do people need so much text? Why do we put it everywhere, as if nothing can be left without a mark?

Blur

After a few days the illiteracy did not disappear and I realized I would have to learn how to read again. But I could not see the shape of signs, I did not recognize any letter. So I started to do Tangram, the game in which

you make

different

shapes with the same 7 pieces. On and off I would try to make shapes and make the same shape again. Slowly I improved. After about a week I opened a Donald Duck magazine. First the exclamations opened up and bit by bit more letters and even words. It was a strange experience that after another week I could read Donald Duck, but at the same time the newspaper still remained a blur. I remembered this experience from when I was a child: learning to read, but not being able to read *grown up* things. Apparently when you cannot handle a more complex level of the same thing, it goes back to the state of blur.

Looking through

So after Donald Duck I went into the women's magazines and by the time I could read those (advertising especially was fun in the beginning) slowly the newspaper opened up. By now I was training several hours a day and I could read faster and faster. I was immersed in trying to make sense of more blur and more blur, puzzled by how my brain was adapting in this exponential manner. After 4 weeks I even read complex French and German texts that I could hardly read before. My focus and training on *looking through shapes* had a deep impact on my understanding.

Opening up

The experience of letters *opening up* is strange. One has to be able to recognize the shape to be able to read the words. But once reading, you don't see the shape anymore, only words and meaning surface. Learning to read seemed to be learning to look through shapes and not at shapes. Peripheral attention registers the shapes, but words, sounds, and meaning emerge from behind and through the shapes. Letters are like the mise-en-scène of language, setting the stage for the theatre of mediated communication. Only when you grab the mise-en-scène do words acquire meaning and communication flows.

Centre Stage

Letters opening up requires me to move my attention into the place where letters are located. On the many devices connecting to the Internet, however, letters pass by in instantaneous configurations of a never ending mise-en-scène. I am put centre stage, where mobile letter carriers embrace my body with their bliebs and sounds and colour my personal environment. No looking through is required here; opening up one's self is the only way in or out. All is here. What is it that we do not look at now?

--

Caroline Nevejan is a researcher and designer focusing on the implications of technology on society.

45

Achievement Unlocked!

David B. Nieborg

371 words | 1:29 mins

It is a question that keeps recurring among game critics. What if games had the same social status as literature? A gamer can search through the supplements of the Dutch quality newspapers and although there is well-wrought literary criticism, there is remarkably little intellectual reflection about games. And that is a pity for fervent readers and hardcore gamers have a lot to tell each other.

There is a world to be gained in the way in which stories are told in the average blockbuster game, such as the popular first-person shooter games Call of Duty, Medal of Honor, or Halo. The stories in these games can be summarized in one sentence and act as an excuse to paste a series of explosions and game locations one after another. There is seldom any narrative depth. Yet these games are played a lot. In fact, it is probable that many young gamers gain greater insight into modern warfare through digital games, than through books about the war in Fallujah, Baghdad, or the Korengal Valley.

The how (they fight) question is answered rather precisely by game designers. The why question is seldom addressed. Even though the interactive character of games can present the player with moral dilemmas in a different and more direct way than in books. In a war game, the question *What would you have done?* is translated into *What do you do?* Actually, authors in particular can help create believable characters, ambiguous choices, and applying many shades of grey.

Conversely, game makers can help tempt gamers to dive into war books. For games are not played for no reason. Before, during, and after the game, you constantly receive feedback from the game about how good you have been. Achievement unlocked then appears in the television picture. Such virtual medals can then be seen by all gaming friends.

Structurally speaking, there is nothing to prevent publishers and writers of books from adding such game elements to the book. Perhaps not in its paper form, but the average e-reader, tablet, or digital bookshelf is powerful and networked enough to add so-called *paratextual* elements to the book. What if you could become better in reading books and could share that with the whole world?

--

David B. Nieborg is researcher and teacher at the University of Amsterdam and Utrecht with a focus on online participation and gaming culture.

46

U-turn
Kali Nikitas

117 words | 0:28 mins

Alternative paths towards reading to achieve maximum knowledge, in the shortest period of time, with approval from peers on content consumed and delivery method, tackling any insecurity about missed information or simply not being smart enough, not knowing how to manage time, racing to consume material that will make you more civic, a better conversationalist, a humanitarian, a braggart, fighting the fear of memory loss, and sneaking away into the corners of texts on Lady Gaga, fashion updates when the nagging continues pulling you back to world news even though you can't stand the misfortunes of others and your only concern is *do I really* or rather *can I really take the time to enjoy the comics?*

--

Kali Nikitas is the Chair of MFA Graphic Design + Communication Arts of the Otis College of Art and Design in Los Angeles.

47

The Epitaph or Writing Beyond the Grave
Henk Oosterling

549 words | 2:12 mins

We browse a lot. What used to be written in thick books hidden away in shadowy libraries and which could only be consulted after negotiating a lot of red tape is now available virtually, fully illuminated, for everybody, at any moment. With a single click of the mouse or a gentle stroke of the touch screen, thousands of hits are compiled in a fraction of a second. At the end of the twentieth century, reading was given back, unnoticed and unintentionally, its original significance: collecting

by hand.

This urge
for collecting still echoes in the old Dutch expression *aren lezen* –reading the are. After harvesting, the farmers allowed the crowd of poor creatures who were looking on in hunger to collect the broken, discarded corn stalks.

We are collectors when we read. Not collectors of ideas, but of material symbols. The blind are the most sensitive readers. More even than the are readers, they read with the tips of their fingers. From within their dark universe, they inspect dexterously every pleat, groove, dent, or bump in the material. They stroke graphemes: symbols that are engraved in the world, such as the spoils on the hunter's stake, to reverse the volatility of transitory existence. The grapheme offers resistance to oblivion. That is why the world's graphic design is, in a literal sense, the material basis for a script culture. The grapheme is a grave in which the past is buried. But paradoxically, this epitaph gives eternal life to all that is past.

The reader is a laser. The seer touches the material with his eyes. First his eye flash back and forth across the medium on which the symbols string together meaninglessly. But unlike the illiterate person who, searching in panic for meaning like a Dutch tourist lost in China or Libya, only gathers senseless symbols, the reader sees meaning at the same time that he scans. The reader reads the world. Collecting is one of the meanings of the Ancient Greek legein that also means *reading*. Logos is derived from this. In logic, collecting becomes calculating. In science, calculating becomes, via registering, chronicling. Counting becomes recounting. Sciences arise from the urge to manage in rulers thirsting for power, the coquetry of megalomaniac priests, and the urge to collect of inquisitive world travellers. Through this combination, every form of systematic collecting eventually changes into an authoritarian -logy: astrology, archaeology, psychology, neurology. Knowledge is power. World is truth.

With the World Wide Web, we are back to the beginning and yet far past it. The circle closes. Data is meaningless and information contains no truth. Information is friction-less. WWW is like a sixteenth-century collection of knick-knacks. But through cunning communication technology, an ICTheological message is given: somewhere there is a resistance-less, eternal world. A world in which each fact is itself in a virtual current event where everything is possible. The world of pure potentiality is not made up of atoms packed together into matter. They punctually unite in a brightly lit, shimmering 1-dimensionality that is created by double passes between infotomes. We are beyond the depth and with it the epitaph. On the touch screen we stroke, without meeting resistance, as if reaching for Michelangelo's The Creation on the ceiling of the Sistine Chapel, the foundation of our existence.

--

Henk Oosterling is a philosopher, and associate professor at Erasmus University Rotterdam.

48

Jumping Frames
David Ottina

533 words | 2:08 mins

My experience of reading is dominated by the experience of browsing the web. I meander, dipping into conversations then jumping out to essays, sometimes settling into books. Yet ultimately it is a linear way of reading and although it may branch, the path I follow is only visible to me from ground level. I think this is changing though.

Every word that travels through the Internet is parsed and stored. Every touch sensed and recorded. Every connection routed and logged. We are identified and located. Our meanings and moods are derived and noted. Profiles are built. Our relationships are graphed and analyzed. Histories are compiled. As we read, so we are read.

The question is what sorts of texts are being written with these traces? Who are their authors? Who are their readers? And how are they being read?

We can think of the authors of these computed texts as the people who write the algorithms that set the conditions of narrative possibility. Rather than writing the stories themselves, they simply create the frames in which stories can occur. The readers are the ones who extract the narratives from this multidimensional space to create a coherent story. The creative role of the reader has of course been theorized, but for these sorts of texts, it's an imperative. The reader comes to the foreground while authorship recedes into the shadows, a purely technical function.

These texts are read in the hopes of monetizing our every communication, of securing a perpetual rent on culture. As long as the texts are created for exploitation and control, it seems unlikely they will lead to new understandings of ourselves. In this context, the social can only be cast in the image of the individual, like the aggregate figure in the frontispiece of Leviathan.

However, algorithmic authorship and creative readership can be put to other uses. What interests me is the potential of multidimensional texts. The ability to read/see a text through multiple contexts at once. The chance to try out different frames. The opportunity to see discourses from a perspective other than ground level. Such a thing is difficult to envision, but it can be analogized to the current media implosion/genre explosion.

Digitization undoes the materiality separating media, collapsing them into one, multifaceted medium. This, in turn, erodes the barriers under which genres have developed. All of a sudden we are free to mix genres, causing an explosion of possibilities.

Through the same kind of move, barriers between texts/readers can also be eroded. Of course we can and do mix contexts and jump frames with texts already, but the process is laborious and difficult. This is compounded by the fact that our discursive traditions make transcending disciplines near impossible. Computational media have the potential to make such frame jumping easier, to become a normal part of reading.

What would such networked texts look like if not framed by the conditions of capital, but by free and open cultural production? One certain outcome would be the massive proliferation of frames that flow from the diversity that openness invites. Might we see another image of ourselves in this process, not as an aggregation of individuals but as a social entity?

--

David Ottina is an interaction designer, free culture advocate, and a co-founder of Open Humanities Press.

49

Pictures and Words
Peter Pontiac

352 words | 1:25 mins

Asked to share his or her views on reading, no serious comic strip artist can ignore the bad reputation comic art (or *sequential art* as Will *The Spirit* Eisner preferred to call it) appeared to have and still does:

it spoils

young

readers and makes them unqualified for reading true literature.

In the fifties Dr. Fredric Wertham proposed a total ban on comics in his book Seduction of the innocent. A Dr. Schückler claimed that comics were *the Esperanto of the illiterate*. And to this day the comic book is generally deemed the defective cousin of the pictureless novel. Pictures, however successful in telling a story, are simply considered inferior to words.

Neither the *Classics Illustrated* comic series that started in 1957 with its boasting motto *Lees feestelijk, groei geestelijk* (*When reading pleases, knowledge increases*), featuring stories by Shakespeare, Verne, Homer, et al (not always drawn by the most inspired artist, I'm afraid), nor the fashionable new label *graphic novel* (also coined by Eisner) have yet changed this arrogant view.

Presumably *word art* is seen as superior to *picture art* because a writer, simply by using well-put phrases, provokes the reader's imagination to breathe life into a story and its characters, whereas the drawing storyteller shortchanges the reader, leaving less elements to the imagination. According to this way of thinking, film should have even less value than comic art, as film is one of many art forms that use more than just words to touch the beholder –art's core business after all.

(By the way, the fact can't be denied that those who cherish the Word and disdain the Picture find themselves in the company of bad-ass bearded bigots...)

But as long as the reader is moved, how this is achieved shouldn't be of consequence. Pictures and words are simply equal in their storytelling skills. A picture paints a thousand words, so they say, but –frankly– one word might just as well paint a thousand pictures.

One thing though is certain: only a pitiful blind man wouldn't agree with the conclusion that a novel is a comic without pictures!

--

Peter Pontiac is a comic strip artist.

50

The Grammar of Images

Ine Poppe

518 words | 2:04 mins

When I was asked to write something about *the future of reading*, I googled to see what has already been published about this subject and what claims have been made. You could think up most of what I found in an afternoon.

A number of articles claimed that we were rushing headlong into an image culture and that the reading culture was disappearing or at least subject to intense change. The latter is certainly true. But language is still the spindle of our thinking. Our image culture is based on language, but now that language directs ones and zeros (just look at the code, commands, and software that serve as the basis of the web).

But image is also a culture-linked language that you have to master, and this is shown by Werner Herzog in his 1969 documentary about the Flying Doctors. The doctors who Herzog follows in East Africa use pictures to teach the isolated population about vaccination and malaria. Large boards show a greatly magnified mosquito, and also a man, a woman, and a child. Herzog hangs up a number of these prints, and he hangs up one of them upside down. Next, Herzog asks the Africans one by one which print is upside down. Nobody is able to point out the correct print: nobody is capable, in fact, of *reading* the picture. When Herzog asks them to point out a picture

of a man, they do not understand that the black line on the paper is a representation (and a condensed one at that) of a human. After all, a human is much taller than on the picture and doesn't fit on a board that's just a couple of feet high, and we aren't made up of a line. The same applies to the magnified mosquito. Is that a small creature? In villages with some schooling, things are better; people there have learned to interpret pictures.

Reading image language is linked to culture: you need schooling, practice, and explanation. Reading written language requires more effort and a longer learning process; writing is abstract and complex. Through globalization, we have access to several image languages, and some are more dominant than others. Our current image language develops extremely rapidly, is becoming in a certain sense more complex, and requires knowledge about the *way of reading*: think of parallel editing and fast transitions in feature films. Virtually always, there are written sources at the foundation of the image: a story, a scenario, a plan for the structure of a web project, or design. That is why it is important that image makers learn to enjoy reading and writing; become fully aware of the cultural links and development of image languages. How pictures are read.

William Burroughs wrote an essay in which he claimed that written language existed before language was spoken. An amusing thought experiment that arises from the idea that it is not possible to think without a language. Much has been written and philosophized about this. I would, as an extension of this, suggest that without intensive reading and writing, image language has no future.

--

Ine Poppe is an artist and journalist with a special interest in digital culture, technology, and art.

51

The Many Readers in My Body
Emilie Randoe

709 words | 2:50 mins

My father was a passionate typographer who, during his time at the academy, managed to pick up an antique English printing press and, during his life, collected a complete print shop. He taught us the basic principles of the art of printing. All three of us, because then we would at least be able to print a newspaper should there be ongoing problems in the future with power cuts. After his death, I kept the mini-printing shop together. A newspaper isn't really possible, but a daily pamphlet should be all right. And I've got enough ink to last me at least 150 years –all of superior German überkwalität.

My mother grew up in a period when children were strictly discouraged from reading comic books. As pedagogue herself, she felt that it really didn't matter how we absorbed information or knowledge, as long as we learned something and did something with it. Thanks to her, when I was a young grammar school pupil, I collected all the Asterix and Obelix albums –in Latin. Nowadays, I can't read them any more, but they still stand in a row in my bookcase.

People in my circle know me as somebody who is pretty smart about applications of new media and their carriers. But since the appearance of the iPad, I doubt whether I can still justify this. You see, I don't own one and every time I go into the shop to buy one, I'm struck with doubt. If I were a designer, photographer, or model, I'd get one at once. But as change manager, I don't see the added value, except that it's a bit of a conversation piece when you get one. For the time being, that is, because at every congress I attend, the consultants wander round with their iPads under their arm. But

every time

I am

just about to buy one, I simply can't come up with the answer to what the iPad adds to my MacBook and iPhone.

So this is the context in which I ponder the future of reading. A confrontational question. I have kept track of my reading behaviour during the past few weeks and what do you know: for real reading, simply give me a book made of real paper. I can scribble in the margin, stick mini post-its at the important passages, and, very important, I can see how far I am and whether I have to hurry up –for a book I really want to finish– or actually slow down –because some books you never want to end. So for a week in Barcelona, I stuffed my bag with books which, naturally, I took home practically unread. The pile on my bedside table gave me a comforting feeling when I turned out the reading lamp at night. And how enjoyable it was –when I got back home– to sit at the table after dinner with my beloved reading the newspaper, tearing out articles, and passing sections to each other. The first thing I read is that my favourite newspaper is losing two hundred readers per week.

So I am one of the last of the Mohicans. Because in that very same Barcelona, my sixteen-year-old daughter explained to me how she saw the future of reading. She's wrestling at the moment with the mandatory book list. She reads quite a bit, but few titles on the book list interest her. But fortunately that's not a problem, she explains cheerfully, for you simply watch the film and download the summary from somewhere.

In Barcelona, the iPad once again pursued us. There we were, fiddling with our paper guidebook and the fold out metro map, and we see those clever boys –no clever girls, strangely enough– who really do have everything about the metro within hand's reach on the iPad: the metro map, the information from the tourist guides, the newspaper from home, the latest news on Facebook. In the cafés you see that the iPad really does make sure that reading –consuming– goes hand in hand with writing –producing. And all that takes place in much shorter texts than the ones I grew up with and used in my training.

--

Emilie Randoe is director of Randoe Verandermanagement and founder of the Institute of Interactive Media at the Hogeschool Amsterdam.

52

Arrangements
Bernhard Rieder

215 words | 0:52 mins

Having been part of collections, libraries, and catalogues for centuries, the book is increasingly embedded into digital databases of various kinds. As a data object it is not only an expression of cultural ingenuity, but also an arrangement of words, sentences, and paragraphs that can be counted and processed in innumerable ways. By comparing word frequency distributions, degrees of similarity between books can be calculated in a heartbeat; *modeled* knowledge allows for the extraction of names, places, dates, and more abstract concepts from millions of pages per second; with the help of shopping profiles, customer reviews, and statistical representations of actual reading patterns, extracted from data collected by eBook readers, database companies like Amazon and Google rank, filter, connect, and suggest in real time. These techniques have become part of our routine: they structure the way we find books, decide whether and how to read them, explore their contents. Access to the universe of books now leads more often through an

algorithm

than

through a library door –and the new mediators are mostly private companies that seek to transform the *computational potential* (Jean-Claude Guédon) of vast book collections into sale and click streams rather than explore the immense opportunities for new ways of knowing. Is it time to put *data politics* on the agenda?

--

Bernhard Rieder is an assistant professor for New Media at the Media Studies department at the University of Amsterdam.

53

Desecration of Reading
Paul Rutten

168 words | 0:40 mins

Information consumption, and that includes reading, can in principle take place everywhere. Electronic networks offer information to the farthest corners of the world. Efforts by research institutes and companies are aimed at making information omnipresent; a cloud of permanently available and accessible intelligence. With this, we arrive in the era of unbound information. The marriage between specific information and dedicated media has been finally dissolved through digitization. With digitization, the relationship between printed media and reading has definitely come to an end, we read from walls and coins, and from screens and streets. The current technology development is on the point of final desecration, by digitizing the icon of enlightened culture, the printed book. In this process, reading is stripped of both its status and its form. Some cultural critics see this as a degeneration of culture, while others celebrate it as the final unlocking of information and culture for everybody. The greatest challenge is to provide everybody with access, regardless of the institutional, commercial, and social barriers.

--

Paul Rutten is independent researcher and visiting professor Creative INDUSTRIES at University of Antwerp.

54

Epi-phany Plea for a Counter-culture of Un-reading and Un-writing
Johan Sanctorum

488 words | 1:57 mins

The advance of Internet and the new *social networks* regularly leads to culture-pessimistic deliberations: we shall no longer be capable of understanding texts and making links. But the comprehension of a text is acquired and pre-conditioned by power relationships. The links are always conventional, and determined by tradition, fashion, or the hype culture. The radical break with the cultural conventions would then consist of un-associating and not making links. That leads to a double counter culture: that of the *un-writing* and the *un-reading*.

Today, we find ourselves in an infinite network of images, texts, stories. We are terrorized, partly via the mandatory social intercourse, by the intertext, the communication hysteria, the obsessive neurosis to have to link everything together. The counter movement is that of striking things out.

The new writer escapes from all stories and also decomposes his own stories. He is the absolute amateur or *man-without-qualities*. Everything remains one-off, unrecognizable for the outside world, awkward and jagged, in the stage of experimentation. The ultimate boundary is the writer of the unwritten book, that only exists as an intention. The best book is the unwritten book.

The existing scientific, cultural, artistic, or political domains, always working with selection norms and communicative criteria, completely ignore the epiphany –the own interpretation. The Internet is an enormous biotope for this trans-communicative amateurism, that on the other hand possibly contains the germ of a new, non-levelling mass culture. The blog in that sense is not an individual Internet newspaper (that is a typical media-sociological confusion), but rather a diary left laying around which accidentally comes across a reader, who is aware of his indiscretion and the impossibility of decoding. In this way, a new reader also emerges: the *surfer* who appreciates the text as a mystery and thus respects it, as an *absent-minded* passerby.

I like people who read books they don't understand. I prefer to read books in a language I do not master: sentences, words, symbols that reveal nothing, preferably in a different alphabet, Chinese, Arabic, or Sanskrit. The new reader is an un-reader, an accidental finder of inscriptions that cannot be decoded, which he may momentarily touch but further leaves intact. Everything that presents itself as public, communicable, able to be integrated is then mercilessly exposed. I un-read only a certain type of book, which I suspect were not written in order to be understood. Epiphanies, texts that have never been published, but have appeared, or perhaps not. I respect them as a labyrinth of words that only have a meaning inside the mind of their inventor.

In a technopolis dominated by speed and immediacy, we may wish to create delay, search for mystery, and send messages to an intermediate space that offers comfort to both message and the messenger. Completely on the outskirts of cyberspace, a meeting can take place between the un-writer and the un-reader. Accidental, perhaps. Do we call this a moment of fortune?

--

Johan Sanctorum is a Flemish columnist, essayist, and philosopher.

55

Savouring Thoughts
Louise Sandhaus

183 words | 0:44 mins

I admit it. I've stopped reading. Well, not really perhaps. I consume words. That's not the issue. They come in through my ears, my eyes, and occasionally I have to eat them. Is it age? The age of many media? A bit of both I suspect. And what I do consume –are they morsels to sustain or just to entertain... or soothe?

Sleepless nights and long drives, I listen. Mysteries are for the road, while light-hearted banter is best on the pillow. (I blush at my disclosure.) But in one ear and out the other.

Sustenance it seems still needs to come through the eyes. Something about the shape and space of words. Yes, on a page; materialized into ink-like-ness on flat white rectangles of permanence or it remains reconfigurable bits in my brain –flotsam and jetsam of thoughts that don't add up.

Give me complex thought elaborated on a folio and I'll get out my knife and fork, savouring every bit and relish it as I ingest the experience!

And, by the way, did I mention my fear of phones.

--

Louise Sandhaus is owner of LSD (Louise Sandhaus Design), full-time faculty at CalArts and board member of AIGA.

56

The Stutter in Reading (Call for a New Quality of Reading)

Niels Schrader

189 words | 0:46 mins

Reading is the process of consuming information. It cannot exist without the action of producing information and the two can simply not be addressed separately. Therefore, to understand how reading will change, we should consider the act of communication in general.

Based on the concept of history, reading and writing unfold into an ever-evolving linear code. As communication habits keep adapting to new lifestyles and technological developments, communicating through and with computers stimulates a new, numerical, structure of information. Here, concepts are displayed as a mosaic of numbers (Latin calculi) rather than a sequence.

The ease of use and the pace of technological developments stimulate the fragmentation of texts. The linearity is being broken up as browsing effectively means navigation through short fragments distributed over multiple accessible sources. Chunks of different style, form, language, or format.

Consequently the future of reading lies in learning how to lay a thread of reasoning between these disconnected fragments. We will have to learn hyperlinking in communication and, eventually, speaking HTML. Otherwise communication will undoubtedly evolve into stuttering. Only those who develop a new quality of reading, will continue to understand the world.

--

Niels Schrader is founder of Mind Design in Amsterdam and lecturer at the Royal Academy of Art in The Hague.

57

I Read in the Mind
Ray Siemens

173 words | 0:41 mins

I read in the mind. For all the physical locations of reading one might choose (at home, at the office, in the garden), for all the bodily points of interaction (eye, fingers, hands, sometimes the tongue to wet a finger to turn a page), for all the material manifestations of reading devices (scroll, book, letter, napkin even, iPad), and for all the affordance-oriented technological apparatus associated with reading (eyeglasses, candle or light, manuscript marginalia, indexes, wordless, tweets, search screens, and distribution lists, database back-end with pertinent corpora)... For all this, the place of reading ultimately is, for me, in my mind, with reading as a technologically-facilitated, intellectually-centred emotional and physical act, one in which acts of community are established and shared across time and space. The most prominent advances made in reading technologies over time have been pragmatic interventions that ultimately facilitate, serve, and support the ability of the mind to act as a place of reading; we would do best to look in this direction for our next advances in reading-related resources.

--

Ray Siemens holds the Canada Research Chair in Humanities Computing at the University of Victoria and leads the Electronic Textual Cultures Laboratory (ETCL).

58

Full Circle
Karin Spaink

590 words | 2:22 mins

I used to read whenever and wherever I could. You were only allowed to borrow four books a week

from the library –for me, a measly ration. Once I had finished the children's section, I cheated a bit with the age groups; the lady behind the desk sometimes turned a blind eye to that.

When my parents were out for the evening, I would sit for hours on end on the wc with a book. At least that light wouldn't betray me when they came home. As soon as they started fiddling with the front door, I hid my book under my pyjamas, sanctimoniously flushed the wc, and pretended to be intoxicated by sleep. In the weekend, when they had a lie-in, I would take book after book from the shelves in the living room. At breakfast, I read the labels on the jam jars.

Later, I would read at least two or three books a week and the greatest attraction about holidays was that you could read even more. When around my thirtieth birthday I was suddenly struck half blind –fortunately only temporarily– my first concern was how I could carry on reading. I considered Braille. When my sight cleared up, I triumphantly read the screaming advertisements and billboards that disfigured public roads.

All around me, in my five by five living room, there are now more than fifty metres of books: almost three walls full. It looks impressive, but I hardly ever read them. Nowadays, I read at most a couple of pages before going to sleep, in order to ease the transition from waking to snoozing. I also seem more and more unable to keep up with the newspapers and magazines to which I subscribe. (I do obsessively read the T-shirts of people I meet.)

It's the computer. I sit at it day and night, I read myself silly on mails, news groups, forums, blogs, websites, newspapers, wikis, Facebook updates, summaries, and tweets, and naturally all the reactions to that. Internet has turned me into a short-track reader. I would conscientiously keep the longer pieces that I came across on my way for that same later in which I would read all those unread books that had, in the meantime, piled themselves up everywhere.

That continued for years.

Until I saw a Kindle and immediately fell in love. Four days later, Amazon delivered mine, which I immediately stuffed full of books. Longer pieces that I encounter on the Internet are sent, with just a few clicks, to my Kindle, and would you believe it, now I do get round to them. Hours on end on the sofa, in bed, or in the train; during stolen minutes in the smoking breaks, or waiting in the café at the cinema for the film to start –I'm again reading books wherever and whenever I can.

And again –plus ça change– I often read illegally. I exchange as I have always done books with my friends, but that isn't allowed now that they are digital. I have to break the copy protection on the books I purchased in the Netherlands in order to read them. (Dutch books shops only serve the market for Sony e-readers.)

My Kindle is in a red leather case; as soon as I open it, I have two hundred books at my disposal. There is a reading lamp built into that same case. In bed, in the dark, I read books –and my cats suspect nothing when they come home at night.

--

Karin Spaink is a writer, columnist, and feminist. She is a free speech advocate and social critic.

59

Books
Erik Spiekermann

221 words | 0:53 mins

Lots of important people have pronounced the book dead. And lots of less important people –the average consumer– believe them

because

they want

to be seen as progressive and on top of the latest trends. Tablets, smartphones, and other gadgets are sexy; printed books are tired.

I disagree. Nothing is sexier for the promotion of knowledge than printed books. The decisive factor is the typographic arrangement in all its depth and detail and adequate production. Books are objects, not surfaces. Badly designed and produced books will quickly be superceded by letters on screen.

A book, however, that has been properly designed in all its parameters, from the format, the paper, the binding, and the other materials to all its complex typographic parameters, offers a physical experience far beyond the mere transfer of facts. 500 years of typographic experience cannot be emulated by a reader's swipe of a finger. There are only so many ways to set a beautiful, legible and readable page in a given size and format and most readers wouldn't be able to improve on it.

As long as our brains and eyes have to compensate for technical and typographic defects instead of dedicating all our brainpower to the comprehension of content, we'll need books. If their design and production have been carefully considered, they can be perfect objects.

--

Erik Spiekermann is typographer and graphic designer. He is co-founder of MetaDesign design consultancy.

60

The New Orality and the Empty House
Matthew Stadler

466 words | 1:52 mins

There is anxiety about the book, but little about writing. Text flourishes. We read and write everywhere. Recall sitting in a room with a half-dozen friends on laptops, passing messages in chat boxes; or texting a loved one in another room of the house. No more phone calls; in Japan and South Korea per-capita minutes talking on the phone are down almost 300 percent. Never has literacy been so ascendant over orality. Or so it would seem.

Contrarily, bookstores close and sales numbers drop, throwing shadows of doom over the evolving enterprise of the book. People worry and assemble conferences.

In fact, the book is robust and ascendant while literacy threatens to collapse under the weight of a new orality. The New Orality. Digitized and freed from the inertia of the printed page, the written word has become fluid. Just as solid ground liquifies in an earthquake, the written word turns oral within the rhythmic convulsions of digital transmission. Text corrects itself. It is withdrawn, resent, and then doubled. Links burst open; feedback loops chatter; spelling dissolves and is reassembled. Digital transmission is, thus, performative, contextual, social, additive (rather than subordinative), aggregative (rather than analytic), copious, and homeostatic –in Walter Ong's analysis, oral.

The printed page is static. Like an empty house, the book does not change while you are away. It waits, making meaning only in the strangely private relationship called reading. Digitized text lives and changes constantly, vibrant in its hive mind. Ong, writing thirty years ago, predicted that electronic techonology would hasten a *secondary orality*. Though he had in mind books-on-tape, rather than digitization, his analysis remarkably predicts the condition we find ourselves in: *This new orality has striking resemblances to the old in its participatory mystique, its fostering of a communal sense, its concentration on the present moment.*

Paradoxically, the new orality recovers the book as an enduring and meaningful technology by freeing it from a host of awkwardly performed duties. During the age of mechanical reproduction books became home to image culture; their flat pages hosted the illusion of three-dimensional space and were sometimes manipulated to convey action or motion, as in flip-books or the sequential illustrations of comic strips. Their covers became movie stills and their interiors art galleries in which were hung that ultimate expression of the contemporary artist, his photo documentation.

No longer. Now the unfolding capacities of digital transmission will free the printed page from these awkwardly performed duties. As image culture –whatever that is– moves into its spacious new home (digital transmission), it will bed down with its true lover, orality. And literacy will be left to reside comfortably in the flat static pages of the book –home alone, at last. The book lies closed, recumbent and still, waiting for its reader. Who wouldn't want that?

--

Matthew Stadler is a writer and editor living in Portland, Oregon. Together with Patricia No he founded Publication Studio.

61

Letter and Spirit
F. Starik

160 words | 0:38 mins

There are two types of people: readers and lookers. And all just push against doors on which scribbles are scrawled, everyone does it. The reader will only go into the toilet after carefully studying which scribble is the man

Which the woman: pictograms are meant for illiterates and not intended for you, who just wants to know where to piss. The reader can't know what the train door is saying if the picture explains that the door is half open

And the **arrows point downwards** or do they **point upwards**,
it's all over the **place.** The **reader just loves giving**
meaning, but **never attaches** an **action**, a **consequence** to what
he has **just finished reading.** When the **reader leaves** his **flat**

he **reads** all the **names** on the **doors** of the other tenants
and also the words on the doormat with the bleeding heart
of the girl on the first floor: *You look nice today*.
The looker rings that bell. (© F. Starik, 2003)

--

Letter en geest

Er zijn twee soorten mensen: lezers en kijkers. Allen
duwen tegen deuren waarop trekken staat geschreven,
dat doet echt iedereen. De lezer stapt het toilet pas binnen
na zorgvuldige bestudering van wie de man moet voorstellen

wie de vrouw: pictogrammen zullen wel voor analfabeten
zijn bedoeld en niet voor jou, die gewoon wil weten waar
te pissen. De lezer snapt niet wat de treindeur wil zeggen
als het plaatje hem vertelt dat de deur half openstaat

en de pijlen naar binnen of juist naar buiten wijzen,
dat kan nog alle kanten op. De lezer geeft gretig betekenis,
maar verbindt nooit een gevolg, een handeling, aan wat
hij zojuist gelezen heeft. Als de lezer zijn huis verlaat

leest hij alle namen op de deuren van de overige bewoners
en ook het opschrift op de deurmat met het bloedend hart
van het meisje op één hoog: *You look nice today*.
De kijker belt daar aan. (© F. Starik, 2003)

--

F. Starik is a writer, poet, singer, and artist.
He is the current city poet laureate of Amsterdam.

62

Social Reading
Bob Stein

626 words | 2:30 mins

Beginning in 2005 The Institute for the
Future of the Book began a series of experi-
ments

under

the rubric of *networked books*. This was the moment of the blog and we were exploring what would happen if we applied the concept of *reader comments* to essays and books. Our first attempt, McKenzie Wark's Gamer Theory turned out to be a remarkably lucky choice. The book's structure –numbered paragraphs rather than numbered pages– required my colleagues to come up with an innovative design allowing readers to make comments at the level of the paragraph rather than the page. Their solution to what at the time seemed like a simple graphical UI problem, was to put the comments to the right of each of Wark's paragraphs rather than follow the standard practice of placing them underneath the author's text.

Within a few hours of putting Gamer Theory online, a vibrant discussion emerged in the margins. We realized that moving comments from the bottom to the side, a change that at the time seemed minor, in fact had profound implications. Largely because Wark took a very active role in the unfolding discussion, our understanding at first focused on the ways in which this new format upends the traditional hierarchies of print which place the author on a pedestal and the reader at her adoring feet. With the side-by-side layout of Gamer Theory's text and comments, author and reader were suddenly occupying the same visual space; which in turn shifted their relationship to one of much greater equality. As the days went by it became clear that author and reader were engaged in a collaborative effort to increase their collective understanding.

Later experiments in classrooms and reading groups were just as successful even though no author was involved, leading us to realize we were witnessing much more than a shift in the relationship between author and reader.

The reification of ideas into printed, persistent objects obscures the social aspect of both reading and writing, so much so, that our culture portrays them as among the most solitary of behaviours. This is because the social aspect traditionally takes place outside the pages –around the water cooler, at the dinner table, and on the pages of other publications in the form of reviews or references and bibliographies. In that light, moving texts from page to screen doesn't make them social so much as it allows the social components to come forward and to multiply in value.

And once you've engaged in a social reading experience the value is obvious. Contemporary problems are sufficiently complex that individuals can rarely understand them on their own. More eyes, more minds collaborating on the task of understanding will perhaps yield better, more comprehensive answers.

The difficult thing however about predicting the future of reading is that everything I've said so far presumes that what is being read is an *n-page* article or essay or an *n-page*, *n-chapter* book, when realistically, the forms of expression will change dramatically as we learn to exploit the unique affordances of new electronic media. Ideally, the boundaries between reading and writing will become ever more porous as readers take a more active role in the production of knowledge and ideas.

And lest, you think this shift applies only to non-fiction, please consider huge multi-player games such as World of Warcraft as a strand of future-fiction where the author describes a world and the players/readers write the narrative as they play the game.

Our grandchildren will assume that reading with others, i.e. social reading, is the *natural* way to read. They will be amazed to

realize

that

in our day reading was something one did alone. Reading by one's self will seem as antiquated as silent movies are to us.

--

Bob Stein is founder and co-director of the Institute for the Future of the Book.

63

Is the Role of Libraries in Reading Innovation Fading?

Michael Stephens & Jan Klerk

522 words | 2:06 mins

Michael Stephens and Jan Klerk share some thoughts about the future of reading and libraries.

Michael, I would like you to consider the following lines: I think reading is the mother of time consuming activities. To understand a book fully you'll need to read it in private for many hours from start to finish. Of course you can try to understand a text by *diagonal* reading. Compare it to trying to know a Bach cello suite by just listening to part 1, 3, and 6. But you can only fully comprehend a Bach piece in a slow way. Time-consuming activities are under increasing pressure. There are more and more things that come up for distraction: we are living in times where you are constantly challenged to do things you actually don't want to do. In my personal life this has led to a totally fragmented but dynamic information and media experience spending many small bits of time on different sorts of writing, reading, watching, and listening.

I've always loved libraries for the *slow* experience. In a library you can easily forget about time. But times have changed. Last year most of the books, DVDs, and CDs I borrowed from my library remained unread, unseen, unlistened to. Instead I've spent an increasing number of hours reading and commenting on various texts on various online screens. Libraries have always been the guardians and perhaps even the personification of time-consuming activities. You could say that libraries therefore may not fit all to well into the Zeitgeist. What would you say Michael about the perspectives of libraries? How will libraries survive when reading, watching, and listening is becoming more and more a digital and social experience by using personal mobile devices?

Jan –I spent much of the morning reading Bilton's I Live in the Future on my Kindle for a class this weekend –highlighting and sharing interesting passages to my followers on Twitter and Facebook. The potential for reading to become a social act of sharing/ commenting and remixing is great. Then, I jumped into YouTube and reviewed a few videos for the class, using the favourite command to save them and share them. Imagine a future where an eBook, a video, audio, et cetera might seamlessly be shared and utilized to educate and entertain. As you note, the solitary concept of reading wanes whilst a media rich experience blooms across multiple channels and networks. These changes will not contribute to the dumbing down of our culture. The opposite is true: media savvy consumers and creators of content will be the renaissance stars of this future scenario.

Sadly, the library playing a strong role in this equation might be fading. I'm writing this the day the news broke in the US about publisher Harper Collins enacting borrowers limits on eBooks through the OverDrive service as well as requesting access to borrower data. This only muddles the waters further for librarians and readers with Kindles, Nooks, mobiles, et cetera. It may mean that the content available via the

library

may

rely more on creators and less on publishers stuck in old models of distribution and economics.

--

Jan Klerk and Michael Stephens wrote columns together about the future of libraries for the Dutch journal Digitale Bibliotheek.

64

Slow Reading

Carolyn Strauss

252 words | 1:04 mins

By definition, *reading* goes well beyond the grasping of written characters and the realm of ideas they express. Applied to environments, systems, and relationships, *reading* is an act of interpreting, intuiting, even foretelling what may be.

Not surprisingly, today's fast world has taken its toll on all manner of reading. More *connected* than we've ever been, we're increasingly disengaged from territories of thought, personal experience, and creativity that I believe are essential to *reading* the world accurately and authentically. As the ubiquitous web, messaging, chat, friending, and tweeting force us into a constant state of reacting, we are left little or no time for turning inward, reflecting, losing, and then finding ourselves again to arrive at what we truly think and believe in.

Psychologist/author Guy Claxton warns that while today we have become very good at solving analytical and technological problems, we've lost touch with the *Slow mind*– the one more suited to addressing ecologies and systems. Two centuries prior, Goethe promoted *intuitive imagining* as a tool of scientific research to reveal relationships and underlying patterns; he believed we should read the world around us not at face value, but in terms of *flowing processes*.

Both point to what I call *slower ways of knowing* that can enable an expanded (maybe unexpected) set of *readings/interpretations* of a given situation, place, or relationship. We need both *slow reading* (verb> active process) and *slow readings* (noun> understanding emerging from process) to arrive at information and tools for moving forward in an increasingly complex world.

--

Carolyn Strauss is founder and director of slowLab (US/NL), a laboratory for Slow design research and creative activism.

65

Cyclops iPad
Dick Tuinder

433 words | 1:44 mins

When we open the classic book, it has the proportions of a landscape. The way that landscape-like format works is not only determined by what we see, but also what we miss as we concentrate on a section of the show. What is outside our immediate field of vision determines our idea of landscapeness more than what we do see. Because it implies that there is something larger than can be immediately observed by our senses.

It is seductive, and perhaps not even nonsense, to imagine that the landscape size of the paper book has influenced the form which literature has assumed over the centuries. That it has given that literature a perspective and stratification which had to be achieved at the time of the clay tablet in totally different ways.

There are more matters connected with the classic book that must have supported subconsciously not only the reader but also the writer in his imagination.

Subtle sensations that make reading a physical experience. Naturally there is the smell of paper and ink. The bonus that is becoming increasingly rare of text set in lead. The fact that a book is not only a carrier of words, but also a unique object. But also the slowly shifting balance from right to left (or from left to right depending on where you live) the more one progresses in the story. A shift in weight that, with increments of a half a gram of paper for each page turned, also propels the reader faster in the direction of the end of the story.

It is also of the utmost importance that the opened book should fall into two halves. The left and right page. Naturally that is a logical consequence of the form of the book, and it would only be that if it were not coincidentally a conceptually flawless visualization of the core of just about all the dramas written down in books. Jekyll & Hyde, plus and minus, conscious and subconscious, will and imagination, war and peace.

You ask yourself why a medium that is so well equipped for its task should have to be replaced by something new.

Naturally there are all sorts of practical reasons for the school slate like format of the iPad and its cousins, but the symbolism is too coincidental to ignore. If the paper book should ever disappear then that will not be because the e-reader is a better idea, but because the landscape has lost its significance for the modern reader and his interest is primarily directed at the single upright format of the portrait photograph.

--

Dick Tuinder is a visual artist, illustrator, writer, and producer of (short) movies.

66

Context Is King; Content Is Queen
Lian van de Wiel

329 words | 1:19 mins

Tablet, e-reader, laptop, smartphone. Add to that the information overload from Google, Twitter, and Facebook, combined with the overruling image culture and the trend towards a decline in reading. The changes in the information society take place at a rapid rate. But nevertheless, a number of fixed values and needs are still around. And that is the importance we attach to fine stories, useful information, and valuable knowledge.

The question many publishers pose today is how those stories are going to reach us, how we shall gather information, and how we can best learn. Reading in the old meaning of the world –namely, with a *paper book in a quiet place*– is still one of the methods for doing that. But it is not always the most effective, up-to-date, or appealing way.

Text, image, and sound now exist in all sorts of combinations. From hardcover print books via printing app with sound effects to on-demand animation films. The choice depends on what you want to achieve: stimulating the fantasy, discovering things yourself, or escaping for a moment from reality.

The activities around this content are also influenced by technique and will increasingly be absorbed into the content: reading can become a continuous process of scanning, assessing, sharing, learning, noting, talking, adding, watching, writing, reacting, et cetera.

Content is and remains the basis, but context is going to offer real added value. And whether you obtain that content from paper or from a screen is not the most interesting question... The question is how you, as user in the information wilderness, can find your way to the right content. So it can be rather nice if

there is

a publisher

who builds up such a good contact with you –personally or via an online profile– that they know better even than yourself what you want to read or learn. And then to offer you the appropriate content via the proper medium and at the right moment.

--

Lian van de Wiel is business consultant with the Dutch educative publisher ThiemeMeulenhoff, and focuses on the influence of digital developments on learning tools.

67

Reading Becomes Looking
Bregtje van der Haak

678 words | 2:43 mins

Recently, a friend (26) told me that when reading a book, her eyes will intuitively drift to the top right-hand corner of the page, as she expects to find a window there with the Google search function. Rather than having to work her way through the whole book, she wants to zoom in on the essentials and she fully expects to be directed there instantly, effortlessly, and free of charge. When standing in front of a bookcase, again she casts a look upwards to the right, eagerly in search of an entry point for the liberating key word to create order in the chaos of book covers and to find the needle in the haystack.

How do we create order in the chaos? How do we find what we need? These questions are crucial in how we will relate to reading in the future. Linear methods of organization, based on text, reading, and alphabet, will lose ground to visual methods based on looking and image recognition. After all, when confronted with *massive information*, looking is a faster and more efficient strategy than reading. In addition, looking overcomes the awkward problem of all those different languages.

In the West, reading is by definition linear: if you change the sequence of the letters, the words mean nothing anymore, or something very different. It is a harness and an arrangement along an established pattern one can hardly escape from. If you mix the ingredients of this recipe in the wrong order, the recipe will simply be wrong too.

Looking is more free and therefore faster, more flexible, and more contemporary. When you read an image you can also start at the right-hand side or at the bottom as the ingredients of an image can be mixed in many different ways to get meaning. My son (7) approaches letters and numbers as pictures. While looking at them he combines them into something that makes sense to him.

In China, every word is a picture. With enormous effort, Chinese boys and girls learn by heart thousands of *word pictures* (characters) and the meanings attached to them. There is no alphabet and no fixed link between signs and sounds. You can start reading a Chinese book at the front or back or on the left or right pages. This is changeable and the reader construes structure and meaning from the context.

The Chinese engineer Yunhe Pan is leader of The Million Book Project (CADAL), which aims to digitize a million books and ultimately all books in the world. He uses the term *Data Ocean* for the rapidly expanding total amount of information in the world and works on the concept of the *Smart Library': *a needs-centered, rather than a books-centered information service*.

Pan thinks that reading will ultimately be too slow to satisfy our informational needs. He calculates that human beings – providing they live to be a hundred and read one book every single day–

are able to read 36,500 books during their lifetime. This is simply not enough, says Pan. He predicts that books will become increasingly *multi-modal* and *multi-medial* (integrated with videos, photos, drawings, music, and animations) to accelerate the transfer of knowledge *because visuals can sometimes more quickly explain an issue than text*. With the shift towards e-reading, books and digital archives will increasingly include open, dynamic, and informal sources such as construction drawings, web pages, video news, and statistics.

Pan ascertains that considerable progress has been made in recent years concerning computer-driven recognition, translation, and visual comparison of Chinese calligraphy and that this knowledge could presently be applied to navigate more efficiently in the *data ocean*. Searching on the basis of pictures rather than words will undoubtedly become more important. Today, my friend still has a search word in mind when she stands in front of a bookcase, but for my son this will probably be a *search picture* flashing through his mind. The time is right for intellectuals and scholars to set aside their fear, dislike, and disdain for pictures and to learn to picture-read and picture-write.

--

Bregtje van der Haak is a documentary filmmaker, journalist, and writer on contemporary culture.

68

The Library Is As Large As One Half of the Brain
Els van der Plas

722 words | 2:53 mins

If an old man dies in Africa, a library disappears. This is a well-known African proverb, where oral tradition ensures that history and stories survive.

Libraries are rare in many African countries. Illiteracy is high, 39 percent of the population to the south of the Sahara cannot read or write. Stories are told orally. So if an old man dies, a library really does disappear.

In Africa, they have been looking for a solution to this problem for decades; libraries exist (in, for example, Egypt, Senegal, and South Africa) but are scarce, just like the old wise men. They work hard at combating illiteracy, organize bus libraries that reach people who would otherwise never read or borrow a book, and have started rescue operations for libraries such as those in Sudan and Yemen, where mainly Islamic clerics have ensured that the ancient papyrus rolls have survived and been passed down through the centuries. But the old man is still the best option. You ask him about the history of your family, the stories of other people, and he begins his narration. There are men and women who have made this storytelling their official occupation, generally by passing it on from father to son or from mother to daughter. These are the so-called griots. They have the knowledge because their parents had the knowledge, and they in turn received it from their parents. Repetition is essential here, through the centuries. The knowledge that is managed and imparted by the griots is called jeliya, which means imparting through blood. You are therefore born a griot, with passed down knowledge and stories; it is in your blood, as it were, and therefore in your head.

In Africa, stories are also told through clothing. The Vlisco Dutch Wax fabrics, highly popular in many African countries, tell historical stories through pictures printed on the fabrics about, for example, the release of Nelson Mandela (11 February 1990), the celebration of Independence Day in Ghana (6 March 1967), the relationship between George

Bush and

(two men embracing each other, 2003), or the woman who wants to show with her shawl with lips that her husband is a good lover: *Mon mari est capable* ('my husband knows what he's doing*, 1953). Negative stories about husbands are also told: the dissatisfaction of the women about her adulterous husband, or the shawl with birds flying out of cages with the title *Si tu sors, je sors* –*If you leave, then I'll leave as well*. But there is also good advice: a cloth with a crown and hearts tells of a faithful husband (1973). All these stories, historical events, and wise advice are told in pictures like a moving comic strip. The street with the women in colourful fabrics moving gracefully is a visual library, accessible for everybody, including illiterates.

In the West, knowledge has long been strongly linked with the image of the book. Transfer of knowledge has, both literally and figuratively, an enormous volume with clear contours; libraries represent both in content and in image (rows of books) the enlightenment idea about how knowledge can take us further. That image is now drastically changing; the library can be downloaded and can therefore be accessed and read with a little machine. Do you want to know when Boniface was murdered, where your great-great grandfather lived, or what Eline Vere, the book by Couperus who lived in The Hague, is all about, simply google it. Internet has become a true world library, containing everything, and accessible in every language within a fraction of a second.

In Africa, the library is as small as one half of the old man's brain, enormous because of the interpretation and wisdom of that man, and limited in its reach which goes no farther than the immediate surroundings. In the West, the library is now as small as the iPad or iPhone, with an enormous accessibility. In Africa, the griot, within his collaborating surroundings, live on for a while; the jeliya is directly accessible. They will soon get used to i-information, the mobile telephone is now common property throughout Africa and the best form of communication. That is what you call the law of the handicap of a head start. They will only then truly miss the interpreta-tion and wisdom of the old man.

--

Els van der Plas is the director of Premsela, Dutch Platform for Design and Fashion.

69

Classic Canon
Rick van der Ploeg

137 words | 0:34 mins

By reading, you find peace, you come into a different world, experience and feel things you would otherwise never dream of. Reading is astonishing and enriching. Nowadays, you can download onto your iPod, iPad, or any other mobile screen from, say, the Gutenberg project, the classics of literature completely free-of-charge. And when you have a spare half hour in the train, in the bath, or wher-ever, you can allow Kafka, Austin, Mann, Shakespeare, and the other greats to visit you. By allowing the classic canon to have its way with you in these transitory times, you get ever more insight into and understanding for the greats of literature because your frame of reference becomes ever deeper and broader. Never would have thought that reading things that are really worthwhile could become so simple in the Internet age.

--

Rick van der Ploeg is an economist and politician. From 1998 to 2002 he was Dutch Secretary of State for Culture and Media.

70

Content Economies
Daniel van der Velden

446 words | 1:48 mins

In recent years the economies of offline print and online content have merged as networks invade the book's former sovereignty. Google Books transforms the currencies of page and chapter, and devices like the Amazon Kindle are increasingly viable alternatives to reading on paper. Interactions between book and Internet were eventually to boost book sales, but are of course supplanting the finite, limited nature of the printed object.

To secure the physical economy of book making, publishers resort to techniques of nostalgia that are at odds with the ideas of high efficiency that made the printing press a groundbreaking invention. Coffee table books now assume gargantuan proportions, rather like furniture or architecture –Sexitecture as one is aptly titled. If the end of print is in sight, these are the dinosaurs: a grotesque species that travels the earth, dramatically illuminating the critical condition of contemporary reading. It is a losing game if you consider a book to be the horse and carriage of the information economy, to be preserved because it is slow, heavy, and expensive.

It is conceivable that books will become dispersed entities, *content economies*, of which the physical object constitutes just one aspect. Live events, comments snippets, PDFs, blog postings and discussions, and printed artifacts may operate together in a new coherence. Consumers may purchase the printed book as a centerpiece in the midst of a largely virtual buzz. To design a book may become like the process of coordination required to fine-tune all these online and offline efforts, rather than typesetting pages and creating cover imagery for a paper object.

In 2009, we did an inquiry into the networked space of the book.[1] We targeted the seminal Manuel Castells volume, The Rise of the Network Society, and looked at ways to rebuild it without actually owning it or getting it from a library. Based on online sources (blogs, Amazon, Google Books, professors posting parts of it as classroom PDFs) and pictures taken with a cell phone in a bookstore, we retrieved about seventy percent of the pages, and collected these in between a cover printed from an enlarged Amazon.com jpeg image. The remaining thirty percent of pages were printed black, *informational black holes*. Visualizing the *content economy* of Castell's classic was a helpful exercise in realizing the extent to which the book, in a network society, gets disembodied from its physical presence.

--

Daniel van der Velden is a designer, writer, and co-founder of the design studio Metahaven.

1
The Netbook and its Library was carried out by Daniel van der Velden (Metahaven), Nina Støttrup Larsen, Femke Herregraven, Henrik van Leeuwen, Rozemarijn Koopmans, and Kees de Klein as part of the project *The Architecture of Knowledge*, initiated by the Netherlands Architecture Institute and the Dutch Library Association, in Rotterdam, 2009.

NB:
I am myself quite puzzled by the way this book is conceived; it seems to want to limit the length of texts to as close as possible to zero words. I personally do not think the future is in very short texts; I think the future is in new economies around longer texts, mediated by shorter texts. DvdV

71

Do Images Also Argue?
Adriaan van der Weel

199 words | 0:51 mins

The screens that dominate our lives demand literacy. How else would we utilize our digital tools, or the social media that have become so important to us? In fact we read and write more than ever before. Yet the primacy of text has passed.

Not only are the texts we produce becoming ever shorter, more importantly our communication is becoming multimodal. The populist expansion of audiovisual media we now witness finds parallels in the 1970s, when offset lithography democratized print production. Cutting and pasting text for offset repro-

duction,

which

could even be typewritten, eliminated the expensive investment in cumbersome presses, metal type, and highly skilled typesetters. Offset lithography generated an avalanche of printed matter on culturally and politically *marginal* subjects.

Similarly, anyone can now produce photos and videos, often in preference to textual messages. Just as offset lithography supported –if not fomented– grass-roots movements for social change, the democratization of audio-visual media will prove transformative.

Images can be extremely eloquent, but they do speak differently than texts. If images and sound increasingly merge into the communication stream, what might happen, for example, to sustained discursive prose? Will multimodal communications replace textual argumentation? And if so, how will images argue?

--

Adriaan van der Weel is Professor of Modern Dutch Book History at Leiden University, and lecturer in Book and Digital Media Studies.

72

Read Me First
Erwin van der Zande

475 words | 1:54 mins

I read more today than ever before. This contradicts the general idea that we are currently reading less and less. And yet it's true. I watch less TV in the evenings, and mainly read on the Internet. When I watch something on Internet, generally on YouTube, it never lasts long. What's more, with the arrival of smart phones and tablets, any moment that previously would have been wasted can now be filled with checking the news, feeds, and received messages. We read more and more often, but with less concentration. Ecstasy has made way for distraction, slow media for hypermedia. Thanks to digital technology, we have taken two steps forward and one back. That is, on balance, still progress. But why doesn't it feel like it?

Naturally that has to do with the quality of our reading behaviour. Modern reading consists mainly of glancing over, checking, and scanning headlines. According to publicist Nicolas Carr, this transitory reading behaviour even influences in a worrying way our cognitive abilities. If we don't watch out, he warns us, we will forget the attentive reading that offers room for reflection and insight. We need quality time when it comes to reading. As if you are talking about a couple who, with the arrival of their first child, come to the conclusion that they hardly have any attention for each other.

It is a pattern that we frequently see arise since the digitization of media: there is more, but it is of a lesser quality. Take music. Digitization has brought us into contact with a virtually infinite collection of music. Initially, we exchanged them illegally using Napster; now there is Spotify where you can get millions of numbers free of charge. The audio quality of the music is worse than it was on vinyl or CD, but that doesn't bother us. The same applies to videos on YouTube. The picture quality of the average video is awful, certainly when compared to the high definition pictures of some digital TV channels or Blu-ray discs, but we put up with it.

An e-reader doesn't surpass the interface of a printed book, but with an e-reader you can take more easily more books on holiday with you. For writers, it has become easier to publish a book; they do not necessarily need a publisher and can publish the book themselves.

The

online communities are also very appealing to fervent readers; they cross borders and are stimulating. But we ourselves remain the biggest stimulus. If you believe that you read with too little attention, then you will have to free up some time. It's as simple as that. If that doesn't work –and there's every chance of that– then you will have to be more rigorous: get rid of the TV, leave your laptop in the office, and get a dumb phone.

--

Erwin van der Zande is the founder and current editor-in-chief of Bright magazine.

73

Designing a New Stratification of Information
René van Engelenburg

373 words | 1:29 mins

There may very well be drivers who are an exception, but I think that for most, observing traffic signs along the road is an automatism. You pick up the relevant data: *here the maximum speed limit is 130 kph*. But actually the reverse is true: you *unconsciously* filter out what is not interesting. *Prohibited for vehicles weighing more than 5,000 kg*; whoever saw that sign? And so you *scan* yourself a route through the traffic.

An explosion of screens has engulfed us in recent years; from smartphones, iPads, laptops, touch panels on ticket machines, personal navigation systems, and public signposting, to electronic advertising panels and gigantic urban screens. The physical world at all levels is slowly but surely being devoured and covered by the virtual. Behind all those screens there is a world of *new media* people who invisibly provide content 24/7: make apps, fill websites, do dtp, program RSS-Feeds, transmit broad and narrow casting streams, provide Twitter feeds, and very occasionally make a digital work of art. An incomprehensible stream of text, image, and symbols, which have all been thought up and designed by somebody. All those screens have an enormous impact on the way in which we experience our environment and influence our actions.

In this new world, artists and designers have more chance than ever to think about and to build that approaching *New Babylon*; the modernistic ideal world of CoBrA artist Constant Nieuwenhuis, where the architecture will adapt itself to the changing circumstances so that you, as a completely free and nomad individual, will never return to exactly the same place. Where you, just like the driver, automatically filter what is relevant information for you on your way to your next location.

The reality, however, has not yet arrived in *New Babylon*; the integration of this new media layer and the *old architecture* will demand years of development. Museums, broadcasting companies, cinemas, and theatres, the classic providers of culture content, have the chance, and perhaps the obligation, to play a leading role in that developing world. They could begin by reinventing themselves by integrating all the various media layers into a search for new possibilities for the public that then not only absorbs information, but also shapes it themselves.

--

René van Engelenburg, designer and initiator of DROPSTUFF.nl; Urban Screen Network for the Digital and Interactive Arts.

74

Dancing Words
Francisco van Jole

412 words | 1:39 mins

In the second half of the twentieth century, the arrival of vinyl and the transistor made music permanently available to everybody. And the first thing that perished was the dance. Before this, dancing was subject to rules, encapsulated in formats. Waltz or fox-trot, Charleston or tango. Each had its own demands that the dancer had to satisfy. That drawing up of rules is part of restricted availability: making as efficient and intense use as possible of what is available. Scarcity exacts discipline. *I cannot dance* means: I haven't mastered the rules.

Subsequently, dancing became self-invented rhythmic movements of the body There is practically complete freedom, with no or very few rules. Everybody does whatever they like.

A similar liberation arose with the digitization of language. The computer, thanks to the word processor and email, was the first to ensure that written language, with all its specific format rules, was ousted by spoken language. Then the SMS message appeared and put pay to the most elementary spelling rules, like a sort of house music of written language. It is all about the ability to express instead of mastering skills. For the language purist, it is destruction; for the user it is liberation. More people than ever express themselves in writing.

At the same time, the image is in the ascendancy. When I am searching for the meaning of a word in a foreign language, I make at least as much use of Google Images to be able to see what it is at a glance as Google Translations. YouTube is used more than you think as a search machine or encyclopaedia. Ask yourself the question: *how does the heart work?* and you know why pictures are preferable.

Images also win because language is too complicated, too abstract. The example that stands out the most is the smiley. If you want to replace this with words, you will need considerably more time and thought to do it.

For the lovers of language, that is a horror scenario: the image that suppresses the language. But regardless of the question of whether that suppression really is so complete, it actually leads, in practice, to the opposite development. Image language is not yet levelled out, the proper mastery of it is as yet a scarce skill, the rules are stricter. Image is the new field of the expert. As language once was. And before that the dance. Dancing words, that is automatically an image in your mind.

--

Francisco van Jole is an Internet journalist and writer.

75

Books Are Bullets in the Battle for the Minds of Men

Peter van Lindonk

445 words | 1:47 mins

What inspires more? A picture or a text? Stupid question, of course –sometimes a picture and sometimes a text. But almost everybody thinks that a picture always wins. Who hasn't heard the sentence: *A picture says more than a thousand words*? It was first written by Frederick R. Barnard, the marketing boss of Street Railways Advertising, in the trade magazine Printers Ink of 8 December 1921. Frederick is honest enough to say that this piece of wisdom was not his, but came from a Japanese philosopher. He wasn't, incidentally, completely honest: a few years later,

he had

changed

a thousand words into *ten thousand words*, and the Japanese philosopher suddenly became Chinese.

The answer to the question is: the picture has the potential of winning in all its simplicity from a torrent of words, but that does not mean that it is always the case. The problem is that looking at a picture is, in principle, easier than reading words. I say *in principle*, because just as a child must learn to read and write, a child must also learn to *read* a picture, to analyse it, or even to reject it. In a world full of visual violence, *learning to see* (not learning to look) should be a mandatory subject.

What will certainly happen is that text and image will more frequently be consumed jointly. I used to be able to listen to the radio and do my homework at the same time (something my mother wouldn't or couldn't believe); today, young people can also have their television on and watch CNN on their computer, with two split images and above them one and sometimes even two newsbars. Before I forget: making a phone call or sending an SMS via your mobile telephone can also be put on the list.

What is required is something or someone offering coherence and consistency, a sort of funnel. That function was for a long time the exclusive field of newspapers and magazines, but an end is coming to that. No need to panic: new filters are coming. You increasingly consume news via fast websites and Twitter, discover what your friends and acquaintances are doing via the social media. In short, there's not much news coming, just more of the same. And moving along with greater speed.

And what about that book? The unparalleled brainchild of the individual? The jacket may and will change: the e-Reader, the audio book, the iPad, in Japan 180,000 titles exclusively for the mobile phone etcetera. Distribution is changing (recently, Borders, the bookstore chain in America went bankrupt), but content remains. And I remain posimistic, as my son in America calls it.

--

Peter van Lindonk is a publisher and writer. He annually organizes a congress called PINC (People, Ideas, Nature, Creativity).

76

Reading Surroundings
Koert van Mensvoort

180 words | 0:47 mins

Anybody wishing to know the future of reading must consult the past. I will skip grandma's era; the age of printed paper was nothing more than an intermediary period. Let's go back even further. How did we read 40,000 ago? We didn't! Or so you would think. And yet that isn't true, There were, of course, no media such as we have now. And yet we read. What? We read our surroundings. We read the landscape, the skies, the tracks in the sand of the prey we were hunting. This way of *reading our surroundings* is something we've forgotten –except for a handful of Aboriginals. That's a pity, because reading your surroundings, in which symbols coincide with events and things, has a future. An expensive description for this is Augmented Reality. And it is precisely what it says: increased, magnified reality. We drape a symbolic layer over our physical surroundings which must help us denote them. Buildings and events become text. Our surroundings become our interface. Context is content. And we human beings are evolutionarily perfectly equipped for that.

--

Koert van Mensvoort is founder of Next Nature and assistant professor at the University of Technology, Eindhoven.

77

Reading with Electronic Blinkers
Tjebbe van Tijen

580 words | 2:19 mins

This morning, an academic e-reader (MyiLibrary) again annoyed me by putting me in blinkers and only allowing me to read a few pages. I was so annoyed that I sent the following question to a Flemish scientist in the field of reading perception: *Various so-called e-readers with online book files have, in order to protect commercially the paper book, restricted reading to just a few pages at a time. The familiar, traditional way of reading, with pages open next to each other, has been made impossible, as has leafing through the book or jumping from page to page. A single, slowly loading page at a time –that is what is set before you.*

This causes me, but also many others –see all sorts of protesting users and people who have programmed work-arounds– enormous irritation when reading... That irritation is initially subconscious, but it soon becomes so irksome that reading such presentations is virtually impossible.

I am trying to discover what causes that irritation, also out of interest for what reading actually is. (I have been active for thirty years as a part-time librarian/archivist and I am interested in the history of reading and writing.)

Now my experience with a book is of a somewhat undulating landscape of pages laying next to each other, which appear two-by-two in picture (in which hand/eye synchronization... the tactile and the visual, and also the motoric, all blend into one action). This experience is damaged by the visual exclusion of the expected image of neighbouring pages, the constantly missing other page, which gives the physical, but perhaps also the metaphorical balance to the reading object known as book. Printed text is naturally first and foremost image and only becomes writing when it is read. When reading, my eye wanders, as in a landscape, across words, across graphic indications such as indents, quotation marks, differences in the typography, lists –you name it. Linear reading is but one of the actions that are undertaken. This information landscape seems to have a natural border because it is (often) held by ourselves and the eye moves like a ship on the waves and still knows how to keep its course.

Looking back and forward from one half to the other of the open book. Then the distinguishing localizations of our perception system come into play. The peripheral field of vision perhaps creates the space in which reading becomes a creative act. The current scientific research into what reading really is for you also has more refined terms about how observations at the edges of the shifting field of our focus can play a headstrong role. Parafoveal vision is a term that is used in this context. Could the impossibility of reading at one glance the field of writing on the pages of an opened book perhaps cause our eye to scout constantly the edges of our immediate observation as a form of verification of the meandering progress along the words and through the sentences?

Reading academic orations stimulates –I think– this rapid back and forth movement of our alert eye more than a more linear narrative, when we really don't want to know in advance what is coming... It is certain that the single page of the small eBook and the miserly publishers who offer their electronic book versions in the 1-page format are systematically stealing what is and remains

one

of the

miracles of technique: the book controlled by hand and eye.

--

Tjebbe van Tijen runs Imaginary Museum Projects and is visiting fellow at the School of Creative Media / City University of Hong Kong.

78

Better Tools
Dirk van Weelden

552 words | 2:13 mins

In the past, when most people were only moderately lettered and read slowly and out loud (obeying the rules according to the holy printed word), it was an enormous gift if you could also read differently. Scholars, writers, setters: professional readers mastered techniques that resembled sorcery: diagonal reading, fast reading, pattern recognition reader, and reading between the lines. And what's more, it seems as if they were inexhaustible and so could read all the time and everything at once, without getting at all confused.

That speed reading now seems something that the average fourteen-year-old can easily master. Now we all do it. But the quantity, the speed, and the diversity of the texts passing by would make somebody from the seventeenth century faint. We can write something down while we are phoning, and occasionally follow over our shoulder a screen with news items and in another window scroll through search results.

Reading swiftly and switching, at random and recognizing patterns, gave a lead in a world of slow, straightforward text reading. A lead in terms of freedom, speed, skill. What type of reading gives freedom, speed, and skill if the norm for reading is fast, diagonal, springing, and fragmentary?

In the past, it was the magic of the written word that inspired authority and made them obedient. Now it is the magic of the media circus, with its overwhelming, multicoloured variety, its speed, its humour, and its recognition that make people credulous and docile. It is not Authority but Distraction that keeps us stupid. Resistance to it is a good way to start. Or in other words the ability to be able to choose where to direct your attention and to keep it there as well. Don't bat an eyelid when an e-mail comes in, don't multitask, don't do anything other than read.

The second characteristic of reading that is freer and faster, and makes you stronger is this: take the text literally, read the same sentence again, out loud if necessary. Remember what you have written in this way. Think: how could this be said in a different way? Why do they say it like that? You develop a nose for incompetent, thoughtless bullshit. And an eye for the ingenuity of a surprising phrasing. If you read literally and slowly, you know like lightning whether somebody knows what he's writing about or not. You see the secret vanity of how somebody lays the blame in a subtle way with somebody else. You hear emotions between the facts. The repulsive vagueness, the hideous narrow-mindedness. You don't see all that if you speed read. Somebody who can read slowly learns to think faster. You reach an opinion faster –one that is based on something. Handy!

The sort of reading that can make somebody in today's information society freer, faster, and more skilled works like this: continue to concentrate; look at the language and how it works; wait until the implicit and unintended in a text can organize itself and tell you something that does not coincide with the information in the text. Anybody who can do this has built up a strong immune system

against

the toxin

in the stream of information. But also has a formidable tool in their hand. Your fellow speed readers are jealous of it and sometimes afraid.

--

Dirk van Weelden is a philosopher and author.

79

E-Stone
Jack van Wijk

509 words | 2:02 mins

Text is a fantastic invention. The idea is simple: in its minimal form, text is nothing more than a short or long sequence of around one hundred different symbols. This enables us to save, spread, and absorb information, whereby information can be everything, varying from a sequence of facts to an exciting story, from a business letter to a declaration of love.

Text and technology have a close relationship. Text can be cut in stone: a durable, but not very portable solution. We can still read on the Rosetta Stone how the priests of Memphis thanked ruler Ptolemy V Epiphanes more than 2000 years ago, but if we want to read the original we have to go to London. Paper is a much handier medium and allows us to take texts with us; with electronic and digital technology, we can distribute texts around the world like lightning. The telegraph is an early example of this, followed by inventions such as telex, teletext, e-mail, the web, SMS, and Twitter.

In all these new electronic environments, text is the pioneer that first demands space, followed later by graphics, image, and video. Initially, graphic quality is minimal. Instead of carefully designed texts, carefully set in accurately designed fonts, letters are constructed with a limited number of lines or with a coarse grid of dots. The reader, eager for rapid information, accepts this and reads texts from an illuminated ticker-tape and from grey green mobile phone screens. Perhaps we must accept that new technology restricts graphic possibilities. Wim Crouwel saw this as a challenge and in 1967 designed the New Alphabet: a font with exclusively horizontal and vertical lines, suitable for cathode ray tubes. But in practice it transpires that new technology is developed to offer a higher image fidelity, and a modern smartphone has a colour screen with 300 dots per inch.

With modern technology, text can be quickly produced and distributed by everybody. That gives a deluge of text, in which we could drown. But modern technique also provides solutions for this. Finding a word in a text, finding a text in a collection: that is no problem at all with a search function and a search engine. Visualization makes it possible to get a quick overview of large quantities of text. Examples of this are the tag cloud, or the word cloud, with which key words can be indicated; Vox Civitas, a tool which can analyze, for example, 160,000 tweets during a speech by Obama; and ThemeScapes, coloured mountainscapes in which collections of similar documents appear as mountain tops.

Electronic text is transitory. Often that is no problem, not every SMS is equally important, but sometimes you receive a message that effects you and you want to keep it. I see here a gap in the market. Send your SMS to a service that is newly established with the working name SMS4ever. Your message is sent to a computer-driven milling machine and a day later you receive your message engraved in either granite or marbel as specified, immortalized for eternity!

--

Jack van Wijk is Professor Visualization at the Department of Mathematics and Computer Science of Eindhoven University of Technology (TU/e).

80

Mushrooms and Truffles
Astrid Vorstermans

303 words | 1:13 mins

How do illiterates and young children read? They don't read text, but can often point out pictures with the best of them. I spoke to a woman who had been illiterate until she reached the age of forty and had developed a range of clever tricks to distil information from images and context. Until she started reading lessons and learned the difference between the targeted pointing out of information, and savouring text and image for their own qualities.

Gradually I learn to read information on new carriers: Where do you find what? How do you use various media to give stratification and significance to certain questions and content? How do data branch out and how do tracks merge? I find a way in the sea of possibilities. Internet is an ideal source for the latest news, for the weather forecast, and for train cancellations and delays, and while doing that I learn where I can find more and more exciting things. I notice that I still use Internet only as a targeted way to solutions and answers, and, funnily enough, I often use it in the same way as *old* media: if the information is more profound, then I make a print and read it with much more attention than the information on the screen.

But what to do with smell, taste, rhythm, texture, and so on? The information that I acquire via the path of the screen is, for me, a mushroom: nutritious, light, easily and cheaply produced and consumed, no after-taste. Books offer a different experience: the tension curve and concentration is different, and the paper, the rustling, the texture, and the smell, the suppleness of the cover, the typography invite you not just to absorb information, but can, in the proper case, evoke seduction, delay, greed, introversion, excitement, and eroticism.

--

Astrid Vorstermans is an art historian, and founder, editor and publisher of Valiz.

81

Book It
McKenzie Wark

203 words | 0:49 mins

I define book as any fairly long, more or less continuous act of reading with some more or less consistent thread.

It is probably always the case that a book in this sense is not the same as the bound-together pages of the thing usually called book.

When did we start thinking that the book designated some kind of unity? How many bound books actually ever manage to be consistent and coherent enough to warrant its status as being properly booked?

In English, to make a booking is to add something to a collectively authored book, usually a work of appointments. Why not think of booking more broadly?

A booking could be both the writing and reading that produces a more or less consistent, coherent experience where a book appears.

These days booking is a do-it-yourself business. Read across all sorts of surfaces and eventually you find the coherence and consistency of a situation that really seems worth booking.

Perhaps this is what you are looking for, on your screens. Perhaps you are looking for the threads, links, conjectures that can book sentences together into larger realms of sense.

After the death of *the death of the author* comes the birth of booking.

--

McKenzie Wark teaches at the New School for Social Research and is the author of Gamer Theory and A Hacker Manifesto.

82

Danger: Contains Books
Simon Worthington

438 words | 1:45 mins

The recent proliferation of digital reading devices has led to extreme format paranoia, as if the book is an endangered species, under threat of extinction. This overlooks the fact that there is already a lot of *book* in the digital –the vector of incursion moving as much from print to digital as it does from the digital into our notionally stable, *enshrined* cultural form of the book. As the number of tablets and e-readers in use doubles, and mobiles lose their buttons behind the glass of the screen, the interface behaviour of *the swipe* is in ascendance. Is this not, in the end, also a page turn? And in a similar way, is the tweet not something like a margin note; the cloud *bookmark* just that –a bookmark. If we regarded these categories more openly than we do –as ripe for mutation and adaptation, rather than set in stone, a legacy of history– then we would realize this moment constitutes one of ascendance not death.

More interesting questions, I think, focus on the composition of the publishing market –irrespective of whether that is for digital or print. When it comes to the production of books, the booster mantras –of *long tails* and *here comes everybody*– turn out to be misguided fantasies, distractions from the fact that the top twelve publishers make 65 percent (£1.2 billion) of the revenue, at least in the UK. This situation hasn't significantly changed over the last forty years of publishing innovation and digital *revolutions* and if you look across the EU where, at £20 billion (2009), publishing is the largest creative industry, then it's clear the long tail hasn't been benefiting the small publishers as claimed, but instead serves to consolidate network monopolies.

Smaller players and Joe Public are told it's good to share, while these same network monopolies reap all the associated advertising revenue into their offshore accounts, and social networks just wait for IPO day, their bloated info-bellies replete with our profiles, connections, and traces.

Supporting independent writing and publishing has been Mute's raison d'être since day one. Then as now it's infrastructures that appear a prime zone of contestation. Then as now, collaboration appears to offer a way out of the marginalization imposed upon us via our size. A recent project, Progressive Publishing System, looks to help small publishers distribute into ePublishing platforms, hybrid and expanded books, new book channels, and even walled gardens. Infiltrating every channel available, it attempts to allow content to *follow the reader*, rather than pretending the network can come good on its promise to deliver the reader to us.

--

Simon Worthington is the co-founder and director of digital at Mute Publishing.

Indexes

Index on Related Subjects (drawn from Wikipedia)

A Number 92, 113, 125, 149
A Number is a 2002 play by English playwright Caryl Churchill which addresses the subject of human cloning and identity, especially nature versus nurture. The story, set in the near future, is structured around the conflict between a father (Salter) and his sons (Bernard 1, Bernard 2, and Michael Black) – two of whom are clones of the first – when they are 35 and 40 years old.

A Story 63, 72, 124, 126
A Story is an album by Yoko Ono, recorded in 1974, during 'the lost weekend' sessions in which John Lennon produced Walls and Bridges.

Academic Journals 76
An academic journal is a peer-reviewed periodical in which scholarship relating to a particular academic discipline is published. Academic journals serve as forums for the introduction and presentation for scrutiny of new research, and the critique of existing research. Content typically takes the form of articles presenting original research, review articles, and book reviews.

Access to Information 113
Information access is a term used to describe an area of research at the intersection of informatics, Information Science, Language Technology, Computer Science, and library science.

Accessibility 155
Accessibility is a general term used to describe the degree to which a product, device, service, or environment is available to as many people as possible. Accessibility can be viewed as the ability to access and possible benefit of some system or entity.

Ad Infinitum 101-102
Ad infinitum is a Latin phrase meaning 'to infinity'.

Adaptation 174
Adaptation is the evolutionary process whereby a population becomes better suited to its habitat. This process takes place over many generations, and is one of the basic phenomena of biology.

Addressing 146
In computing, an address space defines a range of discrete addresses, each of which may correspond to a network host, peripheral device, disk sector, a memory cell or other logical or physical entity. The Internet Assigned Numbers Authority (IANA) allocates ranges of numbers to various registries in order to enable them to each manage their particular address space.

Adventure 90, 115
An adventure is defined as an exciting or unusual experience; it may also be a bold, usually risky undertaking, with an uncertain outcome. The term is often used to refer to activities with some potential for physical danger, such as skydiving, mountain climbing and or participating in extreme sports. The term also broadly refers to any enterprise that is potentially fraught with physical, financial or psychological risk, such as a business venture, a love affair, or other major life undertakings.

Adventure Games 90
An adventure game is a video game in which the player assumes the role of protagonist in an interactive story driven by exploration and puzzle-solving instead of physical challenge. The genre's focus on story allows it to draw heavily from other narrative-based media such as literature and film, encompassing a wide variety of literary genres. Nearly all adventure games are designed for a single player, since this emphasis on story and character makes multi-player design difficult.

Advertising 79, 116, 160, 163, 175
Advertising is a form of communication intended to persuade an audience (viewers, readers or listeners) to purchase or take some action upon products, ideas, or services. It includes the name of a product or service and how that product or service could benefit the consumer, to persuade a target market to purchase or to consume that particular brand. These messages are usually paid for by sponsors and viewed via various media. Advertising can also serve to communicate an idea to a large number of people in an attempt to convince them to take a certain action.

Advertising Slogans 79
Advertising slogans are short, often memorable phrases used in advertising campaigns. They are claimed to be the most effective means of drawing attention to one or more aspects of a product. A strapline is a British term used as a secondary sentence attached to a brand name. Its purpose is to emphasize a phrase that the company wishes to be remembered by, particularly for marketing a specific corporate image or connection to a product or consumer base.

Age Groups 136
A demographic profile can be used to determine when and where advertising should be placed so as to achieve maximum results. In all such cases, it is important that the advertiser get the most results for their money, and so careful research is done to match the demographic profile of the target market to the demographic profile of the advertising medium. For instance, shortly after the cancellation of Star Trek in 1969, NBC's marketing department complained that was

premature. They explained that their newly instituted demographic audience profiling techniques indicated that the series' main young urban audience was highly desirable for advertisers. In 1971, CBS acted on their own marketing department's demographic findings about their television network's programming and canceled several series that appealed primarily to older and rural audiences in a move nicknamed the rural purge.

Aggregate 97, 105, 122
An aggregate is a collection of items that are gathered together to form a total quantity.

Album 84
An album or record album is a collection of related audio or music tracks distributed to the public. The most common way is through commercial distribution, although some smaller artists will often distribute directly to the public by selling their albums at live concerts or on their websites. The album is distinguished from the single, which on vinyl records was a single song with another on the other or B side; on post-war vinyl these were easily distinguished as the discs were different physical sizes, and played at different speeds; 33 rpm for albums, which were more formally known as long-playing records.

Algorithm 129
In mathematics and computer science, an algorithm is an effective method expressed as a finite list of well-defined instructions for calculating a function. Algorithms are used for calculation, data processing, and automated reasoning.

All the Names 141
All the Names (Portuguese: Todos os nomes) is a novel by Portuguese author José Saramago. It was written in 1997 and translated to English in 1999 by Margaret Jull Costa winning the Oxford-Weidenfeld Translation Prize.

Alone 70, 74, 76, 96, 111, 140, 144
Alone usually refers to the condition of solitude.

Along for the Ride 86
Along for the Ride is a novel by Sarah Dessen. It was released on June 16, 2009.

Along the Way 104
Along the Way is the first live concert DVD from punk band Bad Religion. The concert footage was taken from fourteen different European stops on their 1989 tour for the album, Suffer, but was not released until three years later. It was released on DVD for the first time in 2004, coinciding with the reissues of the band's pre-Recipe for Hate albums.

Aloud 66, 89
Aloud is an American, Boston-based indie rock band known for its songwriting and vocal prowess as well as using a two lead singer approach.

Alphabetic Writing 61
An alphabet is a standardized set of letters – basic written symbols or graphemes – each of which roughly represents a phoneme in a spoken language, either as it exists now or as it was in the past. There are other systems, such as logographies, in which each character represents a word, morpheme, or semantic unit, and syllabaries, in which each character represents a syllable.

Alphabetical 66
Collation is the assembly of written information into a standard order. One common type of collation is called alphabetization, though collation is not limited to ordering letters of the alphabet. Collating lists of words or names into alphabetical order is the basis of most office filing systems, library catalogs and reference books.

Alphanumeric 103
Alphanumeric (sometimes shortened to alphameric) is a combination of alphabetic and numeric characters, and is used to describe the collection of Latin letters and Arabic digits or a text constructed from this collection. There are either 36 (single case) or 62 (case-sensitive) alphanumeric characters. The alphanumeric character set consists of the numbers 0 to 9 and letters A to Z.

Although 64, 67–68, 70, 73, 84, 90, 97, 110, 114, 117, 121
In classical logic, a contradiction consists of a logical incompatibility between two or more propositions. It occurs when the propositions, taken together, yield two conclusions which form the logical, usually opposite inversions of each other. Illustrating a general tendency in applied logic, Aristotle's law of noncontradiction states that 'One cannot say of something that it is and that it is not in the same respect and at the same time'.

Amateurism 132
An amateur (French amateur 'lover of', from Old French and ultimately from Latin amatorem nom. amator, 'lover') is generally considered a person attached to a particular pursuit, study, or science, without pay and often without formal training.

Amazon.com 157
Amazon.com, Inc. is a US-based multinational electronic commerce company. Headquartered in Seattle, Washington, it is the largest online retailer in the United States, with nearly three times the Internet sales revenue of the runner up, Staples, Inc., as of January 2010.

Ambiguous 118

Ambiguity is a term used in writing and math, and under conditions where information can be understood or interpreted in more than one way and is distinct from vagueness, which is a statement about the lack of precision contained or available in the information. Context may play a role in resolving ambiguity. For example the same piece of information may be ambiguous in one context and unambiguous in another.

Amusement 84

Amusement is the state of experiencing humorous and usually entertaining events or situations, and is associated with enjoyment, happiness, laughter and pleasure. The word Amuse is so named from the opposite of 'Muse' -to learn or to think.

An Age 57, 104

An Age (published in the U.S. as Cryptozoic!) is a 1967 science fiction novel by Brian Aldiss. The book, set principally in 2093, combines the popular science fiction themes of time travel, totalitarian dystopia, and the untapped potential of the human mind. It was nominated for an Ditmar Award in 1969 in the Best International Science Fiction of any length or collection category.

Analysis 97, 108, 139

Analysis is the process of breaking a complex topic or substance into smaller parts to gain a better understanding of it. The technique has been applied in the study of mathematics and logic since before Aristotle (384-322 B.C.), though analysis as a formal concept is a relatively recent development.

Annotate 105

An annotation is a note that is made while reading any form of text. This can be as simple as underlined or highlighted passages.

Announcement 113

An announcement (ANN) is a Usenet, mailing list or e-mail message sent to notify subscribers that a software project has made a new release version. Newsgroup announcement recipients often have a name like comp.somegroup.announce. Mailing list announcement recipients often have a name like 'toolname-announce'. Most software projects that make announcements are open source.

Another 53, 63, 66, 73, 79, 83, 87, 92, 106, 116, 118, 123, 139, 168

In hacker jargon, the use of yet another as a way of padding out an acronym is fairly common. It was first used by Stephen C. Johnson in the late 1970s in naming yacc, as a humorous reference to the proliferation of such compiler-compilers at the time.

Antagonists 53

An antagonist is a character opposing the protagonist in literature.

Antique 87, 127

An antique (Latin: antiquus; old) is an old collectible item. It is collected or desirable because of its age (see definition), beauty, rarity, condition, utility, personal emotional connection, and/or other unique features. It is an object that represents a previous era or time period in human society.

Applied 142, 146, 152

Research can be defined as the search for knowledge, or as any systematic investigation, with an open mind, to establish novel facts, usually using a scientific method. The primary purpose for basic research (as opposed to applied research) is discovering, interpreting, and the development of methods and systems for the advancement of human knowledge on a wide variety of scientific matters of our world and the universe.

Appropriation 104

Appropriation in sociology is, according to James J. Sosnoski, 'the assimilation of concepts into a governing framework [the] arrogation, confiscation, [or] seizure of concepts'. According to Tracy B. Strong it contains the Latin root proprius, which, carries the connotations not only of property, but also of proper, stable, assured and indeed of common or ordinary. He elaborates: 'I have appropriated something when I have made it mine, in a manner that I feel comfortable with, that is in a manner to which the challenges of others will carry little or no significance. A text, we might then say, is appropriated when its reader does not find himself or herself called into question by it, but does find him or herself associated with it. A successfully appropriated text no longer troubles the appropriator that it has become a part of his or her understanding, and it is recognized by others as "owned," not openly available for interpretation.' According to Gloria Anzaldúa, 'the difference between appropriation and proliferation is that the first steals and harms; the second helps heal breaches of knowledge'.

Archives 81, 89, 152

An archive refers to a collection of historical records, as well as the physical place they are located. Archives contain primary source documents that have accumulated over the course of an individual or organization's lifetime, and are kept to show the function of an organization.

Argumentation 158

Argumentation theory, or argumentation, is the interdisciplinary study of how humans should, can, and do reach conclusions through logical reasoning, that is, claims based, soundly or not, on premises. It includes the arts and sciences of civil debate, dialogue, conversation, and persuasion. It studies rules of inference, logic, and procedural rules in both artificial and real world settings.

Arguments 67, 83

An argument is a claim or set of claims (about e.g. an idea, action or theory), supported by more or less defensible reason(s). In logic, this can take the form of one or more declarative sentences (or 'propositions'), known as the premises, along with another meaningful declarative sentence or proposition, known as the conclusion.

Arrangement 129, 138, 151

The American Federation of Musicians defines arranging as 'the art of preparing and adapting an already written composition for presentation in other than its original form. An arrangement may include reharmonization, paraphrasing, and/or development of a composition, so that it fully represents the melodic, harmonic, and rhythmic structure' (Corozine 2002, p. 3). Orchestration differs in that it is only adapting music for an orchestra or musical ensemble while arranging 'involves adding compositional techniques, such as new thematic material for introductions, transitions, or modulations, and endings...Arranging is the art of giving an existing melody musical variety' (ibid).

Art Galleries 140

An art gallery or art museum is a building or space for the exhibition of art, usually visual art. Museums can be public or private, but what distinguishes a museum is the ownership of a collection. Paintings are the most commonly displayed art objects; however, sculpture, decorative arts, furniture, textiles, costume, drawings, pastels, watercolors, collages, prints, artists' books, photographs, and installation art are also regularly shown. Although primarily concerned with providing a space to show works of visual art, art galleries are sometimes used to host other artistic activities, such as performance art, music concerts, or poetry readings.

Art History 107

Art history has historically been understood as the academic study of objects of art in their historical development and stylistic contexts, i.e. genre, design, format, and look.

Artist 71, 113, 123-126, 140-141, 148, 161

An artist is a person engaged in one or more of any of a broad spectrum of activities related to creating art, practicing the arts and/or demonstrating an art. The common usage in both everyday speech and academic discourse is a practitioner in the visual arts only. The term is often used in the entertainment business, especially in a business context, for musicians and other performers (less often for actors). Artiste (the French for artist) is a variant used in English only in this context.

Artistic 84, 132

Art is the product or process of deliberately arranging items (often with symbolic significance) in a way that influences and affects one or more of the senses, emotions, and intellect. It encompasses a diverse range of human activities, creations, and modes of expression, including music, literature, film, photography, sculpture, and paintings. The meaning of art is explored in a branch of philosophy known as aesthetics, and even disciplines such as history and psychology analyze its relationship with humans and generations.

Assumption 95

In logic an assumption is a proposition that is taken for granted, as if it were true based upon presupposition without preponderance of the facts.

Asterix and Obelix 127

Asterix or The Adventures of Asterix (French: Astérix or Astérix le Gaulois) is a series of French comic books written by René Goscinny and illustrated by Albert Uderzo (Uderzo also took over the job of writing the series after the death of Goscinny in 1977). The series first appeared in French in the magazine Pilote on October 29, 1959. As of 2009, 34 comic books in the series have been released.

At Last 140

'At Last' is a 1941 song performed by legendary R&B singer Etta James and written by Mack Gordon and Harry Warren for the musical film Orchestra Wives starring George Montgomery and Ann Rutherford.

Attached 151

'Attached' is the eighth episode of the seventh season of Star Trek: The Next Generation, first broadcast on November 8, 1993. It is episode #160, production #260, written by Nick Sagan and directed by Jonathan Frakes.

Attention 88, 91, 93, 96-97, 101, 108, 116-117, 159-160, 169, 172

Attention is the cognitive process of selectively concentrating on one aspect of the environment while ignoring other things. Attention has also been referred to as the allocation of processing resources.

Attention Economy 97

Attention economics is an approach to the management of information that treats human attention as a scarce commodity, and applies economic theory to solve various information management problems.

Attention Span 96

Attention span is the amount of time that a person can concentrate on a task without becoming distracted. Most educators and psychologists agree that the ability to focus one's attention on a task is crucial for the achievement of one's goals.

Audience 100

An audience is a group of people who participate in a show or encounter a work of art, literature (in which they are called the 'reader'), theatre, music or academics in any medium. Audience members participate in different ways in different kinds of art; some events invite overt audience participation and others allowing only modest clapping and criticism and reception. Media audiences are studied by academics in media audience studies. Audience theory offers scholarly insight into audiences in general. These insights shape our knowledge of just how audiences affect and are affected by different forms of art.

Audio Book 164

An audiobook or audio book is a recording of a text being read. It is not necessarily an exact audio version of a book or magazine.

Audio CD 76

Audio CD is an umbrella term that refers to many standards of means of playing back audio on a CD.

Audio Quality 159

Sound quality is the quality of the audio output from various electronic devices. Sound quality can be defined as the degree of accuracy with which a device records or emits the original sound waves. Sound quality is also the physical pleasure or fatigue experienced by a listener.

Audio-Visual 158

The term audio-visual (AV) may refer to works with both a sound and a visual component, the production or use of such works. Slide tape presentation, films and television program are examples of audio-visual presentations.

Augmented Reality 165

Augmented reality (AR) is a term for a live direct or an indirect view of a physical, real-world environment whose elements are augmented by computer-generated sensory input, such as sound or graphics. It is related to a more general concept called mediated reality, in which a view of reality is modified (possibly even diminished rather than augmented) by a computer. As a result, the technology functions by enhancing one's current perception of reality. By contrast, virtual reality replaces the real world with a simulated one.

Authenticity 87

Authenticity refers to the truthfulness of origins, attributions, commitments, sincerity, devotion, and intentions.

Author 71, 74, 77, 81, 87, 95, 100-101, 104-105, 109, 112, 142-143, 146, 170, 174

An author (sometimes, in reference to a female author, authoress) is broadly defined as 'the person who originates or gives existence to anything' and that authorship determines responsibility for what is created. Narrowly defined, an author is the originator of any written work.

Average 57, 117-118, 137, 159, 168

In mathematics, an average, or central tendency of a data set is a measure of the middle value of the data set.

Away 56, 85, 88, 99, 110, 119, 139

Away is a play written by the Australian playwright Michael Gow. First performed by the Griffin Theatre Company in 1986, it tells the story of three internally-conflicted families holidaying on the coast for Christmas, 1968. It has become one of the most widely produced Australian plays of all time and is part of the Higher School Certificate syllabi or general High School Curriculum in many states, including Western Australia, New South Wales, Queensland and Victoria.

Awful 159

Awful means extremely unpleasant, or of poor quality; also amazing, full of awe, awe-inspiring, awesome.

Back-end 135

Front end and back end are generalized terms that refer to the initial and the end stages of a process. The front end is responsible for collecting input in various forms from the user and processing it to conform to a specification the back end can use. The front end is an interface between the user and the back end.

Barthes 104

Roland Barthes (12 November 1915–25 March 1980) was a French literary theorist, philosopher, critic, and semiotician. Barthes' ideas explored a diverse range of fields and he influenced the development of schools of theory including structuralism, semiotics, existentialism, social theory, Marxism, anthropology and post-structuralism.

BASIC 65, 127

In computer programming, BASIC (an acronym which stands for Beginner's All-purpose Symbolic Instruction Code) is a family of high-level programming languages designed to be easy to use.

Beautiful 91, 138

Beautiful is an adjective used to describe things as possessing beauty.

Behaviour 50, 55, 128, 159, 174

Behavior or behaviour (see American and British spelling differences) refers to the actions of a system or organism, usually in relation to its environment, which includes the other systems or organisms around as well as the physical environment. It is the response of the system or organism to various stimuli or inputs, whether internal or external, conscious or subconscious, overt or covert, and voluntary or involuntary.

Beholder 97, 124

The beholder is a fictional monster in the Dungeons & Dragons fantasy role-playing game. It resembles a floating orb of flesh with a large mouth, single central eye, and lots of smaller eyestalks on top with deadly magical powers.

Benjamin 57

Walter Bendix Schönflies Benjamin (15 July 1892–26 September 1940) was a German-Jewish intellectual, who functioned variously as a literary critic, philosopher, sociologist, translator, radio broadcaster and essayist. His work, combining elements of historical materialism, German idealism and Jewish mysticism, has made enduring and influential contributions to aesthetic theory and Western Marxism, and has sometimes been associated with the Frankfurt School of critical theory. As a literary critic, among his major works are essays on Goethe's novel Elective Affinities; the work of Franz Kafka; translation theory; the stories of Nikolai Leskov; the work of Marcel Proust and perhaps most significantly, the poetry of Charles Baudelaire. He also made major translations into German of the Tableaux Parisiens section of Baudelaire's Les Fleurs du mal and parts of Proust's À la recherche du temps perdu.

Bibliographies 143
Bibliography (from Greek: bibliographia, literally 'book writing'), as a practice, is the academic study of books as physical, cultural objects; in this sense, it is also known as bibliology (from Greek: -logia). On the whole, bibliography is not concerned with the literary content of books, but rather the 'bookness' of books – how they were designed, edited, printed, circulated, reprinted and collected.

Billboards 136
A billboard (archaically a 'hoarding' in the UK) is a large outdoor advertising structure (a billing board), typically found in high traffic areas such as alongside busy roads. Billboards present large advertisements to passing pedestrians and drivers.

Binding 92, 138
Bookbinding is the process of physically assembling a book from a number of folded or unfolded sheets of paper or other material. It usually involves attaching covers to the resulting text-block.

BIT 86, 89, 98, 116, 127-128, 133, 136
BIT was an information service, publisher, travel guide and social centre founded, in 1968, by John 'Hoppy' Hopkins. It pre-dated the internet as a free service that would try to find any information asked for and derived its name from the smallest unit of computer information.

Bitmap 75
In computer graphics, a bitmap or pixmap is a type of memory organization or image file format used to store digital images. The term bitmap comes from the computer programming terminology, meaning just a map of bits, a spatially mapped array of bits. Now, along with pixmap, it commonly refers to the similar concept of a spatially mapped array of pixels. Raster images in general may be referred to as bitmaps or pixmaps, whether synthetic or photographic, in files or memory.

Black and White 76
Black-and-white, often abbreviated B/W or B & W, is a term referring to a number of monochrome forms in visual arts.

Black Holes 157
A black hole is a region of space from which nothing, not even light, can escape. The theory of general relativity predicts that a sufficiently compact mass will deform spacetime to form a black hole. Around a black hole there is an undetectable surface called an event horizon that marks the point of no return.

Blog 78, 93, 108, 132, 142, 156
A blog (a blend of the term web log) is a type of website or part of a website. Blogs are usually maintained by an individual with regular entries of commentary, descriptions of events, or other material such as graphics or video. Entries are commonly displayed in reverse-chronological order. Blog can also be used as a verb, meaning to maintain or add content to a blog.

Body of Knowledge 81
Body of Knowledge (BOK or BoK) is a term used to represent the complete set of concepts, terms and activities that make up a professional domain, as defined by the relevant professional association.

Boniface 154
Saint Boniface (Latin: Bonifacius) (c. 672–5 June 754), the Apostle of the Germans, born Winfrid, Wynfrith, or Wynfryth in the kingdom of Wessex, probably at Crediton (now in Devon, England), was a missionary who propagated Christianity in the Frankish Empire during the 8th century. He is the patron saint of Germany and the first archbishop of Mainz. He was killed in Frisia in 754. His remains were returned to Fulda, where they rest in a sarcophagus which became a site of pilgrimage.

Bonus 148
The word Bonus refers to extra pay due to good performance.

Book Bag 74
A book bag is a durable bag, satchel, or backpack that is used to carry books and sometimes other supplies such as notebooks, ring binders, and file folders, particularly by students. Typical designs include backpacks, hand-carried briefcases, bags with drawstring closures that can be hand-carried or worn over one shoulder, and messenger bags that are typically worn over one shoulder.

Book Club 101
Book discussion club is a group of people who meet to discuss a book or books that they have read and express their opinions, likes, dislikes, etc. It is more often called simply a book club, a term that is also used to describe a book sales club, which can cause confusion. Other frequently used terms to describe a book discussion club include reading group, book group, and book discussion group. Book discussion clubs may meet in private homes, libraries, bookstores, online forums, pubs, and in cafes or restaurants over meals or drinks.

Book Covers 150
A book cover is any protective covering used to bind together the pages of a book. Beyond the familiar distinction between hardcovers and paperbacks, there are further

alternatives and additions, such as dust jackets, ring-binding, and older forms such as the nineteenth-century paper-boards and the traditional types of hand-binding. This article is concerned with modern mechanically produced covers.

Bookcase 127, 150, 152

A bookcase, or bookshelf, is a piece of furniture, almost always with horizontal shelves, used to store books. A bookcase consists of a unit including two or more shelves which may not all be used to contain books or other printed materials. Shelves may be fixed or adjustable to different positions in the case. In rooms entirely devoted to the storage of books they may be permanently fixed to the walls and/or floor. Bookcases frequently have doors that should be closed to protect the books from air pollution, and bookshelves are open-fronted. These doors are almost always glazed, so as to allow the spines of the books to be read. Especially valuable books may be kept in locked cases with wooden or glazed doors. A bookshelf normally stands on some other piece of furniture such as a desk or chest. Larger books are more likely to be kept in horizontal piles and very large books flat on wide shelves.

Booksellers 54

Bookselling is the commercial trading of books, the retail and distribution end of the publishing process. People who engage in bookselling are called booksellers or bookmen.

Borges 112-113

Jorge Francisco Isidoro Luis Borges Acevedo (August 24, 1899–June 14, 1986), best known as Jorge Luis Borges, was an Argentine writer, essayist, and poet born in Buenos Aires. In 1914 his family moved to Switzerland where he attended school and traveled to Spain. On his return to Argentina in 1921, Borges began publishing his poems and essays in surrealist literary journals. He also worked as a librarian and public lecturer. In 1955 he was appointed director of the National Public Library (Biblioteca Nacional) and professor of Literature at the University of Buenos Aires. In 1961 he came to international attention when he received the first International Publishers' Prize, the Prix Formentor. In 1971 he won the Jerusalem Prize. His work was translated and published widely in the United States and in Europe. Borges himself was fluent in several languages. He died in Geneva, Switzerland, in 1986.

Borrow 135, 153

Borrow or borrowing can mean: to receive (something) from somebody temporarily, expecting to return it.

Borrowers 145

The Borrowers is a series of children's fantasy novels by Mary Norton about tiny people who live in the homes of big people and 'borrow' things to survive while keeping their existence unknown.

Bound 53, 74, 106, 173

Bound, a descriptor of a book that has gone through the bookbinding process

Braille 136

The Braille system is a method that is widely used by blind people to read and write, and was the first digital form of writing.

Brain 83, 86, 90, 116, 133, 152, 154

The brain is the center of the nervous system in all vertebrate and most invertebrate animals. Some primitive animals such as jellyfish and starfish have a decentralized nervous system without a brain, while sponges lack any nervous system at all. In vertebrates the brain is located in the head, protected by the skull and close to the primary sensory apparatus of vision, hearing, balance, taste, and smell.

Brand 54, 93

A brand is the identity of a specific product, service, or business.

Breaking News 93

Breaking news, also known as a special report or news bulletin, is a current event that broadcasters feel warrants the interruption of scheduled programming in order to report its details. Many times, breaking news is used after the news network has already reported on this story. When a story has not been reported on previously, the graphic and phrase Just In is sometimes used instead. Its use is often loosely assigned to the most significant story of the moment or a story that is being covered live. It could be a story that is simply of wide interest to viewers and has little impact otherwise.

Breaks 137

Breakbeat (sometimes breakbeats or breaks) is a term used to describe a collection of sub-genres of electronic music, usually characterized by the use of a non-straightened 4/4 drum pattern (as opposed to the steady beat of house). These rhythms may be characterized by their intensive use of syncopation and polyrhythms.

Broadcasting 161

Broadcasting is the distribution of audio and video content to a dispersed audience via radio, television, or other. Receiving parties may include the general public or a relatively large subset of thereof.

Build 77, 161

The Build engine is a first-person shooter engine created by Ken Silverman for 3D Realms. Like the Doom engine, the Build engine represents its world on a two-dimensional grid using closed 2D shapes called sectors, and uses simple flat objects called sprites to populate the world geometry with objects. It is generally considered to be a 2.5D engine as the basic world geometry is two-dimensional, with an added height component, allowing each sector to have a different ceiling and floor height, and allowing them to be angled along one line of the sector.

The engine renders the world in a way that looks three-dimensional; however, the sizing for perspective only depends on the horizontal distance. This is noticeable in that wall vertices are always straight vertical lines on screen, regardless of the angle of view. This can cause noticeable distortion when looking up and down; as such, most Build games restrict this to a fairly limited range.

Bump 120

To bump a thread on an internet forum is to post a reply to it purely in order to raise the thread's profile. This will typically return it to the top of the list of active threads. The term 'to push-up' a thread is also used to describe this type of action. It has been suggested that 'bump' is an acronym of 'bring up my post', however this is almost certainly a backronym and the usage is entirely consistent with the verb 'bump' which means 'to knock to a new position'. It can also be used in personal messages (PMs) or instant messages (IMs) on the Web, to return an older message to the top of the list.

Burroughs 126

William Seward Burroughs II (also known by his pen name William Lee; February 5, 1914(1914-02-05)–August 2, 1997(1997-08-02)) was an American novelist, poet, essayist and spoken word performer. Burroughs was a primary figure of the Beat Generation and a major postmodernist author who affected popular culture as well as literature.

Business 99, 124, 150, 170, 173

A business (also known as enterprise or firm) is an organization designed to provide goods, services, or both to consumers. Businesses are predominant in capitalist economies, in which most of them are privately owned and formed to earn profit to increase the wealth of their owners. Businesses may also form not-for-profit or be state-owned. A business owned by multiple individuals may be referred to as a company, although that term also has a more precise meaning.

Business Letter 170

A commercial business letter is a letter written in formal language, usually used when writing from one business organization to another, or for correspondence between such organizations and their customers, clients and other external parties. The overall style of letter will depend on the relationship between the parties concerned.

But Why 97, 159

But Why is one of Christina Rossetti's early works, thought to have been written in the mid-1800s.

Buzz 156

A buzz can be a rapidly oscillating two-tone noise caused by vibration or other source, such as that produced by bees or wasps. It can also refer to a generally excited hubbub, or background noise – see for example marketing buzz.

Bytes 51

The byte is a unit of digital information in computing and telecommunications, that most commonly consists of eight bits. Historically, a byte was the number of bits used to encode a single character of text in a computer and it is for this reason the basic addressable element in many computer architectures.

Calculating 120

A calculation is a deliberate process for transforming one or more inputs into one or more results, with variable change.

Calculi 134

Calculus (Latin for pebble, pl. calculi) in its most general sense is any method or system of calculation.

Call of Duty 117

Call of Duty is a first-person and third-person shooter video game series franchise, created by Ben Chichoski. The series began on the PC, and later expanded to consoles and handhelds, and several spin-off games have also been released alongside the main series. The majority of the games in the series have been set primarily in World War II, with the exception of Call of Duty 4: Modern Warfare, Call of Duty: Modern Warfare 2 which are set in modern times, and Call of Duty: Black Ops which is set in the Cold War era.

Calligraphy 75, 152

Calligraphy is a type of visual art. It is often called the art of fancy lettering (Mediavilla 1996: 17). A contemporary definition of calligraphic practice is 'the art of giving form to signs in an expressive, harmonious and skillful manner' (Mediavilla 1996: 18). The story of writing is one of aesthetic evolution framed within the technical skills, transmission speed(s) and material limitations of a person, time and place (Diringer 1968: 441). A style of writing is described as a script, hand or alphabet (Fraser and Kwiatkowski 2006; Johnston 1909: Plate 6). Modern calligraphy ranges from functional hand-lettered inscriptions and designs to fine-art pieces where the abstract expression of the handwritten mark may or may not compromise the legibility of the letters (Mediavilla 1996). Classical calligraphy differs from typography and non-classical hand-lettering, though a calligrapher may create all of these; characters are historically disciplined yet fluid and spontaneous, at the moment of writing (Pott 2006 and 2005; Zapf 2007 and 2006).

Camus 73

Albert Camus (7 November 1913–4 January 1960) was a French Algerian author, philosopher and journalist. He was a key philosopher of the 20th-century, his most famous work being the novel The Stranger (L'Étranger).

Can It Be 80

Can It Be? is a 1995 album by rapper Gangsta Blac. track number 3 samples a part of a song by Notorious B.I.G.

Capitalist 82
Capitalism is an economic system in which the means of production are privately owned and operated for profit. Income in a Capitalist system takes at least two forms, profit on the one hand and wages on the other. There is also a tradition that treats rent, income from the control of natural resources, as a third phenomenon distinct from either of those. In any case, profit is what is received by virtue of control of the tools of production, by the capitalists (those who provide the capital). Wages are received by those who sell their labor with those tools, i.e. the workers.

Carr 83, 159
Nicholas G. Carr (born 1959) is an American writer who has published books and articles on technology, business, and culture. He was educated at Dartmouth College and Harvard University.

Carrier 92, 114, 148
A telephone company (also known as a telco, telecommunications operator, communications service provider, or CSP) is a service provider of telecommunications services such as telephony and data communications access. Many were at one time nationalized or state-regulated monopolies. These monopolies are often referred to, primarily in Europe, as Postal Telegraph and Telephones (PTTs).

Castells 157
Manuel Castells (Spanish name: Manuel Castells Oliván, born in Hellín, Albacete, Spain, in 1942) is a sociologist especially associated with information society and communications research. The 2000–09 research survey of the Social Sciences Citation Index ranks him as the world's fifth most-cited social sciences scholar, and the foremost-cited communications scholar.

Categorized 96
Categorization is the process in which ideas and objects are recognized, differentiated and understood. Categorization implies that objects are grouped into categories, usually for some specific purpose. Ideally, a category illuminates a relationship between the subjects and objects of knowledge. Categorization is fundamental in language, prediction, inference, decision making and in all kinds of environmental interaction.

Cause 167
Causality is the relationship between an event (the cause) and a second event (the effect), where the second event is understood as a consequence of the first.

CD 76, 159
A Compact Disc (also known as a CD) is an optical disc used to store digital data. It was originally developed to store and playback sound recordings exclusively, but later expanded to encompass data storage CD-ROM, write-once audio and data storage CD-R, rewritable media CD-RW, Video Compact Discs (VCD), Super Video Compact Discs (SVCD), PhotoCD, PictureCD, CD-i, and Enhanced CD. Audio CDs and audio CD players have been commercially available since October 1982.

Ceiling of the Sistine Chapel 121
The Sistine Chapel ceiling, painted by Michelangelo between 1508 and 1512, at the commission of Pope Julius II, is one of the most renowned artworks of the High Renaissance. The ceiling is that of the large Papal Chapel built within the Vatican between 1477 and 1480 by Pope Sixtus IV after whom it is named the Sistine Chapel. The chapel is the location for Papal Conclaves and many important services.

Chair 57, 60, 89, 91, 119, 135
A chair is a stable, raised surface used to sit on, commonly for use by one person. Chairs are most often supported by four legs; however, a chair can have three legs (in a triangle shape) or could have a different shape depending on the criteria of the chair specifications. A chair without a back or arm rests is a stool, or when raised up, a bar stool. A chair with arms is an armchair and with folding action and inclining footrest, a recliner. A permanently fixed chair in a train or theater is a seat or airline seat; when riding, it is a saddle and bicycle saddle, and for an automobile, a car seat or infant car seat. With wheels it is a wheelchair and when hung from above, a swing.

Chapter 156
Chapter, as an organizational class title.

Chapters 114
Chapters is a Canadian big box bookstore banner owned by Indigo Books and Music. Formerly a company in its own right competing with Indigo, the combined company has continued to operate both banners since their merger in 2001.

Cheerful 88
Cheering is the uttering or making of sounds encouraging, stimulating or exciting to action, indicating approval or acclaiming or welcoming persons, announcements of events and the like.

Chinese Calligraphy 152
East Asian calligraphy is a form of calligraphy widely practised and revered in the Sinosphere. This most often includes China, Japan, Korea, and Vietnam. The East Asian calligraphic tradition originated and developed from China. There is a general standardization of the various styles of calligraphy in this tradition. East Asian calligraphy and ink and wash painting are closely related, since accomplished using similar tools and techniques. Chinese painting and calligraphy distinguishes themselves from onther culture's arts by their emphasis on motion, and their charge with dynamic life. According to Stanley-Baker : 'Calligraphy is sheer life experienced through energy in motion that is registered as traces on silk or paper, with time and rhythm in shifting space its main

ingredients'. Calligraphy has also led to the development of many forms of art in East Asia, including seal carving, ornate paperweights, and inkstones.

Choice 63, 142, 149

Choice consists of the mental process of judging the merits of multiple options and selecting one of them. While a choice can be made between imagined options ('what would I do if ...?'), often a choice is made between real options, and followed by the corresponding action. For example, a route for a journey is chosen based on the preference of arriving at a given destination as soon as possible. The preferred (and therefore chosen) route is then derived from information about how long each of the possible routes take. This can be done by a route planner. If the preference is more complex, such as involving the scenery of the route, cognition and feeling are more intertwined, and the choice is less easy to delegate to a computer program or assistant.

Chronological 86

Chronology (from Latin chronologia, from Ancient Greek: chronos, 'time'; and -logia) is the science of arranging events in their order of occurrence in time, such as the use of a timeline. It is also 'the determination of the actual temporal sequence of past events'.

Cinemas 161

A movie theater, cinema, movie house, picture theater, film theater is a venue, usually a building, for viewing motion pictures (movies or 'films').

Citation 81

Broadly, a citation is a reference to a published or unpublished source (not always the original source). More precisely, a citation is an abbreviated alphanumeric expression (e.g. [Newell84]) embedded in the body of an intellectual work that denotes an entry in the bibliographic references section of the work for the purpose of acknowledging the relevance of the works of others to the topic of discussion at the spot where the citation appears. Generally the combination of both the in-body citation and the bibliographic entry constitutes what is commonly thought of as a citation (whereas bibliographic entries by themselves are not).

Classic 79, 83, 102, 147-148, 155, 157, 161

The word classic means something that is a perfect example of a particular style, something of lasting worth or with a timeless quality. The word can be an adjective (a classic car) or a noun (a classic of English literature). It denotes a particular quality in art, architecture, literature and other cultural artifacts. In commerce, products are named 'classic' to denote a long standing popular version or model, to distinguish it from a newer variety. Classic is used to describe many major, long-standing sporting events. Colloquially, an everyday occurrence (e.g. a joke or mishap) may be described as 'an absolute classic'.

Classic Book 79, 147-148

A classic book is a book accepted as being exemplary or noteworthy, either through an imprimatur such as being listed in any of the Western canons or through a reader's own personal opinion. The term itself is closely related to Western Canon and to various college/university Senior Comprehensive Examination Reading Lists. What makes a book 'classic' is a concern that has occurred to various authors ranging from Italo Calvino to Mark Twain and the related questions of 'Why Read the Classics?' and 'What Is a Classic?' have been essayed by authors from different genres and eras (Calvino, T.S. Eliot, Charles Saint-Beuve). The ability of a classic book to be reinterpreted, to seemingly be renewed in the interests of generations of readers succeeding its creation, is a theme that is seen in the writings of literary critics including Michael Dirda, Saint-Beuve and Ezra Pound.

Classical 66

The word classical has several meanings. In general, these meanings refer to some past time, works of that era or later works influenced by that time. Classical things are often seen as ordered and part of high culture or a golden age, and contrasted to earlier or later things which may be seen as chaotic, elaborate or emotional.

Classics Illustrated 124

Classics Illustrated is a comic book series featuring adaptations of literary classics such as Moby Dick, Hamlet, and The Iliad. Created by Albert Kanter, the series began publication in 1941 and finished its first run in 1971, producing 169 issues. Following the series' demise, various companies reprinted its titles. This series is different from the Great Illustrated Classics, which is an adaptation of the classics for young readers that includes illustrations, but is not in the comic book form.

Clay Tablet 147

In the Ancient Near East, clay tablets were used as a writing medium, especially for writing in cuneiform, throughout the Bronze Age and well into the Iron Age.

Close Reading 107

Close reading describes, in literary criticism, the careful, sustained interpretation of a brief passage of text. Such a reading places great emphasis on the particular over the general, paying close attention to individual words, syntax, and the order in which sentences and ideas unfold as they are read.

CNN 164

Cable News Network (CNN) is a U.S. cable news channel founded in 1980 by Ted Turner. Upon its launch, CNN was the first channel to provide 24-hour television news coverage, and the first all-news television channel in the United States. While the news channel has numerous affiliates, CNN primarily broadcasts from its headquarters at the CNN Center in Atlanta, the Time Warner Center in New York City, and studios in Washington, D.C. and Los Angeles. CNN is owned by parent company Time Warner, and the U.S. news channel is a division of the Turner Broadcasting System.

Code 65, 125, 134

A code is a rule for converting a piece of information (for example, a letter, word, phrase, or gesture) into another form or representation (one sign into another sign), not necessarily of the same type.

CoffeeTable Book 156

A coffee table book is a hardcover book that is intended to sit on a coffee table or similar surface in an area where guests sit and are entertained, thus inspiring conversation or alleviating boredom. They tend to be oversized and of heavy construction, since there is no pressing need for portability. Subject matter is generally confined to non-fiction, and is usually visually-oriented. Pages consist mainly of photographs and illustrations, accompanied by captions and small blocks of text, as opposed to long prose. Since they are aimed at anyone who might pick the book up for a light read, the analysis inside is often more basic and with less jargon than other books on the subject. Because of this, the term coffee table book can be used pejoratively to indicate a superficial approach to the subject.

Cognitive Processes 106

Cognition is the scientific term for 'the process of thought'. Usage of the term varies in different disciplines; for example in psychology and cognitive science, it usually refers to an information processing view of an individual's psychological functions. Other interpretations of the meaning of cognition link it to the development of concepts; individual minds, groups, and organizations.

CoINS 130

ContextObjects in Spans, commonly abbreviated COinS, is a method to embed bibliographic metadata in the HTML code of web pages. This allows bibliographic software to publish machine-readable bibliographic items and client reference management software to retrieve bibliographic metadata. The metadata can also be sent to an OpenURL resolver. This allows, for instance, searching for a copy of a book in one's own library.

Collaboration 175

Collaboration is working together to achieve a goal, but in its negative sense it is working as a traitor. It is a recursive process where two or more people or organizations work together to realize shared goals, (this is more than the intersection of common goals seen in co-operative ventures, but a deep, collective, determination to reach an identical objective) – for example, an intruiging endeavor that is creative in nature – by sharing knowledge, learning and building consensus. Most collaboration requires leadership, although the form of leadership can be social within a decentralized and egalitarian group. In particular, teams that work collaboratively can obtain greater resources, recognition and reward when facing competition for finite resources. Collaboration is also present in opposing goals exhibiting the notion of adversarial collaboration, though this is not a common case for using the word.

Collaborative Writing 93

The term collaborative writing refers to projects where written works are created by multiple people together (collaboratively) rather than individually. Some projects are overseen by an editor or editorial team, but many grow without any oversight.

Collected 63, 127, 129, 157

Collected is a best of album by British trip-hop collective Massive Attack.

Collecting 119-120

Collecting includes seeking, locating, acquiring, organizing, cataloging, displaying, storing, and maintaining whatever items are of interest to the individual collector. Some collectors are generalists, accumulating merchandise, or stamps from all countries of the world. Others focus on a subtopic within their area of interest, perhaps 19th century postage stamps, milk bottle labels from Sussex, or Mongolian harnesses and tack.

Collective 82, 110, 142

A collective is a group of entities that share or are motivated by at least one common issue or interest, or work together on a specific project(s) to achieve a common objective. Collectives differ from cooperatives in that they are not necessarily focused upon an economic benefit or saving (but can be that as well). There may be some issues with meaningfully describing the qualities of a collective.

Colour 117, 171

Color or colour (see spelling differences) is the visual perceptual property corresponding in humans to the categories called red, green, blue and others. Color derives from the spectrum of light (distribution of light energy versus wavelength) interacting in the eye with the spectral sensitivities of the light receptors. Color categories and physical specifications of color are also associated with objects, materials, light sources, etc., based on their physical properties such as light absorption, reflection, or emission spectra. By defining a color space, colors can be identified numerically by their coordinates.

Combination 84, 96, 103, 120

In mathematics a combination is a way of selecting several things out of a larger group, where (unlike permutations) order does not matter. In smaller cases it is possible to count the number of combinations. For example given three fruit, an apple, orange and pear say, there are three combinations of two that can be drawn from this set: an apple and a pear; an apple and an orange; or a pear and an orange. More formally a k-combination of a set S is a subset of k distinct elements of S. If the set has n elements the number of k-combinations is equal to the binomial coefficient

Comic 84, 123-125, 127, 140, 154

Comics is a graphic medium in which images convey a sequential narrative. The term derives from the mostly humorous early work in the medium, and came to apply to that form of the medium including those far from comic. The sequential nature of the pictures, and the predominance of pictures over words, distinguishes comics from picture books, though there is some overlap between the two. Most comics combine words with images, often indicating speech in the form of word balloons, but pantomime strips, such as The Little King, are not uncommon. Words other than dialogue, captions for example, usually expand upon the pictures, but sometimes act in counterpoint. Early precursors of comic as they are known today include Trajan's Column and the work of William Hogarth. By the 19th century, the medium as we know it today began to take form among European and American artists. Comics as a real mass medium started to emerge in the United States in the early 20th century with the newspaper comic strip, where its form began to be standardized (image-driven, speech balloons, etc.), first in Sunday strips and later in daily strips. The combination of words and pictures proved popular and quickly spread throughout the world.

Comic Art 123-124

Comic Art is a magazine, edited by Todd Hignite, which surveys newspaper comic strips, magazine cartoon panels and comic book art, both historical and contemporary. Daniel Zimmer is the publication's graphic design and art director.

Comic Book 124

A comic book or comicbook (often shortened to simply comic and sometimes called a funny book, comic paper, or comic magazine) is a magazine made up of comics, narrative artwork in the form of separate panels that represent individual scenes, often accompanied by dialog (usually in word balloons, emblematic of the comic book art form) as well as including brief descriptive prose. The first comic book appeared in the United States in 1932, reprinting the earlier newspaper comic strips, which established many of the storytelling devices used in comics. The term 'comic book' arose because the first comic books reprinted humor comic strips.

Comic Strip 84, 123, 125, 154

A comic strip is a sequence of drawings arranged in interrelated panels to display brief humor or form a narrative, often serialized, with text in balloons and captions.

Comic Strip Artist 123, 125

A cartoonist is a person who specializes in drawing cartoons. Much of this work is humorous, usually created for entertainment, political commentary or advertising. Throughout the 20th century, cartoons were widely published in print media of various kinds, featured in magazines such as The New Yorker and Punch and distributed to newspapers through such organizations as King Features Syndicate. Today, both original cartoons and vintage cartoons can be found online.

Command Line 65

A command-line interface (CLI) is a mechanism for interacting with a computer operating system or software by typing commands to perform specific tasks. This text-only interface contrasts with the use of a mouse pointer with a graphical user interface (GUI) to click on options, or menus on a text user interface (TUI) to select options. This method of instructing a computer to perform a given task is referred to as entering a command: the system waits for the user to conclude the submitting of the text command by pressing the 'Enter' key (a descendant of the 'carriage return' key of a typewriter keyboard).

Comment 107

A comment is generally a verbal or written remark often related to an added piece of information, or an observation or statement. These are usually marked with an abbreviation, such as 'obs.' or 'N.B.'.

Communication 62, 66, 73, 96, 117, 119, 121-122, 131, 134, 155, 158

Communication is the activity of conveying information. Communication requires a sender, a message, and an intended recipient, although the receiver need not be present or aware of the sender's intent to communicate at the time of communication; thus communication can occur across vast distances in time and space. Communication requires that the communicating parties share an area of communicative commonality.

Communication Technology 121

Information and communications technology or information and communication technology, usually called ICT, is often used as an extended synonym for information technology (IT) but is usually a more general term that stresses the role of unified communications and the integration of telecommunications (telephone lines and wireless signals), intelligent building management systems and audio-visual systems in modern information technology. ICT consists of all technical means used to handle information and aid communication, including computer and network hardware, communication middleware as well as necessary software. In other words, ICT consists of IT as well as telephony, broadcast media, all types of audio and video processing and transmission and network based control and monitoring functions. The expression was first used in 1997 in a report by Dennis Stevenson to the UK government and promoted by the new National Curriculum documents for the UK in 2000.

Compatible 63

A family of computer models is said to be compatible if certain software that runs on one of the models can also be run on all other models of the family. The computer models may differ in performance, reliability or some other characteristic. These differences may affect the outcome of the running of the software.

Compiled 77, 92, 119, 122
A compiler is a computer program (or set of programs) that transforms source code written in a programming language (the source language) into another computer language (the target language, often having a binary form known as object code). The most common reason for wanting to transform source code is to create an executable program.

Complexity 83
In general usage, complexity tends to be used to characterize something with many parts in intricate arrangement. The study of these complex linkages is the main goal of network theory and network science. In science there are at this time a number of approaches to characterizing complexity, many of which are reflected in this article. In a business context, complexity management is the methodology to minimize value-destroying complexity and efficiently control value-adding complexity in a cross-functional approach.

Computational Resources 108
In computational complexity theory, a computational resource is a resource used by some computational models in the solution of computational problems.

Computer 63, 66-67, 76, 82, 84, 104, 106, 108, 136, 162, 164, 171
A computer is a programmable machine designed to sequentially and automatically carry out a sequence of arithmetic or logical operations. The particular sequence of operations can be changed readily, allowing the computer to solve more than one kind of problem.

Computer Literacy 66
Computer literacy is defined as the knowledge and ability to use computers and related technology efficiently, with a range of skills covering levels from elementary use to programming and advanced problem solving. Computer literacy can also refer to the comfort level someone has with using computer programs and other applications that are associated with computers. Another valuable component of computer literacy is knowing how computers work and operate. Having basic computer skills is a significant asset in the developed countries.

Computer Science 108, 171
Computer science or computing science (abbreviated CS) is the study of the theoretical foundations of information and computation and of practical techniques for their implementation and application in computer systems. Computer scientists invent algorithmic processes that create, describe, and transform information and formulate suitable abstractions to model complex systems.

Computer Screen 84, 106
A monitor or display (sometimes called a visual display unit) is an electronic visual display for computers. The monitor comprises the display device, circuitry, and an enclosure. The display device in modern monitors is typically a thin film transistor liquid crystal display (TFT-LCD) thin panel, while older monitors use a cathode ray tube about as deep as the screen size. Originally computer monitors were used for data processing and television receivers for entertainment; increasingly computers are being used both for data processing and entertainment and TVs implement some typical computer functionality. Displays exclusively for data use tend to have an aspect ratio of 4:3; those used also (or solely) for entertainment are usually 16:9 widescreen, Sometimes a compromise is used, e.g. 16:10.

Concept 66, 73, 109, 134, 142, 145, 151
A concept (abstract term: conception) is a cognitive unit of meaning – an abstract idea or a mental symbol sometimes defined as a 'unit of knowledge,' built from other units which act as a concept's characteristics. A concept is typically associated with a corresponding representation in a language or symbology such as a single meaning of a term.

Configurations 62, 106, 117
Configurations is an academic journal established in 1993 and the official publication of the Society for Literature, Science, and Arts. It is the only journal devoted to the study of discourse in science, technology, and medicine. The journal investigates the relationship between literature and the arts and science and technology.

Consciousness 61, 97
Consciousness is a term that has been used to refer to a variety of aspects of the relationship between the mind and the world with which it interacts. It has been defined, at one time or another, as: subjective experience; awareness; the ability to experience feelings; wakefulness; having a sense of selfhood; or as the executive control system of the mind. Despite the difficulty of definition, many philosophers believe that there is a basic underlying intuition about consciousness that is shared by nearly all people.

Consumers 70, 105, 145, 156
Consumer is a broad label for any individuals or households that use goods and services generated within the economy. The concept of a consumer occurs in different contexts, so that the usage and significance of the term may vary.

Consumption 52, 102-103, 110, 130
Consumption is a common concept in economics, and gives rise to derived concepts such as consumer debt. Generally, consumption is defined in part by opposition to production. But the precise definition can

vary because different schools of economists define production quite differently. According to mainstream economists, only the final purchase of goods and services by individuals constitutes consumption, while other types of expenditure – in particular, fixed investment and government spending – are placed in separate categories. See consumer choice. Other economists define consumption much more broadly, as the aggregate of all economic activity that does not entail the design, production and marketing of goods and services (e.g. the selection

Contemporary 61, 97, 102, 104, 106, 140, 143, 151-152, 156

Contemporary means coexistent in time. This time can be in the past. As a secondary meaning, contemporary can mean modern, and refer to the present age.

Controlled 168

Control is the ability to purposefully direct, or suppress, change.

Conventional 131

A convention is a set of agreed, stipulated or generally accepted standards, norms, social norms or criteria, often taking the form of a custom.

Conversations 107-108, 121

Conversation is interactive, more-or-less spontaneous, communication between two or more conversants. Interactivity occurs because contributions to a conversation are response reactions to what has previously been said. Spontaneity occurs because a conversation must proceed, to some extent, and in some way, unpredictably. (Contrast with a scripted conversation, which falls outside this definition.) (However, the scope of that spontaneity may legitimately be somewhat pre-limited for the purpose of expediency, e.g. a talk show or a debate.)

Coordinated 111

Motor coordination is the combination of body movements created with the kinematic (such as spatial direction) and kinetic (force) parameters that result in intended actions. Such movements usually smoothly and efficiently work together. Motor coordination can occur between subsequent parts of the same movement and movements of several limbs. Motor coordination involves the integration of processes ranging from how muscles interact with the skeletal system to neural processes controlling them both in the spine and the brain.

Coordination 156

Coordination is the act of coordinating, making different people or things work together for a goal or effect.

Copy Protection 137

Copy protection, also known as content protection, copy obstruction, copy prevention and copy restriction, refer to techniques used for preventing the reproduction of software, films, music, and other media, usually for copyright reasons.

Copying 56

Copying is the duplication of information or an artifact based only on an instance of that information or artifact, and not using the process that originally generated it. With analog forms of information, copying is only possible to a limited degree of accuracy, which depends on the quality of the equipment used and the skill of the operator.

Core Business 124

The core business of an organization is an idealized construct intended to express that organization's 'main' or 'essential' activity.

Counter Movement 131

By definition, a countermovement in sociology means a social movement opposed to another social movement. Whenever one social movement starts up, another group establishes themselves to undermine the previous group. Many social movements start out as an affect of political activism towards issues that a group disagrees with. 'Researchers have used resource mobilization to study all manner of social and political movements such as environmentalism, father's rights groups, religious movements, and abortion righth.' The reason for the start of countermovement groups is that people are competing for resources for political influence. Countermovement groups are a part of American society that try to compete for government legislation to support their own views.

Counterculture 54

Counterculture (also written counter-culture) is a sociological term used to describe the values and norms of behavior of a cultural group, or subculture, that run counter to those of the social mainstream of the day, the cultural equivalent of political opposition. Counterculture can also be described as deviating away from the norm of society, or what is perceived to be normal. This deviation takes a group or behavior to be segregated from the norms. It is a neologism attributed to Theodore Roszak.

Counting 90, 120

Counting is the action of finding the number of elements of a finite set of objects. The traditional way of counting consists of continually increasing a (mental or spoken) counter by a unit for every element of the set, in some order, while marking (or displacing) those elements to avoid visiting the same element more than once, until no unmarked elements are left; if the counter was set to one after the first object, the value after visiting the final object gives the desired number of elements. Counting is also used (primarily by children) to demonstrate knowledge of the number names and the number system. The related term enumeration refers to determining the number of elements of a finite (combinatorial) set in some manner, not necessarily by explicitly counting in the above sense.

Craft 92

A craft is a branch of profession that requires some particular kind of skilled work. In historical sense, particularly as pertinent to the Medieval history and earlier, the term is usually applied towards people occupied in small-scale production of goods.

Creative 73, 83, 105, 122, 131, 147, 167-168, 175

Creative (noun, in advertising), referring to materials, imagery, or collateral prescriptively produced through creativity and the creative process.

Creative Industry 175

The creative industries refers to a range of economic activities which are concerned with the generation or exploitation of knowledge and information. They may variously also be referred to as the cultural industries (especially in Europe (Hesmondhalgh 2002, p.160;14) or the creative economy (Howkins 2001).

Crime and Punishment 52

Crime and Punishment (Russian: Pryestupleniye i nakazaniye) is a novel by the Russian author Fyodor Dostoevsky. It was first published in the Russian literary journal The Russian Messenger in twelve monthly installments during 1866. It was later published in a single volume. This is the second of Dostoevsky's full-length novels following his return from five years of exile in Siberia, where he was serving his sentence in Katorga camps, the Tsarist forced-labor system and predecessor to the Soviet Gulag. Crime and Punishment is the first great novel of his 'mature period' of writing.

Critics 58, 101, 117, 130

A critic is anyone who expresses a value judgement. Informally, criticism is a common aspect of all human expression and need not necessarily imply skilled or accurate expressions of judgement. Critical judgements, good or bad, may be positive (in praise of an object of attention), negative (in dispraise), or balanced (weighing a combination of factors both for and against). Since all criticism must be regarded as having a purpose, a critic may also be definable by his or her specific motivation. At its simplest, and for whatever reason, a critic may have either constructive or destructive intent.

Critique 65

Critique is a method of disciplined, systematic analysis of a written or oral discourse. Critique is an accepted format of written and oral debate. Critique differs from (is not) criticism in that critique is never personalized nor ad hominem, but is instead the analyses of the structure of the thought in the content of the item critiqued. This analysis then offers by way of the critique method either a rebuttal or a suggestion of further expansion upon the problems presented by the topic of that specific written or oral argumentation.

Crouwel 171

Willem Hendrik (Wim) Crouwel (Groningen, 1928) is a Dutch graphic designer and typographer. Between 1947 and 1949 he studied Fine Arts at Academie Minerva in Groningen, the Netherlands. In addition to that, he studied typography at what is now the Gerrit Rietveld Academie in Amsterdam.

Cultural 61, 66, 69, 90, 97, 101, 103, 107-108, 123, 126, 129-132, 174

Culture (from the Latin cultura stemming from colere, meaning to cultivate) is a term that has various meanings.

Culture Industry 65

Culture industry is a term coined by critical theorists Theodor Adorno (1903–1969) and Max Horkheimer (1895–1973), who argued in the final chapter of their book Dialectic of Enlightenment, 'The Culture Industry: Enlightenment as Mass Deception'. Adorno and Horkheimer saw this mass-produced culture as a danger to the more difficult high arts. Culture industries may cultivate false needs; that is, needs created and satisfied by capitalism. True needs, in contrast, are freedom, creativity, or genuine happiness. This was reference to an earlier demarcation in needs by Herbert Marcuse (see Eros and Civilization (1955)).

Culture Media 65

A growth medium or culture medium is a liquid or gel designed to support the growth of microorganisms or cells, or small plants like the moss Physcomitrella patens. There are different types of media for growing different types of cells.

Curation 72

Curation is generally the selection of, care for and presentation of the objects entered into a collection, whether that collection is physical (such as items in a museum) or digital (such as entries in Wikipedia).

Curators 71

Curator (from Latin cura, care), means manager, overseer.

Customer 51, 129

A customer (also known as a client, buyer, or purchaser) is usually used to refer to a current or potential buyer or user of the products of an individual or organization, called the supplier, seller, or vendor. This is typically through purchasing or renting goods or services. However, in certain contexts, the term customer also includes by extension any entity that uses or experiences the services of another. A customer may also be a viewer of the product or service that is being sold despite deciding not to buy them. The general distinction between a customer and a client is that a customer purchases products, whereas a client purchases services.

Cut-and-Paste 67

In human-computer interaction, cut and paste and copy and paste offer user-interface paradigms for transferring text, data, files or objects from a source to a destination. Most ubiquitously, users require the ability to cut and paste sections of plain text. This paradigm has close associations with graphical user interfaces that use pointing devices such as a computer mouse (by drag and drop, for example).

Cyberspace 132

Cyberspace is the electronic medium of computer networks, in which online communication takes place.

Daldry 101

Stephen David Daldry, CBE (born 2 May 1961) is an English theatre and film director and producer, as well as a three-time Academy Award nominated and Tony Award winning director.

DASH 89

A dash is a punctuation mark.

Data 51, 57, 59, 61-64, 71-72, 81, 92, 107-108, 121, 129-130, 145, 151-152, 160, 172

The term data refers to qualitative or quantitative attributes of a variable or set of variables. Data (plural of 'datum') are typically the results of measurements and can be the basis of graphs, images, or observations of a set of variables. Data are often viewed as the lowest level of abstraction from which information and then knowledge are derived. Raw data, i.e. unprocessed data, refers to a collection of numbers, characters, images or other outputs from devices that collect information to convert physical quantities into symbols.

Data Analysis 108

Analysis of data is a process of inspecting, cleaning, transforming, and modeling data with the goal of highlighting useful information, suggesting conclusions, and supporting decision making. Data analysis has multiple facets and approaches, encompassing diverse techniques under a variety of names, in different business, science, and social science domains.

Data Mining 108

Data mining (also known as Knowledge Discovery in Data, or KDD), a relatively young and interdisciplinary of computer science, is the process of extracting patterns from large data sets by combining methods from statistics and artificial intelligence with database management.

Data Object 129

In computer science, an object is any entity that can be manipulated by the commands of a programming language, such as a value, variable, function, or data structure. (With the later introduction of object-oriented programming the same word, 'object', refers to a particular instance of a class).

Data Set 63

A data set (or dataset) is a collection of data, usually presented in tabular form. Each column represents a particular variable. Each row corresponds to a given member of the data set in question. Its values for each of the variables, such as height and weight of an object or values of random numbers. Each value is known as a datum. The data set may comprise data for one or more members, corresponding to the number of rows.

Data Visualization 62-64, 71

Data visualization is the study of the visual representation of data, meaning 'information which has been abstracted in some schematic form, including attributes or variables for the units of information'. According to Friedman (2008) the 'main goal of data visualization is to communicate information clearly and effectively through graphical means. It doesn't mean that data visualization needs to look boring to be functional or extremely sophisticated to look beautiful. To convey ideas effectively, both aesthetic form and functionality need to go hand in hand, providing insights into a rather sparse and complex data set by communicating its key-aspects in a more intuitive way. Yet designers often fail to achieve a balance between design and function, creating gorgeous data visualizations which fail to serve their main purpose – to communicate information'.

Database 129, 135

A database is a system intended to organize, store, and retrieve large amounts of data easily. It consists of an organized collection of data for one or more uses, typically in digital form. One way of classifying databases involves the type of their contents, for example: bibliographic, document-text, statistical. Digital databases are managed using database management systems, which store database contents, allowing data creation and maintenance, and search and other access.

De Volkskrant 55

De Volkskrant (literally 'the people's paper') is a national daily Dutch morning newspaper, the leading left-of-center broadsheet (albeit now in tabloid size).

De-facto 65

De facto is a Latin expression that means by [the] fact.

Debate 70

Debate or debating is a formal method of interactive and representational argument. Debate is a broader form of argument than logical argument, which only examines consistency from axiom, and factual argument, which only examines what is or isn't the case or rhetoric which is a technique of persuasion. Though logical consistency, factual accuracy and some degree of emotional appeal to the audience are important elements of the art of persuasion, in debating, one side often prevails over the other side by presenting a superior 'context' and/or framework of the issue, which is far more subtle and strategic.

Deciphering 98

Decipherment is the analysis of documents written in ancient languages, where the language is unknown, or knowledge of the language has been lost.

Declare 113

Declare (2001) is a supernatural spy novel by Tim Powers. It presents a secret history of the Cold War in which an agent for a secret British spy organization learns the true nature of several beings living on Mount Ararat. In this he is opposed by real-life communist traitor Kim Philby, who did travel extensively in the region. Philby's father, St. John Philby, was a noted Arabist whose book The Empty Quarter (on the Rub' al Khali) was extensively used as source material for the novel.

Decoding 132

In computer science and linguistics, parsing, or, more formally, syntactic analysis, is the process of analyzing a text, made of a sequence of tokens (for example, words), to determine its grammatical structure with respect to a given (more or less) formal grammar. Parsing can also be used as a linguistic term, especially in reference to how phrases are divided up in garden path sentences. Parsing is also an earlier term for the diagramming of sentences of natural languages, and is still used for the diagramming of inflected languages, such as the Romance languages or Latin. The term parsing comes from Latin pars, meaning part (of speech). Parsing is a common term used in psycholinguistics when describing language comprehension. In this context, parsing refers to the way that human beings, rather than computers, analyze a sentence or phrase (in spoken language or text) 'in terms of grammatical constituents, identifying the parts of speech, syntactic relations, etc.' This term is especially common when discussing what linguistic cues help speakers to parse garden-path sentences.

Deconstructionism 61

Deconstruction is a term that French philosopher Jacques Derrida introduced in 1967, with the purpose of translating and adapting to his own ends Martin Heidegger's German word Destruktion or Abbau. Heidegger's word was used in the sense of historicize the tradition, its categories and concepts, overcoming its conceal and blocks to our access to its primordial 'sources'.

Definition 70, 75, 146, 151, 159

A definition is a passage that explains the meaning of a term (a word, phrase or other set of symbols), or a type of thing. The term to be defined is the definiendum. A term may have many different senses or meanings. For each such specific sense, a definiens is a cluster of words that defines that term.

Degeneration 130

The idea of degeneration had significant influence on science, art and politics from the 1850s to the 1950s. The social theory developed consequently from Charles Darwin's Theory of Evolution. Evolution meant that mankind's development was no longer fixed and certain, but could change and evolve or degenerate into an unknown future, possibly a bleak future that clashes with the analogy between evolution and civilization as a progressive positive direction.

Demarcated 115

A demarcation line means simply a boundary around a specific area, but is commonly used to denote a temporary geopolitical border, often agreed upon as part of an armistice or ceasefire.

Democratization 158

Democratization (or democratisation) is the transition to a more democratic political regime. It may be the transition from an authoritarian regime to a full democracy, a transition from an authoritarian political system to a semi-democracy or transition from a semi-authoritarian political system to a democratic political system. The outcome may be consolidated (as it was for example in the United Kingdom) or democratization may face frequent reversals (as it has faced for example in Argentina). Different patterns of democratization are often used to explain other political phenomena, such as whether a country goes to a war or whether its economy grows. Democratization itself is influenced by various factors, including economic development, history, and civil society.

Denote 165

In semiotics, denotation is the surface or literal meaning encoded to a signifier, and the definition most likely to appear in a dictionary.

Deprogram 68

Deprogramming refers to actions that attempt to force a person to abandon allegiance to a religious, political, economic, or social group. Methods and practices may involve kidnapping and coercion. Similar actions, when done without force, are called exit counseling.

Derived 64, 120, 122

In phylogenetics, a derived trait is a trait that is present in an organism, but was absent in the last common ancestor of the group being considered. This may also refer to structures that are not present in an organism, but were present in its ancestors, i.e. traits that have undergone secondary loss. Here the lack of a structure is a derived trait.

Derrida 61, 79, 104

Jacques Derrida (15 July 1930–9 October 2004) was a French philosopher, born in French Algeria. He developed the critical theory known as deconstruction, his work has been labeled as post-structuralism and associated with postmodern philosophy. His prolific output of more than 40 published books, together with essays and public speaking, has had a significant impact upon the humanities, particularly on literary theory and continental philosophy. Perhaps Derrida's most quoted and famous assertion ever, is the axial statement of his whole essay on Rousseau (part of his highly influential Of Grammatology,

1967), is 'there is nothing outside the text' (il n'y a pas de hors-texte), meaning that there is nothing outside context. Critics of Derrida have countless times quoted it as a slogan to characterize and stigmatize deconstruction.

Description 107, 165
Description is one of four rhetorical modes (also known as modes of discourse), along with exposition, argumentation, and narration. Each of the rhetorical modes is present in a variety of forms and each has its own purpose and conventions.

Designer 60, 72, 75, 77-78, 110, 117, 123, 127, 138, 157, 161
A designer is a person who designs. More formally, a designer is an agent that 'specifies the structural properties of a design object'. In practice, anyone who creates tangible or intangible objects, such as consumer products, processes, laws, games and graphics, is referred to as a designer. Classically, the main areas of design were only Painting, Sculpture and Architecture, which were understood as the major arts. The design of clothing, furniture and other common artifacts were left mostly to tradition or artisans specializing in hand making them. With the increasing complexity of today's society, and due to the needs of mass production where more time is usually associated with more cost, the production methods became more complex and with them the way designs and their production is created. The classical areas are now subdivided in smaller and more specialized domains of design (Landscape Design, Urban Design, Exterior Design, Interior Design, Industrial Design, Furniture Design, Cloth Design, and many more) according to the product designed or perhaps its means of production.

Designs 54
Design as a noun informally refers to a plan for the construction of an object or a system (as in architectural blueprints, engineering drawing, business process, circuit diagrams and sewing patterns) while 'to design' (verb) refers to making this plan. No generally-accepted definition of 'design' exists, and the term has different connotations in different fields (see design disciplines below). However, one can also design by directly constructing an object (as in pottery, engineering, management, cowboy coding and graphic design).

Desk 76, 78, 95, 136
A desk is a furniture form and a class of table often used in a work or office setting for reading or writing on or using a computer. Desks often have one or more drawers to store office supplies and papers. Unlike a regular table, usually only one side of a desk is suitable to sit on (though there are some exceptions, such as a partners desk). Not all desks have the form of a table. For instance, an armoire desk is a desk built within a large wardrobe-like cabinet, and a portable desk is light enough to be placed on a person's lap. Since many people lean on a desk while using it, a desk must be sturdy.

Desmond 85
Norma Desmond is the fictional main character in Billy Wilder's film Sunset Boulevard.

DeviantART.com 109
DeviantArt (official typeset as deviantART; commonly abbreviated as dA) is an online community showcasing various forms of user-made artwork. It was first launched on August 7, 2000 by Scott Jarkoff, Matthew Stephens, Angelo Sotira and others. deviantArt, Inc. is headquartered in the Hollywood area of Los Angeles, California, United States.

Diagram 69, 89
A diagram is a two-dimensional geometric symbolic representation of information according to some visualization technique. Sometimes, the technique uses a three-dimensional visualization which is then projected onto the two-dimensional surface. The word graph is sometimes used as a synonym for diagram.

Dialogues 70
Dialogue (sometimes spelled dialog in American English) is a literary and theatrical form consisting of a written or spoken conversational exchange between two or more people.

Diary 88, 132
A diary is a record (originally in handwritten format) with discrete entries arranged by date reporting on what has happened over the course of a day or other period. Diaries undertaken for institutional purposes play a role in many aspects of human civilization, including government records (e.g., Hansard), business ledgers and military records.

Digital Connectivity 105
Digital Connectivity is a DVD by Los Angeles industrial metal band Fear Factory released in 2001 on Roadrunner Records.

Digital Display 105
A display device is an output device for presentation of information in visual or tactile form. When the input information is supplied as an electrical signal, the display is called an electronic display. Tactile electronic displays (aka refreshable Braille display) are usually intended for the blind. They use electro-mechanical parts to dynamically update a tactile image (usually of text) so that the image may be felt by the fingers.

Digital Domain 110
Digital Domain is a visual effects and animation company founded by film director James Cameron, Stan Winston and Scott Ross. It is based in Venice, Los Angeles, California. The company is known for creating state-of-the-art digital imagery for feature films, television advertising, interactive visual media and the video game industry.

Digital Information 113
A digital system is a data technology that uses discrete (discontinuous) values. By contrast, non-digital (or analog) systems use a continuous range of values to represent

information. Although digital representations are discrete, the information represented can be either discrete, such as numbers, letters or icons, or continuous, such as sounds, images, and other measurements of continuous systems.

Digital Media 55, 158
Digital media is a form of electronic media where data is stored in digital (as opposed to analog) form. It can refer to the technical aspect of storage and transmission (e.g. hard disk drives or computer networking) of information or to the 'end product', such as digital video, augmented reality or digital art.

Digital Network 52
Digital electronics represent signals by discrete bands of analog levels, rather than by a continuous range. All levels within a band represent the same signal state. Relatively small changes to the analog signal levels due to manufacturing tolerance, signal attenuation or parasitic noise do not leave the discrete envelope, and as a result are ignored by signal state sensing circuitry.

Digital Research 77
Digital Research, Inc. (aka DR or DRI; originally Intergalactic Digital Research) was the company created by Dr. Gary Kildall to market and develop his CP/M operating system and related products. It was the first large software company in the microcomputer world. Digital Research was based in Pacific Grove, California.

Digital Revolution 84
The Digital Revolution is the change from analog mechanical and electronic technology to digital technology that has taken place since c. 1980 and continues to the present day. Implicitly, the term also refers to the sweeping changes brought about by digital computing and communication technology during the latter half of the 20th century. Analogous to the Agricultural Revolution and Industrial Revolution, the Digital Revolution marked the beginning of the Information Age.

Digital Technology 101, 159, 170
Digital electronics represent signals by discrete bands of analog levels, rather than by a continuous range. All levels within a band represent the same signal state. Relatively small changes to the analog signal levels due to manufacturing tolerance, signal attenuation or parasitic noise do not leave the discrete envelope, and as a result are ignored by signal state sensing circuitry.

Digital Traces 107
A digital footprint is a trail left by an entity's interactions in a digital environment; including their usage of TV, mobile phone, internet and world wide web, mobile web and other devices and sensors. Digital footprints provide data on what an entity has performed in the digital environment; and are valuable in assisting behavioural targeting, personalization, targeted marketing, digital reputation, and other social media or social graphing services.

Digital Transmission 139-140
Data transmission, digital transmission, or digital communications is the physical transfer of data (a digital bit stream) over a point-to-point or point-to-multipoint communication channel. Examples of such channels are copper wires, optical fibres, wireless communication channels, and storage media. The data is represented as an electromagnetic signal, such as an electrical voltage, radiowave, microwave, or infrared signal.

Digital TV 159
Digital television (DTV) is the transmission of audio and video by digital signals, in contrast to the analog signals used by analog TV. Many countries are replacing over-the-air broadcast analog television with digital television to allow other uses of the radio spectrum formerly used for analog TV broadcast.

Digitality 68
Digitality is used to mean the condition of living in a digital culture, derived from Nicholas Negroponte's book Being Digital in analogy with modernity and post-modernity.

Discipline 162
In its original sense, discipline referred to systematic instruction given to a disciples to train them as students in a craft or trade, or to follow a particular code of conduct or order.

Discourse 72
Discourse (from Latin discursus, meaning running to and from) generally refers to 'written or spoken communication or debate'.

Discourses 122
Discourse is a term used in semantics, philosophy and discourse analysis.

Disguise 60
A disguise can be anything which conceals or changes a person's physical appearance, including a wig, glasses, makeup, costume or other ways. Camouflage is one type of disguise for people, animals and objects. Hats, glasses, change in hair style or wigs, plastic surgery, and make-up are also used. Internationally Fancy Dress Costumes are described as Disguises.

Dissemination 96
To disseminate, in terms of the field of communication, means to broadcast a message to the public without direct feedback from the audience. Dissemination takes on the theory of the traditional view of communication, which involves a sender and receiver. The traditional communication view point is broken down into a sender sending information, and receiver collecting the information processing it and sending information back, like a telephone line.

Dissertations 104
A dissertation or thesis is a document submitted in support of candidature for an academic degree or professional qualification presenting the author's research and findings.

Distance 61, 73
Distance is a numerical description of how far apart objects are. In physics or everyday discussion, distance may refer to a physical length, or an estimation based on other criteria (e.g. 'two counties over').

Distracted 83, 102
Distraction is the divided attention of an individual or group from the chosen object of attention onto the source of distraction. Distraction is caused by: the lack of ability to pay attention; lack of interest in the object of attention; or the great intensity, novelty or attractiveness of something other than the object of attention. Distractions come from both external sources, and internal sources. Multitasking could also be considered as distraction in situations requiring full attention on a single object (e.g. sports, academic tests, performance).

Distributed Systems 80
Distributed computing is a field of computer science that studies distributed systems. A distributed system consists of multiple autonomous computers that communicate through a computer network. The computers interact with each other in order to achieve a common goal. A computer program that runs in a distributed system is called a distributed program, and distributed programming is the process of writing such programs.

Distribution Channels 55
Product distribution (or place) is one of the four elements of the marketing mix. An organization or set of organizations (go-betweens) involved in the process of making a product or service available for use or consumption by a consumer or business user.

Distribution Lists 135
Distribution list is a term sometimes used for a function of email clients where lists of email addresses are used to email everyone on the list at once. This can be referred to as an electronic mailshot. It differs from a mailing list, electronic mailing list or the email option found in an Internet forum as it is usually for one way traffic and not for coordinating a discussion. In effect, only members of a distribution list can send mails to the list.

Do-It-Yourself 173
Do it yourself (or DIY) is a term used to describe building, modifying, or repairing of something without the aid of experts or professionals. The phrase 'do it yourself' came into common usage in the 1950s in reference to home improvement projects which people might choose to complete independently.

Doctoral 104
A doctorate is an academic degree or professional degree that in most countries refers to a class of degrees which qualify the holder to teach in a specific field, (e.g. a Doctor of Philosophy (Ph.D.).

Document 106
A document is a work of non-fiction writing intended to store and communicate information, thus acting as a recording. Documents are often the focus and concern of business administration and government administration. The word is also used as a verb as documenting describes the process of making a document.

Documentary 90, 125, 152
Documentary film is a broad category of motion pictures intended to document some aspect of reality. A documentary film was originally a movie shot on film stock – the only medium available – but now includes video and digital productions that can be either direct-to-video or made for a television program.

Documentation 140
Documentation is a general term for a multiplicity of documents in a chosen mix of media and with a certain collection. Purpose of documentation is the use to support a tool or a process.

Donald Duck 116
Donald Fauntleroy Duck is an American cartoon character from The Walt Disney Company. Donald is a white anthropomorphic duck with a yellow-orange bill, legs, and feet. He usually wears a sailor shirt, cap, and a red bow tie, but no trousers (except when he goes swimming). Donald's most famous personality trait is his easily provoked and explosive temper. Donald Duck has been officially honored as the third most popular cartoon character of all time with Bugs Bunny of Warner Bros. Looney Tunes/Merrie Melodies at number two and fellow Disney creation Mickey Mouse who is number one. Donald Duck was first known as Donald Oliver Duckling.

Dots per Inch 171
Dots per inch (DPI) is a measure of spatial printing or video dot density, in particular the number of individual dots that can be placed in a line within the span of 1 inch (2.54 cm). The DPI value tends to correlate with image resolution, but is related only indirectly.

Download 51, 88, 128, 155
In computer networks, to download means to receive data to a local system from a remote system, or to initiate such a data transfer. Examples of a remote system from which a download might be performed include a webserver, FTP server, email server, or other similar systems. A download can mean either any file that is offered for downloading or that has been downloaded, or the process of receiving such a file.

Drawing 124, 162

Drawing is a visual art that makes use of any number of drawing instruments to mark a two-dimensional medium. Common instruments include graphite pencils, pen and ink, inked brushes, wax color pencils, crayons, charcoals, chalk, pastels, markers, stylus, or various metals like silverpoint. An artist who practices or works in drawing may be referred to as a draughtsman or draftsman.

DTP 160

Desktop publishing (also known as DTP) combines a personal computer and WYSIWYG page layout software to create publication documents on a computer for either large scale publishing or small scale local multi-function peripheral output and distribution.

Dumbing Down 96, 145

Dumbing down is a pejorative term for a perceived over-simplification of education, news and television (among other things), or as a statement of truth about real cultural trends in education and culture. According to John Algeo, former editor of American Speech, the neologism dumb down 'revise so as to appeal to those of little education or intelligence' was first recorded in 1933 as movie slang and dumb up in 1928.

Dvds 144

DVD (Digital Versatile Disk) is an optical disc storage media format, invented and developed by Philips, Sony, Toshiba, and Time Warner in 1995. DVD discs offer higher storage capacity than compact discs while having the same dimensions.

E-mail 63, 66, 169-170

Electronic mail, commonly called email or e-mail, is a method of exchanging digital messages from an author to one or more recipients. Modern email operates across the Internet or other computer networks. Some early email systems required that the author and the recipient both be online at the same time, a la instant messaging. Today's email systems are based on a store-and-forward model. Email servers accept, forward, deliver and store messages. Neither the users nor their computers are required to be online simultaneously; they need connect only briefly, typically to an email server, for as long as it takes to send or receive messages.

E-Reader 114, 118, 148, 159, 164, 166

E-Reader may refer to: An eBook reader, also called an eBook device or eReader, is a portable electronic device that is designed primarily for the purpose of reading digital books and periodicals.

Ease of Use 134

Usability is the ease of use and learnability of a human-made object. The object of use can be a software application, website, book, tool, machine, process, or anything a human interacts with. A usability study may be conducted as a primary job function by a usability analyst or as a secondary job function by designers, technical writers, marketing personnel, and others. It is widely used in consumer electronics, communication, and knowledge transfer objects (such as a cookbook, a document or online help) and mechanical objects such as a door handle or a hammer.

East and West 94

The East-West dichotomy is a sociological concept used to describe perceived differences between Western cultures and the Eastern world. Cultural rather than geographical in division, the boundaries of East and West are not fixed, but vary according to the criteria adopted by individuals using the term. Historically, Islamic and Asian nations have been regarded as East, while the United States and Western Europe are regarded as West. Used in discussing such studies as management, economics and linguistics, the concept is criticized for overlooking regional hybridity.

Ebook Readers 129

An e-book reader, also called an eBook device or eReader, is a portable electronic device that is designed primarily for the purpose of reading digital books and periodicals.

Editing 94-95, 126

Editing is the process of selecting and preparing written, visual, audible, and film medium used to convey information through the processes of correction, condensation, organization, and other modifications in various media, performed with an intention of producing a correct, consistent, accurate, and complete output.

Editorial 63, 78, 95, 102, 104

An editorial is an opinion piece written by the senior editorial staff or publisher of a newspaper or magazine. Editorials are usually unsigned and may be supposed to reflect the opinion of the periodical. In the UK, these unsigned columns are known as 'leading articles'. In major United States newspapers, such as The New York Times and the Boston Globe, editorials are classified under the heading 'opinion'. Editorials may also be in the form of editorial cartoons. Typically, a newspaper's editorial board evaluates which issues are important for their readership to know the newspaper's opinion. In the field of fashion publishing especially, the term has been adapted to usually refer to photo-editorials in particular – features with often full-page photographs on a particular theme, designer, model or other single topic, with or (as a photo-essay) without accompanying text.

Editors 71

Editors are a British indie rock band based in Birmingham, who formed in 2002. Previously known as Pilot, The Pride and Snowfield, the band consists of Tom Smith (lead vocals, rhythm guitar, piano), Chris Urbanowicz (lead guitar, synthesizer), Russell Leetch (bass guitar, backing vocals) and Ed Lay (drums, percussion).

Educating 83

Education in the largest sense is any act or experience that has a formative effect on the mind, character or physical ability of an individual. In its technical sense, education is the process by which society deliberately transmits its accumulated knowledge, skills and values from one generation to another.

Eisner 123-124

William Erwin 'Will' Eisner (March 6, 1917–January 3, 2005) was an American comics writer, artist and entrepreneur. He is considered one of the most important contributors to the development of the medium and is known for the cartooning studio he founded; for his highly influential series The Spirit; for his use of comics as an instructional medium; for his leading role in establishing the graphic novel as a form of literature with his book A Contract with God and Other Tenement Stories; and for his educational work about the medium as exemplified by his book Comics and Sequential Art.

Electronic Book 167

An electronic book (also eBook, ebook, digital book) is a text and image-based publication in digital form produced on, published by, and readable on computers or other digital devices. Sometimes the equivalent of a conventional printed book, eBooks can also be born digital. The Oxford Dictionary of English defines the eBook as 'an electronic version of a printed book,' but eBooks can and do exist without any printed equivalent. eBooks are usually read on dedicated hardware devices known as eReaders or eBook devices. Personal computers and some cell phones can also be used to read eBooks.

Electronic Devices 87

Electronics is the branch of science and technology that deals with electrical circuits involving active electrical components such as vacuum tubes, transistors, diodes and integrated circuits. The nonlinear behaviour of these components and their ability to control electron flows makes amplification of weak signals possible, and is usually applied to information and signal processing.

Electronic Media 101, 115, 143

Electronic media are media that use electronics or electromechanical energy for the end-user (audience) to access the content. This is in contrast to static media (mainly print media), which today are most often created electronically, but don't require electronics to be accessed by the end-user in the printed form. The primary electronic media sources familiar to the general public are better known as video recordings, audio recordings, multimedia presentations, slide presentations, CD-ROM and online content. Most new media are in the form of digital media. However, electronic media may be in either analog or digital format.

Electronic Networks 130

An electronic communication network (ECN) is the term used in financial circles for a type of computer system that facilitates trading of financial products outside of stock exchanges. The primary products that are traded on ECNs are stocks and currencies. The first ECN, Instinet, was created in 1969. ECNs increase competition among trading firms by lowering transaction costs, giving clients full access to their order books, and offering order matching outside of traditional exchange hours. ECN's are sometimes also referred to as Alternative Trading Networks.

Electronic Paper 99

Electronic paper, e-paper and electronic ink are a range of display technologies which are designed to mimic the appearance of ordinary ink on paper. Unlike conventional backlit flat panel displays, electronic paper displays reflect light like ordinary paper. Many of the technologies can hold text and images indefinitely without using electricity, while allowing images to be changed later. Flexible electronic paper uses plastic substrates and plastic electronics for the display backplane.

Elitist 73, 98

Elitism is the belief or attitude that some individuals, who form an elite – a select group of people with intellect, wealth, specialized training or experience, or other distinctive attributes – are those whose views on a matter are to be taken the most seriously or carry the most weight or those who view their own views as so; whose views and/or actions are most likely to be constructive to society as a whole; or whose extraordinary skills, abilities or wisdom render them especially fit to govern.

Elocution 75

Elocution is the study of formal speaking in pronunciation, grammar, style, and tone.

Eloquent 158

Eloquence (from Latin eloquentia) is fluent, forcible, elegant or persuasive speaking. It is primarily the power of expressing strong emotions in striking and appropriate language, thereby producing conviction or persuasion. The term is also used for writing in a fluent style.

Embedding 104

In mathematics, an embedding (or imbedding) is one instance of some mathematical structure contained within another instance, such as a group that is a subgroup.

Emergence 61, 81, 107

In philosophy, systems theory, science, and art, emergence is the way complex systems and patterns arise out of a multiplicity of relatively simple interactions. Emergence is central to the theories of integrative levels and of complex systems.

Empirical Research 50

Empirical research is a way of gaining knowledge by means of direct observation or experience. Empirical evidence (the record of one's direct observations or experiences) can be analyzed quantitatively or qualitatively. Through quantifying the evidence or making sense of it in qualitative form, a researcher can answer empirical questions, which should be clearly defined and answerable with the evidence collected (usually called data). Research design varies by field and by the question being investigated. Many researchers combine qualitative and quantitative forms of analysis to better answer questions which cannot be studied in laboratory settings, particularly in the social sciences and in education.

Emulated 138

An emulator in computing duplicates (provides an emulation of) the functions of one system using a different system, so that the second system behaves like (and appears to be) the first system. This focus on exact reproduction of external behavior is in contrast to some other forms of computer simulation, which can concern an abstract model of the system being simulated.

Encyclopaedia 162

An encyclopaedia (also spelled encyclopedia or encyclopædia) is a type of reference work, a compendium holding a summary of information from either all branches of knowledge or a particular branch of knowledge.

Engineer 151

An engineer is a professional practitioner of engineering, concerned with applying scientific knowledge, mathematics and ingenuity to develop solutions for technical problems. Engineers design materials, structures, machines and systems while considering the limitations imposed by practicality, safety and cost. The word engineer is derived from the Latin root ingenium, meaning cleverness.

Engraved 120, 171

Engraving is the practice of incising a design on to a hard, usually flat surface, by cutting grooves into it. The result may be a decorated object in itself, as when silver, gold, steel, or glass are engraved, or may provide an intaglio printing plate, of copper or another metal, for printing images on paper as prints or illustrations; these images are also called engravings.

Enigma 97

An Enigma machine is any of a family of related electro-mechanical rotor machines used for the encryption and decryption of secret messages. The first Enigma was invented by German engineer Arthur Scherbius at the end of World War I. This model and its variants were used commercially from the early 1920s, and adopted by military and government services of several countries – most notably by Nazi Germany before and during World War II. Several different Enigma models were produced, but the German military models, the Wehrmacht Enigmas, are the ones most commonly discussed.

Envision 122

Envision means to conceive or see something within one's mind; to imagine.

Epitaph 119-121

An epitaph (from Greek epitaphion 'a funeral oration' from epi 'at, over' and taphos 'tomb') is a short text honouring a deceased person, strictly speaking that is inscribed on their tombstone or plaque, but also used figuratively. Some are specified by the dead person beforehand, others chosen by those responsible for the burial. An epitaph may be in poem verse; poets have been known to compose their own epitaphs prior to their death, as W.B. Yeats did.

Equivalents 54

'Equivalents' is a series of photographs of clouds taken by Alfred Stieglitz from 1925 to 1934. They are generally recognized as the first photographs intended to free the subject matter from literal interpretation, and, as such, are some of the first completely abstract photographic works of art.

Ergonomics 51

Ergonomics is the study of designing equipment and devices that fit the human body, its movements, and its cognitive abilities.

Espresso Book Machine 87

The Espresso Book Machine (EBM) is a print on demand (POD) machine that prints, collates, covers, and binds a single book in a few minutes. A single machine can cost from $97,000 plus printer.

Essay 126, 143

An essay is a short piece of writing which is often written from an author's personal point of view. Essays can consist of a number of elements, including: literary criticism, political manifestos, learned arguments, observations of daily life, recollections, and reflections of the author. The definition of an essay is vague, overlapping with those of an article and a short story. Almost all modern essays are written in prose, but works in verse have been dubbed essays (e.g. Alexander Pope's An Essay on Criticism and An Essay on Man). While brevity usually defines an essay, voluminous works like John Locke's An Essay Concerning Human Understanding and Thomas Malthus's An Essay on the Principle of Population provide counterexamples.

Ethics 70

Ethics, also known as moral philosophy, is a branch of philosophy that addresses questions about morality – that is, concepts such as good and evil, right and wrong, virtue and vice, justice, etc.

Evenings 158

De Avonden, international title Evenings, is a 1988 Dutch film directed by Rudolf van den Berg. It is based on the novel of the same title by Gerard Reve.

Everything is Possible 121

Everything is Possible: The Best of Os Mutantes is a best of compilation by the Brazilian tropicalia band Os Mutantes. Compiled by David Byrne of Talking Heads, it was released by his world music record label Luaka Bop in 1999. Aimed towards an English-speaking market, its track selection differs much from other Mutantes compilations. It includes an abridged version of Ando Meio Desligado.

Expanded Books 175

The Expanded Books Project was an undertaking at The Voyager Company during 1991, that investigated ideas on how a book could be presented on a computer screen in a way that would be both familiar and useful to regular book readers. A lot of time was spent thinking about font choice, font size, line spacing, margin notes, book marks, and so on.

Expert 63, 163

An expert (Audio (US) (help·info)) is someone widely recognized as a reliable source of technique or skill whose faculty for judging or deciding rightly, justly, or wisely is accorded authority and status by their peers or the public in a specific well-distinguished domain. An expert, more generally, is a person with extensive knowledge or ability based on research, experience, or occupation and in a particular area of study. Experts are called in for advice on their respective subject, but they do not always agree on the particulars of a field of study. An expert can be, by virtue of credential, training, education, profession, publication or experience, believed to have special knowledge of a subject beyond that of the average person, sufficient that others may officially (and legally) rely upon the individual's opinion. Historically, an expert was referred to as a sage (Sophos). The individual was usually a profound thinker distinguished for wisdom and sound judgment.

Extrapolate 114

In mathematics, extrapolation is the process of constructing new data points outside a discrete set of known data points. It is similar to the process of interpolation, which constructs new points between known points, but the results of extrapolations are often less meaningful, and are subject to greater uncertainty. It may also mean extension of a method, assuming similar methods will be applicable. Extrapolation may also apply to human experience to project, extend, or expand known experience into an area not known or previously experienced so as to arrive at a (usually conjectural) knowledge of the unknown (e.g. a driver extrapolates road conditions beyond his sight while driving).

Eyeglasses 135

Glasses (eyeglasses, spectacles, specs) are frames bearing lenses worn in front of the eyes for vision correction or eye protection. Safety glasses are a kind of eye protection against flying debris or against visible and near visible light or radiation. Sunglasses allow better vision in bright daylight, and may protect against damage from high levels of ultraviolet light. Other types of glasses may be used for viewing visual information (such as stereoscopy) or simply just for aesthetic or fashion values.

Face Value 147

The Face value is the value of a coin, stamp or paper money, as printed on the coin, stamp or bill itself by the minting authority. While the face value usually refers to the true value of the coin, stamp or bill in question (as with circulation coins) it can sometimes be largely symbolic, as is often the case with bullion coins. For example, a one troy ounce (31 g) American Gold Eagle bullion coin was worth and sold for about $1200 USD during 2009 market prices (as of November 14, 2009) and yet has a face value of only $50 USD.

Facebook 56, 65, 81, 103, 129, 136, 145, 149

Facebook (stylized facebook) is a social networking service and website launched in February 2004, operated and privately owned by Facebook, Inc. As of January 2011[update], Facebook has more than 600 million active users. Users may create a personal profile, add other users as friends, and exchange messages, including automatic notifications when they update their profile. Additionally, users may join common interest user groups, organized358by workplace, school or college, or other characteristics. The name of the service stems from the colloquial name for the book given to students at the start of the academic year by university administrations in the United States to help students get to know each other better. Facebook allows anyone who declares themselves to be at least 13 years old to become a registered user of the website.

Facsimile 87

A facsimile (from Latin fac simile, 'made alike') is a copy or reproduction of an old book, manuscript, map, art print, or other item of historical value that is as true to the original source as possible. It differs from other forms of reproduction by attempting to replicate the source as accurately as possible in terms of scale, color, condition, and other material qualities. For books and manuscripts, this also entails a complete copy of all pages; hence an incomplete copy is a 'partial facsimile'. Facsimiles are used, for example, by scholars to research a source that they do not have access to otherwise and by museums and archives for museum and media preservation. Many are sold commercially, often accompanied by a volume of commentary. They may be produced in limited editions, typically of 500–2,000 copies, and cost the equivalent of a few thousand United States dollars.

Fading 58, 144-145

In wireless communications, fading is deviation of the attenuation that a carrier-modulated telecommunication signal experiences over certain propagation media. The fading may vary with time, geographical position and/or radio frequency, and is often modelled as a random process. A fading channel is a communication channel that experiences fading. In wireless systems, fading may either be due to multipath propagation, referred to as multipath induced fading, or due to shadowing from obstacles affecting the wave propagation, sometimes referred to as shadow fading.

Fake 85

Fake is a seven-volume Boys' Love (shōjo with homosexual male themes) manga by Sanami Matoh. The story focuses in a romance between Randy 'Ryo' Maclean and Dee Laytner, two New York City detectives from the fictitious 27th precinct. An anime version of the fifth act (or chapter) from the second manga is also available, in the form of an OVA.

Fashion 119, 131, 155

Fashion, a general term for a currently popular style or practice, especially in clothing, foot wear or accessories. Fashion references to anything that is the current trend in look and dress up of a person.

Faulkner 101

William Cuthbert Faulkner (September 25, 1897–July 6, 1962) was an American writer of novels, short stories, poetry and occasional screenplays.

Featuring 124

Featuring, often abbreviated to ft., feat. or f/ is a term used in the music industry to credit a musician who is not the main artist for their performance on a song or, on occasion, an album. The number of songs with a featured artist has increased considerably in the 2000s, although artists being featured can be traced back to the start of singles charts, with the first use of the term in the UK Singles Chart in July 1954 by 'The Four Aces featuring Al Alberts' with 'Three Coins In The Fountain' at 5th place.

Feedback 94, 118, 139

Feedback describes the situation when output from (or information about the result of) an event or phenomenon in the past will influence an occurrence or occurrences of the same (i.e. same defined) event / phenomenon (or the continuation / development of the original phenomenon) in the present or future. When an event is part of a chain of cause-and-effect that forms a circuit or loop, then the event is said to feed back into itself.

Feuilleton 72

The feuilleton may be described as a 'talk of the town', and a contemporary English-language example of the form is the 'Talk of the Town' section of The New Yorker. In English newspapers, the term 'feuilleton' instead came to refer to an installment of a serial story printed in one part of a newspaper. The genre of the feuilleton in its French sense was eventually included in English newspapers, but was not referred to as a feuilleton. In contemporary French, feuilleton takes on the definition of 'soap opera,' specifically ones aired for television. German and Polish newspapers still use the term for their literary and arts sections. The term feuilleton was invented by Julien Louis Geoffroy and Bertin the Elder, editors of the French Journal des Débats in 1800.

Field of Vision 147, 167

The field of view (also field of vision, abbreviated FOV) is the (angular or linear or areal) extent of the observable world that is seen at any given moment.

File Formats 105

A file format is a particular way that information is encoded for storage in a computer file.

Filing Cabinets 76

A filing cabinet (or sometimes file cabinet in American English) is a piece of office furniture usually used to store paper documents in file folders. In the most simple sense, it is an enclosure for drawers in which items are stored. The two most common forms of filing cabinets are lateral files and vertical files. A vertical file cabinet has drawers that extend from the short side (typically 15 inches) of the cabinet. A lateral file cabinet has drawers that extend from the long side (various lengths) of the cabinet. These are also called side filers in Great Britain. There are also shelf files. In the United States, file cabinets are usually built to accommodate 8.5 x 11 paper, and in other countries, filing cabinets are often designed to hold other sizes of paper, such as A4 paper.

Finite Space 102

In mathematics, a finite topological space is a topological space for which the underlying point set is finite. That is, it is a topological space for which there are only finitely many points.

First-Person Shooter 117

First-person shooter (FPS) is a video game genre which centers the gameplay around gun and projectile weapon-based combat through the first person perspective; i.e., the player experiences the action through the eyes of a protagonist. Generally speaking, the first-person shooter shares common traits with other shooter games, which in turn fall under the heading action game. From the genre's inception, advanced 3D or pseudo-3D graphics elements have challenged hardware development, and multiplayer gaming has been integral.

Five Years 73

'Five Years' is a song written by David Bowie and released in 1972. It was the opening track on the album The Rise and Fall of Ziggy Stardust and the Spiders from Mars.

Flickr 65, 108

Flickr is an image hosting and video hosting website, web services suite, and online community created by Ludicorp and later acquired by Yahoo!. In addition to being a popular website for users to share and embed personal photographs, the service is widely used by bloggers to host images that they embed in blogs and social media. In September 2010, it reported that it was hosting more than 5 billion images. For mobile users, Flickr has an official app for iPhone, BlackBerry and for Windows Phone 7, but not for other mobile devices. Several third party apps offer alternatives such as flickr hd for the iPad.

Flows 81, 89, 117

In graph theory, a flow network is a directed graph where each edge has a capacity and each edge receives a flow. The amount of flow on an edge cannot exceed the capacity of the edge. Often in Operations Research, a directed graph is called a network, the vertices are called nodes and the edges are called arcs. A flow must satisfy the restriction that the amount of flow into a node equals the amount of flow out of it, except when it is a source, which has more outgoing flow, or sink, which has more incoming flow. A network can be used to model traffic in a road system, fluids in pipes, currents in an electrical circuit, or anything similar in which something travels through a network of nodes.

Fluid 61, 103, 139

FLUID (Fast Light User Interface Designer) is a graphical editor that is used to produce FLTK source code. FLUID edits and saves its state in text .fl files, which can be edited in a text editor for finer control over display and behavior.

Following 50, 65-66, 76, 84, 103, 112, 144, 166

Following is a 1998 British neo-noir film directed by Christopher Nolan. It tells the story of a young man who follows strangers around the streets of London and is drawn into a criminal underworld when he fails to keep his distance. The film was made on a small budget and features an unusual non-linear plot structure which has been a feature in several of Nolan's films.

Fonts 170

In typography, a font (also fount) is traditionally defined as a quantity of sorts composing a complete character set of a single size and style of a particular typeface. For example, the set of all characters for 9-point Bulmer italic is a font, and the 10-point size would be a separate font, as would the 9-point upright.

FoolProof 89

The FoolProof Initiative is a project by America's credit unions that teaches financial literacy to consumers in the United States and Canada through a variety of programs. It uses video and audio, games and music in a modular system to teach complex as well as basic financial concepts such as understanding credit (finance) and credit score, getting a checking account or savings account, and knowing how to use credit cards.

Footage 93

In film and video, footage is the raw, unedited material as it had been originally filmed by movie camera or recorded by a video camera which usually must be edited to create a motion picture, video clip, television show or similar completed work. More loosely, footage can also refer to all sequences used in film and video editing, such as special effects and archive material (for special cases of this, see stock footage and B roll). Since the term originates in film, footage is only used for recorded images, such as film stock, videotapes or digitized clips – on live television, the signals from the cameras are called sources instead.

For All 88, 135

In predicate logic, universal quantification formalizes the notion that something (a logical predicate) is true for everything, or every relevant thing. The resulting statement is a universally quantified statement, and we have universally quantified over the predicate. In symbolic logic, the universal quantifier (a turned A) is the symbol used to denote universal quantification, and is often informally read as "given any" or "for all".

Forecasting 65

Forecasting is the process of making statements about events whose actual outcomes (typically) have not yet been observed. A commonplace example might be estimation for some variable of interest at some specified future date. Prediction is a similar, but more general term. Both might refer to formal statistical methods employing time series, cross-sectional or longitudinal data, or alternatively to less formal judgemental methods.

Foreman 68

Richard Foreman (born in New York on 10 June 1937) is an American playwright and avant-garde theater pioneer. He is the founder of the Ontological-Hysteric Theater.

Forgetful 68

Forgetting (retention loss) refers to apparent loss of information already encoded and stored in an individual's long term memory. It is a spontaneous or gradual process in which old memories are unable to be recalled from memory storage. It is subject to delicately balanced optimization that ensures that relevant memories are recalled. Forgetting can be reduced by repetition and/or more elaborate cognitive processing of information. Reviewing information in ways that involve active retrieval seems to slow the rate of forgetting.

Forms 61-62, 73, 75, 83-84, 100, 113, 124, 143

Plato's theory of Forms or theory of Ideas asserts that non-material abstract (but substantial) forms (or ideas), and not the material world of change known to us through sensation, possess the highest and most fundamental kind of reality. When used in this sense, the word form is often capitalized.

Plato speaks of these entities only through the characters (primarily Socrates) of his dialogues who sometimes suggest that these Forms are the only true objects of study that can provide us with genuine knowledge; thus even apart from the very controversial status of the theory, Plato's own views are much in doubt. Plato spoke of Forms in formulating a possible solution to the problem of universals.

Foucault 104

Michel Foucault, born Paul-Michel Foucault (15 October 1926–25 June 1984), was a French philosopher and historian of ideas. He held a chair at the prestigious Collège de France with the title 'History of Systems of Thought,' and also taught at the University at Buffalo and the University of California, Berkeley. Foucault is best known for his critical studies of social institutions, most notably psychiatry, medicine, the human sciences, and the prison system, as well as for his work on the history of human sexuality. His writings on power, knowledge, and discourse have been widely influential in academic circles. In the 1960s Foucault was associated with structuralism, a movement from which he distanced himself. Foucault also rejected the poststructuralist and postmodernist labels later attributed to him, preferring to classify his thought as a critical history of modernity rooted in Kant. Foucault's project was particularly influenced by Nietzsche, his 'genealogy of knowledge' a direct allusion to Nietzsche's 'genealogy of morality'. In a late interview he definitively stated: 'I am a Nietzschean.'

FoxTrot 162

FoxTrot is an American comic strip written and illustrated by Bill Amend. As of December 2006, FoxTrot was carried by more than 1,000 newspapers worldwide. From its inception in 1988 it was published daily until December 31, 2006, when Amend switched to a Sunday-only format.

Frame of Reference 155

A frame of reference in physics, may refer to a coordinate system or set of axes within which to measure the position, orientation, and other properties of objects in it, or it may refer to an observational reference frame tied to the state of motion of an observer. It may also refer to both an observational reference frame and an attached coordinate system, as a unit.

Frankenstein 83

Frankenstein; or, The Modern Prometheus is a novel written by Mary Shelley. Shelley started writing the story when she was eighteen, and the novel was published when she was twenty-one. The first edition was published anonymously in London in 1818. Shelley's name appears on the second edition, published in France.

Free of Charge 150, 159

Gratis is the process of providing goods or services without compensation. It is often referred to in English as 'free of charge' (FOC) or 'complimentary'.

French Philosophy 97

French philosophy, here taken to mean philosophy in the French language, has been extremely diverse and has influenced Western philosophy as a whole for centuries, from the medieval scholasticism of Peter Abelard, through the founding of modern philosophy by René Descartes, to 20th century existentialism and post-structuralism.

Frequent 63

In grammar, a frequentative form (abbreviated freq or fr) of a word is one which indicates repeated action. The frequentative form can be considered a separate, but not completely independent word, called a frequentative. English frequentative is no longer productive, but in some languages, such as Finnish or Lithuanian, it is.

Frisch 71

Max Rudolf Frisch (May 15, 1911–April 4, 1991) was a Swiss playwright and novelist, regarded as highly representative of German-language literature after World War II. In his creative works Frisch paid particular attention to issues relating to problems of human identity, individuality, responsibility, morality and political commitment. His use of irony is a significant feature of his post-war publications. Frisch was a member of the Gruppe Olten.

From, John 112

John Frum (or Jon Frum, or John From) is a figure associated with cargo cults on the island of Tanna in Vanuatu. He is often depicted as an American World War II serviceman, who will bring wealth and prosperity to the people if they follow him. He is sometimes portrayed as black, sometimes as white; from David Attenborough's report of an encounter: 'E look like you. 'E got white face. 'E tall man. 'E live 'long South America.'

From Left to Right 148

From Left to Right is an album by American jazz pianist Bill Evans, released in 1970.

Front to Back 113

'Front to Back' is a program where artists play one of their most beloved albums, from start to finish, in a live concert which is filmed and then re-broadcast on MySpace. The program began in the fall of 2008 when the alternative rock band Ben Folds Five reunited to play their final album, 1999's The Unauthorized Biography of Reinhold Messner. The show took place on September 18, 2008 at the UNC Memorial Hall in Chapel Hill, North Carolina and stands as the band's only live performance together since breaking up nearly 10 years earlier.

Front-end 94

Front end and back end are generalized terms that refer to the initial and the end stages of a process. The front end is responsible for collecting input in various forms from the user and processing it to conform to a specification the back end can use. The front end is an interface between the user and the back end.

Full Text Search 81
In text retrieval, full text search refers to a technique for searching a computer-stored document or database. In a full text search, the search engine examines all of the words in every stored document as it tries to match search words supplied by the user. Full text searching techniques became common in online bibliographic databases in the 1970s [verification needed]. Many web sites and application programs (such as word processing software) provide full-text search capabilities. Some web search engines such as AltaVista employ full text search techniques while others index only a portion of the web pages examined by its indexing system.

Fungible 54
Fungibility is the property of a good or a commodity whose individual units are capable of mutual substitution. Examples of highly fungible commodities are crude oil, wheat, orange juice, precious metals, and currencies.

Futurologist 69
Futurists (not in the sense of futurism) or futurologists are scientists and social scientists whose speciality is to attempt to systematically predict the future, whether that of human society in particular or of life on earth in general.

Gadgets 138
A gadget is a small technological object (such as a device or an appliance) that has a particular function, but is often thought of as a novelty. Gadgets are invariably considered to be more unusually or cleverly designed than normal technological objects at the time of their invention. Gadgets are sometimes also referred to as gizmos.

Game 61-62, 88, 115, 117-118, 143, 156
A game is structured playing, usually undertaken for enjoyment and sometimes used as an educational tool. Games are distinct from work, which is usually carried out for remuneration, and from art, which is more often an expression of aesthetic or ideological elements. However, the distinction is not clear-cut, and many games are also considered to be work (such as professional players of spectator sports/games) or art (such as jigsaw puzzles or games involving an artistic layout such as Mahjong, solitaire, or some video games).

Game Designers 118
Game design, a subset of game development, is the process of designing the content and rules of a game in the pre-production stage and design of gameplay, environment, and storyline, characters during production stage. The term is also used to describe both the game design embodied in a game as well as documentation that describes such a design. Game design requires artistic and technical competence as well as writing skills.

Gazette 72
A gazette is a newspaper.

Generalize 107
A generalization (or generalisation) of a concept is an extension of the concept to less-specific criteria. It is a foundational element of logic and human reasoning. Generalizations posit the existence of a domain or set of elements, as well as one or more common characteristics shared by those elements. As such, it is the essential basis of all valid deductive inferences. The process of verification is necessary to determine whether a generalization holds true for any given situation.

Genre 95, 123
Genre is the term for any category of literature as well as various other forms of art or culture, e.g., music, based on some loose set of stylistic criteria. Genres are formed by conventions that change over time as new genres are invented and the use of old ones are discontinued. Often, works fit into multiple genres by way of borrowing and recombining these conventions. While the scope of the word 'genre' is commonly confined to art and culture, it also defines individuals' interactions with and within their environments. In order to be recognized as genre these interactions and environments must be recurring.

Geotagged 108
Geotagging (also written as GeoTagging) is the process of adding geographical identification metadata to various media such as photographs, video, websites, SMS messages, or RSS feeds and is a form of geospatial metadata. These data usually consist of latitude and longitude coordinates, though they can also include altitude, bearing, distance, accuracy data, and place names. It is commonly used for photographs, giving geotagged photographs.

Gestures 90
A gesture is a form of non-verbal communication in which visible bodily actions communicate particular messages, either in place of speech or together and in parallel with spoken words. Gestures include movement of the hands, face, or other parts of the body. Gestures differ from physical non-verbal communication that does not communicate specific messages, such as purely expressive displays, proxemics, or displays of joint attention. Gestures allow individuals to communicate a variety of feelings and thoughts, from contempt and hostility to approval and affection, often together with body language in addition to words when they speak.

Getting Better 51
'Getting Better' is a song written mainly by Paul McCartney with lyrical contributions from John Lennon, credited to Lennon/McCartney. It was recorded by The Beatles for the 1967 album Sgt. Pepper's Lonely Hearts Club Band.

Global Networks 102

A global network is any communication network which spans the entire Earth. The term, as exposed in this article refers in a more restricted way to bidirectional communication networks, and to technology-based networks. Early networks such as mail and unidirectional communication networks, such as radio and television, are described elsewhere.

Globalization 126

Globalisation (or globalization) describes the process by which regional economies, societies, and cultures have become integrated through a global network of political ideas through communication, transportation, and trade. The term is most closely associated with the term economic globalization: the integration of national economies into the international economy through trade, foreign direct investment, capital flows, migration, the spread of technology, and military presence. However, globalization is usually recognized as being driven by a combination of economic, technological, sociocultural, political, and biological factors. The term can also refer to the transnational circulation of ideas, languages, or popular culture through acculturation. An aspect of the world which has gone through the process can be said to be globalized.

Gloss 57

A gloss (from Latin: glossa, from Greek: glóssa 'tongue') is a brief notation of the meaning of a word or wording in a text. It may be in the language of the text, or in the reader's language if that is different. A collection of glosses is a glossary. A collection of medieval legal glosses, made by so-called glossators, is called an apparatus. The compilation of glosses into glossaries was the beginning of lexicography, and the glossaries so compiled were in fact the first dictionaries. In modern times a glossary, as opposed to a dictionary, is typically found in a text as an appendix of specialized terms that the typical reader may find unfamiliar. Also, satirical explanations of words and events are called glosses. The German Romantic movement used the expression of gloss for poems commenting a given other piece of poetry, often in the spanish Décima style. Glosses were originally notes made in the margin or between the lines of a text in a Classical language, in which the meaning of a word or passage is explained. As such, glosses vary in thoroughness and complexity, from simple marginal notations of words one reader found difficult or obscure, to interlinear translations of a text with cross references to similar passages.

Goes 116, 129, 146, 154

The Geostationary Satellite system, operated by the United States National Environmental Satellite, Data, and Information Service (NESDIS), supports weather forecasting, severe storm tracking, and meteorology research. Spacecraft and ground-based elements of the system work together to provide a continuous stream of environmental data. The National Weather Service (NWS) uses the GOES system for its United States weather monitoring and forecasting operations, and scientific researchers use the data to better understand land, atmosphere, ocean, and climate interactions.

Goethe 146

Johann Wolfgang von Goethe, 28 August 1749 – 22 March 1832) was a German writer and polymath. Goethe is considered the supreme genius of modern German literature side by side with Schiller. Goethe's works span the fields of poetry, drama, literature, philosophy, and science. His Faust has been called the greatest long poem of modern European literature. Goethe's other well-known literary works include his numerous poems, the Bildungsroman Wilhelm Meister's Apprenticeship, and the epistolary novel The Sorrows of Young Werther.

Google 53, 72, 81, 105, 109, 129, 149-150, 154, 156-157, 162

Google Inc. is an American multinational public corporation invested in Internet search, cloud computing, and advertising technologies. Google hosts and develops a number of Internet-based services and products, and generates profit primarily from advertising through its AdWords program. The company was founded by Larry Page and Sergey Brin, often dubbed the Google Guys, while the two were attending Stanford University as PhD candidates.

Google Books 156-157

Google Books (previously known as Google Book Search and Google Print) is a service from Google that searches the full text of books that Google has scanned, converted to text using optical character recognition, and stored in its digital database. The service was formerly known as Google Print when it was introduced at the Frankfurt Book Fair in October 2004. Google's Library Project, also now known as Google Book Search, was announced in December 2004.

Google Images 162

Google Images is a search service created by Google that allows users to search the Web for image content. The feature was introduced in July 2001. The keywords for the image search are based on the filename of the image, the link text pointing to the image, and text adjacent to the image. When searching for an image, a thumbnail of each matching image is displayed. When the user clicks on a thumbnail, the image is displayed in a box over the website that it came from. The user can then close the box and browse the website, or view the full-sized image.

Google Rank 129

PageRank is a link analysis algorithm, named after Larry Page and used by the Google Internet search engine, that assigns a numerical weighting to each element of a hyperlinked set of documents, such as the World Wide Web, with the purpose of 'measuring' its relative importance within the set. The algorithm may be applied to any collection of entities with reciprocal quotations and references. The numerical weight that it assigns to any given element E is referred to as the PageRank of E and denoted by PR(E).

Google Search 150

Google Search or Google Web Search is a web search engine owned by Google Inc. and is the most-used search engine on the Web. Google receives several hundred million queries each day through its various services. The main purpose of Google Search is to hunt for text in webpages, as opposed to other data, such as with Google Image Search. Google search was originally developed by Larry Page and Sergey Brin in 1997.

Googled 125

The transitive verb to google (also spelled to Google) refers to using the Google search engine to obtain information on the Web. A neologism arising from the popularity and dominance of the eponymous search engine, the American Dialect Society chose it as the 'most useful word of 2002'. It was officially added to the Oxford English Dictionary on June 15 2006.

Goto 68, 170

goto is a statement found in many computer programming languages. It is a combination of the English words go and to. It performs a one-way transfer of control to another line of code; in contrast a function call normally returns control. The jumped-to locations are usually identified using labels, though some languages use line numbers. At the machine code level, a goto is a form of branch or jump statement.

Graffiti 64

Graffiti (singular: graffito; the plural is used as a mass noun) is the name for images or lettering scratched, scrawled, painted or marked in any manner on property. Graffiti is any type of public markings that may appear in the forms of simple written words to elaborate wall paintings. Graffiti has existed since ancient times, with examples dating back to Ancient Greece and the Roman Empire.

Grammar 105, 125, 127

In linguistics, grammar is the set of structural rules that govern the composition of sentences, phrases, and words in any given natural language. The term refers also to the study of such rules, and this field includes morphology, syntax, and phonology, often complemented by phonetics, semantics, and pragmatics. Linguists do not normally use the term to refer to orthographical rules, although usage books and style guides that call themselves grammars may also refer to spelling and punctuation.

Grapheme 120

A grapheme (from the Greek: gráphō, 'write') is a fundamental unit in a written language. Examples of graphemes include alphabetic letters, Chinese characters, numerical digits, punctuation marks, and the individual symbols of any of the world's writing systems.

Graphic Design 75, 105, 119-120

Graphic design is a creative process – most often involving a client and a designer and usually completed in conjunction with producers of form (i.e., printers, programmers, signmakers, etc.) – undertaken in order to convey a specific message (or messages) to a targeted audience. The term 'graphic design' can also refer to a number of artistic and professional disciplines that focus on visual communication and presentation. The field as a whole is also often referred to as Visual Communication or Communication Design.

Graphic Novels 95-97

A graphic novel is a narrative work in which the story is conveyed to the reader using sequential art in either an experimental design or in a traditional comics format. The term is employed in a broad manner, encompassing non-fiction works and thematically linked short stories as well as fictional stories across a number of genres.

Graphical User Interface 65

In computing a graphical user interface (GUI, sometimes pronounced gooey,) is a type of user interface that allows users to interact with electronic devices with images rather than text commands. GUIs can be used in computers, hand-held devices such as MP3 players, portable media players or gaming devices, household appliances and office equipment. A GUI represents the information and actions available to a user through graphical icons and visual indicators such as secondary notation, as opposed to text-based interfaces, typed command labels or text navigation. The actions are usually performed through direct manipulation of the graphical elements.

Graphics 62, 71-72, 103, 170

Graphics (from Greek: graphikos) are visual presentations on some surface, such as a wall, canvas, computer screen, paper, or stone to brand, inform, illustrate, or entertain. Examples are photographs, drawings, Line Art, graphs, diagrams, typography, numbers, symbols, geometric designs, maps, engineering drawings, or other images. Graphics often combine text, illustration, and color. Graphic design may consist of the deliberate selection, creation, or arrangement of typography alone, as in a brochure, flier, poster, web site, or book without any other element. Clarity or effective communication may be the objective, association with other cultural elements may be sought, or merely, the creation of a distinctive style.

Great Books 113

Great Books refers primarily to a group of books that tradition, and various institutions and authorities, have regarded as constituting or best expressing the foundations of Western culture (the Western canon is a synonymous designation); derivatively the term also refers to a curriculum or method of education based around a list of such books. Mortimer Adler lists three criteria for including a book on the list: the book has contemporary significance; that is, it has relevance to the problems and issues of our times; the book is inexhaustible; it can be read again and again with benefit. 'This is an exacting criterion, an ideal that is fully attained by only a small number of the 511 works that we selected. It is approximated in varying degrees by the rest.'; the book is relevant to a large number of the great ideas and great issues that have occupied the minds of thinking individuals for the last 25 centuries.

Griot 153, 155
A griot is a West African historian. The griot delivers history as a poet, praise singer, and wandering musician. The griot is a repository of oral tradition. As such, they are sometimes also called bards.

Groundbreaking 156
Groundbreaking, also known as cutting, sod-cutting, turning the first sod or a sod-turning ceremony, is a traditional ceremony in many cultures that celebrates the first day of construction for a building or other project. Such ceremonies are often attended by dignitaries such as politicians and business-men. The actual shovel or spade used during the actual groundbreaking is often a special ceremonial shovel meant to be saved for sub-sequent display. Commemorative information may be subsequently engraved on the shovel.

Guide 79, 94
A guide is a person who leads anyone through unknown or unmapped country. This includes a guide of the real world (such as someone who conducts travellers and tour-ists through a place of interest), as well as a person who leads someone to more abstract places (such as to knowledge or wisdom).

Guru 54
A guru is one who is regarded as having great knowledge, wisdom and authority in a certain area, and who uses it to guide others (teacher). Other forms of manifestation of this principle also include parents, school teachers, non-human objects (books) and even one's own intellectual discipline.

Handwriting 92
Penmanship or handwriting is the technique of writing with the hand and a writing instrument. Styles of handwriting are also called hands or scripts. Writing as an art is called calligraphy.

Happening 64, 94
A happening is a performance, event or situation meant to be considered art, usually as performance art. Happenings take place anywhere (from basements to studio lofts and even street alley ways), are often multi-disciplinary, with a nonlinear narrative and the active participation of the audience. Key ele-ments of happenings are planned, but artists sometimes retain room for improvisation. This new media art aspect to happenings eliminates the boundary between the artwork and its viewer. Henceforth, the interactions between the audience and the artwork makes the audi-ence, in a sense, part of the art.

Hara 54
Kenya Hara (born 1958) is a Japanese graphic designer and curator. Hara is art direc-tor of Muji since 2001 and designed the opening and closing ceremony programs of the Nagano Winter Olympic Games 1998.

Hard Disk 76
A hard disk drive (HDD) is a non-volatile, random access device for digital data. It fea-tures rotating rigid platters on a motor-driven spindle within a protective enclosure. Data is magnetically read from and written to the plat-ter by read/write heads that float on a film of air above the platters.

Hardcover 149
A hardcover, hardback or hardbound is a book bound with rigid protective covers (typi-cally of cardboard covered with cloth, heavy paper, or sometimes leather). They may have flexible sewn spines which allow the book to lie flat on a surface when opened, although most modern commercial hardcover books have glued spines.

Hardware 85, 105-106
Hardware is a general term for the physi-cal artifacts of a technology. It may also mean the physical components of a computer system, in the form of computer hardware.

Harper Collins 145
HarperCollins is a publishing company owned by News Corporation. It is the combina-tion of the publishers William Collins, Sons and Co Ltd, a British company, and Harper & Row, an American company, itself the result of an earlier merger of Harper & Brothers and Row, Peterson & Company. The worldwide CEO of HarperCollins is Brian Murray. The company publishes under many different imprints, and publishes the Collins English Dictionary.

Headlines 57, 159
The headline is the text at the top of a newspaper article, indicating the nature of the article below it.

Hearing 90
Hearing (or audition; adjectival form: 'auditory' or 'aural') is the ability to perceive sound by detecting vibrations through an organ such as the ear. It is one of the traditional five senses. The inability to hear is called deafness.

Helping 72
Helping behavior refers to voluntary actions intended to help the others, with reward regarded or disregarded. It is a type of prosocial behavior (voluntary action intended to help or benefit another individual or group of individu-als, such as sharing, comforting, rescuing and helping).

Here Comes Everybody 174

Here Comes Everybody: The Power of Organizing Without Organizations is a book by Clay Shirky published by Penguin Press in 2008, which evaluates the effect of the Internet on modern group dynamics. The author considers examples such as Wikipedia and MySpace in his analysis.

Hermeneutics 98

In religious studies and social philosophy, hermeneutics is the study of interpretation theory, and can be either the art of interpretation, or the theory and practice of interpretation. Traditional hermeneutics refers to the study of the interpretation of written texts, especially texts in the areas of literature, religion and law. Contemporary, or modern, hermeneutics encompasses not only issues involving the written text, but everything in the interpretative process. This includes verbal and nonverbal forms of communication as well as prior aspects that affect communication, such as presuppositions, preunderstandings, the meaning and philosophy of language, and semiotics. Philosophical hermeneutics refers primarily to Hans-Georg Gadamer's theory of knowledge as developed in Truth and Method, and sometimes to Paul Ricoeur. Hermeneutic consistency refers to analysis of texts for coherent explanation. A hermeneutic (singular) refers to one particular method or strand of interpretation.

Herzog 125

Werner Herzog Stipetić, born 5 September 1942, known as Werner Herzog, is a German film director, producer, screenwriter, actor, and opera director.

Hierarchy 58-59

A hierarchy (Greek: hierarchia, from hierarches, 'leader of sacred rites') is an arrangement of items (objects, names, values, categories, etc.) in which the items are represented as being 'above,' 'below,' or 'at the same level as' one another. Abstractly, a hierarchy is simply an ordered set or an acyclic directed graph.

High Definition 75, 159

HDMI (High-Definition Multimedia Interface) is a compact audio/video interface for transmitting uncompressed digital data. It is a digital alternative to consumer analog standards, such as radio frequency (RF) coaxial cable, composite video, S-Video, SCART, component video, D-Terminal, or VGA. HDMI connects digital audio/video sources (such as set-top boxes, upconvert DVD players, HD DVD players, Blu-ray Disc players, AVCHD camcorders, personal computers (PCs), video game consoles such as the PlayStation 3 and Xbox 360, and AV receivers) to compatible digital audio devices, computer monitors, video projectors and digital televisions.

Highbrow 100

Used colloquially as a noun or adjective, highbrow is synonymous with intellectual; as an adjective, it also means elite, and generally carries a connotation of high culture. The word draws its metonymy from the pseudoscience of phrenology, and was originally simply a physical descriptor. 'Highbrow' can be applied to music, implying most of the classical music tradition and much of post-bebop jazz; to literature, i.e. literary fiction; to films in the arthouse line; and to comedy that requires significant understanding of analogies or references to appreciate. As the former buzzword highbrow has lost some currency and sounds slightly passé, its use now gives an impression of mild irony.

Historical Events 154

Those who cannot remember the past are condemned to repeat it.

History of Art 111

The history of art refers to the history of the arts, including the literary, visual, musical and performing arts. Literary arts include poetry, prose and scripts (theatrical scripts, screenplays, comics scripts). The visual arts include painting, sculpture and architecture. Performing arts include theatrical and dance spectacles. Art is also part of the humanities. The humanities also include theory of art or aesthetics, which is the study of the appreciation of all forms of art. In the past, performing arts were excluded from the fine arts and considered minor arts, but the currently the dominant view is that there are no minor arts, only minor artists or artworks.

Hollywood Films 111

The cinema of the United States has had a profound effect on cinema across the world since the early 20th century. Its history is sometimes separated into four main periods: the silent film era, classical Hollywood cinema, New Hollywood, and the contemporary period. Since the 1920s, the American film industry has grossed more money every year than that of any other country.

Homer 124

In the Western classical tradition Homer is the author of the Iliad and the Odyssey, and is revered as the greatest ancient Greek epic poet. These epics are at the beginning of the Western canon of literature, and have had an enormous influence on the history of literature.

Homework 164

Homework, or homework assignment, refers to tasks assigned to students by their teachers to be completed mostly outside of class, and derives its name from the fact that most students do the majority of such work at home. Common homework assignments may include a quantity or period of reading to be performed, writing or typing to be completed, problems to be solved, a school project to be built (such as a diorama or display), or other skills to be practiced.

House Music 162

House music is a style of electronic dance music that originated in Chicago, Illinois, United States in the early 1980s. It was initially popularized in mid-1980s discothèques catering to the African-American, Latino American, and gay communities; first in Chicago circa 1984, then in other cities such as New York City, Toronto, Montreal, London, Detroit, San Francisco, Los Angeles and Miami. It then reached Europe largely due to the infamous House Music Tour visiting England. England played a pivotal role in the development of house music throughout Europe. Since the early to mid-1990s, it has become infused in mainstream pop and dance music worldwide.

How to 83, 110, 115, 119, 129, 134, 167
A how-to or a how to is an informal, often short, description of how to accomplish some specific task. A how-to is usually meant to help non-experts, may leave out details that are only important to experts, and may also be greatly simplified from an overall discussion of the topic. One of the earliest How-to books was published in 1519 by Thomas Wight and entitled, A booke of the arte and maner, how to plant and graffe all sortes of trees: With divers other new practise, by one of the Abbey of Saint Vincent in Fraunce by Leonard Mascall.

How We Think 69
How We Think is a book written by John Dewey, published in 1910.

HTML 82, 134
HTML, which stands for HyperText Markup Language, is the predominant markup language for web pages. HTML is the basic building-blocks of webpages.

Human History 115
Recorded history (sometimes called record history) is a part of human history that has been written down or recorded by the use of language. It starts in the 4th millennium BC, with the invention of writing. The period before this is known as prehistory.

Human Is 126
'Human Is' is a science fiction short story by Philip K. Dick. It was first published in Startling Stories, Winter 1955. The plot centers on the crisis facing a woman whose cold and emotionally abusive husband returns, from a survey mission to the dying planet Rexor IV, changed for the better – due to his psyche being replaced by a Rexorian glad to have escaped the confines of its dying planet.

Humour 169
Humour is the tendency of particular cognitive experiences to provoke laughter and provide amusement. The term derives from the humoral medicine of the ancient Greeks, which taught that the balance of fluids in the human body, known as humourous (Latin: húmor, 'body fluid'), control human health and emotion.

Hyperlinking 134
In computing, a hyperlink (or link) is a reference to a document that the reader can directly follow, or that is followed automatically. A hyperlink points to a whole document or to a specific element within a document. Hypertext is text with hyperlinks. A software system for viewing and creating hypertext is a hypertext system, and to create a hyperlink is to hyperlink (or simply to link). A user following hyperlinks is said to navigate or browse the hypertext.

Hypermedia 159
Hypermedia is used as a logical extension of the term hypertext in which graphics, audio, video, plain text and hyperlinks intertwine to create a generally non-linear medium of information. This contrasts with the broader term multimedia, which may be used to describe non-interactive linear presentations as well as hypermedia. It is also related to the field of Electronic literature. The term was first used in a 1965 article by Ted Nelson.

Hypertext Fiction 83
Hypertext fiction is a genre of electronic literature, characterized by the use of hypertext links which provides a new context for non-linearity in 'literature' and reader interaction. The reader typically chooses links to move from one node of text to the next, and in this fashion arranges a story from a deeper pool of potential stories. Its spirit can also be seen in interactive fiction. The term can also be used to describe traditionally-published books in which a nonlinear narrative and interactive narrative is achieved through internal references. Enrique Jardiel Poncela's La Tournée de Dios (1932), Vladimir Nabokov's Pale Fire (1962) and Julio Cortázar's Rayuela (1963; translated as Hopscotch) are early examples predating the word 'hypertext', while a common pop-culture example is the Choose Your Own Adventure series in young adult fiction and other similar gamebooks.

I Am One 128
'I Am One' is the debut single by The Smashing Pumpkins. It was the band's first ever release and remains the only single issued by the band with co-writing credits to both Billy Corgan and James Iha. It charted on the UK Singles Chart at a peak position of number 73.

I Will Be Back 95
'I'll be back' is a catch phrase associated with Arnold Schwarzenegger.

Iconic 65
A cultural icon can be a symbol, logo, picture, name, face, person, building or other image that is readily recognized and generally represents an object or concept with great cultural significance to a wide cultural group. A representation of an object or person, or that object or person may come to be regarded as having a special status as particularly representative of, or important to, or loved by, a particular group of people, a place, or a period in history.

Icons 65, 102
An icon (from Greek 'image') is a religious work of art, most commonly a painting, from Eastern Orthodox Christianity and Catholicism.

More broadly the term is used in a wide number of contexts for an image, picture, or representation; it is a sign or likeness that stands for an object by signifying or representing it either concretely or by analogy, as in semiotics; by extension, icon is also used, particularly in modern culture, in the general sense of symbol – i.e. a name, face, picture, edifice or even a person readily recognized as having some well-known significance or embodying certain qualities: one thing, an image or depiction, that represents something else of greater significance through literal or figurative meaning, usually associated with religious, cultural, political, or economic standing.

Ideology 82

An ideology is a set of ideas that constitutes one's goals, expectations, and actions. An ideology can be thought of as a comprehensive vision, as a way of looking at things (compare worldview), as in common sense (see Ideology in everyday society below) and several philosophical tendencies (see Political ideologies), or a set of ideas proposed by the dominant class of a society to all members of this society (a 'received consciousness' or product of socialization).

Idolatry 112

Idolatry is the worship of a physical object as a god. In monotheistic religions it is also the error of giving undue honour and regard to created forms rather than their Creator who is the source of any excellence or beauty that any created form may possess. In the Abrahamic religions idolatry is a cardinal sin. In religions where such activity is not considered a sin, the term 'idolatry' itself is absent.

If I Were 127

Rock It is a Chuck Berry album released in 1979 by Atco Records; Atco was only the third label for which Berry recorded studio material after two tenures with Chess Records and a brief 1960s stint at Mercury Records. It is, to date, his most recent studio album (although he has released some live recordings since).

Illustration 89

An illustration is a displayed visualization form presented as a drawing, painting, photograph or other work of art that is created to elucidate or dictate sensual information (such as a story, poem or newspaper article) by providing a visual representation graphically.

Image Recognition 150

Computer vision is the science and technology of machines that see, where see in this case means that the machine is able to extract information from an image that is necessary to solve some task. As a scientific discipline, computer vision is concerned with the theory behind artificial systems that extract information from images. The image data can take many forms, such as video sequences, views from multiple cameras, or multi-dimensional data from a medical scanner.

Imagery 157

Imagery is a collection of images. It is the usage of details and descriptions in order to create a sensory experience for the reader. Imagery/Image are the elements in a literary work used to evoke mental images, not only of the visual sense, but of sensation and emotion as well. While most commonly used in reference to figurative language, imagery is a variable term which can apply to any and all components of a poem that evoke sensory experience and emotional response, whether figurative or literal, and also applies to the concrete things so imaged.

Imagination 74, 107, 112, 114, 124, 148

Imagination, also called the faculty of imagining, is the ability of forming mental images, sensations and concepts, in a moment when they are not perceived through sight, hearing or other senses. Imagination is the work of the mind that helps create. Imagination helps provide meaning to experience and understanding to knowledge; it is a fundamental facility through which people make sense of the world, and it also plays a key role in the learning process. A basic training for imagination is listening to storytelling (narrative), in which the exactness of the chosen words is the fundamental factor to evoke worlds.

Imprint 95

In the publishing industry, an imprint can mean several different things: As a piece of bibliographic information about a book, it refers to the name and address of the book's publisher and its date of publication as given at the foot or on the verso of its title page; It can mean a trade name under which a work is published. One single publishing company may have multiple imprints; the different imprints are used by the publisher to market works to different demographic consumer segments. In some cases, the diversity results from the takeover of smaller publishers (or parts of their business) by a larger company. This usage of the word has evolved from the first meaning given above; It can also refer to a finer distinction of a book's version than 'edition'. This is used to distinguish, for example different printings, or printing runs of the same edition, or to distinguish the same edition produced by a different publisher or printer. With the creation of the 'ISBN' identification system, which is assigned to a text prior to its printing, a different imprint has effectively come to mean a text with a different ISBN – if one had been assigned to it; The word imprint or masthead is sometimes used on international websites, normally translated from German. This usually contains an 'Impressum' that contains legal information, such as website details with information on the responsible person or entity.

In One Ear 133

In One Ear was a late-night alternative comedy sketch show, broadcast between 1984 and 1986, on BBC Radio 4 in the United Kingdom, broadcast live from the BBC Paris

Studio in London, with a (sometimes edited) repeat later in the week.

In the Margins 66, 142

'In the Margins' is a single by Echo & the Bunnymen that was released on 31 October 2005 in the UK and on 3 November 2005 in the U.S. It was the second single to be released from the 2005 album Siberia.

In the Room 89

'In the Room' is episode 118 of The West Wing.

In the Street 81

In The Street is an album by the Village People. It features both original cop Victor Willis and the cop currently in the group Ray Simpson as lead singers. The G.I. Alex Briley also sings the lead for one song, and the re-release in 1999 featured the bonus track America with Miles J. Davis singing the lead vocals. Fox On The Box and In The Street contain the same songs, but Fox On The Box was released by RCA records in 1982 and In The Street by Casablanca Records a year later.

Indeed 95, 114

Indeed.com is a metasearch engine for job listings launched in November 2004. As a single-topic search engine, it is also an example of vertical search. The site aggregates job listings from thousands of websites, including job boards, newspapers, associations, and company career pages. Job seekers do not apply for jobs through Indeed; they simply see job postings. Applicants can then decide which jobs are of interest and then go to the corresponding sites to apply. Indeed is currently available in 53 countries. Indeed is the only site available on 7 continents. In October, 2010, Indeed.com slipped past Monster.com to become the largest job site in the United States.

Index 66, 114

An index is a system used to make finding information easier.

Indexical 65

In linguistics and in philosophy of language, an indexical behavior or utterance points to (or indicates) some state of affairs. For example, I refers to whomever is speaking; now refers to the time at which that word is uttered; and here refers to the place of utterance. For Charles Sanders Peirce, indexicality is one of three sign modalities (see further down), and is a phenomenon far broader than language; that which, independently of interpretation, points to something – such as smoke (an index of fire) or a pointing finger – works indexically for interpretation. Social indexicality in the human realm has been regarded as including any sign (clothing, speech variety, table manners) that points to, and helps create, social identity.

Information 52, 54-55, 64, 66, 68, 71-72, 76, 80-81, 87, 92-98, 100-104, 108-110, 113, 119, 121, 127-128, 130, 134, 144, 147, 149-151, 156, 160-161, 167, 169-170, 172

Information in its most restricted technical sense is an ordered sequence of symbols that record or transmit a message. It can be recorded as signs, or conveyed as waves. Information is any kind of event that affects the state of a dynamic system. As a concept, however, information has many meanings. Moreover, the concept of information is closely related to notions of constraint, communication, control, data, form, instruction, knowledge, meaning, mental stimulus, pattern, perception, representation, and even entropy.

Information Economy 156

Information economy is a term that characterizes an economy with an increased emphasis on informational activities and information industry.

Information Graphics 71-72

Information graphics or infographics are graphic visual representations of information, data or knowledge. These graphics present complex information quickly and clearly, such as in signs, maps, journalism, technical writing, and education. With an information graphic, computer scientists, mathematicians, and statisticians develop and communicate concepts using a single symbol to process information.

Information Overload 52, 149

Information overload is a term popularized by Alvin Toffler in his bestselling book Future Shock. It refers to the difficulty a person can have understanding an issue and making decisions that can be caused by the presence of too much information. The term itself is mentioned in a 1964 book by Bertram Gross, The Managing of Organizations.

Information Service 151

An information broker, also known as an independent information professional or information consultant, is a person or business that researches information for clients. Common uses for information brokers include market research and patent searches, but can include practically any type of information research.

Information Society 97, 149, 169

An information society is a society in which the manipulation of information is a significant and sometimes measured amount of personal activity.

Information Wants to be Free 54

Information wants to be free is a slogan of technology activists typically invoked against any efforts to limit access to or charge money for information. According to contemporary criticism of intellectual property rights, the system of governmental control of exclusivity is in conflict with the development of a public domain of information.

Initial 55, 77

In a written or published work, an initial is a letter at the beginning of a work, a chapter, or a paragraph that is larger than the rest of the text. The word is derived from the Latin initialis, which means standing at the beginning. An initial often is several lines in height and in older books or manuscripts, sometimes ornately decorated.

Ink 82, 127, 148, 163

Ink is a semi liquid solid/paste that contains pigments and/or dyes and is used to color a surface to produce an image, text, or design. Ink is used for drawing and/or writing with a pen, brush, or quill. Thicker inks, in paste form, are used extensively in letterpress and lithographic printing.

Input 71, 105

Input is the term denoting either an entrance or changes which are inserted into a system and which activate/modify a process. It is an abstract concept, used in the modeling, system(s) design and system(s) exploitation. It is usually connected with other terms, e.g., input field, input variable, input parameter, input value, input signal, input port, input device and input file (file format).

Inquiry 157

An inquiry is any process that has the aim of augmenting knowledge, resolving doubt, or solving a problem. A theory of inquiry is an account of the various types of inquiry and a treatment of the ways that each type of inquiry achieves its aim.

Inscriptions 132

Epigraphy (from the Greek: epi-graphē, literally 'on-writing', 'inscription') is the study of inscriptions or epigraphs as writing; that is, the science of identifying the graphemes and of classifying their use as to cultural context and date, elucidating their meaning and assessing what conclusions can be deduced concerning the writing and the writers. Specifically excluded from epigraphy is the historical significance of an epigraph as a document or the artistic value of a literary composition.

Instant Messaging 106

Instant messaging (IM) is a form of real-time direct text-based communication between two or more people using personal computers or other devices, along with shared clients. The user's text is conveyed over a network, such as the Internet. More advanced instant messaging software clients also allow enhanced modes of communication, such as live voice or video calling.

Intellectual 117

An intellectual is a person who uses intelligence (thought and reason) and critical or analytical reasoning in either a professional or a personal capacity.

Intensive 80, 126

In grammar, an intensive word form is one which denotes stronger or more forceful action relative to the root on which the intensive is built. Intensives are usually lexical formations, but there may be a regular process for forming intensives from a root. Intensive formations, for example, existed in Proto-Indo-European, and in many of the Semitic languages.

Interaction 74, 96, 123, 135

Interaction is a kind of action that occurs as two or more objects have an effect upon one another. The idea of a two-way effect is essential in the concept of interaction, as opposed to a one-way causal effect. A closely related term is interconnectivity, which deals with the interactions of interactions within systems: combinations of many simple interactions can lead to surprising emergent phenomena. Interaction has different tailored meanings in various sciences. All systems are related and interdependent. Every action has a consequence.

Interactive 106, 111, 118, 129, 161

In the fields of information science, communication, and industrial design, there is debate over the meaning of interactivity. In the 'contingency view' of interactivity, there are three levels: 1. Noninteractive, when a message is not related to previous messages; 2. Reactive, when a message is related only to one immediately previous message; 3. Interactive, when a message is related to a number of previous messages and to the relationship between them.

Interfaces 102, 105

In the industrial design field of human–machine interaction, the user interface is the space where interaction between humans and machines occurs. The goal of interaction between a human and a machine at the user interface is effective operation and control of the machine, and feedback from the machine which aids the operator in making operational decisions. Examples of this broad concept of user interfaces include the interactive aspects of computer operating systems, hand tools, heavy machinery operator controls, and process controls. The design considerations applicable when creating user interfaces are related to or involve such disciplines as ergonomics and psychology.

Interiors 140

Interiors is a 1978 drama film written and directed by Woody Allen. Featured performers are Kristin Griffith, Mary Beth Hurt, Richard Jordan, Diane Keaton, E. G. Marshall, Geraldine Page, Maureen Stapleton and Sam Waterston.

Intermediary 165

An intermediary is a third party that offers intermediation services between two trading parties. The intermediary acts as a conduit for goods or services offered by a supplier to a consumer. Typically the intermediary offers some added value to the transaction that may not be possible by direct trading.

Internet 50, 52, 55, 65, 68, 94, 113-114, 117, 122, 131-132, 136-137, 154-156, 158, 163, 172

The Internet is a global system of interconnected computer networks that use the standard Internet Protocol Suite (TCP/IP) to serve billions of users worldwide. It is a network of networks that consists of millions of private, public, academic, business, and government networks, of local to global scope, that are linked by a broad array of electronic, wireless and optical networking technologies. The Internet carries a vast range of information resources and services, such as the inter-linked hypertext documents of the World Wide Web (WWW) and the infrastructure to support electronic mail.

Internet Browser 68, 113

A web browser or Internet browser is a software application for retrieving, presenting, and traversing information resources on the World Wide Web. An information resource is identified by a Uniform Resource Identifier (URI) and may be a web page, image, video, or other piece of content. Hyperlinks present in resources enable users to easily navigate their browsers to related resources.

Interpreting 97, 146

Language interpretation is the facilitating of oral or sign-language communication, either simultaneously or consecutively, between users of different languages. The process is described by both the words interpreting and interpretation.

Interruption 98

In computing, an interrupt is an asynchronous signal indicating the need for attention or a synchronous event in software indicating the need for a change in execution.

Interventions 135

Interventions is a book by Noam Chomsky, an American linguist, MIT professor, and political activist. Published in May 2007, Interventions is a collection of 44 op-ed articles, post-9/11, from September 2002, through March 2007.

Interview 84

An interview is a conversation between two people (the interviewer and the interviewee) where questions are asked by the interviewer to obtain information from the interviewee.

Invention of Writing 68

The history of writing regards the development of expressing language by letters or other marks. In the history of how systems of representation of language through graphic means have evolved in different human civilizations, more complete writing systems were preceded by proto-writing, systems of ideographic and/or early mnemonic symbol. True writing, in which the entire content of a linguistic utterance is encoded so that another reader can reconstruct, with a fair degree of accuracy, the exact utterance written down, is a later development, and is distinguished from proto-writing in that the latter typically avoids encoding grammatical words and affixes, making it difficult or impossible to confidently reconstruct the exact meaning intended by the writer unless a great deal of context is already known in advance.

IP 95

The Internet Protocol (IP) is the principal communications protocol used for relaying datagrams (packets) across an internetwork using the Internet Protocol Suite. Responsible for routing packets across network boundaries, it is the primary protocol that establishes the Internet.

iPhone 128, 155

The iPhone (pronounced: EYE-fohn) is a line of Internet and multimedia-enabled smartphones designed and marketed by Apple Inc. The first iPhone was unveiled on January 9, 2007, and released on June 29, 2007. Steve Jobs, head of Apple announced iPhone to the world in San Francisco, California at the Moscone Center.

iPod 155

iPod is a line of portable media players designed and marketed by Apple and launched on October 23, 2001. The product line-up currently consists of the hard drive-based iPod Classic, the touchscreen iPod Touch, the compact iPod Nano, and the ultra-compact iPod Shuffle. iPod Classic models store media on an internal hard drive, while all other models use flash memory to enable their smaller size (the discontinued Mini used a Microdrive miniature hard drive). As with many other digital music players, iPods can also serve as external data storage devices. Storage capacity varies by model, ranging from 2 GB for the iPod Shuffle to 160 GB for the iPod Classic. All of the models have been redesigned multiple times since their introduction. The most recent iPod redesigns were introduced on September 1, 2010.

Irony 73

Irony (from the Ancient Greek: eirōneía, meaning dissimulation or feigned ignorance) is a rhetorical device, literary technique, or situation in which there is a sharp incongruity or discordance that goes beyond the simple and evident intention of words or actions. Ironic statements (verbal irony) usually convey a meaning exactly opposite from their literal meaning. A situation is often said to be ironic (situational irony) if the actions taken have an effect exactly opposite from what was intended. The discordance of verbal irony is created as a means of communication (as in art or rhetoric). Descriptions or depictions of situational ironies, whether in fiction or in non-fiction, serve a communicative function of sharpening or highlighting certain discordant features of reality.

Itinerary 60

Travel literature is travel writing of literary value. Travel literature typically records the experiences of an author touring a place for the pleasure of travel. An individual work is sometimes called a travelogue or itinerary. Travel literature may be cross-cultural or transnational in focus, or may involve travel to different regions within the same country. Accounts of spaceflight may also be considered travel literature.

iTunes 76
iTunes is a proprietary digital media player application, used for playing and organizing digital music and video files. The application is also an interface to manage the contents on Apple's iPod and iPhone lines, as well as the iPad.

Journal 77, 81, 146
A journal (through French from Latin diurnalis, daily) has several related meanings: a daily record of events or business; a private journal is usually referred to as a diary; a newspaper or other periodical, in the literal sense of one published each day; many publications issued at stated intervals, such as magazines, or scholarly pacific journals, academic journals, or the record of the transactions of a society, are often called journals. Although journal is sometimes used, erroneously, as a synonym for 'magazine', in academic use, a journal refers to a serious, scholarly publication, most often peer-reviewed. A non-scholarly magazine written for an educated audience about an industry or an area of professional activity is usually [citation needed] called a professional magazine. The word 'journalist' for one whose business is writing for the public press has been in use since the end of the 17th century.

Journalism 52-53, 95
Journalism is the practice of investigation and reporting of events, issues, and trends to a broad audience. Although there is much variation within journalism, the ideal is to inform the citizenry. Besides covering organizations and institutions such as government and business, journalism also covers cultural aspects of society such as arts and entertainment. The field includes jobs such as editing, photojournalism, and documentary.

Journalist 53, 71, 126, 152, 163
A journalist collects and disseminates information about current events, people, trends, and issues. His or her work is acknowledged as journalism.

Journals 76, 87
A written medium, for instance: an academic journal; a diary; a literary magazine, a periodical devoted to literature; a daily newspaper; a scientific journal; a bound paper book with blank lined pages into which accounting transactions were written by pen and ink.

JPEG Image 157
In computing, JPEG is a commonly used method of lossy compression for digital photography (image). The degree of compression can be adjusted, allowing a selectable tradeoff between storage size and image quality. JPEG typically achieves 10:1 compression with little perceptible loss in image quality.

Kafka 155
Franz Kafka (3 July 1883–3 June 1924) was a culturally influential German-language novelist. Contemporary critics and academics [who?] regard Kafka as one of the best writers of the 20th century. The term 'Kafkaesque' has become part of the English vernacular.

Keywords 77
Keywords are the words that are used to reveal the internal structure of an author's reasoning. While they are used primarily for rhetoric, they are also used in a strictly grammatical sense for structural composition, reasoning, and comprehension. Indeed, they are an essential part of any language.

Kittler 96
Friedrich A. Kittler (born 1943 in Rochlitz, Saxony) is a literary scholar and a media theorist. His works relate to media, technology, and the military.

Know How 58, 99
Procedural knowledge, also known as imperative knowledge, is the knowledge exercised in the performance of some task. See below for the specific meaning of this term in cognitive psychology and intellectual property law.

Knowledge 51, 74, 79-81, 91, 107-109, 113-114, 119, 121, 124, 126-127, 129, 138, 143, 149, 152-154, 157
Knowledge is a detailed familiarity with, or understanding of, a person, thing or situation. It can include facts and information, as well as understanding that is gained through experience, education or reason. It can be implicit (as with practical skill or expertise) or explicit (as with the theoretical understanding of a subject); and it can be more or less formal or systematic. In philosophy, the study of knowledge is called epistemology, and the philosopher Plato famously defined knowledge as justified true belief. There is however no single agreed upon definition of knowledge.

Knowledge is Power 121
The famous phrase scientia potentia est is a Latin maxim meaning 'knowledge is power'. It is commonly attributed to Sir Francis Bacon; however, there is no known occurrence of this precise phrase in Bacon's English or Latin writings. The closest expression in Bacon's works is 'Human knowledge and human power meet in one; for where the cause is not known the effect cannot be produced. Nature to be commanded must be obeyed; and that which in contemplation is as the cause is in operation as the rule.'

KPN 92
KPN (in full Koninklijke KPN N.V., also Royal KPN N.V.) is a Dutch landline and mobile telecommunications company, including both 2G and 3G mobile operations. The company is based in The Hague.

Lady Gaga 119

Stefani Joanne Angelina Germanotta (born March 28, 1986), better known by her stage name Lady Gaga, is an American pop singer-songwriter. After performing in the rock music scene of New York City's Lower East Side in 2003 and later enrolling at New York University's Tisch School of the Arts, she soon signed with Streamline Records, an imprint of Interscope Records. During her early time at Interscope, she worked as a songwriter for fellow label artists and captured the attention of Akon, who recognized her vocal abilities, and signed her to his own label, Kon Live Distribution.

Lament 59

A lament or lamentation is a song, poem, or piece of music expressing grief, regret, or mourning.

Language 54, 64, 69, 79, 96, 109-110, 113, 116, 125-126, 132, 134, 154, 162-163, 169

Language may refer either to the specifically human capacity for acquiring and using complex systems of communication, or to a specific instance of such a system of complex communication. The scientific study of language in any of its senses is called linguistics.

Lap 60, 66

A lap is the area on top of the thighs of a sitting person.

Laptop 149, 160

A laptop (notebook) is a personal computer for mobile use. A laptop integrates most of the typical components of a desktop computer, including a display, a keyboard, a pointing device (a touchpad, also known as a trackpad, and/or a pointing stick) and speakers into a single unit. A laptop is powered by mains electricity via an AC adapter, and can be used away from an outlet using a rechargeable battery. A laptop battery in new condition typically stores enough energy to run the laptop for three to five hours, depending on the computer usage, configuration and power management settings. When the laptop is plugged into the mains, the battery charges, whether or not the computer is running.

Latin Root 59

The following is an alphabetical list of Greek and Latin roots, stems, suffixes, and prefixes commonly used in English.

Latour 107

Bruno Latour (born 22 June 1947, Beaune, Côte-d'Or) is a French sociologist and anthropologist and an influential theorist in the field of Science and Technology Studies (STS). After teaching at the École des Mines de Paris (Centre de Sociologie de l'Innovation) from 1982 to 2006, he is now Professor and vice-president for research at the Institut d'études politiques de Paris (2007), where he is associated with the Centre de sociologie des organisations (CSO).

Layout 78, 91, 96, 142

Page layout is the part of graphic design that deals in the arrangement and style treatment of elements (content) on a page.

Lead In 168

Optical disc authoring, including DVD and Blu-ray Disc authoring (often referred to colloquially as burning), is the process of assembling source material – video, audio or other data – into the proper logical volume format to then be recorded (burned) onto an optical disc (typically a compact disc or DVD).

Leading 65, 74, 76, 78, 142, 161

In typography, leading refers to the distance between the baselines of successive lines of type. The term originated in the days of hand-typesetting, when thin strips of lead were inserted into the formes to increase the vertical distance between lines of type. The term is still used in modern page layout software such as QuarkXPress and Adobe InDesign.

Learn to Read 96, 164, 172

'Learn to Read' is an adult educational TV series that consists of 30 programs, hosted by entrepreneur and literacy advocate Wally Amos. Co-instructors include Doris Biscoe (who was an anchorwoman for WXYZ-TV in Detroit, Michigan) and Charlotte Scot. Bruce Jenner guest-starred on the first episode. This was based on 27 million Americans having almost no reading skills. On Friday, there is a review of the week. The final program reviews the entire series.

Learning 80, 116, 126, 134, 149-150, 164

Learning is acquiring new or modifying existing knowledge, behaviors, skills, values, or preferences and may involve synthesizing different types of information. The ability to learn is possessed by humans, animals and some machines. Progress over time tends to follow learning curves.

Lecture 59, 67

A lecture is an oral presentation intended to present information or teach people about a particular subject, for example by a university or college teacher. Lectures are used to convey critical information, history, background, theories and equations. A politician's speech, a minister's sermon, or even a businessman's sales presentation may be similar in form to a lecture. Usually the lecturer will stand at the front of the room and recite information relevant to the lecture's content.

Lecture Hall 67

A lecture hall (or lecture theatre) is a large room used for instruction, typically at a college or university. Unlike a traditional classroom with a capacity from one to four dozen, the capacity of lecture halls is typically measured in the hundreds. Lecture halls almost always have a pitched floor, so that those in the rear are sat higher than those at the front, allowing them to see the lecturer. The importance of lecture halls is so significant that some schools of architecture have offered courses exclusively centered on their design. The noted Boston architect Earl Flansburgh wrote numerous articles focusing on achieving efficacious lecture hall design.

Legislator 104

A legislator (or lawmaker) is a person who writes and passes laws, especially someone who is a member of a legislature. Legislators are usually politicians and are often elected by the people. Legislatures may be supra-national (for example, the United Nations General Assembly), national (for example, the United States Congress), regional (for example, the National Assembly for Wales) or local for example, local authorities.

Letter Carriers 117

A mail carrier, mailman (US), postman/postwoman (UK), letter carrier (in American English and in New Zealand) or postie (in Australia, New Zealand) is an employee of the post office or postal service, who delivers mail and parcel post to residences and businesses. The term 'mail carrier' came to be used as a gender-neutral substitute for 'mailman' soon after women began performing the job.

Librarians 145

A librarian is an information professional trained in library and information science, which is the organization and management of information services or materials for those with information needs. Typically, librarians work in a public or college library, an elementary or secondary school media center, a library within a business or company, or another information-provision agency like a hospital or law firm. Some librarians are independent entrepreneurs working as information specialists, catalogers, indexers and other professional, specialized capacities. Librarians may be categorized as a public, school, correctional, special, independent or academic librarian.

Library 50, 71, 73-74, 81, 112-113, 130, 136, 144-145, 152-154, 157

A library is a collection of sources, resources, and services, and the structure in which it is housed; it is organized for use and maintained by a public body, an institution, or a private individual. In the more traditional sense, a library is a collection of books. It can mean the collection itself, the building or room that houses such a collection, or both. The term 'library' has itself acquired a secondary meaning: 'a collection of useful material for common use'. This sense is used in fields such as computer science, mathematics, statistics, electronics and biology. It can also be used by publishers in naming series of related books, e.g. The Library of Anglo-Catholic Theology.

Libre 82

Libre in English is adopted from the various Romance languages, ultimately descending from the Latin word lībere; its origin is closely related to liberty. It denotes 'the state of being free', as in 'liberty' or 'having freedom'. The Oxford English Dictionary (OED) considers libre to be obsolete, but the word has come back into limited use. Unlike gratis, libre appears in few English dictionaries, although there is no other English single-word adjective signifying 'liberty' exclusively, without also meaning 'at no monetary cost'.

Libre Software 82

Free software, software libre or libre software is software that can be used, studied, and modified without restriction, and which can be copied and redistributed in modified or unmodified form either without restriction, or with minimal restrictions only to ensure that further recipients can also do these things and that manufacturers of consumer-facing hardware allow user modifications to their hardware. Free software is generally available without charge, but can have a fee, such as in the form of charging for CDs or other distribution medium among other ways.

Life 70, 85, 87, 99-101, 109, 114-115, 120, 124, 127, 144

Life can refer to three American magazines: A humor and general interest magazine published from 1883 to 1936. Time founder Henry Luce bought the magazine in 1936 solely so that he could acquire the rights to its name; A weekly news magazine launched by Luce in 1936, with a strong emphasis on photojournalism. Life was published until 1972; as an intermittent 'special' until 1978; and as a monthly from 1978 to 2000.; A weekly newspaper supplement published by Time Inc. from 2004 to 2007 and included in some American newspapers.

Light-Hearted 133

Jack the Ripper, Light-Hearted Friend is a 1996 book by Richard Wallace in which Wallace proposed a theory that British author Lewis Carroll, whose real name was Charles L. Dodgson (1832–1898), and his colleague Thomas Vere Bayne (1829–1908) were responsible for the Jack the Ripper murders.

Likes 53, 90

In the English language, the word like has a very flexible range of uses, ranging from conventional to non-standard. It can be used as a noun, verb, adverb, adjective, preposition, particle, conjunction, hedge, interjection, and quotative.

Limitations 55

Limitations is a novel by Scott Turow which was published in 2006. It is by far his shortest novel (197 pages) and prior to publication as a novel was released as a serial story in the Sunday New York Times Magazine.

Linear Code 134

In coding theory, a linear code is an error-correcting code for which any linear combination of codewords is another codeword of the code. Linear codes are traditionally partitioned into block codes and convolutional codes, although Turbo codes can be seen as a hybrid of these two types. Linear codes allow for more efficient encoding and decoding algorithms than other codes (cf. syndrome decoding).

Linearity 115, 134

The word linear comes from the Latin word linearis, which means created by lines.

Linguistic 50, 54

Linguistics is the scientific study of human language. Linguistics can be broadly broken into three categories or subfields: the study of language form, of language meaning, and of language in context. The first is the study of language structure, or grammar. This focuses on the system of rules followed by the speakers (or hearers) of a language. It encompasses morphology (the formation and composition of words), syntax (the formation and composition of phrases and sentences from these words), and phonology (sound systems). Phonetics is a related branch of linguistics concerned with the actual properties of speech sounds, nonspeech sounds, and how they are produced and perceived. The study of language meaning is concerned with how languages employ logical structures and real-world references to convey, process and assign meaning, as well as to manage and resolve ambiguity. This subfield encompasses semantics (how meaning is inferred from words and concepts) and pragmatics (how meaning is inferred from context).

Literacy 66, 72, 83, 139-140, 157

Literacy has traditionally been described as the ability to read and write. It is a concept claimed and defined by a range of different theoretical fields.

Literal 120

Literal and figurative language is a distinction in traditional systems for analyzing language. Literal language refers to words that do not deviate from their defined meaning. Figurative language refers to words, and groups of words, that exaggerate or alter the usual meanings of the component words. Figurative language may involve analogy to similar concepts or other contexts, and may involve exaggerations. These alterations result in figures of speech.

Live chat 95

Live Support Software (aka Live person, Live chat, Live help) is a popular term for instant messaging applications designed specifically to provide online assistance to users of a web site.

Long Tail 175

The phrase the Long Tail was, according to Chris Anderson, first coined by him. The concept drew in part from a February 2003 essay by Clay Shirky, 'Power Laws, Weblogs and Inequality', which noted that a relative handful of weblogs have many links going into them but 'the long tail' of millions of weblogs may have only a handful of links going into them. Beginning in a series of speeches in early 2004 and culminating with the publication of a Wired magazine article in October 2004, Anderson described the effects of the Long Tail on current and future business models. Anderson later extended it into the book The Long Tail: Why the Future of Business is Selling Less of More (2006).

Look and Feel 102

In software design, look and feel is a term used in respect of a graphical user interface and comprises aspects of its design, including elements such as colors, shapes, layout, and typefaces (the 'look'), as well as the behavior of dynamic elements such as buttons, boxes, and menus (the 'feel'). The term can also refer to aspects of an API, mostly to parts of an API which are not related to its functional properties. The term is used in reference to both software and websites. Look and feel applies to other products. In documentation, for example, it refers to the graphical layout (document size, color, font, etc.) and the writing style. In the context of equipment, it refers to consistency in controls and displays across a product line. Look and feel in operating system user interfaces serves two general purposes. First, it provides branding, helping to identify a set of products from one company. Second, it increases ease of use, since users will become familiar with how one product functions (looks, reads, etc.) and can translate their experience to other products with the same look and feel.

Looker 141

Looker is a 1981 science fiction film written and directed by Michael Crichton. It starred Albert Finney, Susan Dey, James Coburn and featured former NFL linebacker Tim Rossovich as the villain's main henchman.

Lost 57, 67, 102, 110, 115, 120, 146, 148

'Lost' is an American television series that originally aired on the American Broadcasting Company (ABC) between 2004 and 2010, consisting of six seasons. Lost is a drama series that follows the lives of various individuals and groups of people, most importantly the survivors of the crash of a commercial passenger jet flying between Sydney and Los Angeles, on a mysterious tropical island somewhere in the South Pacific Ocean. Episodes typically feature a primary storyline on the island, as well as a secondary storyline from another point in a character's life.

Loved 139, 144

'Loved' is a song recorded by Kim Wilde as a 'new' track for the compilation album The Very Best of Kim Wilde released in 2001.

MacBook 128

The MacBook is a brand of Macintosh notebook computers built by Apple Inc. First introduced in May 2006, it replaced the iBook and 12-inch PowerBook series of notebooks as a part of the Apple-Intel transition. Positioned as the low end of the MacBook family, the MacBook is aimed at the consumer and education markets. It is the best-selling Macintosh in history, and according to the sales-research organization NPD Group in October 2008, the mid-range model of the MacBook was the single best-selling laptop of any brand in U.S. retail stores for the preceding five months.

Magazine 50, 90-92, 103, 108, 112, 116, 160, 163

Magazines, periodicals, glossies or serials are publications, generally published on a regular schedule, containing a variety of articles. They are generally financed by advertising, by a purchase price, by pre-paid magazine subscriptions, or all three.

Mail 56, 63

Mail, or post, is a method for transmitting information and tangible objects, wherein written documents, typically enclosed in envelopes and also small packages are delivered to destinations around the world. Anything sent through the postal system is called mail or post.

Mandela 153

Nelson Rolihlahla Mandela; born 18 July 1918) served as President of South Africa from 1994 to 1999, and was the first South African president to be elected in a fully representative democratic election. Before his presidency, Mandela was an anti-apartheid activist, and the leader of Umkhonto we Sizwe, the armed wing of the African National Congress (ANC). In 1962 he was arrested and convicted of sabotage and other charges, and sentenced to life in prison. Mandela served 27 years in prison, spending many of these years on Robben Island. Following his release from prison on 11 February 1990, Mandela led his party in the negotiations that led to multi-racial democracy in 1994. As president from 1994 to 1999, he frequently gave priority to reconciliation.

Manga 109

Manga consist of comics and print cartoons (sometimes also called komikku), in the Japanese language and conforming to the style developed in Japan in the late 19th century. In their modern form, manga date from shortly after World War II, but they have a long, complex pre-history in earlier Japanese art.

Mantras 174

A mantra is a sound, syllable, word, or group of words that is considered capable of creating transformation (cf. spiritual transformation). Their use and type varies according to the school and philosophy associated with the mantra.

Manuscript 87, 135

A manuscript or handwrit is a recording of information that has been manually created by someone or some people, such as a hand-written letter, as opposed to being printed or reproduced some other way. The term may also be used for information that is hand-recorded in other ways than writing, for example inscriptions that are chiselled upon a hard material or scratched (the original meaning of graffiti) as with a knife point in plaster or with a stylus on a waxed tablet, (the way Romans made notes), or are in cuneiform writing, impressed with a pointed stylus in a flat tablet of unbaked clay.

Map 60, 63-64, 128

A map is a visual, often 2-dimensional, representation of a space – e.g. as a navigational aid.

Marginalia 57, 135

Marginalia are scribbles, comments, and illuminations in the margins of a book.

Marked 56

Marked is a television program produced by NorthSouth Productions for History that premiered August 27, 2009. MARKED explores the world of tattoos belonging to modern day tribes that operate at the edges of society, including motorcycle clubs, urban gangs, and hardcore prisoners. The show takes the viewer into the minds of members as they explain what the mysterious symbols decorating their bodies mean on the street, and mean to them personally. Initiation rites, turf wars, and the fierce pride of belonging to an outlaw family are all part of the territory. Tattoo artists and cultural experts explain the technique and history behind the ink and the groups it adorns, putting the personal experiences of the main characters into perspective.

Marketplace 69

A marketplace is the space, actual, virtual or metaphorical, in which a market operates. The term is also used in a trademark law context to denote the actual consumer environment, ie. the 'real world' in which products and services are provided and consumed.

Mass Marketing 52

Mass marketing is a market coverage strategy in which a firm decides to ignore market segment differences and go after the whole market with one offer. It is type of marketing (or attempting to sell through persuasion) of a product to a wide audience. The idea is to broadcast a message that will reach the largest number of people possible. Traditionally mass marketing has focused on radio, television and newspapers as the medium used to reach this broad audience. By reaching the largest audience possible exposure to the product is maximized. In theory this would directly correlate with a larger number of sales or buy in to the product.

Mass Media 52, 65

Mass media refers collectively to all media technologies, including the Internet, television, newspapers, and radio, which are used for mass communications, and to the organizations which control these technologies.

Mastering 162

Mastering, a form of audio post-production, is the process of preparing and transferring recorded audio from a source containing the final mix to a data storage device (the master); the source from which all copies will be produced (via methods such as pressing, duplication or replication). Recently, the format choice includes using digital masters although analog masters, such as audio tapes, are still being used by the manufacturing industry and by a few engineers who have chosen to specialize in analog mastering.

Materialized 133

In philosophy, the theory of materialism holds that the only thing that exists is matter; that all things are composed of material and all phenomena (including consciousness) are the result of material interactions. In other words, matter is the only substance. To many philosophers, not only is 'physicalism' synonymous with 'materialism', but they use both even if they are talking about more than matter (like anti-matter or gravity). Therefore much of the generally philosophical discussion below on materialism may be relevant to physicalism.

McGurk effect 65

The McGurk effect is a perceptual phenomenon which demonstrates an interaction between hearing and vision in speech perception. It suggests that speech perception is multimodal, that is, that it involves information from more than one sensory modality. The McGurk effect is sometimes called the McGurk-MacDonald effect. It was first described in a paper by Harry McGurk and John MacDonald in 1976.

McLuhan, Marshall 113-114

Herbert Marshall McLuhan, CC (July 21, 1911–December 31, 1980) was a Canadian educator, philosopher, and scholar – a professor of English literature, a literary critic, a rhetorician, and a communication theorist. McLuhan's work is viewed as one of the cornerstones of the study of media theory, as well as having practical applications in the advertising and television industries.

Media Circus 169

Media circus describes a news event where the media coverage is perceived to be out of proportion to the event being covered, such as the number of reporters at the scene, the amount of news media published or broadcast, and the level of media hype. The term is meant to critique the media by comparing it to a circus and, as such, is an idiom and not an objective observation. Media hype, orgy, and feeding frenzy are similar terms used in reference to a critique of news and entertainment media.

Media Ecology 50

Media ecology is a contested term within media studies having different meanings within European and North American contexts. The North American definition refers to an interdisciplinary field of media theory and media design involving the study of media environments. According to the Media Ecology Association, media ecology can be defined as 'the study of media environments, the idea that technology and techniques, modes of information and codes of communication play a leading role in human affairs.'

Media Outlets 72

The news media refers to the section of the mass media that focuses on presenting current news to the public. These include print media (newspapers, magazines); broadcast media (radio stations, television stations, television networks), and increasingly Internet-based media (World Wide Web pages, blogs).

Mediated 69-70, 75, 111, 117

Mediated: How the Media Shapes Your World and the Way You Live in It is a non-fiction book by anthropologist Thomas de Zengotita published in 2005 by Bloomsbury about the effect of the media in the Western world.

Medium 56, 65-66, 73, 84, 102-103, 111-112, 114, 120, 123, 148, 150, 170

In communications, media (singular medium) are the storage and transmission channels or tools used to store and deliver information or data. It is often referred to as synonymous with mass media or news media, but may refer to a single medium used to communicate any data for any purpose.

Memoir 95

A memoir (from the French: mémoire from the Latin memoria, meaning 'memory', or a reminiscence), is a literary genre, forming a subclass of autobiography – although the terms 'memoir' and 'autobiography' are almost interchangeable. Memoir is autobiographical writing, but not all autobiographical writing follows the criteria for memoir set out below. The author of a memoir may be referred to as a memoirist.

Memory 57, 97, 114, 119

In psychology, memory is an organism's ability to store, retain, and recall information and experiences. Traditional studies of memory began in the fields of philosophy, including techniques of artificially enhancing memory. The late nineteenth and early twentieth century put memory within the paradigms of cognitive psychology. In recent decades, it has become one of the principal pillars of a branch of science called cognitive neuroscience, an interdisciplinary link between cognitive psychology and neuroscience.

Memory Loss 119

Memory loss can be partial or total and it is normal when it comes with aging. Sudden memory loss is usually a result of brain trauma and it may be permanent or temporary. When it is caused by medical conditions such as Alzheimer's disease, the memory loss is gradual and tends to be permanent. Otherwise the condition is temporary [contradiction] and only affects memories relating to a portion of one's experience.

Message 82, 93, 109, 121, 132, 162, 171

A message in its most general meaning is an object of communication. It is a vessel which provides information. Yet, it can also be this information. Therefore, its meaning is dependent upon the context in which it is used; the term may apply to both the information and its form. A communiqué is a brief report or statement released by a public agency.

Metadata 76, 85

The term Metadata is an ambiguous term which is used for two fundamentally different concepts (Types). Although an expression 'data about data' is often used, it does not apply to both in the same way. Structural metadata, the design and specification of data structures, cannot be about data, because at design time the application contains no data. In this case the correct description would be 'data about the containers of data'. Descriptive metadata on the other hand, is about individual instances of application data, the data content. In this case, a useful description (resulting in a disambiguating neologism) would be 'data about data contents' or 'content about content' thus metacontent.

Metaphors 62

Metaphor is the concept of understanding one thing in terms of another. A metaphor is a figure of speech that constructs an analogy between two things or ideas; the analogy is conveyed by the use of a metaphorical word in place of some other word. For example: 'Her eyes were glistening jewels.' Metaphors compare things without using 'like' or 'as'.

Microsoft Word 82

Microsoft Word is a non-free commercial word processor designed by Microsoft. It was first released in 1983 under the name Multi-Tool Word for Xenix systems. Subsequent versions were later written for several other platforms including IBM PCs running DOS (1983), the Apple Macintosh (1984), the AT & T Unix PC (1985), Atari ST (1986), SCO UNIX, OS/2, and Microsoft Windows (1989). It is a component of the Microsoft Office system; it is also sold as a standalone product and included in Microsoft Works Suite. The current versions are Microsoft Word 2010 for Windows and 2011 for Mac.

Million Book Project 151

The Million Book Project (or the Universal Library), is a book digitization project, led by Carnegie Mellon University School of Computer Science and University Libraries. Working with government and research partners in India (Digital Library of India) and China, the project is scanning books in many languages, using OCR to enable full text searching, and providing free-to-read access to the books on the web.

MIX 123, 151

MIX is a hypothetical computer used in Donald Knuth's monograph, The Art of Computer Programming (TAOCP). MIX's model number is 1009, which was derived by combining the model numbers and names of several contemporaneous, commercial machines deemed significant by the author. ('MIX' also has the value 1009 in Roman numerals.)

Mobile Devices 94, 145

A mobile device (also known as a handheld device, handheld computer or simply handheld) is a pocket-sized computing device, typically having a display screen with touch input and/or a miniature keyboard. In the case of the personal digital assistant (PDA) the input and output are often combined into a touch-screen interface. Smartphones and PDAs are popular amongst those who require the assistance and convenience of certain aspects of a conventional computer, in environments where carrying one would not be practical. Enterprise digital assistants can further extend the available functionality for the business user by offering integrated data capture devices like barcode, RFID and smart card readers.

Mobile Phone 164, 171

A mobile phone (also called mobile, cellular telephone, or cell phone) is an electronic device used to make mobile telephone calls across a wide geographic area. Mobile phones are different from cordless telephones, which only offer telephone service within a limited range of a fixed land line, for example within a home or an office.

Modern Typography 82

Modern Typography was a reaction against the perceived decadence of typography and design of the late 19th century. It is mostly associated with the works of Jan Tschichold and Bauhaus typographers Herbert Bayer, Laszlo Moholy-Nagy, El Lissitzky and others.

Monetizing 122

Monetization is the process of converting or establishing something into legal tender. It usually refers to the printing of banknotes by central banks, but things such as gold, diamonds and emeralds, and art can also be monetized. Even intrinsically worthless items can be made into money, as long as they are difficult to make or acquire. Monetization may also refer to exchanging securities for currency, selling a possession, charging for something that used to be free or making money on goods or services that were previously unprofitable.

Monks 66

A monk (from Greek: monachos, 'single, solitary') is a person who practices religious asceticism, living either alone or with any number of monks, while always maintaining some degree of physical separation from those not sharing the same purpose. The concept is ancient and can be seen in many religions and in philosophy.

Monocle 72

A monocle is a type of corrective lens used to correct or enhance the vision in only one eye. It consists of a circular lens, generally with a wire ring around the circumference that can be attached to a string. The other end of the string is then connected to the wearer's clothing to avoid losing the monocle. The antiquarian Philipp von Stosch wore a monocle in Rome in the 1720s, in order to closely examine engravings and antique engraved gems, but the monocle did not become an article of gentlemen's apparel until the nineteenth century. It was introduced by the dandy's quizzing glass of the 1790s, as a sense of high fashion.

Monopolies 175

In economics, a monopoly (from Greek monos (alone or single) + polein (to sell)) exists when a specific individual or an enterprise has sufficient control over a particular product or service to determine significantly the terms on which other individuals shall have access to it. (This is in contrast to a monopsony which relates to a single entity's control over a market to purchase a good or service, and contrasted with oligopoly where a few entities exert considerable influence over an industry) Monopolies are thus characterised by a lack of economic competition to produce the good or service and a lack of viable substitute goods. The verb monopolise refers to the process by which a firm gains persistently greater market share than what is expected under perfect competition.

Morse Code 65

Morse code is a method of transmitting textual information as a series of on-off tones, lights, or clicks that can be directly understood by a skilled listener or observer without special equipment. The International Morse Code encodes the Roman alphabet, the Arabic numerals and a small set of punctuation and procedural signals as standardized sequences of short and long signals called 'dots' and 'dashes' respectively, or 'dits' and 'dahs'. Because many non-English natural languages use more than the 26 Roman letters, extensions to the Morse alphabet exist for those languages.

MOSAIC 113, 134

Each character (letter or numeral) is represented by a unique sequence of dots and dashes. The duration of a dash is three times the duration of a dot. Each dot or dash is followed by a short silence, equal to the dot duration. The dot duration is the basic unit of time measurement in code transmission.

Motto 124

A motto (Italian for pledge, sentence; plural: mottos or mottoes) is a phrase meant to formally describe the general motivation or intention of a social group or organization. A motto may be in any language, but Latin is the most used. The local language is usual in the mottos of governments. In informal ways, it can be a rule or slogan someone follows, or lives their life by.

Mouse pad 68

A mousepad (US) or mouse mat (UK) is a surface for enhancing the usability of a computer mouse.

Movable Type 61

Movable Type is a weblog publishing system developed by the company Six Apart. It was publicly announced on September 3, 2001; version 1.0 was publicly released on October 8, 2001. On 12 December 2007, Movable Type was relicensed as free software under the GNU General Public License. The current version is 5.04.

MP3 files 76

MPEG-1 or MPEG-2 Audio Layer III, more commonly referred to as MP3, is a patented digital audio encoding format using a form of lossy data compression. It is a common audio format for consumer audio storage, as well as a de facto standard of digital audio compression for the transfer and playback of music on digital audio players.

Mrs Dalloway 101

Mrs Dalloway (published on 14 May 1925) is a novel by Virginia Woolf that details a day in the life of Clarissa Dalloway in post-World War I England. It is one of Woolf's best-known novels.

Multi-player 143

A multiplayer game is a game which is played by several players. The players might be independent opponents, formed into teams or be just a single team pitted against the game. Games with many independent players are difficult to analyse formally in a game-theoretical way as the players may form coalitions.

Multitask 169

Human multitasking is the performance by an individual of appearing to handle more than one task at the same time. The term is derived from computer multitasking. An example of multitasking is listening to a radio interview while typing an email. Some believe that multitasking can result in time wasted due to human context switching and apparently causing more errors due to insufficient attention.

Multitude 68

Multitude is a political term first used by Machiavelli and reiterated by Spinoza. Recently the term has returned to prominence because of its conceptualization as a new model of resistance against the global capitalist system as described by political theorists Michael Hardt and Antonio Negri in their international best-seller Empire (2000) and expanded upon in their recent Multitude: War and Democracy in the Age of Empire (2004). Other theorists which have recently used the term include political thinkers associated with Autonomist Marxism and its sequelae, including Sylvère Lotringer, Paolo Virno, and thinkers connected with the eponymous review Multitudes.

Museum 161

A museum is an institution that houses and cares for a collection of artifacts and other objects of scientific, artistic, or historical importance and makes them available for public viewing through exhibits that may be permanent or temporary.

Mutually Exclusive 85, 102

In layman's terms, two events are mutually exclusive if they cannot occur at the same time (i.e., they have no common outcomes). An example is tossing a coin, which can result in either heads or tails, but not both. Both outcomes cannot happen simultaneously. Incidentally, both outcomes are collectively exhaustive, which means that at least one of the outcomes must happen (ignoring the possibility that the coin will land on its edge). Not all mutually exclusive events are collectively exhaustive. For example, the outcomes 1 and 4 of rolling a six-sided die are mutually exclusive (cannot happen at the same time) but not collectively exhaustive (there are other possible outcomes).

My Book 136

'My Book' is the solo debut for K-Ci of Jodeci and K-Ci & JoJo. There was only one single released off the album called It's All Love featuring KansasCali.

My Day 89

'My Day' was a newspaper column that was written by first lady Eleanor Roosevelt six days a week from 1935 to 1962. In her column, she discussed issues such as race, women, and key events (Pearl Harbor, Prohibition, H Bomb, etc.). This column allowed Mrs. Roosevelt to spread her ideas and thoughts to millions of Americans and give them a new view on the issues they faced every day. George T. Bye, Eleanor Roosevelt's literary agent, encouraged her to write the column.

My Friend 152

'My Friend' is a song written and recorded by Jimi Hendrix in New York City in 1968 during the recording sessions for Electric Ladyland. The song was first released in 1971 on the posthumous album The Cry of Love and later appeared on the CD First Rays of the New Rising Sun. It was mixed posthumously by Hendrix's engineer Eddie Kramer. Because it was left unreleased at the time it was recorded some people have raised doubts if Hendrix had ever intended to use that song on any of his albums.

Napster 159

Napster is an online music store and a Best Buy company. It was originally founded as a pioneering peer-to-peer file sharing internet service that emphasized sharing audio files that were typically digitally encoded music as MP3 format files. The original company ran into legal difficulties over copyright infringement, ceased operations and was eventually acquired by Roxio and later by Best Buy. For more information about the current service, see Napster (pay service).

Narration 153

A narrator is, within any story (literary work, movie, play, verbal account, etc.), the person who tells the story to the audience. When the narrator is also a character within the story, he or she is sometimes known as the viewpoint character. The narrator is one of three entities responsible for story-telling of any kind. The others are the author and the audience; the latter called the reader when referring specifically to literature.

Narrative 118, 122, 143, 167

A narrative is a story that is created in a constructive format (as a work of speech, writing, song, film, television, video games, in photography or theatre) that describes a sequence of fictional or non-fictional events. The word derives from the Latin verb narrare, 'to recount', and is related to the adjective gnarus, 'knowing' or 'skilled'. Ultimately its origin is found in the Proto-Indo-European root gnō-, 'to know'. The word 'story' may be used as a synonym of 'narrative', but can also be used to refer to the sequence of events described in a narrative. A narrative can also be told by a character within a larger narrative. An important part of narration is the narrative mode, the set of methods used to communicate the narrative through a process called narration.

Network Society 157

The term Network Society describes several different phenomena related to the social, political, economic and cultural changes caused by the spread of networked, digital information and communications technologies. A number of academics (see below) are credited with coining the term since the 1990's and several competing definitions exist. The intellectual origins of the idea can be traced back to the work of early social theorists such as Georg Simmel who analyzed the effect of modernization and industrial capitalism on complex patterns of affiliation, organization, production and experience.

Networking 68

Business networking is a socioeconomic activity by which groups of like-minded businesspeople recognize, create, or act upon business opportunities. A business network is a type of social network whose reason for existing is business activity. There are several prominent business networking organizations that create models of networking activity that, when followed, allow the business person to build new business relationships and generate business opportunities at the same time. A professional network service is an implementation of information technology in support of business networking.

New Media 51, 53, 62, 69, 82, 86, 96, 101, 109, 113, 127, 130, 160-161

New media is a broad term in media studies that emerged in the later part of the 20th century to encompass the amalgamation of traditional media such as film, images, music, spoken and written word, with the interactive power of computer and communications technology, computer-enabled consumer devices and most importantly the Internet. There are many promises related to the term. For example, new media holds out a possibility of on-demand access to content any time, anywhere, on any digital device, as well as interactive user feedback, creative participation and community formation around the media content. Another important promise of New Media is the 'democratization' of the creation, publishing, distribution and consumption of media content. What distinguishes new media from traditional media is the digitizing of content into bits. There is also a dynamic aspect of content production which can be done in real time.

New Technologies 69

In the history of technology, emerging technologies are contemporary advances and innovation in various fields of technology. Various converging technologies have emerged in the technological convergence of different systems evolving towards similar goals. Convergence can refer to previously separate technologies such as voice (and telephony features), data (and productivity applications) and video that now share resources and interact with each other, creating new efficiencies.

News 53, 73, 88-89, 93-94, 119, 129, 136, 145, 152, 159, 164, 168, 172

News is the communication of selected information on current events which is presented by print, broadcast, Internet, or word of mouth to a third party or mass audience.

News Groups 136

A usenet newsgroup is a repository usually within the Usenet system, for messages posted from many users in different locations. The term may be confusing to some, because it is usually a discussion group. Newsgroups are technically distinct from, but functionally similar to, discussion forums on the World Wide Web. Newsreader software is used to read newsgroups.

News Items 168

News Items (French: Faits divers) is a 1983 French documentary film directed by Raymond Depardon. It was screened in the Un Certain Regard section at the 1983 Cannes Film Festival.

Newspaper 55, 57, 116, 127-129, 132

A newspaper is a regularly scheduled publication containing news of current events, informative articles, diverse features and advertising. It usually is printed on relatively inexpensive, low-grade paper such as newsprint. By 2007, there were 6580 daily newspapers in the world selling 395 million copies a day. The worldwide recession of 2008, combined with the rapid growth of web-based alternatives, caused a serious decline in advertising and circulation, as many papers closed or sharply retrenched operations.

NewsRoom 93-94

CNN Newsroom is an American news program on CNN/US.

Non-Fiction 71, 143

Non-fiction or nonfiction is an account, narrative, or representation of a subject which a person presents as fact. This presentation may be accurate or not; that is, it can give either a true or a false account of the subject in question. However, it is generally assumed that the authors of such accounts believe them to be truthful at the time of their composition. Note that reporting the beliefs of others in a non-fiction format is not necessarily an endorsement of the ultimate veracity of those beliefs, it is simply saying that it is true that people believe that (for such topics as mythology, religion). Non-fiction can also be written about fiction, giving information about these other works.

Non-linear 50, 77, 86

In mathematics, a nonlinear system is a system which is not linear, that is, a system which does not satisfy the superposition principle, or whose output is not directly proportional to its input. Less technically, a nonlinear system is any problem where the variable(s) to be solved for cannot be written as a linear combination of independent components. A nonhomogeneous system, which is linear apart from the presence of a function of the independent variables, is nonlinear according to a strict definition, but such systems are usually studied alongside linear systems, because they can be transformed to a linear system of multiple variables.

Nonsense 147

Nonsense is a communication such as speech, writing or other symbolic system that lacks any coherent meaning. Sometimes in ordinary usage, nonsense is synonymous with absurdity or the ridiculous. Many poets, novelists and songwriters have used nonsense in their works, often creating entire works using it for reasons ranging from pure comic amusement or satire, to illustrating a point about language or reasoning. In the philosophy of language and philosophy of science, nonsense is distinguished from sense or meaningfulness, and attempts have been made to come up with a coherent and consistent method of distinguishing sense from nonsense. It is also an important field of study in cryptography regarding separating a signal from noise.

Nooks 145

The Barnes & Noble Nook (styled nook) is a brand of electronic-book readers developed by American book retailer Barnes & Noble, based on the Android platform. The original device was announced in the United States on 20 October 2009, and was released 30 November 2009 for US$259. The original Nook includes Wi-Fi and AT&T 3G wireless connectivity, a six-inch E Ink display, and a separate, smaller color touchscreen that serves as the primary input device. On June 21,

2010 Barnes & Noble reduced the Nook's price to US$199 and announced the launch of a new Wi-Fi-only model for US$149.

Normative 52, 68

Normative has specialized meanings in several academic disciplines. Generically, it means relating to an ideal standard or model. In practice, it has strong connotations of relating to a typical standard or model (see also normality).

Nostalgia 156

The term nostalgia describes a yearning for the past, often in idealized form. The word is a learned formation of a Greek compound, consisting of (nóstos), meaning 'returning home', a Homeric word, and (álgos), meaning 'pain, ache'. It was described as a medical condition, a form of melancholy, in the Early Modern period, and came to be an important topic in Romanticism. Nostalgia, in its most common meaning, caused the old front desk of The Beverly Hills Hotel (from 1942 to 1979) to be made into a bar. In common, less clinical usage, nostalgia sometimes includes a general interest in past eras and their personalities and events, especially the 'good old days' of a few generations back recast in an idyllic light, such as the Belle Époque, Merry England, Neo-Victorian aesthetics, the US 'Antebellum' Old South, etc. Sometimes it is brought on by a sudden image, or remembrance of something from one's childhood.

Notification 93

A modern notification system is a combination of software and hardware that provides a means of delivering a message to a set of recipients. For example, notification systems can send an e-mail when a new topic has been added to Wikipedia. The complexity of the notification system is often dependent on the types of messages that must be sent. An e-mail noting when a page has been inserted into Wikipedia is adequate for such a straightforward task. However, notifying individuals when a building is on fire would require real-time interaction, escalation, scheduling, rosters, and fail-over scenarios.

Number 92, 95, 112–113, 125, 144, 149, 170, 174

A number is a mathematical object used to count and measure. A notational symbol that represents a number is called a numeral but in common use, the word number can mean the abstract object, the symbol, or the word for the number. In addition to their use in counting and measuring, numerals are often used for labels (telephone numbers), for ordering (serial numbers), and for codes (e.g., ISBNs). In mathematics, the definition of number has been extended over the years to include such numbers as zero, negative numbers, rational numbers, irrational numbers, and complex numbers.

Obsolescence 96

Obsolescence is the state of a being which occurs when an object, service or practice is no longer wanted even though it may still be in good working order. Obsolescence frequently occurs because a replacement has become available that is superior in one or more aspects. Obsolete refers to something that is already disused or discarded, or antiquated. Typically, obsolescence is preceded by a gradual decline in popularity.

Offset Lithography 157–158

Offset printing is a commonly used printing technique where the inked image is transferred (or 'offset') from a plate to a rubber blanket, then to the printing surface. When used in combination with the lithographic process, which is based on the repulsion of oil and water, the offset technique employs a flat (planographic) image carrier on which the image to be printed obtains ink from ink rollers, while the non-printing area attracts a water-based film (called 'fountain solution'), keeping the non-printing areas ink-free. Development of the offset press came in two versions: in 1875 by Robert Barclay of England for printing on tin, and in 1903 by Ira Washington Rubel of the United States for printing on paper.

Old Dutch 120

In linguistics, Old Dutch (aka Old West Low Franconian) is the forms of West Franconian spoken and written during the early Middle Ages (c. 600–1150) in the Netherlands and the northern part of present-day Belgium. Old Dutch is considered the first stage in the development of a separate Dutch language and is succeeded by Middle Dutch in the later Middle Ages.

Old Media 62

The old media or legacy media are traditional means of communication and expression that have existed since before the advent of the new medium of the Internet. Industries that are generally considered part of the old media are broadcast and cable television, radio, movie and music studios, newspapers, magazines, books and most print publications.

Omnipresent 130

Omnipresence or ubiquity is the property of being present everywhere. According to eastern theism, God is present everywhere. Divine omnipresence is thus one of the divine attributes, although in western theism it has attracted less philosophical attention than such attributes as omnipotence, omniscience, or being eternal.

On Our Way 68

On Our Way is a studio album by American hardcore punk band Time Flies.

On the Blog 78

'On the Blog' is a BBC Radio comedy series starring Caroline Quentin (Men Behaving Badly), Simon Greenall (I'm Alan Partridge) and Andy Taylor (Red Dwarf). It is written by Kris Dyer, Dave Marks and Andy Taylor and is an Above The Title Production for BBC Radio 2.

On the Internet 52, 113-114, 137, 158

'On the Internet, nobody knows you're a dog' is an adage which began as the caption of a cartoon by Peter Steiner published by The New Yorker on July 5, 1993. The cartoon features two dogs: one sitting on a chair in front of a computer, speaking the caption to a second dog sitting on the floor. As of 2000 [update], the panel was the most reproduced cartoon from The New Yorker, and Steiner has earned over US$50,000 from its reprinting.

Ones 88-89, 122, 125, 129

Ones is a collection of Selena's Spanish and English hits. The Limited Edition version also has a bonus DVD which contains all her videos. The album has been certified 5x Platinum (Latin type) by RIAA with shipments of 500,000 copies.

Online and Offline 156

The terms 'online' and 'offline' (also stylized as 'on-line' and 'off-line') have specific meanings in regard to computer technology and telecommunications. In general, 'online' indicates a state of connectivity, while 'offline' indicates a disconnected state. In common usage, 'online' often refers to the Internet or the World Wide Web.

Online Book 166

An on-line book is a resource in book-like form that is only available to read online. It differs from the common idea of an ebook, which is usually available to download and read locally or on an ebook reader.

Online Communities 160

An online community is a virtual community that exists online whose members enable its existence through taking part in membership ritual. An online community can take the form of an information system where anyone can post content, such as a Bulletin board system or one where only a restricted number of people can initiate posts, such as Weblogs. Online communities have also become a supplemental form of communication between people who know each other primarily in real life. Many means are used in social software separately or in combination, including text-based chat rooms and forums that use voice, video text or avatars. Significant socio-technical change may have resulted from the proliferation of such Internet-based social networks.

Online Journal 81

Electronic journals, also known as ejournals, e-journals, and electronic serials, are scholarly journals or intellectual magazines that can be accessed via electronic transmission. In practice, this means that they are usually published on the Web. They are a specialized form of electronic document: they have the purpose of providing material for academic research and study, and they are formatted approximately like journal articles in traditional printed journals. Being in electronic form, articles sometimes contain metadata that can be entered into specialized databases, such as DOAJ or OACI, as well as the databases and search-engines for the academic discipline concerned.

Open Access 81

Open access (OA) refers to unrestricted online access to articles published in scholarly journals, and increasingly also book chapters or monographs. Open Access comes in two forms, Gratis versus Libre: Gratis OA is no-cost online access, while Libre OA offers some additional usage rights. Open content is similar to OA, but usually includes the right to modify the work, whereas in scholarly publishing it is usual to keep an article's content intact and to associate it with a fixed author. Creative Commons licenses can be used to specify usage rights. The Open Access idea can be extended to the learning objects and resources provided in e-learning.

Open Data 81

Open data is a philosophy and practice requiring that certain data be freely available to everyone, without restrictions from copyright, patents or other mechanisms of control. It has a similar ethos to a number of other 'Open' movements and communities such as open source and open access. However these are not logically linked and many combinations of practice are found. The practice and ideology itself is well established (for example in the Mertonian tradition of science) but the term 'open data' itself is recent. Much of the emphasis in this entry is on data from scientific research and from the data-driven web. In some cases open data may be considered as more properly Open Metadata and there is not yet a consistent formalization. This article uses recent publications and activities to define the scope of the concept and term.

Open Education 81

Open education is a collective term that refers to educational organizations that seek to eliminate barriers to entry. Such institutions, for example, would not have academic admission requirements. Such universities include Open University in Britain and Athabasca University in Canada. Such programs are commonly distance learning programs, but not necessarily.

Open Science 81

Open research is research, conducted in the spirit of free and open source software. If the research is scientific in nature it is frequently referred to as open science; open research can also include social sciences and the humanities.

Open Source 82, 109

The term open source describes practices in production and development that promote access to the end product's source materials. Some consider open source a philosophy, others consider it a pragmatic methodology. Before the term open source became widely adopted, developers and producers used a variety of phrases to describe the concept; open source gained hold with the rise of the Internet, and the attendant need for massive retooling of the computing source code. Opening the source code enabled a self-enhancing diversity of production models, communication paths, and interactive communities. Subsequently, the new phrase 'open-source software' was born to describe the environment that the new copyright, licensing, domain, and consumer issues created.

Openness 123

Openness is a very general philosophical position from which some individuals and organizations operate, often highlighted by a decision-making process recognizing communal management by distributed stakeholders (users/producers/contributors) rather than a centralized authority (owners, experts, boards of directors, etc.)

Opportunities 130

'Opportunities (Let's Make Lots of Money)' is a song by UK synthpop duo Pet Shop Boys, released as a single in 1985 and then in 1986, gaining greater popularity in both the UK and U.S. with its second release. Written as a satire of Thatcherism and its embodiment in conspicuous consumption and yuppies in the United Kingdom during the 1980s, the song's indirect attack on its subject matter has come to exemplify the Pet Shop Boys as ironists in their songwriting.

Oral Tradition 152

Oral tradition, oral culture and oral lore is cultural material and traditions transmitted orally from one generation to another. The messages or testimony are verbally transmitted in speech or song and may take the form, for example, of folktales, sayings, ballads, songs, or chants. In this way, it is possible for a society to transmit oral history, oral literature, oral law and other knowledges across generations without a writing system.

Orality 138–140

Orality is thought and verbal expression in societies where the technologies of literacy (especially writing and print) are unfamiliar to most of the population. The study of orality is closely allied to the study of oral tradition. However, it has broader implications, implicitly touching every aspect of the economics, politics, institutional development, and human development of oral societies. The study of orality has important implications for international development, especially as it relates to the goal of eradicating poverty, as well as to the process of globalization.

Orations 167

Public speaking is the process of speaking to a group of people in a structured, deliberate manner intended to inform, influence, or entertain the listeners. It is closely allied to 'presenting', although the latter has more of a commercial connotation.

Organizing 77

Organizing (also spelled organising) is the act of rearranging elements following one or more rules.

Original 63, 79, 87, 105, 113, 119, 141, 170

Originality is the aspect of created or invented works by as being new or novel, and thus can be distinguished from reproductions, clones, forgeries, or derivative works. An original work is one not received from others nor one copied based on the work of others. The term 'originality' is often applied as a compliment to the creativity of artists, writers and thinkers.

Original Language 113

The origin of language is the onset in prehistory of human spoken language. It also represents the acquisition of the human ability to use language. There are a number of hypotheses surrounding the origin of language, but each is speculative. Being located so early in human prehistory, the relevant developments have left no direct historical traces and no comparable processes can be observed today.

Our Day 144

Our Day is a silent documentary short film directed by Wallace Kelly in 1938, about a day in the life of the Kelly family in Lebanon, Kentucky. It starred his mother, wife, brother, pet dog, and Wallace himself. The film countered the contemporary stereotypes of impoverished Southerners eking out a living during the Depression, by documenting a modern home inhabited by adults with sophisticated interests.

Out 1 125

Out 1 is a 1971 film directed by Jacques Rivette, one of the major filmmakers of the French New Wave. Notorious for its unwieldy length of twelve hours and forty minutes, it is also referred to as Out 1: Noli me tangere. When asked why the film is called Out 1, Rivette responded, 'I choose "Out" as the opposite of the vogue word "in", which had caught in France and which I thought was silly. The action of the film is rather like a serial which could continue through several episodes, so I gave it the number "One".' The Spectre subtitle for the shorter version was similarly chosen for its ambiguous and various indistinct meanings, while the Noli me tangere subtitle ('don't touch me') for the original version is clearly a reference to it being the full length film as intended by Rivette.

Output 72, 105

Output is the term denoting either an exit or changes which exit a system and which activate/modify a process. It is an abstract concept, used in the modeling, system(s) design and system(s) exploitation.

Output device 72

An output device is any piece of computer hardware equipment used to communicate the results of data processing carried out by an information processing system (such as a computer) to the outside world.

Page In 138

In computer operating systems, paging is one of the memory-management schemes by which a computer can store and retrieve data from secondary storage for use in main memory. In the paging memory-management scheme, the operating system retrieves data from secondary storage in same-size blocks called pages. The main advantage of paging is that it allows the physical address space of a process to be noncontiguous. Before the time paging was used, systems had to fit whole programs into storage contiguously, which caused various storage and fragmentation problems.

Page to Screen 143

Page to Screen is an American documentary television series hosted by Peter Gallagher, and narrated by David Hibbard. The series premiered October 28, 2002 on Bravo. Page to Screen explores the process of translating novels into films.

Pamphlet 127

A pamphlet is an unbound booklet (that is, without a hard cover or binding). It may consist of a single sheet of paper that is printed on both sides and folded in half, in thirds, or in fourths (called a leaflet), or it may consist of a few pages that are folded in half and saddle stapled at the crease to make a simple book. In order to count as a pamphlet, UNESCO requires a publication (other than a periodical) to have at least 5 but not more than 48 pages exclusive of the cover pages; a longer item is a book.

Paper 55, 57, 67-68, 73, 76-77, 87-88, 91, 99, 102, 114, 118, 126, 128, 138, 147-149, 156-157, 165-166, 170, 172

Paper is a thin material mainly used for writing upon, printing upon or for packaging. It is produced by pressing together moist fibers, typically cellulose pulp derived from wood, rags or grasses, and drying them into flexible sheets.

Paperback 99

Paperback, softback or softcover describe and refer to a book by the nature of its binding. The covers of such books are usually made of paper or paperboard, and are usually held together with glue rather than stitches or staples. Inexpensive books bound in paper have existed since at least the 19th century and exist in a number of formats that have specific names, such as pamphlets, yellowbacks, dime novels and airport novels. Most paperbacks are either 'mass-market paperbacks' or 'trade paperbacks'. In contrast, books with hardcover or hardback are bound with cardboard covered with cloth; although more expensive, hardbacks are more durable.

Papyrus 153

Papyrus is a thick paper-like material produced from the pith of the papyrus plant, Cyperus papyrus, a wetland sedge that was once abundant in the Nile Delta of Egypt.

Paradoxically 120, 140

A paradox is a seemingly true statement or group of statements that lead to a contradiction or a situation which seems to defy logic or intuition. The term is also used for an apparent contradiction that actually expresses a non-dual truth such as two true sentences which put together seem incompatible as both being true (cf. Catuskoti). Typically however, quoted paradoxical statements do not imply a real contradiction and the puzzling results can be rectified by demonstrating that one or more of the premises themselves are not really true, a play on words, faulty and/or cannot all be true together. But many paradoxes, such as Curry's paradox, do not yet have universally accepted resolutions. The word paradox is often used interchangeably with contradiction. Literary and other artistic uses of paradoxes imply no contradiction and may be used to describe situations that are ironic. Sometimes the term paradox is used for situations that are merely surprising.

Paragraph 67, 142

A paragraph (from the Greek paragraphos, 'to write beside' or 'written beside') is a self-contained unit of a discourse in writing dealing with a particular point or idea. Paragraphs consist of one or more sentences. The start of a paragraph is indicated by beginning on a new line. Sometimes the first line is indented. At various times, the beginning of a paragraph has been indicated by the pilcrow: ¶. A written work – be it an essay or a story – is about an idea or concept. An essay explains it; a story narrates it. To help the reader understand and enjoy it, the explanation or narration is broken down into units of text, the paragraph. In an essay, each paragraph explains or demonstrates a key point or thought of the central idea, usually to inform or persuade. In fiction, each paragraph serves to advance the plot, develop a character, describe a scene or narrate an action – all to entertain the reader. All paragraphs support each other, leading the reader from the first idea to the final resolution of the written work.

Parameters 138

In mathematics, statistics, and the mathematical sciences, a parameter (G: auxiliary measure) is a quantity that serves to relate functions and variables using a common variable when such a relationship would be difficult to explicate with an equation. In different contexts, the term may have special uses. Parameter- is a computation from data values recorded- but it is not actually a data value recorded from a subject. Example: for a population of test scores, a parameter would not be an actual score, but perhaps an average computed from all scores, or a percent computed from all scores.

Paraphrase 54

Paraphrase is restatement of a text or passages, using other words. The term 'paraphrase' derives via the Latin 'paraphrasis' from the Greek para phraseïn, meaning 'additional manner of expression'. The act of paraphrasing is also called 'paraphrasis'. A paraphrase typically explains or clarifies the text that is being paraphrased. For example, 'The signal was red' might be paraphrased as

'The train was not allowed to proceed.' When accompanying the original statement, a paraphrase is usually introduced with a verbum dicendi – a declaratory expression to signal the transition to the paraphrase. For example, in 'The signal was red, that is, the train was not allowed to proceed,' the 'that is' signals the paraphrase that follows.

Participatory 139

Participation in social science refers to different mechanisms for the public to express opinions – and ideally exert influence – regarding political, economic, management or other social decisions. Participatory decision making can take place along any realm of human social activity, including economic (i.e. participatory economics), political (i.e. participatory democracy or parpolity), management (i.e. participatory management), cultural (i.e. intercommunalism) or familial (i.e. feminism).

Passages 128, 145

Passages is a musical album in the style of chamber music co-composed by Ravi Shankar and Philip Glass and released in 1990 by RCA Victor. The album's content is a hybrid of Ravi Shankar's signature sitar playing and Hindustani classical music and Philip Glass's distinct American minimalist contemporary classical style.

Pattern 107, 151, 159, 168

A pattern, from the French patron, is a type of theme of recurring events or objects, sometimes referred to as elements of a set of objects.

Pattern Recognition 107, 168

In machine learning, pattern recognition is the assignment of some sort of output value (or label) to a given input value (or instance), according to some specific algorithm. An example of pattern recognition is classification, which attempts to assign each input value to one of a given set of classes (for example, determine whether a given email is 'spam' or 'non-spam').

Pedagogue 127

Pedagogy is the study of being a teacher or the process of teaching. The term generally refers to strategies of instruction, or a style of instruction.

Period of Time 81, 119

Time is a part of the measuring system used to sequence events, to compare the durations of events and the intervals between them, and to quantify rates of change such as the motions of objects. The temporal position of events with respect to the transitory present is continually changing; future events become present, then pass further and further into the past. Time has been a major subject of religion, philosophy, and science, but defining it in a non-controversial manner applicable to all fields of study has consistently eluded the greatest scholars.

Peripheral 116, 167

A peripheral is a device attached to a host computer, but not part of it, and is more or less dependent on the host. It expands the host's capabilities, but does not form part of the core computer architecture.

Personalize 88

Personalization involves using technology to accommodate the differences between individuals. Once confined mainly to the Web, it is increasingly becoming a factor in education, health care (i.e. personalized medicine), television, and in both 'business to business' and 'business to consumer' settings.

Personification 145

Personification is an ontological metaphor in which a thing or abstraction is represented as a person.

Photo 140

A photograph (often shortened to photo) is an image created by light falling on a light-sensitive surface, usually photographic film or an electronic imager such as a CCD or a CMOS chip. Most photographs are created using a camera, which uses a lens to focus the scene's visible wavelengths of light into a reproduction of what the human eye would see. The process and practice of creating photographs is called photography.

Photography 92

Photography is the art, science, and practice of creating pictures by recording radiation on a radiation-sensitive medium, such as a photographic film, or electronic image sensors. Photography uses foremost radiation in the UV, visible and near-IR spectrum. For common purposes the term light is used instead of radiation. Light reflected or emitted from objects form a real image on a light sensitive area (film or plate) or a FPA pixel array sensor by means of a pin hole or lens in a device known as a camera during a timed exposure. The result on film or plate is a latent image, subsequently developed into a visual image (negative or diapositive). An image on paper base is known as a print. The result on the FPA pixel array sensor is an electrical charge at each pixel which is electronically processed and stored in a computer (raster)-image file for subsequent display or processing. Photography has many uses for business, science, manufacturing (f.i. Photolithography), art, and recreational purposes.

Phrase 71

In everyday speech, a phrase may refer to any group of words. In linguistics, a phrase is a group of words which form a constituent and so function as a single unit in the syntax of a sentence. A phrase is lower on the grammatical hierarchy than a clause.

Phrasing 169

Phrasing refers to an expressive shaping of music, and relates to the shaping of notes in time. Phrasing relates to the manner of playing the individual notes of a particular group of consecutive notes; and the way they are weighted and shaped relative to one another. It does not refer to the idealized note values/durations as represented in sheetmusic; but to the multitude of deviations that the performer needs to make from sheetmusic, if a performance is to be expressive, in a particular style and culturally aware. An example may be an acceleration of a group of notes, but there are many more. This shaping of notes is creatively performed by the musician with the aim of expressing (feelings), and can be distinguished by the listener – not only factually, but in music, as emotional expression.

Picture 58, 71, 78-79, 84, 98, 118, 124-126, 140, 151-152, 159, 163-164, 166

An image (from Latin: imago) is an artifact, for example a two-dimensional picture, that has a similar appearance to some subject – usually a physical object or a person.

Picture and Text 84

Picture and Text is a collection of essays by Henry James on the art of illustration, published in 1893. The essays are brief profiles of the principal illustrators for Harper and Brothers books and magazines, and has been remembered for extensive and perceptive essays on John Singer Sargent and Honoré Daumier. Included with the essays on black-and-white illustration of texts is a discussion in dialogue form about the similar relation between scenery and play in the theater.

Placebo 111

A placebo (Latin: I shall please) is a sham or simulated medical intervention. Sometimes patients given a placebo treatment will have a perceived or actual improvement in a medical condition, a phenomenon commonly called the placebo effect.

Plagiarism 105

Plagiarism is defined in dictionaries as the 'wrongful appropriation,' 'close imitation,' or 'purloining and publication' of another author's 'language, thoughts, ideas, or expressions,' and the representation of them as one's own original work, but the notion remains problematic with nebulous boundaries. The modern concept of plagiarism as immoral and originality as an ideal emerged in Europe only in the 18th century, particularly with the Romantic movement, while in the previous centuries authors and artists were encouraged to 'copy the masters as closely as possible' and avoid 'unnecessary invention'.

Platform 65, 74, 85, 94, 96, 155

A computing platform is some sort of hardware architecture and software framework (including application frameworks) that allows software to run. Typical platforms include a computer's architecture, operating system, programming languages and related user interface (run-time system libraries or graphical user interface).

Pleasure 64, 71, 99

Pleasure describes the broad class of mental states that humans and other animals experience as positive, enjoyable, or worth seeking. It includes more specific mental states such as happiness, entertainment, enjoyment, ecstasy, and euphoria. In psychology, the pleasure principle describes pleasure as a positive feedback mechanism, motivating the organism to recreate in the future the situation which it has just found pleasurable. According to this theory, organisms are similarly motivated to avoid situations that have caused pain in the past.

Pleat 120

A pleat (older plait) is a type of fold formed by doubling fabric back upon itself and securing it in place. It is commonly used in clothing and upholstery to gather a wide piece of fabric to a narrower circumference.

Poetics 111

Poetics refers generally to the theory of literary discourse and specifically to the theory of poetry, although some speakers use the term so broadly as to denote the concept of theory itself.

Popular Culture 95

Popular culture (commonly known as pop culture) is the totality of ideas, perspectives, attitudes, images and other phenomena that are deemed preferred per an informal consensus within the mainstream of a given culture, especially Western culture of the early to mid 20th century and the emerging global mainstream of the late 20th and early 21st century. Heavily influenced by mass media, this collection of ideas permeates the everyday lives of the society.john f

Portable 53, 74, 170

A portable computer is a computer that is designed to be moved from one place to another and includes a display and keyboard. Portable computers, by their nature, are microcomputers. Portable computers, because of their size, are also commonly known as 'Lunchbox' or 'Luggable' computers. They can also be called a 'Portable Workstation' or 'Portable PC'.

Post-Its 128

A Post-it note is a piece of stationery with a re-adherable strip of adhesive on the back, designed for temporarily attaching notes to documents and other surfaces. Although now available in a wide range of colors, shapes, and sizes, Post-it notes are most commonly a 3-inch (76 mm) square, canary yellow in color. A unique low-tack adhesive allows the notes to be easily attached and removed without leaving marks or residue, unless used on white boards.

Post-synchronization 79

Dubbing is the post-production process of recording and replacing voices on a motion picture or television soundtrack subsequent to the original shooting. The term most commonly refers to the substitution of the voices of the actors shown on the screen by those of different performers, who may be speaking a different language. The procedure was sometimes practised in musicals when the actor had an unsatisfactory singing voice, and remains in use to enable the screening of audio-visual material to a mass audience in countries where viewers do not speak the same language as the original performers. 'Dubbing' also describes the process of an actor's re-recording lines spoken during filming and which must be replaced to improve audio quality or reflect dialog changes.

Postulated 86

In traditional logic, an axiom or postulate is a proposition that is not proved or demonstrated but considered to be either self-evident, or subject to necessary decision. That is to say, an axiom is a logical statement that is assumed to be true. Therefore, its truth is taken for granted, and serves as a starting point for deducing and inferring other (theory dependent) truths.

Powerful 52, 73, 101, 118

Power is a measure of an entity's ability to control its environment, including the behavior of other entities. The term authority is often used for power, perceived as legitimate by the social structure. Power can be seen as evil or unjust, but the exercise of power is accepted as endemic to humans as social beings. In the corporate environment, power is often expressed as upward or downward. With downward power, a company's superior influences subordinates. When a company exerts upward power, it is the subordinates who influence the decisions of the leader (Greiner & Schein, 1988). Often, the study of power in a society is referred to as politics.

Practical 61, 82, 148

Pragmatism is an American philosophical practice founded, roughly, on the following hypotheses: that knowledge is a social phenomenon rather than introspective; that an object of knowledge must consider the conceivable effects upon our actions in order to conceive of the object in its entirety; that truth can only be found through ongoing investigation, in which we check our experiences against one another; that truth is never complete, as the future is always uncertain and may alter a current truth; that all knowledge is primarily a call to action, wherein we recheck it, build upon it, or use it to shape our society; that all learning changes the world, for part of its effect will be causing us to act differently than had we not learned. It espouses theories of truth which give preference on practicality rather then theoretical discourses.

Predetermined 62

Determinism (specifically causal determinism) is the concept that events within a given paradigm are bound by causality in such a way that any state (of an object or event) is completely, or at least to some large degree, determined by prior states. In physics, this principle is known as cause-and-effect.

Prediction 65, 70

A prediction or forecast is a statement about the way things will happen in the future, often but not always based on experience or knowledge. While there is much overlap between prediction and forecast, a prediction may be a statement that some outcome is expected, while a forecast may cover a range of possible outcomes.

Presentation 93

Presentation is the practice of showing and explaining the content of a topic to an audience or learner. A presentation program, such as Microsoft PowerPoint, Apple Keynote, OpenOffice.org Impress or Prezi, is often used to generate the presentation content. The development of information technology has made the use of these solutions possible, but overhead transparencies are still used widely.

Presenter 78

A presenter, or host (sometimes hostess, in feminine form), is a person or organization responsible for running an event. A museum or university, for example, may be the presenter or host of an exhibit. Likewise, a master of ceremonies (also MC, emcee, or host) is a person that hosts or presents a show. In films, a presenter (but not a host) is a usually well-known executive producer credited with introducing a film or filmmaker to a larger audience. In broadcast media, especially British, a presenter is the person who hosts, narrates, presents, or takes the main role in the program.

Presents 132

A gift or a present is the transfer of something without the expectation of receiving something in return. Although gift-giving might involve an expectation of reciprocity, a gift is meant to be free. In many human societies, the act of mutually exchanging money, goods, etc. may contribute to social cohesion. Economists have elaborated the economics of gift-giving into the notion of a gift economy. By extension the term gift can refer to anything that makes the other happier or less sad, especially as a favor, including forgiveness and kindness.

Preservation 102

Preservation is to protect something, that might include endangered animals, to keep them safe or to preserve food, remaining fresh for longer periods of time.

Press 52-53, 69, 99, 104, 123, 127, 156

The press, otherwise known as the journalism business, the newspaper business, the news media, the Fourth Estate or the mass media.

Print Shop 127

The Print Shop is a basic desktop publishing software package developed in the early 1980s by Brøderbund. It was unique in that it provided libraries of clip-art and templates through a simple interface to build signs, posters and banners with household dot-matrix printers. Over the years the software has been updated to accommodate changing file formats and printer technologies.

Print-on-Demand 102, 105

Print on demand (POD), sometimes called publish on demand, is a printing technology and business process in which new copies of a book (or other document) are not printed until an order has been received. 'Print on Demand' developed only after digital printing began, because it was not economical to print single copies using traditional printing technology such as letterpress and offset printing. Many traditional small presses have replaced their traditional printing equipment with POD equipment or contract their printing out to POD service providers. Many academic publishers, including university presses, use POD services to maintain a large backlist; some even use POD for all of their publications. Larger publishers may use POD in special circumstances, such as reprinting older titles that had been out of print or for performing test marketing.

Printed 50-51, 54-55, 61, 73, 77, 99-100, 103, 106, 130, 138-140, 143, 153, 156-159, 165, 167-168

Printing is a process for reproducing text and image, typically with ink on paper using a printing press. It is often carried out as a large-scale industrial process, and is an essential part of publishing and transaction printing.

Printed Matter 158

Printed matter is a term to describe printed material produced by printers or publishers, such as books, magazines, booklets, brochures and other publicity materials and in some cases, newspapers. Because much of this material is mailed, it is also a category of mail, accepted for delivery by a postal administration, that is not considered to be first-class mail and therefore qualifies for a special reduced printed matter postal rate. Depending on the specific postal regulations of the country, it is usually non-personal correspondence and printed in multiple quantities. Most postal authorities do not permit additional services, like registration or express services, to be added to items mailed as printed matter.

Printed Paper 73, 165

Thomas Carlyle (4 December 1795–5 February 1881) was a Scottish satirical writer, essayist, historian and teacher during the Victorian era. He called economics 'the dismal science', wrote articles for the Edinburgh Encyclopedia, and became a controversial social commentator. Printed Paper was Carlyle's satirical name for the literature of France prior to the Revolution.

Printers 55, 163

In publishing, printers are both companies providing printing services and individuals who directly operate printing presses. With the invention of the moveable type printing press by Johannes Gutenberg around 1450, printing – and printers – proliferated throughout Europe. Today, printers are found throughout the world. They include: Newspaper printers are often owned by newspaper publishers; Magazine printers are usually independent of magazine publishers; Book printers, often not directly connected with book publishers; Stationery printers; Packaging printers; Commercial printers, often offering digital and traditional printing services. An artist who operates a printing press to execute their own works, especially by hand in limited runs, is usually distinguished from other printers by the term printmaker.

Printing 50, 52-53, 61, 75, 88, 99, 127, 149, 156

Printing is a process for reproducing text and image, typically with ink on paper using a printing press. It is often carried out as a large-scale industrial process, and is an essential part of publishing and transaction printing.

Printing Press 53, 99, 127, 156

A printing press is a device for applying pressure to an inked surface resting upon a print medium (such as paper or cloth), thereby transferring the ink. Typically used for texts, the invention and spread of the printing press are widely regarded as the most influential events in the second millennium AD, revolutionizing the way people conceive and describe the world they live in, and ushering in the period of modernity.

Processing 66

Process or processing typically describes the act of taking something through an established and usually routine set of procedures or steps to convert it from one form to another, such as processing milk into cheese, or processing paperwork to grant a mortgage loan, or converting computer data from one form to another. A process involves steps and decisions in the way work is accomplished.

Project Gutenberg 54

Project Gutenberg, abbreviated as PG, is a volunteer effort to digitize and archive cultural works, to 'encourage the creation and distribution of eBooks'. Founded in 1971 by Michael S. Hart, it is the oldest digital library. Most of the items in its collection are the full texts of public domain books. The project tries to make these as free as possible, in long-lasting, open formats that can be used on almost any computer. As of November 2010, Project Gutenberg claimed over 34,000 items in its collection. Project Gutenberg is affiliated with many projects that are independent organizations which share the same ideals, and have been given permission to use the Project Gutenberg trademark.

Propaganda 102

Propaganda is a form of communication that is aimed at influencing the attitude of a community toward some cause or position so as to benefit oneself.

Proverb 152

A proverb (from Latin: proverbium) is a simple and concrete saying popularly known and repeated, which expresses a truth, based on common sense or the practical experience of humanity. They are often metaphorical. A proverb that describes a basic rule of conduct may also be known as a maxim. If a proverb is distinguished by particularly good phrasing, it may be known as an aphorism.

Public 67, 78, 132, 136, 160-161, 175

The Public is the people and society of a nation or community, or the whole of mankind.

Publication 78, 140

To publish is to make content available to the public. While specific use of the term may vary among countries, it is usually applied to text, images, or other audio-visual content on any medium, including paper or electronic publishing forms such as websites, eBooks, Compact Discs and MP3s. The word publication means the act of publishing, and also refers to any copies.

Publicist 159

A publicist is a person whose job is to generate and manage publicity for a public figure, especially a celebrity, a business, or for a work such as a book, film or album. Most top-level publicists work in private practice, handling multiple clients.

Publishers 55, 74, 76, 103, 118, 146, 149, 156, 167, 174-175

Publishing is the process of production and dissemination of literature or information – the activity of making information available to the general public. In some cases, authors may be their own publishers, meaning: originators and developers of content also provide media to deliver and display the content.

Purist 162

A purist is one who desires that an item remain true to its essence and free from adulterating or diluting influences. The term may be used in almost any field, and can be applied either to the self or to others. Use of the term may be either pejorative or complimentary, depending on context.

Pynchon 71

Thomas Ruggles Pynchon, Jr. (born May 8, 1937) is an American novelist. For his most praised novel, Gravity's Rainbow, Pynchon received the National Book Award, and is regularly cited as a contender for the Nobel Prize for Literature. Pynchon is a MacArthur Fellow noted for his dense and complex novels, and both his fiction and non-fiction writings encompass a vast array of subject matter, styles and themes, including (but not limited to) the fields of history, science, and mathematics.

Quality Time 159

'Quality time' (QT) is an informal reference to time spent with loved ones (e.g., close family, partners or friends) which is in some way important, special, productive or profitable. It is time that is set aside for paying full and undivided attention to the person/matter at hand. It may also refer to time spent performing some favored activity (e.g., a hobby or packing suitcases to move across the world with loved ones). The opportunity to experience quality time, or the actual time available to enjoy quality time is often limited. However, this is outweighed by the importance, intensity or value attached to events or interactions which occur during quality time. Quality time therefore has a degree of emotional or social 'quality' which other aspects of personal life may lack. Busy parents may also use the term to justify the limited amount of overall time they spend with their children.

Quantities of Information 101

The mathematical theory of information is based on probability theory and statistics, and measures information with several quantities of information. The choice of logarithmic base in the following formulae determines the unit of information entropy that is used. The most common unit of information is the bit, based on the binary logarithm. Other units include the nat, based on the natural logarithm, and the hartley, based on the base 10 or common logarithm.

Question 50, 83, 95, 117-118, 122, 128, 149, 163-164, 166

A question may be either a linguistic expression used to make a request for information, or else the request itself made by such an expression. This information is provided with an answer.

QWERTY Keyboard 68

QWERTY is the most common modern-day keyboard layout. The name comes from the first six letters (keys) appearing in the top letter row of the keyboard, read left to right: Q-W-E-R-T-Y. The QWERTY design is based on a layout created by Christopher Latham Sholes in 1873 in Milwaukee, Wisconsin for the Sholes and Glidden typewriter and sold to Remington in the same year, when it first appeared in typewriters. It became popular with the success of the Remington No. 2 and No. 3 and No. 389 of 1878, and remains in use on electronic keyboards due to the network effect of a standard layout and a belief that alternatives fail to provide very significant advantages. The use and adoption of the QWERTY keyboard is often viewed as one of the most important case studies in open standards because of the widespread, collective adoption and use of the product, particularly in the United States.

Radio 92, 164

Radio is the transmission of signals by modulation of electromagnetic waves with frequencies below those of visible light.

Electromagnetic radiation travels by means of oscillating electromagnetic fields that pass through the air and the vacuum of space. Information is carried by systematically changing (modulating) some property of the radiated waves, such as amplitude, frequency, phase, or pulse width. When radio waves pass an electrical conductor, the oscillating fields induce an alternating current in the conductor. This can be detected and transformed into sound or other signals that carry information.

Random 168

Randomness has somewhat disparate meanings as used in several different fields. It also has common meanings which may have loose connections with some of those more definite meanings.

Read In 50, 75, 122, 135

The process of being read into a compartmented program generally entails being approved for access to particularly sensitive and restricted information about a classified program, receiving a briefing about the program, and formally acknowledging the briefing, usually by signing a non-disclosure agreement describing restrictions on the handling and use of information concerning the program. Officials with the required security clearance and a need to know may be read into a covert operation or clandestine operation they will be working on. For code-word–classified programs, an official would not be aware a program existed with that codeword until being read in, because the codewords themselves are classified.

Readable 138

Readability can mean how easy it is to read and to make sense of a text. Or it can mean how easy it is to recognise words on a page, sign, or display. In English, this is often called legibility. A third meaning is about whether computer program code can be read by humans through e.g. embedded documentation.

Readers 50, 57-58, 74, 94-96, 98, 100-101, 105, 117, 120, 122-124, 127-129, 138, 140, 142-143, 145, 160, 168, 170

Reader can mean a person who is reading a text, or a basal reader, a book used to teach reading.

Reading 50-52, 54-60, 62, 64-66, 70-75, 77, 80-81, 83-94, 97-101, 106-107, 109-111, 114, 116, 118-121, 123-130, 133-137, 139, 141-151, 155-156, 158-159, 164-169, 172-174

Reading' is a complex cognitive process of decoding symbols for the intention of constructing or deriving meaning (reading comprehension). It is the mastery of basic cognitive processes to the point where they are automatic so that attention is freed for the analysis of meaning. Reading is a means of language acquisition, of communication, and of sharing information and ideas. Like all language, it is a complex interaction between the text and the reader which is shaped by the reader's prior knowledge, experiences, attitude, and language community which is culturally and socially situated. The reading process requires continuous practices, development, and refinement. Readers use a variety of reading strategies to assist with decoding (to translate symbols into sounds or visual representations of speech) and comprehension. Readers may use morpheme, semantics, syntax and context clues to identify the meaning of unknown words. Readers integrate the words they have read into their existing framework of knowledge or schema (schemata theory). Other types of reading are not speech based writing systems, such as music notation or pictograms. The common link is the interpretation of symbols to extract the meaning from the visual notations.

Reality 59, 69-70, 73, 79, 100, 111-112, 149, 161, 165

Reality is the state of things as they actually exist, rather than as they may appear or may be thought to be. In its widest definition, reality includes everything that is and has been, whether or not it is observable or comprehensible.

Recipe 151

A recipe is a set of instructions that describe how to prepare or make something, especially a culinary dish.

Recognition 90, 107, 150, 152, 168-169

Recognition is identification of something already known or acknowledgement of something as valid. The term and similar may have the following specialized meanings.

Recommendation systems 108

Recommender systems, recommendation systems, recommendation engines, recommendation frameworks, recommendation platforms or simply recommender form or work from a specific type of information filtering system technique that attempts to recommend information items (movies, TV program/show/episode, video on demand, music, books, news, images, web pages, scientific literature such as research papers etc.) that are likely to be of interest to the user.

Recorded 122

Recording is a process of capturing data or translating information to a format stored on a storage medium often referred to as a record.

Red 88, 119, 137

Red is a color.

Reference 98, 111, 155

A reference, is derived from Middle English referren, from Middle French rèférer, from Latin referre, 'to carry back' formed from a prefix re- and ferre, 'to bear'. A large number of words derive from this root, including referee, reference, referendum, all retaining the basic meaning of the original Latin as 'a point, place or source of origin' that something of comparable nature can be defined in terms of. A referee is the provider of this source of origin, and a referent is the possessor of the source of origin, whether it is knowledge, matter or energy.

Registers 116

A register, among other definitions, is a record in writing. As a verb it is to record or to be recorded in an official list. Registration is the act of registering or being registered.

Relaxing 90

Leisure, or free time, is time spent away from business, work, and domestic chores. It is also the periods of time before or after necessary activities such as eating, sleeping and, where it is compulsory, education.

Report 71-72

Written reports are documents which present focused, salient content to a specific audience. Reports are often used to display the result of an experiment, investigation, or inquiry. The audience may be public or private, an individual or the public in general. Reports are used in government, business, education, science, and other fields.

Representations 71, 129

Representations is an interdisciplinary journal in the humanities published quarterly by the University of California Press. The journals was established in 1983 and is the founding publication of the New Historicism movement of the 1980s. It covers topics including literary, historical, and cultural studies. The founding editorial board was chaired by Stephen Greenblatt and Svetlana Alpers. Representations frequently publishes thematic special issues, for example, the 2007 issue on the legacies of American Orientalism, the 2006 issue on cross-cultural mimesis, and the 2005 issue on political and intellectual redress.

Research Paper 77

In academic publishing, a paper is an academic work that is usually published in an academic journal. It contains original research results or reviews existing results. Such a paper, also called an article, will only be considered valid if it undergoes a process of peer review by one or more referees (who are academics in the same field) in order to check that the content of the paper is suitable for publication in the journal. A paper may undergo a series of reviews, edits and re-submissions before finally being accepted or rejected for publication. This process typically takes several months. Next there is often a delay of many months (or in some subjects, over a year) before publication, particularly for the most popular journals where the number of acceptable articles outnumbers the space for printing. Due to this, many academics self-archive a 'pre-print' copy of their paper for free download from their personal or institutional website.

Resource 60

A resource is any physical or virtual entity of limited availability that needs to be consumed to obtain a benefit from it. In most cases, commercial or even non-commerial factors require resource allocation through resource management. There are two types of resources; renewable and non-renewable.

Results 81, 99, 168

Results is the 1989 Liza Minnelli album produced by Pet Shop Boys and Julian Mendelsohn. The album was a huge success in the UK, where it reached #6 on the UK Albums Chart (promoted by the lead single 'Losing My Mind,' which reached #6 on the UK Singles Chart). The album was less successful in the US, peaking only at #128 on the Billboard Top 200 albums. According to Minnelli, the album's title came to be when she was at a bar and she complimented a woman on her dress. The woman thanked Minnelli and explained that it was her 'results' dress. 'When I wear this dress, I get results.'

Reverse Engineering 75

Reverse engineering is the process of discovering the technological principles of a human made device, object or system through analysis of its structure, function and operation. It often involves taking something (e.g., a mechanical device, electronic component, or software program) apart and analyzing its workings in detail to be used in maintenance, or to try to make a new device or program that does the same thing without using or simply duplicating (without understanding) the original.

Reviews 129, 143

A review is an evaluation of a publication, such as a movie (a movie review), video game, musical composition (music review of a composition or recording), book (book review); a piece of hardware like a car, home appliance, or computer; or an event or performance, such as a live music concert, a play, musical theater show or dance show. In addition to a critical evaluation, the review's author may assign the work a rating to indicate its relative merit. More loosely, an author may review current events, trends, or items in the news. A compilation of reviews may itself be called a review. The New York Review of Books, for instance, is a collection of essays on literature, culture, and current affairs. National Review, founded by William F. Buckley, Jr., is an influential conservative magazine, and Monthly Review is a long-running socialist periodical. It often is an opinion.

Revolutions 175

A revolution (from the Latin revolutio, 'a turn around') is a fundamental change in power or organizational structures that takes place in a relatively short period of time. Its use to refer to political change dates from the scientific revolution occasioned by Copernicus' famous De Revolutionibus Orbium Coelestium.

Rhetorical 97

A rhetorical question is a figure of speech in the form of a question posed for its persuasive effect without the expectation of a reply. Rhetorical questions encourage the listener to think about what the (often obvious) answer to the question must be.

Rhythmic 139, 162

Rhythm (from Greek: rhythmos, 'any regular recurring motion, symmetry') is a 'movement marked by the regulated succession of strong and weak elements, or of opposite or different conditions'. In other words, rhythm is simply the timing of the musical sounds and silences. While rhythm most commonly applies to sound, such as music and spoken language, it may also refer to visual presentation, as 'timed movement through space'.

Right to Left 148

A language is described as right-to-left (or RTL) if writing starts from the right of the page, and continues to the left.

Right-hand side 151

In mathematics, LHS is informal shorthand for the left-hand side of an equation. Similarly, RHS is the right-hand side. Each is solely a name for a term as part of an expression; and they are in practice interchangeable, since equality is symmetric. This abbreviation is seldom if ever used in print; it is very informal.

Rosetta Stone 170

The Rosetta Stone is an Ancient Egyptian granodiorite stele inscribed with a decree issued at Memphis, Egypt in 196 BC on behalf of King Ptolemy V. The decree appears in three scripts: the upper text is Ancient Egyptian hieroglyphs, the middle portion demotic script, and the lowest Ancient Greek. Because it presents essentially the same text in all three scripts (with some minor differences between them), it provided the key to the modern understanding of Egyptian hieroglyphs.

RSS Feeds 80, 108

RSS (most commonly expanded as Really Simple Syndication) is a family of web feed formats used to publish frequently updated works – such as blog entries, news headlines, audio, and video – in a standardized format. An RSS document (which is called a 'feed', 'web feed', or 'channel') includes full or summarized text, plus metadata such as publishing dates and authorship. Web feeds benefit publishers by letting them syndicate content automatically. They benefit readers who want to subscribe to timely updates from favored websites or to aggregate feeds from many sites into one place. RSS feeds can be read using software called an 'RSS reader', 'feed reader', or 'aggregator', which can be web-based, desktop-based, or mobile-device-based. A standardized XML file format allows the information to be published once and viewed by many different programs. The user subscribes to a feed by entering into the reader the feed's URI or by clicking a feed icon in a web browser that initiates the subscription process. The RSS reader checks the user's subscribed feeds regularly for new work, downloads any updates that it finds, and provides a user interface to monitor and read the feeds. RSS allows users to avoid manually inspecting all of the websites they are interested in, and instead subscribe to websites such that all new content is pushed onto their browsers when it becomes available.

Rubric 142

A rubric is a word or section of text which is traditionally written or printed in red ink to highlight it. The word derives from the Latin: rubrica, meaning red ochre or red chalk, and originates in Medieval illuminated manuscripts from the 13th century or earlier. In these, red letters were used to highlight initial capitals (particularly of psalms), section headings and names of religious significance, a practice known as rubrication, which was a separate stage in the production of a manuscript.

Ruler 170

A ruler, sometimes called a rule or line gauge, is an instrument used in geometry, technical drawing, printing and engineering/building to measure distances and/or to rule straight lines. Strictly speaking, the ruler is essentially a straightedge used to rule lines, but typically the ruler also contains calibrated lines to measure distances.

Rules of the Game 61–62

The Rules of the Game (original French title: La Règle du jeu) is a 1939 French film directed by Jean Renoir about upper-class French society just before the start of World War II. As a point of departure he began with Alfred de Musset's Les Caprices de Marianne, a popular 19th-century comedy of manners: 'My first intention was to film a transposition of Caprices de Marianne to our time. It is the story of a tragic mistake: the lover of Marianne is taken for someone else and is bumped off in an ambush'.

Scalability 75

In telecommunications and software engineering, scalability is the ability of a system, network, or process, to handle growing amounts of work in a graceful manner or its ability to be enlarged to accommodate that growth. For example, it can refer to the capability of a system to increase total throughput under an increased load when resources (typically hardware) are added. An analogous meaning is implied when the word is used in a commercial context, where scalability of a company implies that the underlying business model offers the potential for economic growth within the company.

Scarcity 55, 162

Scarcity is the fundamental economic problem of having seemingly unlimited human needs and wants, in a world of limited resources. It states that society has insufficient productive resources to fulfill all human wants and needs. Alternatively, scarcity implies that not all of society's goals can be pursued at the same time; trade-offs are made of one good against others. In an influential 1932 essay, Lionel Robbins defined economics as the science which studies human behavior as a relationship between ends and scarce means which have alternative uses.

Scenario 126, 145, 163

A scenario (from Italian: that which is pinned to the scenery) is a synthetic description of an event or series of actions and events. In the Commedia dell'arte it was an outline of entrances, exits, and action describing the plot of a play that was literally pinned to the back of the scenery. It is also known as canovaccio or that which is pinned to the canvas of which the scenery was constructed.

Scholar 83

Scholarly method or scholarship – is the body of principles and practices used by scholars to make their claims about the world as valid and trustworthy as possible, and to make them known to the scholarly public.

School 67, 76, 89-90, 92, 97, 127, 148, 168, 174

A school is an institution designed for the teaching of students (or 'pupils') under the supervision of teachers.

Sciences 70, 98, 107, 120

Science (from the Latin scientia, meaning 'knowledge') is an enterprise that builds and organizes knowledge in the form of testable explanations and predictions about the world. An older and closely related meaning still in use today is that of Aristotle, for whom scientific knowledge was a body of reliable knowledge that can be logically and rationally explained.

Scientific Research 146, 167

Scientific method refers to a body of techniques for investigating phenomena, acquiring new knowledge, or correcting and integrating previous knowledge. To be termed scientific, a method of inquiry must be based on gathering observable, empirical and measurable evidence subject to specific principles of reasoning. The Oxford English Dictionary says that scientific method is: 'a method of procedure that has characterized natural science since the 17th century, consisting in systematic observation, measurement, and experiment, and the formulation, testing, and modification of hypotheses.'

Scientist 71, 166

Social roles that partly correspond with the modern scientist can be identified going back at least until 17th century natural philosophy, but the term scientist is much more recent. Until the late 19th or early 20th century, those who pursued science were called 'natural philosophers' or 'men of science'.

Screen Readers 105

A screen reader is a software application that attempts to identify and interpret what is being displayed on the screen (or, more accurately, sent to standard output, whether a video monitor is present or not). This interpretation is then re-presented to the user with text-to-speech, sound icons, or a Braille output device. Screen readers are a form of assistive technology (AT) potentially useful to people who are blind, visually impaired, illiterate or learning disabled, often in combination with other AT, such as screen magnifiers.

Screen Reading 50

Screen reading is the act of reading a text on a computer screen, smartphone, eBook reader, etc. It is often contrasted with the act of reading a text on paper, in particular a printed text.

Screening 88-90

One meaning of screening is the investigation of a great number of something (for instance, people) looking for those with a particular problem or feature.

Scribble 128, 140

A scribble is a drawing composed of random and abstract lines, generally without ever lifting the drawing device off of the paper. Scribbling is most often associated with young children and toddlers, because their lack of hand–eye coordination and lower mental development often make it very difficult for any young child to keep their coloring attempts within the line art of the subject.

Scribes 75

A scribe is a person who writes books or documents by hand as a profession and helps the city keep track of its records. The profession, previously found in all literate cultures in some form, lost most of its importance and status with the advent of printing. The work could involve copying books, including sacred texts, or secretarial and administrative duties such as taking of dictation and the keeping of business, judicial and historical records for kings, nobility, temples and cities. Later the profession developed into public servants, journalists, accountants, typists, and lawyers. In societies with low literacy rates, such as India, street corner letter-writers (and readers) may still be found providing a service. Scribes have also reappeared as assistants to doctors using electronic health records.

Scroll 135, 168

A scroll is a roll of papyrus, parchment, or paper which has been written, drawn or painted upon for the purpose of transmitting information or using as a decoration. It is distinguished from a roll by virtue of being intended for repeated use rather than continuous, but once-only use of the roll.

Search Engine 105, 114, 171

A web search engine is designed to search for information on the World Wide Web and FTP servers. The search results are generally presented in a list of results and are often called hits. The information may consist of web pages, images, information and other types of files. Some search engines also mine data available in databases or open directories. Unlike web directories, which are maintained by human editors, search engines operate algorithmically or are a mixture of algorithmic and human input.

Search Engine Optimization 105

Search engine optimization (SEO) is the process of improving the visibility of a website or a web page in search engines via the 'natural' or un-paid ('organic' or 'algorithmic') search results. Other forms of search engine marketing (SEM) target paid listings.

Second Life 109

Second Life (SL) is an online virtual world developed by Linden Lab which was launched on June 23, 2003. A number of free client programs called Viewers enable Second Life users, called Residents, to interact with each other through avatars. Residents can explore the world (known as the grid), meet other residents, socialize, participate in individual and group activities, and create and trade virtual property and services with one another. Second Life is intended for people aged 13 and over, and as of 2011 has more than 20 million registered user accounts.

Secondary Orality 139

In his book Orality and Literacy: The Technologizing of the Word, published in 1982 (2nd ed. 2002), Walter J. Ong works with the contrast between oral and literate cultures. In this book, he used the phrase 'secondary orality', describing it as 'essentially a more deliberate and self-conscious orality, based permanently on the use of writing and print' (Ong, 1982, p. 136). According to his way of thinking, secondary orality is not primary orality, the orality of pre-literate cultures. Oral societies operated on polychronic time, with many things happening at once – socialization played a great role in the operation of these cultures, memory and memorization were of greater importance, increasing the amount of copiousness and redundancy. Oral cultures were additive rather than subordinate, closer to the human life world, and more situational and participatory than the more abstract qualities of literate cultures.

Seduction of the Innocent 124

Seduction of the Innocent is a book by German-American psychiatrist Fredric Wertham, published in 1954, that warned that comic books were a negative form of popular literature and a serious cause of juvenile delinquency. The book was a minor bestseller that created alarm in parents and galvanized them to campaign for censorship. At the same time, a U.S. Congressional inquiry was launched into the comic book industry. Subsequent to the publication of Seduction of the Innocent, the Comics Code Authority was voluntarily established by publishers to self-censor their titles.

Semiotician 65

Semiotics, also called semiotic studies or (in the Saussurean tradition) semiology, is the study of signs and sign processes (semiosis), indication, designation, likeness, analogy, metaphor, symbolism, signification, and communication. Semiotics is closely related to the field of linguistics, which, for its part, studies the structure and meaning of language more specifically.

Senses 75, 96, 102, 147

Senses are the physiological capacities within organisms that provide inputs for perception. The senses and their operation, classification, and theory are overlapping topics studied by a variety of fields, most notably neuroscience, cognitive psychology (or cognitive science), and philosophy of perception. The nervous system has a specific sensory system or organ, dedicated to each sense.

Sensorimotor 106

Piaget's theory of cognitive development is a comprehensive theory about the nature and development of human intelligence first developed by Jean Piaget. It is primarily known as a developmental stage theory, but in fact, it deals with the nature of knowledge itself and how humans come gradually to acquire it, construct it, and use it. Moreover, Piaget claims the idea that cognitive development is at the centre of human organism and language is contingent on cognitive development. Below, there is first a short description of Piaget's views about the nature of intelligence and then a description of the stages through which it develops until maturity.

Sentiment analysis 108

Sentiment analysis or opinion mining refers to the application of natural language processing, computational linguistics, and text analytics to identify and extract subjective information in source materials.

Sequence 89, 114, 134, 151, 170

In mathematics, a sequence is an ordered list of objects (or events). Like a set, it contains members (also called elements or terms), and the number of terms (possibly infinite) is called the length of the sequence. Unlike a set, order matters, and exactly the same elements can appear multiple times at different positions in the sequence. A sequence is a discrete function.

Sequential Art 123

Sequential art refers to the art form of using a train of images deployed in sequence to graphic storytelling or convey information. The best-known example of sequential art is comics, which are a printed arrangement of art and balloons, especially comic books and comic strips.

Sexier 138

Sexual attractiveness or sex appeal refers to an individual's ability to attract the sexual or erotic interest of another person. The attraction can be to the physical or other qualities or traits of a person, or to such qualities in the context in which they appear. The attraction may be to a person's looks or movements or to their voice or smell, besides other factors. The attraction may be enhanced by a person's adornments, clothing, perfume, hair style, and anything else which can attract the sexual interest of another person. It can also be influenced by individual genetic, psychological, or cultural factors, or to other, more amorphous qualities of the person. Sexual attraction is also a response to another person that depends on a combination of the person possessing the traits and also on the criteria of the person who is attracted.

Sexy 69, 138
Sexy is an adjective that describes sexual attraction in humans, and other species.

Shackled 74
Shackled was a bondage magazine published by London Enterprises and distributed by Lyndon Distributors. It depicted bound and disciplined women.

Shakespeare 124, 155
William Shakespeare (baptised 26 April 1564; died 23 April 1616) was an English poet and playwright, widely regarded as the greatest writer in the English language and the world's pre-eminent dramatist. He is often called England's national poet and the Bard of Avon.

Sharing 57, 145, 149
Sharing the joint use of a resource or space. In its narrow sense, it refers to joint or alternating use of an inherently finite good, such as a common pasture or a shared residence. It is also the process of dividing and distributing. Apart from obvious instances, which we can observe in human activity, we can also find many examples of this happening naturally in nature. When an organism takes in nutrition or oxygen for instance, its internal organs are designed to divide and distribute the energy taken in, to supply parts of its body that need it. Flowers divide and distribute their seeds. In a broader sense, it can also include the free granting of use rights to a good that is capable of being treated as a nonrival good, such as information. Still more loosely, 'sharing' can actually mean giving something as an outright gift: for example, to 'share' one's food really means to give some of it as a gift.

Sheet Music 67
Sheet music is a hand-written or printed form of music notation that uses Modern musical symbols; like its analogs – books, pamphlets, etc. – the medium of sheet music typically is paper (or, in earlier times, parchment), although the access to musical notation in recent years includes also presentation on computer screens.

Shifting 148, 167
Shift generally means to change (position).

Shooter Games 117
Shooter games are a subgenre of action game, which often test the player's speed and reaction time. Because shooters make up the majority of action games, it is a fairly wide subgenre. It includes many subgenres that have the commonality of focusing on the actions of the avatar using some sort of weapon.

Signals 91-92
Signal, signals, signaling, or signalling may refer to a concept of information – a signal is a discrete part of a communication.

Silent Movies 85, 144
A silent film is a film with no synchronized recorded sound, especially spoken dialogue. In silent films for entertainment the dialogue is transmitted through muted gestures, pantomime and title cards. The idea of combining motion pictures with recorded sound is nearly as old as film itself, but because of the technical challenges involved, synchronized dialogue was only made practical in the late 1920s with the perfection of the audion amplifier tube and the introduction of the Vitaphone system. After The Jazz Singer in 1927, talkies became more and more commonplace and within a decade silent films had died out due to technology.

Simulations 104
Simulation is the imitation of some real thing, state of affairs, or process. The act of simulating something generally entails representing certain key characteristics or behaviours of a selected physical or abstract system.

Sketch 60
A sketch story, or sketch, is a piece of writing that is generally shorter than a short story, and contains very little, if any, plot. The term was most popularly-used in the late nineteenth century. As a literary work, it is also often referred to simply as the sketch.

Skills 71, 81, 124, 162
A skill is the learned capacity to carry out pre-determined results often with the minimum outlay of time, energy, or both. Skills can often be divided into domain-general and domain-specific skills. For example, in the domain of work, some general skills would include time management, teamwork and leadership, self motivation and others, whereas domain-specific skills would be useful only for a certain job. Skill usually requires certain environmental stimuli and situations to assess the level of skill being shown and used.

Slogans 79, 113
A slogan is a memorable motto or phrase used in a political, commercial, religious and other context as a repetitive expression of an idea or purpose.

Slow 90, 128, 144, 146-147, 151, 156, 159, 168
In kinematics, the speed of an object is the magnitude of its velocity (the rate of change of its position); it is thus a scalar quantity. The average speed of an object in an interval of time is the distance traveled by the object divided by the duration of the interval; the instantaneous speed is the limit of the average speed as the duration of the time interval approaches zero.

Slow Reading 146-147

Slow reading is the intentional reduction in the speed of reading, carried out to increase comprehension or pleasure. The concept appears to have originated in the study of philosophy and literature as a technique to more fully comprehend and appreciate a complex text. More recently, there has been increased interest in slow reading as result of the slow movement and its focus on decelerating the pace of modern life.

Smartphone 93-94, 149, 171

A smartphone is a mobile phone that offers more advanced computing ability and connectivity than a contemporary feature phone. Smartphones and feature phones may be thought of as handheld computers integrated with a mobile telephone, but while most feature phones are able to run applications based on platforms such as Java ME, a smartphone usually allows the user to install and run more advanced applications. Smartphones run complete operating system software providing a platform for application developers. Thus, they combine the functions of a camera phone and a personal digital assistant (PDA).

Smiley 163

A smiley, or happy face, is a stylized representation of a smiling human face. It is commonly represented as a yellow (many other colors are also used) circle (or sphere) with two black dots representing eyes and a black arc representing the mouth. 'Smiley' is also sometimes used as a generic term for any emoticon.

SMS 65, 92, 104, 162, 164, 170-171

Short Message Service (SMS) is the text communication service component of phone, web, or mobile communication systems, using standardized communications protocols that allow the exchange of short text messages between fixed line or mobile phone devices. SMS text messaging is the most widely used data application in the world, with 2.4 billion active users, or 74% of all mobile phone subscribers. The term SMS is used as a synonym for all types of short text messaging as well as the user activity itself in many parts of the world.

Social 55-56, 61, 69, 74, 80, 93, 98, 102-103, 107, 117, 122-123, 131, 137, 139, 141, 143, 145, 157-158, 164, 174-175

The term Social refers to a characteristic of living organisms (humans in particular, though biologists also apply the term to populations of other animals). It always refers to the interaction of organisms with other organisms and to their collective co-existence, irrespective of whether they are aware of it or not, and irrespective of whether the interaction is voluntary or involuntary.

Social Change 158

Social change refers to an alteration in the social order of a social group or society; a change in the nature, social institutions, social behaviours or social relations of a society.

Social Media 56, 107, 157, 164

Social media are media for social interaction, using highly accessible and scalable communication techniques. Social media is the use of web-based and mobile technologies to turn communication into interactive dialogue.

Social Networks 80, 131, 175

A social network is a social structure made up of individuals (or organizations) called 'nodes', which are tied (connected) by one or more specific types of interdependency, such as friendship, kinship, common interest, financial exchange, dislike, sexual relationships, or relationships of beliefs, knowledge or prestige.

Software 51, 71, 77, 82, 85, 102, 105, 108-109, 125

Computer software, or just software, is a collection of computer programs and related data that provide the instructions telling a computer what to do and how to do it. We can also say software refers to one or more computer programs and data held in the storage of the computer for some purposes. In other words software is a set of programs, procedures, algorithms and its documentation. Program software performs the function of the program it implements, either by directly providing instructions to the computer hardware or by serving as input to another piece of software. The term was coined to contrast to the old term hardware (meaning physical devices). In contrast to hardware, software is intangible, meaning it cannot be touched.

Software Options 102

In communications or computer systems, a configuration is an arrangement of functional units according to their nature, number, and chief characteristics. Often, configuration pertains to the choice of hardware, software, firmware, and documentation. The configuration affects system function and performance.

Software Studies 108-109

Software studies is an academic research field which studies software systems and their cultural effects.

Software Tools 108

A programming tool or software development tool is a program or application that software developers use to create, debug, maintain, or otherwise support other programs and applications. The term usually refers to relatively simple programs that can be combined together to accomplish a task, much as one might use multiple hand tools to fix a physical object.

Some Are 94, 126

'Some Are' is a song by David Bowie recorded during the Low sessions in 1976. It was released as a bonus track on the Rykodisc CD release of Low in 1991 and more recently on the iSelect compilation given away free with British newspaper The Mail on Sunday on 29 June 2008. The symphonic version by Philip Glass was featured on the Bowie instrumental compilation All Saints (2001).

SONY 137
Sony Corporation or commonly referred to as Sony, is a Japanese multinational conglomerate corporation headquartered in Minato, Tokyo, Japan and the world's fifth largest media conglomerate with US$77.20 billion (FY2010). Sony is one of the leading manufacturers of electronics, products for the consumer and professional markets.

Sound 55, 85, 149, 158
Sound is a mechanical wave that is an oscillation of pressure transmitted through a solid, liquid, or gas, composed of frequencies within the range of hearing and of a level sufficiently strong to be heard, or the sensation stimulated in organs of hearing by such vibrations.

Sound Effects 149
Sound effects or audio effects are artificially created or enhanced sounds, or sound processes used to emphasize artistic or other content of films, television shows, live performance, animation, video games, music, or other media. In motion picture and television production, a sound effect is a sound recorded and presented to make a specific storytelling or creative point without the use of dialogue or music. The term often refers to a process applied to a recording, without necessarily referring to the recording itself. In professional motion picture and television production, dialogue, music, and sound effects recordings are treated as separate elements. Dialogue and music recordings are never referred to as sound effects, even though the processes applied to them, such as reverberation or flanging effects, often are called sound effects.

SoundTrack 84
A soundtrack can be recorded music accompanying and synchronized to the images of a motion picture, book, television program or video game; a commercially released soundtrack album of music as featured in the soundtrack of a film or TV show; or the physical area of a film that contains the synchronized recorded sound.

Source 82, 109, 172
A source is the start, beginning, or origin of something.

Spatial 109
Space is the boundless, three-dimensional extent in which objects and events occur and have relative position and direction. Physical space is often conceived in three linear dimensions, although modern physicists usually consider it, with time, to be part of the boundless four-dimensional continuum known as spacetime. In mathematics one examines 'spaces' with different numbers of dimensions and with different underlying structures. The concept of space is considered to be of fundamental importance to an understanding of the physical universe although disagreement continues between philosophers over whether it is itself an entity, a relationship between entities, or part of a conceptual framework.

Speech 104-105, 137, 171
Speech is the vocalized form of human communication. It is based upon the syntactic combination of lexicals and names that are drawn from very large (usually > 10,000 different words) vocabularies. Each spoken word is created out of the phonetic combination of a limited set of vowel and consonant speech sound units. These vocabularies, the syntax which structures them, and their set of speech sound units, differ creating the existence of many thousands of different types of mutually unintelligible human languages. Human speakers (polyglots) are often able to communicate in two or more of them. The vocal abilities that enable humans to produce speech also provide humans with the ability to sing.

Speed 63, 86, 90, 132, 160, 164, 168-170
Speed is the rate of motion, change, or activity.

Speed Reading 86, 168
Speed reading is a collection of reading methods which attempt to increase rates of reading without greatly reducing comprehension or retention. Methods include chunking and eliminating subvocalization. No absolute distinct 'normal' and 'speed-reading' types of reading exist in practice, since all readers use some of the techniques used in speed reading (such as identifying words without focusing on each letter, not sounding out all words, not sub-vocalizing some phrases, or spending less time on some phrases than others, and skimming small sections). Speed reading is characterized by an analysis of trade-offs between measures of speed and comprehension, recognizing that different types of reading call for different speed and comprehension rates, and that those rates may be improved with practice. There are many speed reading training programs available including books, videos, software, and seminars.

Spell Checker 68
In computing, a spell checker (or spell check) is an application program that flags words in a document that may not be spelled correctly. Spell checkers may be stand-alone capable of operating on a block of text, or as part of a larger application, such as a word processor, email client, electronic dictionary, or search engine.

Spelling Rules 162
In Russian, the term spelling rule is used to describe a number of rules relating to the spelling of words in the language that would appear in most cases to deviate from a strictly phonetic transcription.

Spirit 123, 140

The Spirit (Denny Colt) is a crime-fighting fictional character created by writer-artist Will Eisner. He first appeared June 2, 1940 in 'The Spirit Section', the colloquial name given to a seven-page insert into American Sunday-newspaper comics sections. In the 2000s, following Eisner's death, the Spirit appears in comic books published by DC Comics.

Spoken Language 162

Spoken language is a form of human communication in which words derived from a large vocabulary (usually at least 10,000) together with a diverse variety of names are uttered through or with the mouth. All words are made up from a limited set of vowels and consonants. The spoken words they make are stringed into syntactically organized sentences and phrases. The vocabulary and syntax together with the speech sounds it uses define its identity as a particular natural language.

Spoken Word 65, 104

Spoken word is used as a musical or entertainment term, referring to works or performances that consist solely or mostly of one person speaking as if naturally. Musically, this is distinct from rapping, as rapping incorporates rhythm and sometimes melody, whereas spoken word is more akin to narration or speaking as the person would in conversation, as shown in the song 'Everybody's Free (to Wear Sunscreen)' by Baz Luhrmann.

Spotify 159

Spotify is a Swedish music streaming service offering unlimited streaming of selected music from a range of major and independent record labels, including Sony, EMI, Warner Music Group, The Orchard, and Universal. It is presently only available in certain parts of Europe, mostly Western European countries. The system is currently accessible using Microsoft Windows, Mac OS X, Linux, mobile devices and those running iOS, Android, Symbian, Windows Mobile or Palm's HP webOS.

Statistics 52, 94, 107-108, 152

Statistics is the science of the collection, organization, and interpretation of data. It deals with all aspects of this, including the planning of data collection in terms of the design of surveys and experiments.

Story 53, 63, 72, 77-78, 84-85, 89-90, 93-94, 109, 112-114, 122, 124, 126, 148, 170

Story is a common term for a recounting of a sequence of events, or for a statement regarding the facts pertinent to a situation in question (see narrative). Notable cases of stories include: Bedtime story, a traditional form of storytelling, told to children to prepare them for sleep; Organization story, a narrative used in organization studies; Short story, a fictional narrative of briefer length than a novella; 'Stories', or 'my stories', American slang for television soap opera; User story, a method of illustrating software requirements; Storytelling.

Storyline 85

A narrative is a story that is created in a constructive format (as a work of speech, writing, song, film, television, video games, in photography or theatre) that describes a sequence of fictional or non-fictional events.

Storyteller 71, 124

A narrator is, within any story (literary work, movie, play, verbal account, etc.), the person who tells the story to the audience. When the narrator is also a character within the story, he or she is sometimes known as the viewpoint character. The narrator is one of three entities responsible for story-telling of any kind. The others are the author and the audience; the latter called the 'reader' when referring specifically to literature.

Storytelling 71, 124, 153

Storytelling is the conveying of events in words, images and sounds, often by improvisation or embellishment. Stories or narratives have been shared in every culture as a means of entertainment, education, cultural preservation and in order to instill moral values. Crucial elements of stories and storytelling include plot, characters and narrative point of view.

Strict 112

In mathematical writing, the adjective strict is used to modify technical terms which have multiple meanings. It indicates that the exclusive meaning of the term is to be understood. (More formally, one could say that this is the meaning which implies the other meanings.) The opposite is non-strict. This is often implicit but can be put explicitly for clarity. In some contexts the word 'proper' is used as a mathematical synonym for 'strict'.

Structure 62, 68, 91, 96, 111-112, 114, 126, 129, 134, 142, 151

Structure is a fundamental, if intangible, notion referring to the recognition, observation, nature, and stability [disambiguation needed] of patterns and relationships of entities. From a child's verbal description of a snowflake, to the detailed scientific analysis of the properties of magnetic fields, the concept of structure is now often an essential foundation of nearly every mode of inquiry and discovery in science, philosophy, and art. In early 20th-century and earlier thought, form often plays a role comparable to that of structure in contemporary thought. The neo-Kantianism of Ernst Cassirer (cf. his Philosophy of Symbolic Forms, completed in 1929 and published in English translation in the 1950s) is sometimes regarded as a precursor of the later shift to structuralism and poststructuralism.

Students 80, 83

A student is a learner, or someone who attends an educational institution. In some nations, the English term (or its cognate in another language) is reserved for those who attend university, while a schoolchild under the age of eighteen is called a pupil in English (or an equivalent in other languages). In its widest use, student is used for anyone who is learning.

Studying 67, 140

Study skills or study strategies are approaches applied to learning. They are generally critical to success in school, are considered essential for acquiring good grades, and are useful for learning throughout one's life.

Stuttering 134

Stuttering (alalia syllabaris), also known as stammering (alalia literalis or anarthria literalis), is a speech disorder in which the flow of speech is disrupted by involuntary repetitions and prolongations of sounds, syllables, words or phrases, and involuntary silent pauses or blocks in which the stutterer is unable to produce sounds. The term stuttering is most commonly associated with involuntary sound repetition, but it also encompasses the abnormal hesitation or pausing before speech, referred to by stutterers as blocks, and the prolongation of certain sounds, usually vowels and semivowels.

Subject 52, 63, 111, 125, 162, 164

In philosophy, a subject is a being that has subjective experiences, subjective consciousness or a relationship with another entity (or 'object'). A subject is an observer and an object is a thing observed. This concept is especially important in continental philosophy, where 'the Subject' is a central term in debates over human autonomy and the nature of the self. The sharp distinction between subject and object corresponds to the distinction, in the philosophy of René Descartes, between thought and extension. Descartes believed that thought (subjectivity) was the essence of the mind, and that extension (the occupation of space) was the essence of matter.

Subject Line 63

Computer-mediated communication (CMC) is defined as any communicative transaction that occurs through the use of two or more networked computers. While the term has traditionally referred to those communications that occur via computer-mediated formats (e.g., instant messages, e-mails, chat rooms), it has also been applied to other forms of text-based interaction such as text messaging. Research on CMC focuses largely on the social effects of different computer-supported communication technologies. Many recent studies involve Internet-based social networking supported by social software.

Subjectively 63

Subjectivity refers to the subject and his or her perspective, feelings, beliefs, and desires. In philosophy, the term is usually contrasted with objectivity.

Subscribe 136

The subscription business model is a business model where a customer must pay a subscription price to have access to the product/service. The model was pioneered by magazines and newspapers, but is now used by many businesses and websites.

Subtitles 79

Subtitles are textual versions of the dialog in films and television programs, usually displayed at the bottom of the screen. They can either be a form of written translation of a dialog in a foreign language, or a written rendering of the dialog in the same language, with or without added information to help viewers who are deaf and hard-of-hearing to follow the dialog, or people who cannot understand the spoken dialogue or who have accent recognition problems. Television teletext subtitles, which are hidden unless requested by the viewer from a menu or by selecting the relevant teletext page (e.g., p. 888), always carry additional sound representations for deaf and hard of hearing viewers. Teletext subtitle language follows the original audio, except in multi-lingual countries where the broadcaster may provide subtitles in additional languages on other teletext pages.

Summary 56, 128

A summary, synopsis, or recap is a shorter version of the original. Such a simplification highlights the major points from the much longer subject, such as a text, speech, film, or event. The purpose is to help the audience get the gist in a short period of time.

Surplus 97

Surplus means when there is more supply than demand, as in extra resources.

Symbols 65, 89, 120, 132, 161, 165, 170

A symbol is something such as an particular mark that represents some piece of information. For example, a red octagon may be a symbol for 'STOP'. On maps, tables would mean campsite. Numerals are symbols for numbers (amounts). All language consists of symbols. Personal names are symbols representing individuals.

Table of Contents 81

A table of contents, usually headed simply 'Contents' and abbreviated informally as TOC, is a list of the parts of a book or document organized in the order in which the parts appear. The contents usually includes the titles or descriptions of the first-level headers, such as chapter titles in longer works, and often includes second-level or section titles (A-heads) within the chapters as well, and occasionally even third-level titles (subsections or B-heads). The depth of detail in tables of contents depends on the length of the work, with longer works having less. Formal reports (ten or more pages and being too long to put into a memo or letter) also have tables of contents. Documents of fewer than ten pages do not require tables of contents, but often have a short list of contents at the beginning.

Tag Cloud 171

A tag cloud (keyword cloud, or weighted list in visual design) is a visual depiction of user-generated tags, or simply the word content of a site, typically used to describe the content of web sites. Tags are usually single words and are normally listed alphabetically, and the importance of each tag is shown with font size or color. Thus, it is possible to find a tag alphabetically and by popularity. The tags are usually hyperlinks that lead to a collection of items that are associated with a tag. Sometimes, further visual properties are manipulated, such as the font color, intensity, or weight.

Tagging 65, 103

In online computer systems terminology, a tag is a non-hierarchical keyword or term assigned to a piece of information (such as an Internet bookmark, digital image, or computer file). This kind of metadata helps describe an item and allows it to be found again by browsing or searching. Tags are generally chosen informally and personally by the item's creator or by its viewer, depending on the system. Tagging was popularized by websites associated with Web 2.0 and is an important feature of many Web 2.0 services. It is now also part of some desktop software.

Talkies 85

A sound film is a motion picture with synchronized sound, or sound technologically coupled to image, as opposed to a silent film. The first known public exhibition of projected sound films took place in Paris in 1900, but decades would pass before sound motion pictures were made commercially practical. Reliable synchronization was difficult to achieve with the early sound-on-disc systems, and amplification and recording quality were also inadequate. Innovations in sound-on-film led to the first commercial screening of short motion pictures using the technology, which took place in New York City in April 1923.

Tangram 115

The tangram is a dissection puzzle consisting of seven flat shapes, called tans, which are put together to form shapes. The objective of the puzzle is to form a specific shape (given only an outline or silhouette) using all seven pieces, which may not overlap.

Tantamount 63

The Richleighs of Tantamount is a children's historical novel written by British author Barbara Willard. It was originally published in the United Kingdom in 1966 by the publishers, Constable, before being published in the United States by Harcourt, Brace & World in June 1967. C. Walter Hodges drew the line illustrations and painted the cover portrait for the original edition.

Technique 83, 86, 149, 168, 171

A technique is a procedure used to accomplish a specific activity or task.

Technology 50, 69, 75, 96, 101, 103, 117, 121, 126, 130, 140, 159, 165, 170–171

Technology is the usage and knowledge of tools, techniques, crafts, systems or methods of organization in order to solve a problem or serve some purpose.

Telecommunication 66

Telecommunication is the transmission of information, over significant distances, for the purpose of communication. In earlier times, telecommunications involved the use of visual signals, such as beacons, smoke, semaphore telegraphs, signal flags, and optical heliographs, or audio messages via coded drumbeats, lung-blown horns, or sent by loud whistles, for example. In the modern age of electricity and electronics, telecommunications now also includes the use of electrical devices such as telegraphs, telephones, and teletypes, the use of radio and microwave communications, as well as fiber optics and their associated electronics, plus the use of the orbiting satellites and the Internet.

Teletext 170

Teletext (or 'broadcast teletext') is a television information retrieval service developed in the United Kingdom in the early 1970s. It offers a range of text-based information, typically including national, international and sporting news, weather and TV schedules. Subtitle (or closed captioning) information is also transmitted in the teletext signal, typically on page 888 or 777.

Television 78–79, 118, 164

Television (TV) is a telecommunication medium for transmitting and receiving moving images that can be monochromatic (shades of grey) or multicolored. Images are usually accompanied by sound.

Texting 139

Text messaging, or texting, refers to the exchange of brief written messages between fixed-line phone or mobile phone and fixed or portable devices over a network. While the original term (see below) was derived from referring to messages sent using the Short Message Service (SMS) originated from Radio Telegraphy, it has since been extended to include messages containing image, video, and sound content (known as MMS messages). The sender of a text message is known as a texter, while the service itself has different colloquialisms depending on the region: it may simply be referred to as a text in North America, India, Australia, the Philippines and the United Kingdom, an SMS in most of Europe, and a TMS or SMS in the Middle East and Asia.

Textualities 82

Textuality is a concept in linguistics and literary theory that refers to the attributes that distinguish the text (a technical term indicating any communicative content under analysis) as an object of study in those fields. It is associated in both fields with structuralism and post-structuralism.

The Blind 120

The Blind (French: Les aveugles), also known as The Sightless, is a play that was written in 1890 by the Belgian playwright Maurice

Maeterlinck. It is an intense one-act play, which was one of the pieces mentioned in a list of Maeterlinck's most characteristic plays. This list was highlighted in the speech given to honour Maeterlinck with the Nobel Prize in 1911. The play was originally written in French later to be translated into several different languages, such as English and German. The piece is not only a study of human condition in general but it appears to confront its reader with the effect of hope on the latter.

The Books 56-57, 77, 113, 137, 144

The Books are an American duo, formed in New York City in 1999, consisting of guitarist and vocalist Nick Zammuto and cellist Paul de Jong. Their releases typically incorporate samples of obscure sounds and speech. They have released three critically acclaimed albums on the German label Tomlab, and recently released their fourth studio album, The Way Out, on Temporary Residence Limited.

The Bookstore 165

'The Bookstore' is the 173rd episode of the NBC sitcom Seinfeld. This was the 17th episode for the 9th and final season. It aired on April 16, 1998.

The Chaos 150

'The Chaos' is a poem which demonstrates the irregularity of English spelling and pronunciation, written by Dutch writer, traveller and teacher Gerard Nolst Trenité (1870-1946), also known under the pseudonym Charivarius. It includes about 800 examples of irregular pronunciation, and first appeared in an appendix to the author's 1920 textbook Drop Your Foreign Accent: engelsche uitspraakoefeningen. It has appeared in various versions: the author's first version had 164 lines but 'the most complete and authoritative version ever likely to emerge', published by The Spelling Society in 1992-93, has 274 lines.

The Comic 84, 124

The Comic is a 1969 drama/black comedy film co-written, co-produced and directed by Carl Reiner. It stars Dick Van Dyke as Billy Bright (the original title). Reiner wrote the screenplay with Aaron Ruben, which was inspired by the end of silent-era film, and in part, by the life of silent film superstar Buster Keaton.

The Comic Strip 84

The Comic Strip is a group of British comedians, known for their television series The Comic Strip Presents.... The core members are Adrian Edmondson, Dawn French, Rik Mayall, Nigel Planer, Peter Richardson and Jennifer Saunders, with frequent appearances by Keith Allen, Robbie Coltrane and others.

The Consequence 113

Die Konsequenz (English: The Consequence) is a West German film from 1977. It is an adaptation of the 1975 autobiographical novel with the same name by Swiss author Alexander Ziegler and directed by Wolfgang Petersen. The film has a pederastic theme. It has been praised as 'one of the best '70s gay dramas'.

The Context 112, 128, 151

Illustrious Corpses (Italian: Cadaveri eccellenti) is a 1976 thriller film directed by Francesco Rosi and starring Lino Ventura. The film was screened at the 1976 Cannes Film Festival, but was not entered into the main competition. Its title refers to the surrealist game, Cadavre Exquis, invented by André Breton, in which the participants draw consecutive sections of a figure without seeing what the previous person has drawn, leading to unpredictable results, and is meant to describe the meandering nature of the film with its unpredictable foray into the world of political manipulations, as well as the (illustrious) corpses of the murdered judges.

The Death of the Author 174

'The Death of the Author' is a 1967 essay by the French literary critic and theorist Roland Barthes. Barthes's essay argues against traditional literary criticism's practice of incorporating the intentions and biographical context of an author in an interpretation of a text, and instead argues that writing and creator are unrelated.

The Economist 71

The Economist is an English-language weekly news and international affairs publication owned by The Economist Newspaper Ltd. and edited in offices in the City of Westminster, London, England. Continuous publication began under founder James Wilson in September 1843. While The Economist refers to itself as a newspaper, each print edition appears on glossy paper, like a news magazine. In 2009, it reported an average circulation of just over 1.6 million copies per issue, about half of which are sold in North America.

The Enlightenment 154

The Age of Enlightenment (or simply the Enlightenment) is the era in Western philosophy, intellectual, scientific and cultural life, centered upon the 18th century, in which reason was advocated as the primary source for legitimacy and authority. It is also known as the Age of Reason.

The Flying Doctors 125

The Flying Doctors is an Australian drama series produced by Crawford Productions that revolved around the everyday lifesaving efforts of the real Royal Flying Doctor Service of Australia.

The Front 136, 151

The Front is a 1976 film drama about the Hollywood blacklist during the age of live television. It is written by Walter Bernstein, directed by Martin Ritt and stars Woody Allen and Zero Mostel.

The Girl 141

The Girl (1939; 1978) is a novel by Meridel Le Sueur set during Prohibition and chronicling the development of a young woman from a naive small-town girl into a participant in a bank robbery.

The Google 150

Bushisms are unconventional words, phrases, pronunciations, malapropisms, and semantic or linguistic errors that have occurred in the public speaking of former President of the United States George W. Bush and, much less notably, of his father, George H. W. Bush. The term has become part of popular folklore and is the basis of a number of websites and published books. It is often used to caricature the two presidents. Common characteristics include malapropisms, the creation of neologisms, spoonerisms, stunt words and grammatically incorrect subject-verb agreement.

The Graphic 95-96, 105

The Graphic was a British illustrated newspaper, first published on 4 December 1869 by Illustrated Newspapers, Ltd. It continued to be published weekly under this title until 23 April 1932 and then changed title to The National Graphic between 28 April and 14 July 1932; it then ceased publication after 3,266 issues.

The Gutenberg Galaxy 64-65

The Gutenberg Galaxy: The Making of Typographic Man is a book by Marshall McLuhan, in which he analyzes the effects of mass media, especially the printing press, on European culture and human consciousness. It popularized the term global village, which refers to the idea that mass communication allows a village-like mindset to apply to the entire world; and Gutenberg Galaxy, which we may regard today to refer to the accumulated body of recorded works of human art and knowledge, especially books.

The Idea 58, 70, 78, 96, 126, 170

The Idea is a short 2006 black comedy film, a satire of modern societies. The film focuses on the inability to listen beyond the sound of our own voice and ego. It is also a study of contemporary society's insensitivity towards the expression of new ideas and not being willing to give them the appropriate space to grow and form.

The Information Society 149

The Information Society (print: ISSN 0197-2243, online: ISSN 1087-6537) is a peer-reviewed academic journal on sociology, that was established in 1981. It is published five times per year by Routledge and covers topics related to information technologies and changes in society and culture. According to the Journal Citation Reports its 2009 impact factor is 1.111, ranking it 25 out of 65 in the category Information Science & Library Science.

The Last of the Mohicans 128

The Last of the Mohicans: A Narrative of 1757 is a historical novel by James Fenimore Cooper, first published in February 1826. It is the second book of the Leatherstocking Tales pentalogy and the best known. The Pathfinder, published 14 years later in 1840, is its sequel.

The Library of Babel 112

'The Library of Babel' (Spanish: 'La biblioteca de Babel') is a short story by Argentine author and librarian Jorge Luis Borges (1899–1986), conceiving of a universe in the form of a vast library containing all possible 410-page books of a certain format.

The Masses 52-53

The Masses was a graphically innovative magazine of socialist politics published monthly in the U.S. from 1911 until 1917, when Federal prosecutors brought charges against its editors for conspiring to obstruct conscription. It was succeeded by The Liberator and then later The New Masses. It published reportage, fiction, poetry and art by the leading radicals of the time such as Max Eastman, John Reed, Dorothy Day, and Floyd Dell.

The Medium 56, 84, 111-112, 120

The Medium is a short (one hour long) two-act dramatic opera with words and music by Gian Carlo Menotti. Commissioned by Columbia University, its first performance was there on 8 May 1946. The opera's first professional production was presented on a double bill with Menotti's The Telephone at the Heckscher Theater, New York City, February 18-20, 1947 by the Ballet Society. The Broadway production took place on May 1, 1947, at the Ethel Barrymore Theater with the same cast. In 1951, Menotti directed, with the help of filmmaker Alexander Hammid, a film version made to resemble film noir, and starring Anna Maria Alberghetti. A live television production starring Marie Powers took place on 12 December 1948 on the TV series Studio One.

The Message 82

'The Message' is a science fiction short story by American writer Isaac Asimov. It was first published in the February 1956 issue of The Magazine of Fantasy and Science Fiction and reprinted in the 1957 collection Earth is Room Enough. 'The Message' tells the story of how the expression Kilroy was here came to be. A very short story, it runs to 1½ pages in paperback.

The Middle Ages 66

The Middle Ages (adjectival form: medieval or mediæval) was a period of European history from the 5th century to the 15th century. The period followed the fall of the Western Roman Empire in 476, and preceded the Early Modern Era. It is the middle period in a three-period division of history: Classic, Medieval, and Modern. The term 'Middle Ages' first appears in Latin in the 15th century and reflects the view that this period was a deviation from the path of classical learning, a path supposedly reconnected by Renaissance scholarship.

The New Yorker 100

The New Yorker is an American magazine of reportage, commentary, criticism, essays, fiction, satire, cartoons and poetry published by Condé Nast Publications. Starting as a weekly in the mid-1920s, the magazine is now published 47 times annually, with five of these issues covering two-week spans.

The Office 89, 135, 160
The Office is a mockumentary/situation comedy TV show that was first made in the UK and has now been re-made in many other countries. The Israeli version of the show was launched in March 2010. The original version of The Office was created by Ricky Gervais and Stephen Merchant. It starred Gervais as the boss and main character. Initially broadcast on BBC Two on 9 July 2001, the show ran for fourteen episodes – two series of six, plus a two-part Christmas special.

The Paper 68, 87, 126, 138, 147-148, 166, 172
The Paper is a 1994 American comedy-drama film directed by Ron Howard and starring Michael Keaton, Robert Duvall, and Glenn Close. The film depicts 24 hours in a newspaper editor's professional and personal life.

The Reader 57, 63-64, 71, 73, 84, 104-105, 114, 120, 122, 124, 140-142, 148, 151, 170, 175
The Reader (Der Vorleser) is a novel by German law professor and judge Bernhard Schlink, published in Germany in 1995 and in the United States in 1997. The story is a parable, dealing with the difficulties post-war German generations have had comprehending the Holocaust; Ruth Franklin writes that it was aimed specifically at the generation Berthold Brecht called the Nachgeborenen, those who came after. Like other novels in the genre of Vergangenheitsbewältigung, the struggle to come to terms with the past, The Reader explores how the post-war generations should approach the generation that took part in, or witnessed, the atrocities. These are the questions at the heart of Holocaust literature in the late 20th and early 21st century, as the victims and witnesses die and living memory fades.

The Real 59, 71, 112
The Real refers to that which is authentic, the unchangeable truth in reference both to being/the Self and the external dimension of experience, also referred to as the infinite and absolute – as opposed to a reality based on sense perception and the material order.

The Renaissance 145
The Renaissance (Italian: Rinascimento, French: Renaissance, from ri- 'again' and nascere 'be born') is a cultural movement that spanned roughly the 14th to the 17th century, beginning in Florence in the Late Middle Ages and later spreading to the rest of Europe. The term is also used more loosely to refer to the historic era, but since the changes of the Renaissance were not uniform across Europe, this is a general use of the term. As a cultural movement, it encompassed a resurgence of learning based on classical sources, the development of linear perspective in painting, and gradual but widespread educational reform. Traditionally, this intellectual transformation has resulted in the Renaissance being viewed as a bridge between the Middle Ages and the Modern era.

The Screens 88-89, 157
The Screens (French: Les Paravents) is a play by the French dramatist Jean Genet. Its first few productions all used abridged versions, beginning with its world premiere under Hans Lietzau's direction in Berlin in May 1961. Its first complete performance was staged in Stockholm in 1964, two years before Roger Blin directed its French premiere in Paris.

The Search 98
The Search is a 1948 film directed by Fred Zinnemann which tells the story of a young Auschwitz survivor and his mother who search for each other across post-World War II Europe. It stars Montgomery Clift, Ivan Jandl, Jarmila Novotná and Aline MacMahon.

The Sequence 89, 151
The Sequence is a former female old school hip hop trio signed to the Sugar Hill label in the early-1980s. The group consisted of Cheryl Cook (Cheryl The Pearl), Gwendolyn Chisolm (Blondie), and lead singer/rapper Angie Brown Stone (Angie B.). The group originated from Columbia, South Carolina as a group of high school cheerleaders.

The Telegraph 170
The Telegraph was a fan-oriented periodical on musical matters, primarily relating to Bob Dylan. It was published in Manchester, England in 53 issues from November 1981 until the 'Winter' (presumably the final quarter) of 1997. At that point it had a circulation of about 3500, of which England accounted for approximately half.

The Times 104
The Times is a daily national newspaper published in the United Kingdom since 1785, when it was known as The Daily Universal Register.

The Waves 167
The Waves, first published in 1931, is Virginia Woolf's most experimental novel. It consists of soliloquies spoken by the book's six characters: Bernard, Susan, Rhoda, Neville, Jinny, and Louis. Also important is Percival, the seventh character, though readers never hear him speak through his own voice. The monologues that span the characters' lives are broken up by nine brief third-person interludes detailing a coastal scene at varying stages in a day from sunrise to sunset.

The Ways 142
I Modi (The Ways), also known as The Sixteen Pleasures or under the Latin title De omnibus Veneris Schematibus, is a famous erotic book of the Italian Renaissance in which a series of sexual positions were explicitly depicted in engavings. While the original edition was apparently completely

destroyed by the Catholic Church, fragments of a later edition survive. The original illustrations were probably copied by Agostino Caracci, whose version survives. The second edition was accompanied by sonnets written by Pietro Aretino, which described the sexual acts depicted.

The Words 68, 73, 116, 141, 151, 167
The Words (French: Les Mots) is the title of Jean-Paul Sartre's 1963 autobiography.

The Writer 56, 131, 148
The Writer is a monthly magazine for writers published by the Kalmbach Publishing Company of Waukesha, Wisconsin. It was first established by William H. Hills and Robert Luce, two Boston Globe reporters, as 'a monthly magazine to interest and help all literary workers', in April 1887. Until the November 2000 issue, it was published in Boston. It is the oldest magazine for writers currently being published. It is targeted at writers, and includes articles offering advice for writing and resources for publishing.

Thesaurus 68
A thesaurus is a reference work that lists words grouped together according to similarity of meaning (containing synonyms and sometimes antonyms), in contrast to a dictionary, which contains definitions and pronunciations. The largest thesaurus in the world is the Historical Thesaurus of the Oxford English Dictionary, which contains more than 920,000 words.

Thick Description 107
In anthropology and other fields, a thick description of a human behavior is one that explains not just the behavior, but its context as well, such that the behavior becomes meaningful to an outsider.

Things That Are 155
Things That Are is a young adult book by Andrew Clements. Released in 2008 by Philomel, the book is a sequel to Things Hoped For.

Think This 121, 143
Think This is the second studio album by the thrash metal band, Toxik, released in 1989 by Roadracer Records. The album was re-released by Metal Mind Productions and Displeased Records in 2007. Artwork was designed by Ed Repka.

Thinking 60, 69, 91, 124-125, 173
Thought generally refers to any mental or intellectual activity involving an individual's subjective consciousness. It can refer either to the act of thinking or the resulting ideas or arrangements of ideas. Similar concepts include cognition, sentience, consciousness, and imagination.

Thousand Words 71, 78-79, 124, 163-164
Thousand Words is an independent feature film finance and production company founded by Jonah Smith and Palmer West in 2000. The name is a take on the saying 'a picture is worth a thousand words'.

Ticker 93
Ticker can mean: A news ticker (sometimes referred to as a 'crawler') is a small screen space on news television networks dedicated to presenting headlines or minor pieces of news. It may also refer to a long, thin scoreboard-style display seen around the front of some offices or public buildings. The news ticker has been used in Europe in countries such as Britain, Germany and Ireland for some years, and the United States has been catching up recently. It is also used in several Asian countries and Australia.

Ticker-Tape 171
Ticker tape was the earliest digital electronic communications medium, transmitting stock price information over telegraph lines, in use between around 1870 through 1970. It consisted of a paper strip which ran through a machine called a stock ticker, which printed abbreviated company names as alphabetic symbols followed by numeric stock transaction price and volume information.

Time Magazine 108
Time (trademarked in capitals as TIME) is an American news magazine. A European edition (Time Europe, formerly known as Time Atlantic) is published from London. Time Europe covers the Middle East, Africa and, since 2003, Latin America. An Asian edition (Time Asia) is based in Hong Kong. As of 2009, Time no longer publishes a Canadian advertiser edition. The South Pacific edition, covering Australia, New Zealand and the Pacific Islands, is based in Sydney.

Time to Come 114
Time to Come is an anthology of science fiction and fantasy stories edited by August Derleth. It was first published by Farrar, Straus and Young in 1954. The stories are all original to this anthology.

Time-consuming 144-145
In business, retail, and accounting, a cost is the value of money that has been used up to produce something, and hence is not available for use anymore. In economics, a cost is an alternative that is given up as a result of a decision. In business, the cost may be one of acquisition, in which case the amount of money expended to acquire it is counted as cost. In this case, money is the input that is gone in order to acquire the thing. This acquisition cost may be the sum of the cost of production as incurred by the original producer, and further costs of transaction as incurred by the acquirer over and above the price paid to the producer. Usually, the price also includes a mark-up for profit over the cost of production.

Timeless 110
Timeless means the quality of being eternal, ageless, immortal, or not affected by time. Anachronisms can be regarded as timeless or out of time.

Times Higher Education Supplement 107

The Times Higher Education (THE), formerly Times Higher Education Supplement (THES), is a weekly British magazine based in London reporting specifically on news and other issues related to higher education. It is the United Kingdom's leading higher education news publication.

Tintin 84

Tintin is an adventurer who travels around the world in 'The Adventures of Tintin', a series of comic books drawn and written by the Belgian cartoonist Georges Remi, better known as Hergé. The series is one of the most popular comic book series in Europe and the world, especially in Belgium, France, the Netherlands, Denmark and India.

Title 71, 77, 87, 97, 154

A title is a prefix or suffix added to someone's name to signify either veneration, an official position or a professional or academic qualification. In some languages, titles may even be inserted between a first and last name (for example, Graf in German, Cardinal in Catholic usage or clerical titles such as Archbishop). Some titles are hereditary.

To Come 72, 114, 133, 142-143

To Come is a printing and journalism reference abbreviated 'TK'. It is used to signify that additional material will be added at a later date.

To Do 52, 70, 72, 115, 144, 159, 163, 172

Time management is the act or process of exercising conscious control over the amount of time spent on specific activities, especially to increase efficiency or productivity. Time management may be aided by a range of skills, tools, and techniques used to manage time when accomplishing specific tasks, projects and goals. This set encompasses a wide scope of activities, and these include planning, allocating, setting goals, delegation, analysis of time spent, monitoring, organizing, scheduling, and prioritizing. Initially, time management referred to just business or work activities, but eventually the term broadened to include personal activities as well. A time management system is a designed combination of processes, tools, techniques, and methods. Usually time management is a necessity in any project development as it determines the project completion time and scope.

To Survive 87

To Survive is the second album by Joan as Police Woman. It was released on June 9, 2008, and made available on CD, LP and digital download.

Tolstoy 101

Leo Tolstoy, or Count Lyev Nikolayevich Tolstoy (September 9, 1828 ;– November 20, 1910), was a Russian writer of realist fiction and philosophical essays. His works War and Peace and Anna Karenina represent, in their scope, breadth and vivid depiction of 19th-century Russian life and attitudes, a peak of realist fiction.

Too Much Information 102

'Too Much Information' is the third single released from Duran Duran's 1993 album, Duran Duran, popularly known as The Wedding Album. Also known as TMI.

Tool 146, 170-171

A tool is a device that can be used to produce an item or achieve a task, but that is not consumed in the process. Informally the word is also used to describe a procedure or process with a specific purpose. Tools that are used in particular fields or activities may have different designations such as Instrument, Utensil, Implement, Machine, or Apparatus.

Touch Screen 119, 121

A touchscreen is an electronic visual display that can detect the presence and location of a touch within the display area. The term generally refers to touching the display of the device with a finger or hand. Touchscreens can also sense other passive objects, such as a stylus. Touchscreen is common in devices such as all-in-one computers, tablet computers, and smartphones.

Touching 90

The somatosensory system is a diverse sensory system comprising the receptors and processing centres to produce the sensory modalities such as touch, temperature, proprioception (body position), and nociception (pain). The sensory receptors cover the skin and epithelia, skeletal muscles, bones and joints, internal organs, and the cardiovascular system. While touch (also, more formally, tactition; adjectival form: 'tactile' or 'somatosensory') is considered one of the five traditional senses, the impression of touch is formed from several modalities.

Trade Magazine 163

A trade magazine, also called a professional magazine, is a magazine published with the intention of target marketing to a specific industry or type of trade. The collective term for this area of publishing is the trade press.

Tradition 131, 152

A tradition is a ritual, belief or object passed down within a society, still maintained in the present, with origins in the past. Common examples include holidays or impractical but socially meaningful clothes (like lawyer wigs or military officer spurs), but the idea has also been applied to social norms such as greetings. Traditions can persist and evolve for thousands of years.

Traffic Sign 90

Traffic signs or road signs are signs erected at the side of roads to provide information to road users. With traffic volumes increasing over the last eight decades, many countries have adopted pictorial signs or otherwise simplified and standardized their signs to facilitate international travel where language differences would create barriers, and in general to help enhance traffic safety. Such pictorial signs use symbols (often silhouettes) in place of words and are usually based on international protocols. Such signs were first developed in Europe, and have been adopted by most countries to varying degrees.

Trained 58, 102

The term training refers to the acquisition of knowledge, skills, and competencies as a result of the teaching of vocational or practical skills and knowledge that relate to specific useful competencies. It forms the core of apprenticeships and provides the backbone of content at institutes of technology (also known as technical colleges or polytechnics). In addition to the basic training required for a trade, occupation or profession, observers of the labor-market [who?] recognize today [update] the need to continue training beyond initial qualifications: to maintain, upgrade and update skills throughout working life. People within many professions and occupations may refer to this sort of training as professional development.

Trajectories 61

A trajectory is the path a moving object follows through space as a function of time. The object might be a projectile or a satellite, for example. It thus includes the meaning of orbit – the path of a planet, an asteroid or a comet as it travels around a central mass. A trajectory can be described mathematically either by the geometry of the path, or as the position of the object over time.

Transitional Objects 87

A comfort object, transitional object, or security blanket is an item used to provide psychological comfort, especially in unusual or unique situations, or at bedtime for small children. Among toddlers, comfort objects may take the form of a blanket, a stuffed animal, or a favorite toy, and may be referred to by the terms blankey and lovey. Cuddly toys are sometimes carried in emergency vehicles and police patrol cars, to be given to children involved in an accident or traumatic event, to provide them comfort.

Translation 53, 152

Translation is the communication of the meaning of a source-language text by means of an equivalent target-language text. Whereas interpreting undoubtedly antedates writing, translation began only after the appearance of written literature; there exist partial translations of the Sumerian Epic of Gilgamesh (ca. 2000 BCE) into Southwest Asian languages of the second millennium BCE.

Translations 162

Translations is a three-act play by Irish playwright Brian Friel written in 1980. It is set in Baile Beag (Ballybeg), a small village at the heart of 19th- century agricultural Ireland. Friel has said that Translations is 'a play about language and only about language', but it deals with a wide range of issues, stretching from language and communication to Irish history and cultural imperialism. Despite the 1833 setting, there are obvious parallels between Baile Beag and today's world.

Transmit 161

Transmit is an FTP client for Mac OS X and Mac OS Classic (which is unsupported). Developed by Panic, Transmit is shareware – after a seven-day trial period, the product can only be used for seven-minute sessions until it has been purchased.

Travel 99, 115

Travel is movement of people between relatively distant geographical locations for any purpose and any duration, with or without any means of transport. Travel also includes relatively short stays between successive movements. Movements between locations requiring only a few minutes are not considered as travel.

Trivia 90

The trivia (singular trivium, adjective trivial) are the three lower Artes Liberales, i.e. grammar, rhetoric and logic. These were the topics of basic education, foundational to the quadrivia of higher education, and hence the material of basic education, of interest only to undergraduates. The word trivia was also used to describe a place where three roads met in Ancient Rome.

Truth 112, 121

Truth has a variety of meanings, such as the state of being in accord with a particular fact or reality, or being in accord with the body of real things, real events or actualities. It can also mean having fidelity to an original or to a standard or ideal. In a common archaic usage it also meant constancy or sincerity in action or character.

Tumblr 103

Tumblr, sometimes styled as 'tumblr.', is a microblogging platform that allows users to post text, images, videos, links, quotes and audio to their tumblelog, a short-form blog. Users can follow other users, or choose to make their tumblelog private. The service emphasizes ease of use.

Turning 57, 71, 146

Turning is the process whereby a single point cutting tool is parallel to the surface. It can be done manually, in a traditional form of lathe, which frequently requires continuous supervision by the operator, or by using a computer controlled and automated lathe which does not. This type of machine tool is referred to as having computer numerical control, better known as CNC. and is commonly used with many other types of machine tool besides the lathe.

TV In 158
TV IN is a television station in Montenegro. It started working in early 2002. It is based in Podgorica. It is currently one of the most watched TV stations in Montenegro.

Tweet 174
A post on Twitter.

Twenty Years 62, 102
'Twenty Years' was a song recorded to coincide with the 2004 best-of compilation release by Placebo.

Twitter 52, 56, 65, 103, 106, 108, 145, 149, 161, 164, 170
Twitter is a website owned and operated by Twitter Inc. which offers a social networking and microblogging service, enabling its users to send and read messages called tweets. Tweets are text-based posts composed of up to 140 characters displayed on the user's profile page. Tweets are publicly visible by default; however, senders can restrict message delivery to just their followers. Users may subscribe to other users' tweets – this is known as following and subscribers are known as followers or tweeps (Twitter + peeps).

Typeface 82
In typography, a typeface is a set of one or more fonts, in one or more sizes, designed with stylistic unity, each comprising a coordinated set of glyphs. A typeface usually comprises an alphabet of letters, numerals, and punctuation marks; it may also include ideograms and symbols, or consist entirely of them, for example, mathematical or map-making symbols.

Typesetting 82, 156
Typesetting is the composition of text material by means of types.

Typewriter 82
A typewriter is a mechanical or electromechanical device with keys that, when pressed, cause characters to be printed on a medium, usually paper. Typically one character is printed per keypress, and the machine prints the characters by making ink impressions of type elements similar to the pieces of cast metal type (called sorts) used in movable type letterpress printing. From their invention in 1870 through much of the 20th century, typewriters were indispensable tools for many authors and businessmen. By the end of the 1980s, however, word processors and personal computers largely displaced typewriters in the settings where they previously had been ubiquitous in the western world. Nonetheless, typewriters remain in use in various areas of the world.

Typing 68
Typing is the process of inputting text into a device, such as a typewriter, cell phone, computer, or a calculator, by pressing keys on a keyboard. It can be distinguished from other means of input, such as the use of pointing devices like the computer mouse, and text input via speech recognition.

Typography 75, 82, 91, 110, 167, 172
Typography (from the Greek words typos (form) and graphy (writing) is the art and technique of arranging type, type design, and modifying type glyphs. Type glyphs are created and modified using a variety of illustration techniques. The arrangement of type involves the selection of typefaces, point size, line length, leading (line spacing), adjusting the spaces between groups of letters (tracking) and adjusting the space between pairs of letters (kerning).

Ulysses 56
Ulysses is derived from Ulixes, the Latin name for Odysseus, a character in ancient Greek literature.

Unconsciously 160
The unconscious mind is a term coined by the 18th-century German romantic philosopher Sir Christopher Riegel and later introduced into English by the poet and essayist Samuel Taylor Coleridge. The unconscious mind might be defined as that part of the mind which gives rise to a collection of mental phenomena that manifest in a person's mind but which the person is not aware of at the time of their occurrence. These phenomena include unconscious feelings, unconscious or automatic skills, unnoticed perceptions, unconscious thoughts, unconscious habits and automatic reactions, complexes, hidden phobias and concealed desires.

Underline 66
An underline, also called an underscore, is one or more horizontal lines immediately below a portion of writing.

Understanding 64, 74, 90-91, 116, 131, 142-143, 147, 155
Understanding (also called intellection) is a psychological process related to an abstract or physical object, such as a person, situation, or message whereby one is able to think about it and use concepts to deal adequately with that object. Understanding is a relation between the knower and an object of understanding. Understanding implies abilities and dispositions with respect to an object of knowledge sufficient to support intelligent behavior.

Unintended 169
'Unintended' is the fifth single by English alternative rock band Muse.

Unique 53-54, 78, 114, 143, 148
In mathematics and logic, the phrase 'there is one and only one' is used to indicate that exactly one object with a certain property exists.

University Degree 98
An academic degree is a position and title within a college or university that is usually awarded in recognition of the recipient having either satisfactorily completed a prescribed course of study or having conducted a scholarly endeavour deemed worthy of his or her admission to the degree. Academic degrees were first introduced during the Middle Ages and

there was little differentiation between them. Scholarly training could be viewed as analogous to apprenticeship to a guild. The term of study before new teachers were admitted to the 'guild' of 'Master of Arts', was the same as the term of apprenticeship for other occupations. Originally the terms 'master' and 'doctor' were synonymous, but eventually the doctorate came to be regarded as a higher qualification than the master degree.

Upcoming 72

Upcoming (formerly Upcoming.org) is a social event calendar website that launched in 2003, founded by Andy Baio. On October 4, 2005, Upcoming.org was acquired by Yahoo!.

Updates 93, 119, 136

A patch is a piece of software designed to fix problems with, or update a computer program or its supporting data. This includes fixing security vulnerabilities and other bugs, and improving the usability or performance. Though meant to fix problems, poorly designed patches can sometimes introduce new problems (see software regressions).

Upgraded 104

The term upgrade refers to the replacement of a product with a newer version of the same product. It is most often used in computing and consumer electronics, generally meaning a replacement of hardware, software or firmware with a newer or better version, in order to bring the system up to date or to improve its characteristics. Contrast update and replace. See also laptop upgrade.

Urban 160-161

Urban is a Danish free daily newspaper owned by Det Berlingske Officin. It was launched on September 24, 2001, shortly after the competing free daily MetroXpress (the Danish edition of the Metro newspaper). Circulation in second half of 2008 was 196,752.

URGE 120

URGE was opened on May 17, 2006. Downloaded files come with restrictions on their use, enforced by Windows Media DRM, Microsoft's digital rights management. URGE features the music programming of MTV, CMT, and VH1 and provides editorial content for the online music service. URGE currently charges 99¢ a track, or $9.95/month for a subscription. An optional $14.95/month to-go subscription is available for those with PlaysForSure devices. As of May 2008, URGE is not compatible with Microsoft's Zune or Apple's iPod, although the first-generation Zune Marketplace was based on URGE, and had many similarities.

Useful 71, 83, 149

In economics, utility is a measure of relative satisfaction. Given this measure, one may speak meaningfully of increasing or decreasing utility, and thereby explain economic behavior in terms of attempts to increase one's utility. Utility is often modeled to be affected by consumption of various goods and services, possession of wealth and spending of leisure time.

Values 70, 149

A personal and/or cultural value is an absolute or relative ethical value, the assumption of which can be the basis for ethical action. A value system is a set of consistent values and measures. A principle value is a foundation upon which other values and measures of integrity are based. Those values which are not physiologically determined and normally considered objective, such as a desire to avoid physical pain, seek pleasure, etc., are considered subjective, vary across individuals and cultures and are in many ways aligned with belief and belief systems. Types of values include ethical/moral values, doctrinal/ideological (religious, political) values, social values, and aesthetic values. It is debated whether some values which are not clearly physiologically determined are intrinsic such as altruism and whether some such as acquisitiveness should be valued as vices or virtues. Values have typically been studied in sociology; anthropology; social psychology; moral philosophy and business ethics.

Ventures 72

The Ventures are an American instrumental rock band formed in 1958 in Tacoma, Washington. The band, formed by Don Wilson and Bob Bogle, two masonry workers, has had an enduring impact on the development of music worldwide, having sold over 100 million records, and are to date the best-selling instrumental band of all time. In 2008, the Ventures were inducted into the Rock and Roll Hall of Fame.

Verb 104, 147

A verb, from the Latin verbum meaning word, is a word (part of speech) that in syntax conveys an action (bring, read, walk, run, learn), or a state of being (be, exist, stand). In the usual description of English, the basic form, with or without the particle to, is the infinitive. In most languages, verbs are inflected (modified in form) to encode tense, aspect, mood and voice. A verb may also agree with the person, gender, and/or number of some of its arguments, such as its subject, or object.

Video 53, 55, 93, 102, 109, 145, 152, 159, 170

Video is the technology of electronically capturing, recording, processing, storing, transmitting, and reconstructing a sequence of still images representing scenes in motion.

Video-sharing 80

A video hosting service allows individuals to upload video clips to an internet website. The video host will then store the video on its server, and show the individual different types of code to allow others to view this video. The website, mainly used as the video hosting website, is usually called the video sharing website.

View 56, 59, 76, 83, 112, 115, 124

A view is what can be seen in a range of vision. View may also be used as a synonym of point of view in the first sense. View may also be used figuratively or with special significance – for example, to imply a scenic outlook or significant vantage point.

Virtual 59, 89, 93-94, 118, 121, 156, 160

The term virtual is a concept applied in many fields with somewhat differing connotations, and also, differing denotations.

Virtual Desktop 94

In computing, a virtual desktop is a term used with respect to user interfaces, usually within the WIMP paradigm, to describe ways in which the size of a computer's desktop environment is expanded beyond the physical limits of the screen's real estate through the use of software.

Virtually 67, 106, 119, 126, 159, 166

In mathematics, especially in the area of abstract algebra which studies infinite groups, the adverb virtually is used to modify a property so that it need only hold for a subgroup of finite index. Given a property P, the group G is said to be virtually P if there is a finite index subgroup H≤G such that H has property P.

Visual 58-59, 64-65, 71-72, 77, 93, 95-96, 108-109, 142, 148, 150, 152, 154, 164, 166

The visual system is the part of the central nervous system which enables organisms to process visual detail, as well as enabling several non-image forming photoresponse functions. It interprets information from visible light to build a representation of the surrounding world. The visual system accomplishes a number of complex tasks, including the reception of light and the formation of monocular representations; the construction of a binocular perception from a pair of two dimensional projections; the identification and categorization of visual objects; assessing distances to and between objects; and guiding body movements in relation to visual objects. The psychological manifestation of visual information is known as visual perception, a lack of which is called blindness. Non-image forming visual functions, independent of visual perception, include the pupillary light reflex (PLR) and circadian photoentrainment.

Visual Comparison 152

A visual comparison is to compare two or more things by eye. This might be done by placing them side by side; by overlaying them; by alternating an image or by presenting each image to a separate eye.

Visual Design 109

Communication design is a mixed discipline between design and information-development which is concerned with how media intermission such as printed, crafted, electronic media or presentations communicate with people. A communication design approach is not only concerned with developing the message aside from the aesthetics in media, but also with creating new media channels to ensure the message reaches the target audience.

Visual Literacy 72

Visual literacy is the ability to interpret, negotiate, and make meaning from information presented in the form of an image. Visual literacy is based on the idea that pictures can be 'read' and that meaning can be communicated through a process of reading.

Visuals 71, 152

VJing is a broad designation for realtime visual performance. Characteristics of VJing are the creation or manipulation of imagery in realtime through technological mediation and for an audience, in synchronization to music. VJing often takes place at events such as concerts, nightclubs, music festivals and sometimes in combination with other performative arts. This results in a live multimedia performance that can include music, actors and dancers. The term VJing became popular in its association with MTV's Video Jockey but its origins date back to the New York club scene of the 70s. In both situations VJing is the manipulation or selection of visuals, the same way DJing is a selection and manipulation of audio.

Vocabulary 104-105

A person's vocabulary is the set of words within a language that are familiar to that person. A vocabulary usually grows and evolves with age, and serves as a useful and fundamental tool for communication and acquiring knowledge. Acquiring an extensive vocabulary is one of the largest challenges in learning a second language.

Voice-over 79, 95

Voice-over (also known as off-camera or off-stage commentary) is a production technique where a voice which is not part of the narrative (non-diegetic) is used in a radio, television, film, theatre, or other presentation. The voice-over may be spoken by someone who appears elsewhere in the production or by a specialist voice actor.

Waiting For 140

'Waiting For' is Miz's second single from New Day. This one is more rock than all her previous works.

Wander 127

In telecommunication, wander are long-term low-frequency random variations of the significant instants of a digital signal from their ideal positions. Phase variations with a frequency content above 10 Hertz are considered jitter, while those with a frequency below 10 Hz are referred to as wander. Wander variations are those that occur over a period greater than 1 s (second). Jitter, swim, wander, and drift have increasing periods of variation in that order.

War and Peace 148

War and Peace is a novel by the Russian author Leo Tolstoy, published in 1869. The work is epic in scale and is considered one of the most celebrated works of fiction. It is regarded as Tolstoy's finest literary achievement, along with his other famous work Anna Karenina (1873–1877).

War Books 118
A war novel is a novel in which the primary action takes place in a field of armed combat, or in a domestic setting (or home front) where the characters are preoccupied with the preparations for, or recovery from, war. It is sometimes referred to as military fiction.

Warde 75
Beatrice Warde (20 September 1900-16 September 1969, née Beatrice Becker), was a communicator on typography. She was the only daughter of May Lamberton Becker, a journalist on the staff of the New York Herald Tribune, and Gustave Becker, composer and teacher.

Warm Reading 87-88
Cold reading is a series of techniques used by mentalists, illusionists, psychics and con artists to determine or express details about another person, often in order to convince them that the reader knows much more about a subject than they actually do. Without prior knowledge of a person, a practiced cold reader can still quickly obtain a great deal of information about the subject by analyzing the person's body language, age, clothing or fashion, hairstyle, gender, sexual orientation, religion, race or ethnicity, level of education, manner of speech, place of origin, etc. Cold readers commonly employ high probability guesses about the subject, quickly picking up on signals from their subjects as to whether their guesses are in the right direction or not, and then emphasizing and reinforcing any chance connections the subjects acknowledge while quickly moving on from missed guesses.

Watch 60, 85, 89, 95, 128, 158-159, 164
Before wristwatches became popular in the 1920s, most watches were pocket watches, which often had covers and were carried in a pocket and attached to a watch chain or watch fob. In early 1900s, the wristwatch, originally called a Wristlet, was reserved for women and considered more of a passing fad than a serious timepiece. Real gentlemen, who carried pocket watches, were actually quoted as saying they would 'sooner wear a skirt as wear a wristwatch'. This all changed in World War I when soldiers on the battlefield found using a pocket watch to be impractical, so they attached the pocket watch to their wrist by a cupped leather strap.

Watching 57-60, 85, 89, 144-145, 149
Watching is a British television sitcom, produced by Granada Television for the ITV network and broadcast for seven series and four specials between 1987 and 1993.

Wayfinding 60
Wayfinding encompasses all of the ways in which people and animals orient themselves in physical space and navigate from place to place.

Ways of Being 70
In metaphysics (in particular, ontology), the different kinds or ways of being are called categories of being or simply categories. To investigate the categories of being is to determine the most fundamental and the broadest classes of entities. A distinction between such categories, in making the categories or applying them, is called an ontological distinction.

WC 136
WC or Wc commonly refers to a water closet. It may also refer to: Winston Churchill.

Weather Forecast 172
Weather forecasting is the application of science and technology to predict the state of the atmosphere for a given location. Human beings have attempted to predict the weather informally for millennia, and formally since the nineteenth century. Weather forecasts are made by collecting quantitative data about the current state of the atmosphere and using scientific understanding of atmospheric processes to project how the atmosphere will evolve.

WEB 72, 83, 104-105, 121, 125-126, 146, 152, 170
WEB is a computer programming system created by Donald E. Knuth as the first implementation of what he called 'literate programming': the idea that one could create software as works of literature, by embedding source code inside descriptive text, rather than the reverse (as is common practice in most programming languages), in an order that is convenient for exposition to human readers, rather than in the order demanded by the compiler.

Web Pages 152
A web page or webpage is a document or information resource that is suitable for the World Wide Web and can be accessed through a web browser and displayed on a monitor or mobile device. This information is usually in HTML or XHTML format, and may provide navigation to other web pages via hypertext links. Web pages frequently subsume other resources such as style sheets, scripts and images into their final presentation.

Web Templates 105
A web template is a tool used to separate content from presentation in web design, and for mass-production of web documents. It is a basic component of a web template system.

Website 78, 95, 101
A website (also written Web site or simply site) is a collection of related web pages containing images, videos or other digital assets. A website is hosted on at least

one web server, accessible via a network such as the Internet or a private local area network through an Internet address also called URL.

Weight 99, 139, 148

In most physics textbooks, weight is the name given to the force on an object due to gravity. However, some books use an operational definition, defining the weight of an object as the force measured by the operation of weighing it (that is, the force required to support it).

Western Culture 111

Western culture, sometimes equated with Western civilization or European civilization, refers to cultures of European origin, especially western European culture.

Wertham 124

Fredric Wertham (March 20, 1895–November 18, 1981) was a Jewish German-American psychiatrist and crusading author who protested the purportedly harmful effects of violent imagery in mass media and comic books on the development of children. His best-known book was Seduction of the Innocent (1954), which purported that comic books are dangerous to children. Wertham's criticisms of comic books helped spark a U.S. Congressional inquiry into the comic book industry and the creation of the Comics Code.

What The 96, 128, 140

'What The—?!' was a series of Marvel comics parodying the Marvel Universe, similar in vein to the 1960s series Not Brand Echh. It was billed as 'The Marvel mag of mirth and mayhem' and ran for twenty-six issues, with issue #1 having an August 1988 cover date and issue #26 being a 1993 'Fall Special'. It typically contained a series of short stories with comedic takes on Marvel heroes and villains, such as having Spider-Ham substitute for Spider-Man.

When it Started 67

'When it Started' is a song by the garage rock band The Strokes. It appears on Music from and Inspired by Spider-Man. Due to the September 11 terrorist attacks in New York City the song replaced 'New York City Cops' on the US version of the album Is This It after The Strokes witnessed the 'valiant response' of the city's police department during the tragedy. The vinyl release retained the original track list.

When You Write 67

When You Write is a 1998 EP by IBOPA. It is their last release, and was originally printed on red 7 vinyl by Pariah Recrods.

Who is 127, 132

WHOIS (pronounced as the phrase who is) is a query and response protocol that is widely used for querying databases that store the registered users or assignees of an Internet resource, such as a domain name, an IP address block, or an autonomous system, but is also used for a wider range of other information. The protocol stores and delivers database content in a human-readable format. The Whois protocol is documented in RFC 3912.

WiFi 92

Wi-Fi is a trademark of the Wi-Fi Alliance. A Wi-Fi enabled device such as a personal computer, video game console, smartphone, or digital audio player can connect to the Internet when within range of a wireless network connected to the Internet. The coverage of one or more (interconnected) access points – called hotspots when offering public access – generally comprises an area the size of a few rooms but may be expanded to cover many square miles, depending on the number of access points with overlapping coverage.

Wikipedia 81, 109

Wikipedia is a free, web-based, collaborative, multilingual encyclopedia project supported by the non-profit Wikimedia Foundation. Its 18 million articles (over 3.6 million in English) have been written collaboratively by volunteers around the world, and almost all of its articles can be edited by anyone with access to the site. Wikipedia was launched in 2001 by Jimmy Wales and Larry Sanger and has become the largest and most popular general reference work on the Internet, ranking around seventh among all websites on Alexa and having 365 million readers.

Wikis 80, 136

A wiki is a website that allows the creation and editing of any number of interlinked web pages via a web browser using a simplified markup language or a WYSIWYG text editor. Wikis are typically powered by wiki software and are often used to create collaborative works. Examples include community websites, corporate intranets, knowledge management systems, and note services. The software can also be used for personal notetaking.

Winfrey 100

Oprah Winfrey (born Oprah Gail Winfrey; January 29, 1954) is an American television host, actress, producer, and philanthropist, best known for her self-titled, multi-award winning talk show, which has become the highest-rated program of its kind in history. She has been ranked the richest African American of the 20th century, the greatest black philanthropist in American history, and was once the world's only black billionaire. She is also, according to some assessments, the most influential woman in the world.

Wipe 88

Wiping or junking is a colloquial term for action taken by radio and television production and broadcasting companies, in which old audiotapes, videotapes, and telerecordings (kinescopes), are erased, reused, or destroyed after several uses. The practice was prevalent during the 1960s and 1970s, although it is now less common since associated storage costs have decreased, and especially since the advent of domestic audio-visual playback technology (e.g. videocassette and DVD), with broadcasters and production houses realizing both the economic and cultural value of keeping archived material for both rebroadcast and potential profits through release on home video.

Wired 55, 90

Wired is a full-color monthly American magazine and on-line periodical, published since March 1993, that reports on how technology affects culture, the economy, and politics. Owned by Condé Nast Publications, it is headquartered in San Francisco, California.

Wiske 84

Spike and Suzy, the British title for Suske en Wiske in Dutch, is a comics series created by the Belgian comics author Willy Vandersteen. The strip is known as Bob et Bobette in French and Willy and Wanda in the U.S. It was first published in De Nieuwe Standaard in 1945 and soon became popular. Although not in its earlier form, the strip adapted to the Ligne claire style pioneered by Hergé, a change taking place when the strip became serialised in Hergé's comics magazine Tintin (Dutch: Kuifje) from 1948 to 1959.

Without 59-63, 65-68, 73, 80, 83, 93, 101, 103, 106, 110-112, 114-115, 121, 125-126, 134, 157, 168

'Without' (Part 3) is the 163rd episode of the science fiction television series The X-Files.

Word 50-53, 60, 64-65, 79-80, 82, 86, 91, 97, 104-105, 112, 122, 124, 129, 139, 150-152, 162, 168-169, 171

A word is the smallest free form (an item that may be uttered in isolation with semantic or pragmatic content) in a language, in contrast to a morpheme, which is the smallest unit of meaning. A word may consist of only one morpheme (e.g. so, very), but a single morpheme may not be able to exist as a free form (e.g. the English plural morpheme -s).

Word Art 124

WordArt is a text-styling feature that is available in the Microsoft Office suite of products. It allows users to create stylized text with various 'special effects' such as textures, outlines, and many other manipulations that are not available through the standard font formatting. For example, one can create shadows, rotate, 'bend' and 'stretch' the shape of the text. WordArt is available in 30 different preset styles on Microsoft Word, however, it is fully customizable using the tools available on the WordArt toolbar and Drawing toolbar, or on the WordArt tools tab on Office 2007 & 2010. It is also available in Microsoft Excel, Microsoft PowerPoint and Microsoft Publisher. WordArt in Microsoft Office 2010, users can apply formatting effects such as shadow, bevel, glow, gradient glow, and reflection to their text.

Word Processor 162

A word processor (more formally known as document preparation system) is a computer application used for the production (including composition, editing, formatting, and possibly printing) of any sort of printable material.

Words and Pictures 99

Words and Pictures is an album release in 1997 by Bob Snider.

World Literature 115

World literature refers to literature from all over the world, including African literature, American literature, Arabic literature, Asian literature, Australasian literature, Caribbean Literature, English literature, European literature, Indian literature, Latin American literature and Russian literature.

World of Warcraft 143

World of Warcraft, often referred to as WoW, is a massively multiplayer online role-playing game (MMORPG) by Blizzard Entertainment, a subsidiary of Activision Blizzard. It is the fourth released game set in the fantasy Warcraft universe, which was first introduced by Warcraft: Orcs & Humans in 1994. World of Warcraft takes place within the Warcraft world of Azeroth, approximately four years after the events at the conclusion of Blizzard's previous Warcraft release, Warcraft III: The Frozen Throne. Blizzard Entertainment announced World of Warcraft on September 2, 2001. The game was released on November 23, 2004, on the 10th anniversary of the Warcraft franchise.

World Wide Web 121

The World Wide Web, abbreviated as WWW or W3 and commonly known as the Web, is a system of interlinked hypertext documents accessed via the Internet. With a web browser, one can view web pages that may contain text, images, videos, and other multimedia and navigate between them via hyperlinks. Using concepts from earlier hypertext systems, English engineer and computer scientist Sir Tim Berners-Lee, now the Director of the World Wide Web Consortium, wrote a proposal in March 1989 for what would eventually become the World Wide Web. At CERN in Geneva, Switzerland, Berners-Lee and Belgian computer scientist Robert Cailliau proposed in 1990 to use 'HyperText ... to link and access information of various kinds as a web of nodes in which the user can browse at will', and publicly introduced the project in December. 'The World-Wide Web was developed to be a pool of human knowledge, and human culture, which would allow collaborators in remote sites to share their ideas and all aspects of a common project.'

Writer 53, 56-57, 60, 75, 80, 84, 101, 109, 112, 115, 124, 131, 137, 140-141, 148, 152, 157, 163, 165

A writer is a person who produces literary content, including but not limited to stories, poetry, music and other literary art, advertising, procedures, and books.

Writing 52, 61-62, 66-68, 80, 88, 92-93, 104, 119, 122, 126, 129, 134, 138-139, 143-145, 149, 162, 166-167, 169, 173, 175

Writing is the representation of language in a textual medium through the use of a set of signs or symbols (known as a writing system). It is distinguished from illustration, such as cave drawing and painting, and non-symbolic preservation of language via non-textual media, such as magnetic tape audio.

Writing Pad 68

A notebook (also notepad, writing pad, drawing pad, legal pad, etc.) is a book or binder composed of pages of notes, often ruled, that are made out of paper, used for various purposes including recording notes or memoranda, writing, drawing, and scrapbooking.

Written Language 126, 162

A written language is the representation of a language by means of a writing system. Written language is an invention in that it must be taught to children, who will instinctively learn or create spoken or gestural languages.

WYSIWYG 82

WYSIWYG is an acronym for what you see is what you get. The term is used in computing to describe a system in which content displayed during editing appears very similar to the final output, which might be a printed document, web page, or slide presentation.

Yes and No 76

Yes and No is a spoken word game similar to Twenty Questions played in Charles Dickens' A Christmas Carol. In the game, the host (Fred in A Christmas Carol) has something in mind, and the guessers (party guests) ask several simple yes-or-no questions.

You Look Nice Today 141

Merlin Dean Mann III (born November 26, 1966 in Cincinnati, Ohio) writes the blog 43 Folders. He received a B.A. from New College of Florida, and he currently resides in San Francisco, California with his wife, Madeline Mann, and his daughter, Eleanor Flannery Mann.

Young People 104, 164

Youth is the time of life between childhood and adulthood (maturity). Definitions of the specific age range that constitutes youth vary. An individual's actual maturity may not correspond to their chronological age, as immature individuals could exist at all ages.

Youth Culture 65

A youth subculture is a youth-based subculture with distinct styles, behaviors, and interests. Youth subcultures offer participants an identity outside of that ascribed by social institutions such as family, work, home and school. Youth subcultures that show a systematic hostility to the dominant culture are sometimes described as countercultures.

YouTube 65, 85-86, 108-109, 145, 158-159, 162

YouTube is a video-sharing website on which users can upload, share, and view videos, created by three former PayPal employees in February 2005.

Zoom 150

Zoom is an onomatopoeic sound that indicates swiftness.

About this Book

When contemplating what the future of reading may mean, it is one thing to ponder the physical or habitual aspects of reading, but another to consider the shifts in the manner in which texts and literature, and therefore reading, are contextualized. Words and phrases may contain meanings extending past what the author attributes in his or her narrative. For example, temporal or location-dependent contexts may play an increasingly significant role in today's texts.

Literary anthropology, as defined by literary theorist Wolfgang Iser, suggests that while the reader will always have an interpretation of the text he or she reads, the interpretation itself participates in the ongoing development of the reader's self identity. Literary anthropological research is therefore organized by the belief that a relationship to a literary text can become an interesting point for the continued interpretation of culture and the way culture is weighted.

As graphic designers, we are interested in the interpretive practices associated with these reader/text relations. In the past, literary theorists have used literary analytical devices (i.e. codes) to critique literature in order to denote the function of various semantic apparatus. We, as designers, can also use similar methodologies to lay bare the semantic structure of a piece of text.

Except, instead of using literature as our medium, we at LUST prefer to use the ever-growing stream of data we, as a digital society, produce. And instead of using literary methods of critical analysis, we can use self-designed digital tools such as (computational) code, algorithms, and databases to mark large sets of text at a more empirical level. Each time a previously annotated *narrative* is re-visited

–or marked– the context of the last reading changes, therefore also affecting –or changing– the current reading as well. Using similar recursive methodologies, a codex of data (or millions of points of entry) can be developed which supports any research query or interest.

It is this aspect of reading that we have attempted to contextualize in the design and typography of this book. For example, words are colour-coded in a gradient from dark (more) to light (less) as a comparative value of frequency versus uniqueness.

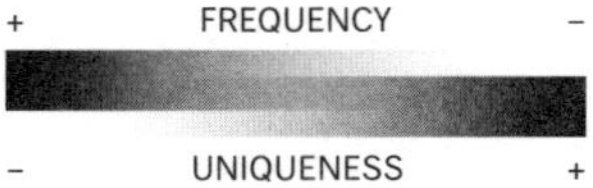

Also, several indexes are featured as random access interfaces to the articles. And finally, the subject matter in the texts is extended beyond the book through comparisons with Wikipedia entries of similar semantic meaning (micro- versus macro-context).

So in essence, in the conceptualization of this book, we are not only trying to produce graphic and typographic design. But, by augmenting code and form with critical language theories, we are also practising what we like to call Digital Anthropology.

--

LUST

The Graphic Design Museum is the first museum in the world for graphic design. The museum exhibits the broad and dynamic area of graphic design and places current graphic design in an historical and cultural context, open to the world and technology. It represents all forms of media, from printed material to interactive web design.

What used to be a culturally defined, craftsmanship based profession has evolved into a popular, democratized discipline permeating all types of media. Today's visual communication landscape functions as a breeding ground for both text and image, which are produced and consumed simultaneously in networked loops. Contemporary practitioners generate their own context and rules, and navigate the world through an array of sampled media, methods, styles, and ideas.

The Graphic Design Museum offers an international podium for established designers and is, in addition, a platform for new top talent.

Visitors get deeper insight into the past and present of the image culture and are brought up to date with the newest developments in visual communication.

--

www.graphicdesign-museum.com

The Institute of Network Cultures was established in 2004 and takes as its focus the Internet and other new forms of media. The INC was founded by Geert Lovink following his appointment as research professor ('lector') within the School of Interactive Media at the Hogeschool van Amsterdam (Amsterdam University of Applied Sciences).

The aim of the INC is to create sustainable research networks. Together with researchers and a group of students, interns and volunteers, events are organized to gather key questions and thinkers.

Each of these events, such as a conference, seminar or workshop, culminates in a publication. Formats of publication may include a printed reader, a book, video interviews, wikis, blogs, print-on-demand titles and special online magazine issues, along with conference documentation. Examples of recent INC research networks are Video Vortex (online video), Society of the Query (culture of search), Critical Point of View (Wikipedia research) and Urban Screens.

--

www.networkcultures.org

Valiz is an international independent publisher and was established to respond to developments in contemporary art, theory, critique, architecture and design in a broad-based and imaginative way. The driving force behind this effort is the publication of books, on its own initiative and in cooperation with others. Valiz produces critical, reflective publications that attempt to explore the subject in a way that is fully in tune with it and to provide relevant links with other disciplines. Roughly speaking, the programme consists of two components:

- Theory and texts on visual culture (art theory, architecture theory, reflection on everyday images, artists' texts);
- Books that are conceived and elaborated in close collaboration with artists, architects, designers and art institutes.

Apart from publishing Valiz organizes cultural projects: debates, conferences, presentations in which certain topics in contemporary art and visual culture can be investigated.

--

www.valiz.nl

LUST is a multidisciplinary graphic design practice established in 1996 by Thomas Castro, Jeroen Barendse, and Dimitri Nieuwenhuizen and based in The Hague. LUST works in a broad spectrum of media including traditional print work and book design, abstract cartography and data-visualizations, new media and interactive installations, and architectural graphics. LUST considers design as a process: each design evolving from a concept resulting from extensive research.

In the course of its existence, LUST has developed a design methodology which has been described as process-based or generative-systems based design. This entails the developing of an analytical process which leads eventually to an end-product that designs itself. Moreover, LUST is deeply interested in exploring new pathways for design at the cutting edge where new media and information technologies, architecture and urban systems, and graphic design overlap. This fascination led to establishing LUSTlab in the summer of 2010. In 2010, LUST published together with Casey Reas and Chandler McWilliam Form+Code in Design, Art & Architecture (Princeton Architectural Press).

--

www.lust.nl

Concept
Graphic Design Museum/Institute of Network Cultures

Editors
Mieke Gerritzen, Geert Lovink, Minke Kampman

Editorial assistance
Morgan Currie

Translation Dutch-English
Jonathan Ellis

Copy-editing
Jonathan Ellis, Hermine Hamhuis

Design
LUST

Production
Valiz

Printing
Albani drukkers

Binding
Binderij Epping

Publisher
Valiz with Graphic Design Museum

I Read Where I Am is part of the INFODECODATA programme in the Graphic Design Museum.

Distribution
NL/BE/LU: Coen Sligting, www.coensligtingbookimport.nl; Centraal Boekhuis, www.boekhuis.nl; Scholtens/Libridis, www.scholtens.nl
USA: D.A.P., www.artbook.com
GB/IE: Art Data, www.artdata.co.uk
Europe/Asia/Australia: Idea Books, www.ideabooks.nl

ISBN 978-90-78088-55-4
Printed and bound in the Netherlands, 2011

Valiz, book and cultural projects
Het Sieraad, Studio K36
Postjesweg 1
NL 1057 DT Amsterdam
T +31.20.6764144
info@valiz.nl
www.valiz.nl

This publication was made possible through the generous support of

SNS REAAL Fonds
Mondriaan Stichting (Mondriaan Foundation)
Provincie Noord-Brabant
Gemeente Breda